Stars and Strikes

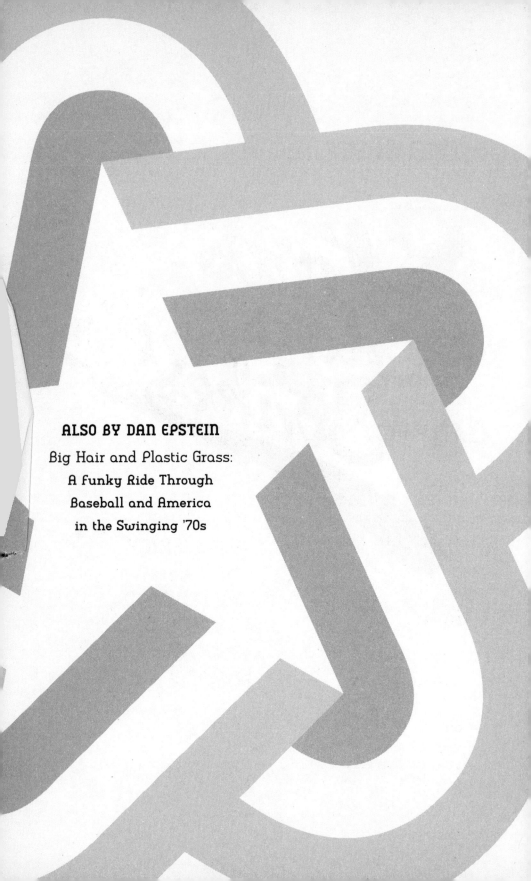

ALSO BY DAN EPSTEIN

Big Hair and Plastic Grass:
A Funky Ride Through
Baseball and America
in the Swinging '70s

DAN EPSTEIN

Stars and Strikes

BASEBALL
AND AMERICA
★ ★ *in the* ★ ★
BICENTENNIAL
SUMMER OF
'76

THOMAS DUNNE BOOKS
ST. MARTIN'S PRESS
NEW YORK

THOMAS DUNNE BOOKS.
An imprint of St. Martin's Press.

STARS AND STRIKES. Copyright © 2014 by Dan Epstein. All rights reserved. Printed in the United States of America. For information, address St. Martin's Press, 175 Fifth Avenue, New York, N.Y. 10010.

www.thomasdunnebooks.com
www.stmartins.com

The Library of Congress Cataloging-in-Publication Data is available upon request.

ISBN 978-1-250-03438-0 (hardcover)
ISBN 978-1-250-03437-3 (e-book)

St. Martin's Press books may be purchased for educational, business, or promotional use. For information on bulk purchases, please contact Macmillan Corporate and Premium Sales Department at 1-800-221-7945, extension 5442, or write specialmarkets@macmillan.com.

First Edition: May 2014

10 9 8 7 6 5 4 3 2 1

For Tanisha

Contents

Stars and Strikes

Introduction

Play That Funky Music

Why 1976? For me, it all goes back to a friend's birthday party in April of that year. Tim's parents, a couple of freethinking post-hippie types, piled a bunch of us fourth graders into their customized Dodge conversion van and took us all to see *The Bad News Bears* at Ann Arbor's Fox Village Theatre. When we returned to their house, our minds suitably blown by the experience of seeing kids who looked and talked (and best of all, *swore*) like us on the big screen, we each received wax packs of Topps baseball cards as party favors. The next day, my father patiently explained to me how to read the stats on the backs of the cards, and my transformation into a full-fledged baseball freak had officially begun.

Nineteen seventy-six was the year I got my first baseball mitt, a cheap two-tone orange-and-burgundy Bud Harrelson model ordered from the Sears catalogue; I attended my first major league games in 1976, and read my first issue of the *Sporting News* while grooving to the Top 40 sounds emanating from my AM transistor radio. By sheer luck, it also happened to be the year in which Mark "The Bird" Fidrych became a bigger pop-cultural sensation than Dorothy Hamill, Bruce Jenner, and "The Fonz" put together, Padres lefty Randy "The Junkman" Jones seemed (for a few months, at least) on course for 30 victories, and Mets slugger Dave "Kong" Kingman pierced the ozone with tape-measure home runs, while new Braves owner Ted Turner and returning White Sox owner Bill Veeck lured fans to their ballparks with one bizarre promotion after another. Billy Martin led the New York Yankees to the postseason for the first time since Lyndon Johnson was president, Danny Ozark's Philadelphia Phillies and the Whitey Herzog–helmed Kansas City Royals emerged as exciting contenders, and Sparky Anderson's Big Red Machine rolled to its second straight World Championship. In other words, it was a tremendously thrilling time to be a ten-year-old boy immersing himself in the myriad joys of the summer game.

Nineteen seventy-six, of course, was also the year of the Bicentennial, that nonstop nationwide party celebrating the United States of America's 200th birthday. But while we were all wrapping ourselves in red, white, and blue and saluting our Founding Fathers, our country was moving through a year of heavy political, social, and cultural transition. We were finally (or so we thought) putting the divisive era of Richard Nixon and the Vietnam War behind us, and searching for a renewed sense of optimism and connection in everything from CB radio and *Frampton Comes Alive!* to Olympic glory, Jimmy Carter's presidential run, and *Rocky*. No longer at war anywhere in the world, and with the Cold War beginning to thaw, we focused our collective paranoia on things like busing, urban crime, swine flu, and Legionnaires' disease. Disco and punk rock, two of the decade's most important—and divisive—musical movements, were cooking in New York City and elsewhere, though they wouldn't reach full boil for another year; hip-hop, which wouldn't explode until the early '80s, was already rocking hard amid the burned-out neighborhoods of the South Bronx.

Nineteen seventy-six was also a crucial transitional year in baseball history, one in which the players finally won their war against the reserve clause despite the best efforts of the owners (and Commissioner Bowie Kuhn), thereby ushering in the free agency era and radically altering the game's economics forever. It was a year in which San Francisco nearly lost the Giants to Toronto, and the city of Seattle successfully sued the American League for a new franchise. It was a year that witnessed the reopening of Yankee Stadium, and the final games of future Hall of Famers Hank Aaron, Frank Robinson, and Billy Williams. It was a year in which Oakland A's owner Charlie Finley—having almost single-handedly built one of the greatest dynasties in baseball history—proceeded to dismantle it like a stolen car in a chop shop.

Yet 1976 is also a year that remains woefully underappreciated by baseball historians—primarily (or so I've long suspected) because its World Series was a one-sided affair that ended an exhilarating season on a dour and chilly note. While writing *Big Hair and Plastic Grass: A Funky Ride Through Baseball and America in the Swinging '70s*, I realized that the 1976 season was so rich with electrifying moments, oddball events, and unforgettable characters—all set against the star-spangled backdrop of the Bicentennial—it truly needed (and deserved) a book of its own. After all, what other season can you name that featured a "Headlock and Wedlock" promotion, major league players wearing Bermuda shorts, and not one but *two* Harpo Marx look-alikes starting against each other in the All-Star Game?

Ah, but I'm getting ahead of myself. Why don't you just kick back on that red-white-and-blue shag rug, pop in that eight-track of the first Boston album, pour yourself a glass of Mateus rosé, and get better acquainted with baseball in the Bicentennial? I'll leave you two alone now . . .

Prologue

More Than a feeling

(October 14, 1976)

"Please do not throw bottles on the field," implored Yankee Stadium PA announcer Bob Sheppard, right as something that looked suspiciously like a freshly emptied bottle of Night Train grazed the leg of Kansas City Royals right fielder Hal McRae.

The restless Bronx crowd—who had already given vent to their tension and frustration over the Yankees' blown lead by hurling paper cups, batteries, empty beer cans, and lit firecrackers onto the playing field—responded to Sheppard's entreaties on this chilly Bronx night with jeers, not to mention additional projectiles.

Over in the Royals' dugout along the third base line, KC skipper Whitey Herzog watched several umpires and members of the stadium grounds crew scramble to pick up the scattered trash, and debated whether to pull his team off the field. Across the diamond in the Yankees' dugout, Billy Martin simply stewed. This was supposed to be the year that the Bronx Bombers returned to postseason glory after over a decade in the doldrums, and Martin was supposed to be the manager that would lead them to the Promised Land. The

Yankees had owned the AL East since the middle of April, and they'd been heavily favored to beat the upstart Royals in this best-of-five American League Championship Series.

And yet, after a series marked by controversy, bad blood, and even bomb threats, here they were: tied 6–6 going into the bottom of the ninth inning in the series' fifth and final game. Tonight's victors would fly to Cincinnati tomorrow to meet the defending World Champion Reds in the World Series. The losers? Martin didn't even want to think about that. He'd already lost 20 pounds over the course of the season, the stress of dealing with Yankee owner George Steinbrenner driving him to subsist largely on a diet of scotch and cigarettes.

The temperature had slid into the mid-30s during the three hours since the game's first pitch, but Telly Savalas didn't seem to mind. The star of the CBS detective drama *Kojak* was seated behind the Yankees' dugout, swathed in a massive fur coat that would have made any uptown pimp turn lime green with envy. Telly remained defiantly hatless despite the cold, his trademark bald dome glistening in the glare of the stadium's lights as he flashed his "Who Loves Ya Baby?" grin at the rival ABC network's cameras.

Over by the Yankees' on-deck circle, Chris Chambliss warmed his left hand in the back pocket of his pinstriped pants, but otherwise appeared equally unfazed by the autumnal chill. The top of the big first baseman's jersey remained casually unbuttoned, hanging open to reveal the top of his undershirt and a thin gold chain around his neck.

"Chambliss is so hot right now, he's got his top button undone," joked Reggie Jackson, the former AL MVP who was spending the ALCS moonlighting as a guest analyst alongside ABC broadcasters Howard Cosell and Keith Jackson. Reggie had a point: not only was Chambliss hitting .500 for the series with 10 hits in 20 at-bats, but he'd already driven in two runs tonight (his sixth and seventh

RBIs of the series) and scored the Yankees' sixth run of the game in the bottom of the sixth, putting himself in scoring position by stealing his second base of the series.

The Yankees' cleanup hitter was hot, all right. But Chambliss looked the very epitome of cool as he leaned back on the handle of his bat and waited for the game to resume. The bat, a 31-ounce blond Hillerich & Bradsby Louisville Slugger, was emblazoned with an image of the Liberty Bell in honor of the nation's Bicentennial. Along with the traditional red, white, and blue bunting that bedecked the newly renovated ballpark, that Liberty Bell logo was about the only visible trace left of the Bicentennial fever that had gripped New York City just a few months earlier.

Tonight was all about *pennant* fever, NYC-style: a win would not only put the Yankees back in the World Series for the first time since 1964, but it would also serve notice to everyone who'd written off New York City in recent years—from President Gerald Ford on down—that the Big Apple was back, and the 56,000 or so Yankee fans in attendance couldn't wait to extend an Empire State Building–sized middle-finger salute to the rest of the country on national television.

But first, their team would have to get past Royals reliever Mark Littell. The 23-year-old righty had been brilliant out of the bullpen all year, going 8–4 with a 2.08 ERA, 16 saves, and 92 strikeouts in 104 innings pitched, and he'd only served up one gopher ball all season. Littell had already breezed through the first five batters he'd faced tonight, but he'd also been distracted from his ninth-inning warm-up tosses by the cleanup efforts on the field, a fact that had not gone unnoticed by Chambliss. Littell was known to have a killer fastball and an equally devastating slider in his arsenal; but between the bone-chilling cold and the pitcher's disrupted rhythm, Chambliss figured Littell wouldn't start him off with the slider.

At 11:13 p.m., with the field finally cleared of the worst of the debris, home plate umpire Art Frantz yelled "Play Ball!" and Chambliss approached the plate. In the on-deck circle behind him, Sandy Alomar—a weak-hitting utility man who'd been brought in earlier to pinch-run for designated hitter Carlos May, and who thus now occupied the fifth slot in the New York lineup—turned to Yankee batboy Joe D'Ambrosio and offered up a prediction. "He's gonna hit it out," Alomar told him. "He's got to hit one out, because if he doesn't do it, I'm on deck."

Chambliss dug in to the left-hand batter's box and waited for the pitch. Catcher Buck Martinez, the only position player left on the Royals from their lowly expansion season of 1969, went into his squat and flashed a sign to Littell. The pitcher nodded, tugged the brim of his hat twice, pushed it back on his head, tugged the brim once more, and went into his windup. Just as Chambliss predicted, the pitch was a fastball, sailing high and inside. His Liberty Bell–emblazoned lumber sliced through the strike zone to meet it, driving the ball on a high arc through the cold night sky toward the right-center-field stands.

Royals center fielder Al Cowens and right fielder Hal McRae converged just to the left of the "353 ft" distance marker on the right-center wall, never once taking their eyes off the flight of the ball. McRae went up for it, turning his back to home plate and extending his gloved left hand as far as it could reach; he returned to earth empty-handed, slumping dejectedly against the fence. Chambliss, initially unsure of the ball's fate, saw Elston Howard jumping ecstatically in the first base coach's box, and realized it had gone out; beyond Howard, he caught sight of hundreds of fans pouring over the right field wall and swarming hungrily toward him . . .

1.

Let's Do It Again

(November–December 1975)

On November 26, 1975, toward the end of a press conference filled with thorny questions about federal spending, Soviet involvement in Angola, Israeli occupancy of the Golan Heights, and the CIA's role in political assassinations, a journalist tossed Gerald R. Ford a softball. "Tomorrow being Thanksgiving Day," asked the reporter, "as the President of the United States, what do you have, number one, to be thankful for?"

"I'm primarily thankful for the fact that this country is at peace on this Thanksgiving," Ford responded, "rather than engaged in a war, as we were for four or five or six years." Though he got the math wrong, this was no mere platitude on the president's part; the traumatic and divisive Vietnam War had come to a close in April 1975 with the fall of Saigon, making this the first Thanksgiving in over a decade where American troops weren't on the ground in Vietnam, nor actively involved in any other foreign war.

America was also largely at peace on the home front, at least in the sense that the race riots and antiwar demonstrations that had been a recurring part of American life from the mid-'60s through the early '70s were now mostly just bitter memories. Armed revolution, once a fashionable concept in various left-wing circles, was no longer a viable threat to the status quo, now that radical organizations like the Black Panther Party, the Weather Underground, and the Puerto Rican liberation collective FALN had been decimated by infighting, heroin addiction, and aggressive law enforcement harassment.

The dark cloud of corruption and paranoia that enveloped the White House during the Nixon administration also seemed to have dissipated during the new commander in chief's tenure, replaced by a fog of amiable incompetence that was relentlessly mocked and parodied by political cartoonists and stand-up comedians alike. Chevy Chase, a cast member of NBC's new late-night sketch comedy/variety program *Saturday Night*, had become the show's first breakout star, partly due to the popularity of his portrayal of President Ford as a bumbling boob who never met a flight of stairs he wouldn't eventually fall down.

The country's unemployment rate had stubbornly refused to dip below 8 percent all year, despite Ford's attempt to shake the U.S. economy out of its mild recession with the Tax Reduction Act of 1975, a one-year tax cut of $22.8 billion that was supposed to stimulate economic growth. When New York City faced bankruptcy in October, the president initially refused NYC's mayor Abraham Beame's pleas for a federal bailout, thus inspiring the infamous New York *Daily News* headline, "Ford to City: Drop Dead." Though Ford—fearing the national, international, and political repercussions of having the country's largest metropolis go into default—eventually relented, the city's long-term prospects appeared pretty grim, as did Ford's prospects in next year's presidential elections.

Still, the overall mood of the country at the end of 1975, if not exactly celebratory, was at least notably lighter than it had been during the bleak closing days of 1974, when the acrid stench of the Watergate scandal was still hanging thickly in the air. Even recent revelations that the late FBI director J. Edgar Hoover had abused his power by illegally ordering the investigation and persecution of thousands of Americans were oddly comforting: though these disclosures offered additional chilling proof of how the nation's highest offices had been befouled by some of the most viciously amoral characters in American history, the mere fact that Hoover's transgressions were coming to light—and provoking considerable outcry from even the most conservative corners of the media—seemed to indicate that sanity was finally creeping back into the national discourse. Maybe Ford had been right when he asserted in his August 1974 speech after being sworn in that "our long national nightmare is over."

This collective sense of relief—mixed with an overwhelming and understandable desire to boogie away the accumulated bad vibes of the past seven years—was widely reflected in late 1975 by the nation's pop charts, where socially conscious hits like Harold Melvin and the Blue Notes' "Wake Up Everybody" were being noticeably muscled out by such blissfully message-free dance tracks as the O'Jays' "I Love Music," the Bee Gees' "Nights on Broadway," and Silver Convention's "Fly Robin Fly," as well as numerous songs whose lyrics seemed entirely devoted to the myriad joys of sex. An article in the December 29 issue of *Time* magazine estimated that 15 percent of airtime on contemporary AM radio was taken up by "sex rock," singling out People's Choice's "Do It Any Way You Wanna," the Staple Singers' "Let's Do It Again," KC and the Sunshine Band's "That's the Way (I Like It)," and Leon Haywood's "I Want'a Do Something Freaky to You" as some of the juicier offenders—along with "Love to Love You Baby," which the magazine prudishly described as "Donna Summer's marathon of 22 orgasms."

When reached for comment on these sybaritic sounds, radio programmer Tom Yates from L.A.'s KLOS-FM simply told *Time*, "People just want to dance and get it on." Or, as the breakthrough hit by grease-painted hard rockers KISS succinctly put it, "I wanna rock and roll all night and party every day."

The lords of baseball should have been celebrating as well, since the game appeared as healthy as it had ever been, perhaps even healthier. Over 29.7 million fans bought tickets to major league ballgames in 1975, the third-highest attendance figure in history, and the season had been capped by an electrifying seven-game World Series between the Boston Red Sox and the Cincinnati Reds—memorably highlighted by Carlton Fisk's game-winning 12th-inning homer in Game Six—during which a record 75.9 million viewers tuned in for what many were already calling the greatest Fall Classic in history.

This World Series ratings bonanza had conveniently occurred right as baseball's four-year, $72 million TV contract with NBC was coming to an end. The new basic broadcasting agreement, split between NBC (which would continue to broadcast Saturday's *Game of the Week* as well as the 1976 World Series) and ABC (which was given the rights to the *Monday Night Baseball* franchise, as well as the '76 League Championship Series broadcasts), would deposit nearly $93 million into the game's coffers over the next four seasons. As *New Yorker* baseball essayist Roger Angell pointed out, the total radio and TV income share for each MLB club "now amounts to one and a half times the total paid out for player salaries and retirement benefits."

But instead of basking in the World Series afterglow, or reclining like contented pashas upon their piles of cash, baseball's owners and executives had more reason to sweat than celebrate as 1975 drew to a close. Despite the overall attendance boom of the last few seasons, at least three major league franchises—the Atlanta Braves, the Chicago White Sox, and the San Francisco Giants—were in dire financial straits. More ominously, a breach of contract lawsuit brought against the American League by the state of Washington in 1970 (which asked for $32.5 million in damages and the return of a major league team to Seattle, as recompense for the city's loss of the Pilots expansion franchise) was about to finally have its day in court.

The lawsuit had already been postponed twice by Washington State attorney general Slade Gorton, in hopes that Commissioner Bowie Kuhn and the American League would make good on their long-standing promise to bring baseball back to Seattle. The King County Multipurpose Domed Stadium, aka the Kingdome, was due to open in the spring of 1976 following three years of construction, but the city still didn't have a baseball team to play there.

Kuhn had repeatedly urged Gorton to forget about the lawsuit, assuring him that Seattle would eventually receive another major league franchise. Gorton, however, had refused to drop it; and now that the suit was scheduled to come to trial in January 1976, Kuhn and the team owners were cringing at the prospect of legal light being shed on baseball's clubby business practices, concerned that it might cause the federal government to put the kibosh on their sport's long-held antitrust exemption.

Kuhn and company's collective mood was further soured by the return of Bill Veeck to Major League Baseball. A good-humored hustler with a mile-wide progressive streak, Veeck—who didn't remotely fit the stodgy profile of a typical major league owner—had long ago established himself as the enemy of conservatism on every level of the sport. During his brief but memorable ownership stints with the Cleveland Indians, St. Louis Browns, and Chicago White Sox, he'd significantly increased attendance in each city with a nonstop barrage of often outlandish promotions, invariably offending the staid sensibilities of his fellow owners, who viewed such irreverent stunts as livestock giveaways and pinch-hitting midgets as affronts to the dignity of the Grand Old Game.

A true populist, Veeck enjoyed making himself accessible to the fans, and could often be seen mingling and drinking with them in the stands—sometimes even letting them stub their cigarettes out on the ashtray he'd had carved into his wooden leg—behavior that only further alienated him from baseball's executive branch. Veeck's round-the-clock preference for casual wear earned him the affectionate nickname "Sport Shirt Bill" from sportswriters, who loved his way with a quote and his generosity with a bottle.

Health issues had forced Veeck to sell off his White Sox ownership shares in the midst of the 1961 season, but baseball fans on Chicago's South Side still remembered him fondly. For them—and for everyone else who appreciated the injection of a little levity into the old ballgame—Christmas came early in 1975, thanks to the December 11 announcement that the 61-year-old Veeck had repurchased the White Sox. After months of rumors that the cash-poor franchise was about to be sold and moved to another city, Veeck and his group of over 40 investors (including *Ebony* and *Jet* publisher John H. Johnson, the first African American to hold an ownership stake in a major league team) stepped in to save the team and keep it in Chicago.

American League president Lee MacPhail and several of the AL owners (including California Angels owner Gene Autry, who'd lobbied hard on behalf of a consortium fronted by fellow Hollywood star Danny Kaye, who wanted to buy the franchise and move it to Seattle) had done their best to prevent the sale of the White Sox to the Veeck group, forcing them to jump through numerous financial and legal hoops before ultimately ratifying the transaction. Veeck, who took control of the team less than 48 hours before baseball's Winter Meetings trading deadline, wasted no time in reestablishing himself as a thorn in the side of his fellow owners, commandeering a desk in the lobby of Hollywood, Florida's, Diplomat Hotel and hanging up a sign reading "Open for Business—The Chicago White Sox, No Reasonable Offer Refused."

The major league team owners and general managers who attended these conventions typically made their deals while sequestered in the privacy of smoke-filled hotel suites and conference rooms, with plenty of liquid refreshment and old boys club backslapping on tap. But Veeck and White Sox general manager Roland Hemond were gleefully making a point of "operating in the open like honest men," as they put it, loudly juggling offers and consummating deals in full view of the assembled media and passing hotel guests alike, and annoying the hell out of their peers in the process. "This is a meat market," huffed Milwaukee Brewers owner Bud Selig. "Why can't he do this in his own room?" complained Houston Astros assistant GM John Mullen, sounding like an appalled parent who'd just caught his longhaired son air-guitaring to Lynyrd Skynyrd in the family den. Even Bowie Kuhn weighed in, disparaging Veeck and Hemond's theatrical display as "gauche."

These gentlemen would have been even more irate had they realized that many of the calls coming in for Veeck were actually being dialed by Hemond from a nearby pay phone. That morning, Veeck had shoved several rolls of dimes into his GM's hands, and instructed him to go off and make calls to their "trading post" whenever there was a lull in the action. Thinking that Veeck's constantly ringing phone meant other teams must be hot to make deals with the Sox, several baseball execs hurriedly joined the fray, setting off what *The New York Times* described as one of "the fastest trading sprees in history"; by the time the Winter Meetings officially came to a close, Veeck had engineered six deals and acquired 11 new players, including speedy outfielder Ralph "Road Runner" Garr, who'd won the 1974 National League batting title as a member of the

Atlanta Braves, and veteran relief pitcher Clay Carroll, who'd just won Game Seven of the 1975 World Series for the Cincinnati Reds.

"I wanted a new ownership, a new team and a new attitude," Veeck explained to Wells Twombly of the *Sporting News*, as the dust from his deal-a-thon began to settle. "I'm not through making changes," he added. "This is only the start."

For all of Veeck's flamboyant dealing, the most significant transactions of the Winter Meetings involved the New York Yankees, who sent slugging right fielder Bobby Bonds to the Angels in exchange for center fielder Mickey Rivers and pitcher Ed Figueroa, and dealt pitcher George "Doc" Medich to the Pittsburgh Pirates for hurlers Dock Ellis and Ken Brett, and a young second baseman named Willie Randolph. The immensely talented Bonds had put up some strong numbers for the Yankees in '75, hitting .270 with 32 homers, 85 RBIs, 93 runs scored, and 30 stolen bases despite playing in near-constant pain after badly injuring his right knee while going after a fly ball in early June. Bonds's speed on the bases and in the outfield suffered accordingly, which caused Yankee fans—and fiery new Yankee manager Billy Martin, who'd replaced skipper Bill Virdon in early August—to accuse Bonds of slacking. Tensions between Bonds and Martin escalated to the point where the outfielder challenged the manager in his office, saying, "If you think you can whup me, fine. I'll beat the shit out of you, plain and simple." Martin, who tended to fight only when someone else was there to hold him back, punched Bonds's ticket out of the Bronx instead.

A second baseman for the Yankees during their 1950s dynastic period, Martin had landed his dream job after successful but tempestuous managerial tenures with the Minnesota Twins, Detroit Tigers, and Texas Rangers. Martin had spent the final months of the '75 season observing his new team, gauging its strengths and weaknesses, and (as befit a man who regularly carried a 1943 silver coin of Italian dictator Benito Mussolini in his pocket) imperiously settling old scores.

Pitcher Larry Gura, who'd clashed with Martin in the spring of '74 when they were both with the Rangers, suddenly found himself the odd man out of the Yankees' starting rotation. Gura further underlined his uselessness in Martin's eyes by playing tennis—which the macho skipper considered a "pussy sport"—with backup outfielder Rich Coggins when the team was on the road; both players' days in pinstripes were accordingly numbered.

Pat Dobson, a former 20-game winner with the Orioles who'd aroused Martin's enmity several years earlier by criticizing his handling of the Tigers' pitching staff, also found himself suddenly unwelcome in the Yankees' rotation. Dobson was the first to go, exiled to the Cleveland Indians in November in exchange for outfielder/DH Oscar Gamble, whose power stroke was nearly as explosive as his luxuriant afro hairdo.

Since his potent left-handed bat matched up well with the short right field porch in Yankee Stadium, Gamble fit in perfectly with Martin's vision for '76. Ditto for Rivers, who'd led the AL with 70 stolen bases in 1975, while 16-game winner Figueroa seemed a sure bet to become a mainstay of the Yankee rotation. Less obvious to many observers, including a high percentage of Yankee players, were the motivations behind the Medich-Ellis-Brett-Randolph deal. Medich, who'd earned the nickname "Doc" via his medical studies at the University of Pittsburgh, had won 49 games in three seasons as a Yankee, and at 27 seemed on the verge of becoming one of the AL's top starters; but when the right-hander committed the cardinal sin of complaining to the press about his team's defense, Martin deemed him expendable.

Still, to the casual observer, the Yankees seemed to be getting little more than a grab bag of spare parts in exchange for Medich. Lefty hurler Brett had only shown occasional flashes of brilliance during his six full years in the bigs, and—though the same age as Medich—already had a history of elbow trouble. Ellis, meanwhile, had a history of trouble, period. The outspoken Ellis had long established himself as one of the game's more colorful and controversial players, a proud black man who wasn't shy about wearing curlers in his hair on the field (sometimes with tightly rolled pin joints hidden inside them) or decrying baseball's racist double standard to the press. After Ellis's well-publicized attempt in August '75 to stage a team-wide insurrection against Bucs manager Danny Murtaugh, the Pirates were only too happy to get rid of him. The very notion of Ellis and Martin occupying the same clubhouse and dugout space had New York pundits scurrying for cover, but both men were mutually respectful in their comments to the press. "We both want to win," Ellis told reporters, while Martin responded to questions about Ellis's alleged bad attitude by saying, "The Hall of Fame is full of tough cases."

The key to the deal, at least from the perspective of Yankees' GM Gabe Paul, was Randolph. Drafted in 1972 out of Brooklyn's Samuel J. Tilden High School, the second baseman had risen quickly in the Pirates' minor league system before being called up to the parent club in the summer of 1975. Unfortunately for Randolph, 24-year-old Rennie Stennett was already firmly ensconced as the Pirates' second sacker, leaving the rookie little opportunity to showcase his skills at the major league level. Paul thought Randolph had the potential to flourish in a full-time situation—and the Yankees, who had trudged through '75 with the weak-hitting Sandy Alomar at second, were more than willing to give him that shot. "This is the jackpot!" commented Paul upon finalizing the deal.

———

But the Yankees' acquisition of Randolph, Ellis, and Brett was nothing compared to the jackpot that the Major League Baseball Players Association hit on December 23, when arbitrator Peter Seitz declared Andy Messersmith and Dave McNally free agents. Messersmith—the Los Angeles Dodgers' best starting pitcher during their NL pennant-winning campaign of 1974—had failed to come to terms on his 1975 contract with Dodgers owner Walter O'Malley, who rejected Messersmith's request for a "no trade" clause. Such clauses were simply unheard of at the time; and O'Malley, despite being one of the most powerful and influential owners in the National League, told Messersmith that the league would never allow him to sign off on such a thing.

Marvin Miller, executive director of the Major League Baseball Players Association, saw Messersmith's situation as another chance to chip away at baseball's infamous reserve clause, which bound players to their teams for perpetuity, and which the union had originally tried to upend in 1970 by backing Curt Flood's unsuccessful lawsuit against Major League Baseball. Miller convinced Messersmith to play the 1975 season without a new contract—he would still get paid, though at only a slight increase from his 1974 salary of $90,000—whereupon he could declare himself a free agent, and file a grievance to bring the case to outside arbitration. Joining Messersmith in his bid for free agency was Dave McNally, a 31-year-old lefty who'd averaged 19 wins per year for the Baltimore Orioles from 1968 through 1974. Traded against his will to the Montreal Expos in late 1974, McNally had asked for a "no-cut" contract from his new team. When the Expos refused, McNally wound up pitching 12 games for Montreal without a contract before shoulder troubles forced him to retire in June 1975. Since the Expos and McNally never had a deal in place (and McNally refused to sign voluntary retirement papers before leaving the club), Miller felt that McNally was now technically a free agent as well—and McNally, a former player representative and a notoriously tough negotiator on his own contracts, was more than happy to go along with Miller's plan and see how it played out. Having already effectively retired from the game to run a successful car dealership in Billings, Montana, McNally literally had nothing to lose.

The owners, on the other hand, knew that they stood to lose plenty, in terms of both money and control. And when Seitz delivered his 64-page opinion declaring that Messersmith and McNally were now free to negotiate with other teams—and that all other players who played for a year without a contract would be eligible to do the same— baseball's old guard reacted as if someone had just pissed in their Sanka. Pirates GM Joe Brown called Seitz's decision "the worst thing to happen to baseball in a long time," while Commissioner Kuhn pronounced himself "enormously disturbed" by the ruling, and promised to appeal it in federal court.

Miller, of course, expressed little sympathy for the panicked state of Kuhn and his cohorts. "I don't think it's becoming to see the commissioner and others wringing their hands just because what they held basic for 100 years is no longer applicable," he said. Since the current Basic Agreement between the players and owners was due to expire at the end of the year, Miller added that he hoped for a "more constructive attitude" on the owners' side of the table when Basic Agreement talks resumed on January 7.

Bill Veeck was trimming the family Christmas tree when he first got the news of Seitz's decision. The new White Sox owner had predicted years earlier that the players would eventually win free agency in the courts—and, ironically, his prediction had come true at the worst possible time for Veeck. Having just purchased a lousy team in a crumbling stadium with capital cobbled together from several dozen investors, the old hustler was poorly equipped to handle the economic changes that the coming year would bring. Sport Shirt Bill would still be smiling plenty in '76; but as with just about everyone else in America during the Bicentennial, those smiles would often require a substantial degree of effort, and occasionally betray a flash or two of anxiety behind the eyes.

2.

Take It to the Limit

(January 1976)

Elvis Presley was fat, 40, and a far cry from the hip-swiveling hit machine he'd once been—it had been over three years since "Burning Love" hunka-hunka'd its way to number two on the *Billboard* singles charts—but he could still make the turnstiles spin. On the evening of December 31, 1975, Michigan's newly opened Pontiac Silverdome was packed tighter than his white jumpsuit (the seat of which would split before the night was out), as over 62,500 adoring fans rang in the New Year with the King of Rock 'n' Roll.

That same night, some 600 miles to the east, Bruce Springsteen and the E Street Band blasted through their final set of 1975 before a smaller but equally enthusiastic crowd at the 3,000-capacity Tower Theater in Upper Darby, Pennsylvania. The Tower show capped a year of frustration and jubilation for the 26-year-old New Jersey native, who'd begun 1975 still mired in the endless sessions for his make-or-break third album, *Born to Run.* Finally released in August, *Born to Run* had transformed Springsteen from scuffling singer-songwriter to bona-fide rock 'n' roll star. Recorded for possible use as a live album, tapes of the incendiary New Year's Eve performance at the Tower Theater—which would be oft-bootlegged, but never officially released—captured him at the perfect midpoint of that transformation from cult hero to major artist.

In downtown Philadelphia, not far from where Springsteen and his gang were raising the roof, another American icon made a memorable New Year's Eve appearance. Pushed slowly forward on a cart loaded with shock-absorbing wet cement by what the Associated Press described as "12 beefy hardhats," and accompanied by a security detail of over a thousand police officers, the Liberty Bell—that cracked, 2,080-pound symbol of American independence—made a 200-yard journey through the freezing rain from its longtime home in Independence Hall to a display platform in the newly built Liberty Bell Pavilion, as at least 20,000 observers looked on. The glass-and-steel pavilion, constructed at a cost of $800,000, was designed to accommodate the estimated 100,000 people per day that Philadelphia tourism officials were predicting would visit the old brass bell during the year-long celebration of the nation's 200th birthday.

America's plans for a major Bicentennial celebration had been in the works since 1966, when the U.S. Congress created the American Revolution Bicentennial Commission to oversee what was originally intended as a single-city exposition to take place in either Boston or Philadelphia. But after more than six years of bitter debate over which city would receive the tourist-dollar windfall that would surely result from hosting the official Bicentennial celebration, Congress—deciding instead that the celebration should be a nation-wide affair—dissolved the ARBC and replaced it with the American Revolution Bicentennial Administration. The ARBA's purpose was to encourage and coordinate locally sponsored Bicentennial events throughout the country that would include everything from parades, fireworks displays, and ice cream socials to the planting of trees, the burial of time capsules, the painting of public fire hydrants and mailboxes (red, white, and blue, of course), and the costumed reenactment of various Revolutionary War battles.

The Bicentennial celebration officially kicked off on April 1, 1975, when the American Freedom Train chugged out of Wilmington, Delaware, beginning what would be a 21-month, 25,388-mile journey through the 48 contiguous states. A traveling exhibition of memorabilia from two centuries of American history, the 26-car train (pulled over the course of its trek by three different restored steam locomotives) contained over 500 artifacts, including George Washington's personal copy of the Constitution, Abraham Lincoln's stovepipe hat, Judy Garland's ruby slippers from *The Wizard of Oz,* and heavyweight champion Smokin' Joe Frazier's boxing trunks. The train's epic journey captured the national imagination, with over seven million Americans eventually boarding the train at its various stops, and another 10 million gathering trackside to watch it thunder past.

Not that you needed to wait for the Freedom Train's arrival to get your Bicentennial fix. By January 1976, it had become virtually impossible to venture anywhere without coming face-to-face with some sort of reminder that, yes, America's 200th birthday was coming right up. The official Bicentennial logo, a white five-pointed star placed in a star-shaped bed of interlaced red, white, and blue ribbons (the work of designer Bruce Blackburn, who'd also recently co-designed NASA's new "worm" logo), was already popping up everywhere, including on the jerseys of the Dallas Cowboys and Pittsburgh Steelers when they faced off on January 18 in Super Bowl X. During the game's halftime segment, the creepy right-wing performance group Up With People presented "200 Years and Just a Baby: A Tribute to America's Bicentennial," a song-and-dance production that included a squeaky-clean medley of such classic American pop hits as

eyes of the world, U.S. citizens could still embrace their inner Ben Franklin, celebrate the intelligence, ingenuity, and fortitude of the Founding Fathers, and wax nostalgic for a war—the American Revolution—in which Americans were not only the victors, but also the underdogs and the indisputable good guys.

Whether you purchased a "Spirit of '76" coffee mug, gorged yourself on a pint of Baskin-Robbins Valley Forge Fudge, or worked off those calories on a walking tour of Philadelphia's "Trail of Freedom," it was all, on some level, about taking a guilt-free hit of American pride. And speaking of hits, a company called Crystal Magick Promotions even put a Bicentennial spin on the push for marijuana legalization, selling "Free the Weed" T-shirts emblazoned with images of marijuana plants growing out of the Statue of Liberty's torch and an upended Liberty Bell. "Get High on 200 Years of America's Freedom," trumpeted the ads for the T-shirts, which ran in such popular counterculture magazines as *High Times* and *National Lampoon*.

Despite the decentralization of the nation's Bicentennial celebration, Philadelphia would be a fixture in the national spotlight throughout 1976. As the site of the Continental Congress and the signing of the Declaration of Independence (not to mention dozens of other events of Revolutionary importance), the city was primed to draw millions of Bicentennial tourists in the coming year. Not coincidentally, Philly was also tapped to host the year's NBA All-Star Game, the NHL All-Star Game, the NCAA Basketball Final Four, and Major League Baseball's All-Star Game—the latter of which would be played at Philadelphia's Veterans Stadium, a modern multipurpose concrete donut opened in 1972 that was bedecked with copious Liberty Bell imagery. As pitcher Ron Reed enthused after being traded to the Philadelphia Phillies in December by the St. Louis Cardinals, "This is going to be a super year in Philadelphia with the All-Star Game, the Bicentennial, and a good chance for a World Series."

The 6′6″ right-hander wasn't just blowing smoke. The '75 Phillies' 86-76 record had been the franchise's best since 1966, earning them a solid second-place finish in the NL East, six and a half games behind their cross-state division rival Pittsburgh Pirates. After nearly a decade of downright awfulness spiked with occasional glimmers of mediocrity, the Phillies looked ready to contend again—just in time for a year when all eyes would be on Philadelphia.

The team's sudden resurgence was led by three young but experienced players: third baseman Mike Schmidt had won his second straight NL home run crown in 1975 by belting 38 round-trippers, while also driving in 95 runs, scoring another 93, and leading the team with 29 stolen bases. Hulking left fielder Greg "The Bull" Luzinski hit .300 with 34 homers and a league-leading 120 RBIs, topping all NL hitters with 322 total bases. And center fielder Garry Maddox, who'd arrived in Philadelphia via a May 1975 trade with the Giants, hit .291 and stole 24 bases. A Vietnam vet, Maddox had been exposed to various chemicals while serving much of 1969 and 1970 at a forward base near the Marine Corps' Chu Lai airfield, resulting in a skin rash that made shaving agonizingly painful; as a result, he sported muttonchop sideburns so large they almost covered his entire face from his eyes to his chin—a fairly radical look for the time, even compared to the hairy likes of the Oakland A's "Mustache Gang." But it was his startling speed and sparkling glove work in the outfield, as opposed to his military service, that earned Maddox the nickname "Secretary of Defense." In 1975, those defensive skills—which inspired Phillies announcer Harry Kalas to memorably quip that, "two-thirds of the Earth is covered by water, the other one-third is covered by Garry Maddox"—also earned him his first Gold Glove award.

The Phillies' lineup was also stocked with talented veterans, including second baseman Dave Cash, shortstop Larry Bowa, and right fielder Jay Johnstone, all of whom were in their late 20s and coming off the best offensive seasons of their respective careers. The oldest member of the Phillies' starting eight was 33-year-old first baseman Dick Allen, who'd been a star with the Phillies during the previous decade, but whose outspokenness (especially on the subject of racism) and tendency to march to his own funky drummer had made him deeply unpopular with both the team's front office and its white ticket holders. Weary of the Philly fans' abuse—he wore a batting helmet while playing first in order to protect himself from the trash hurled at him from the Connie Mack Stadium stands—Allen had demanded to be traded from the team in 1969. But now, after stops in St. Louis, Los Angeles, and Chicago (where he won the 1972 AL MVP award with the White Sox, before shocking the team by suddenly "retiring" in August 1974 to tend to his horse farm), he was back in Philadelphia, playing on the same kind of artificial turf that had once inspired him to quip, "If a horse can't eat it, I don't want to play on it."

Though his 12 home runs and 62 RBIs had been the third-highest totals on the team, Allen's 1975 season was considered a severe disappointment; his .233 batting average and .327 on-base percentage were easily the worst showings of his career. And yet, the Phillies fans that had once jeered Allen gave him a hero's welcome upon his return to Philadelphia, and made him feel far more at home at Veterans Stadium than he'd ever felt at Connie Mack. He also felt far more comfortable in the Phillies' current clubhouse, where the team's black players now had the freedom to be themselves. "Dave Cash, Ollie Brown, and Garry Maddox represented a new generation of black ballplayer," Allen would later reflect in his autobiography. "They were talented and proud of it, and they didn't take a back seat to anybody." Allen also found himself serving as a mentor to Schmidt and Luzinski, both of whom respected Allen's experience and skill enough to seek him out for hitting advice.

Would Allen's own power stroke return to form in 1976? That was one of the big questions hanging over the Phillies heading into the Bicentennial year; the other was the overall effectiveness of their pitching staff, which had posted the fourth-highest ERA (3.82) in the league, thanks to a shaky starting rotation. Thirty-one-year-old staff ace Steve Carlton had gone 15–14 with a 3.56 ERA and 192 strikeouts, looking nothing like the pitcher who'd dominated the NL in 1972, winning 27 games, posting a 1.97 ERA, and striking out 310 for a last-place Phillies team that won only 59 games. Jim Lonborg, who would turn 34 in the spring, had been beset by injuries, winning only eight games in '75 after a 17-victory 1974 campaign. Larry Christenson and Tom Underwood, a pair of 22-year-old hurlers, put up decent numbers during their first full seasons (11–6, 3.67 ERA and 14–13, 4.14 ERA respectively), but didn't exactly look like future Cy Young winners.

Still, Phillies skipper Danny Ozark felt good about his chances going into 1976. Not only did the Phillies have one of the league's most potent offenses, but—thanks to new additions Ron Reed and veteran lefty Jim Kaat (the latter of whom had been obtained from the White Sox during Bill Veeck's winter trade-a-thon)—their rotation also looked considerably stronger. "We should be picked to win the pennant," he told the press. "We have the players to do it."

Down in Atlanta, the coming year looked considerably less exciting than the 1976 Philadelphia was gearing up for. Though the Georgia State Chamber of Commerce urged the state's residents to "stay and see America in Georgia," the likelihood that Bicentennial-frenzied tourists would flock to the southernmost of the 13 original colonies in anything approaching Philadelphia-type numbers was slim, indeed. Even slimmer was the possibility of the Braves being a competitive presence in the National League West.

The Braves' 67-94 record in 1975 was the worst in the 10 years since they'd relocated to Atlanta from Milwaukee, and the team's paid attendance was accordingly dismal, averaging only 6,683 fans per game; only the San Francisco Giants had drawn worse. "At the end of the year, we started buying free tickets from ourselves for twenty-five cents each and calling them paid admissions," Braves publicity director Bob Hope (no relation to the inexplicably popular comedian) later admitted, but even those desperate efforts weren't enough to goose the season's attendance figures higher than 534,672. That was half as many fans as had turned up to Atlanta–Fulton County Stadium in 1974, the year when Hank Aaron broke Babe Ruth's career home run mark and the team played well enough to finish third with an 88–74 record. But with the Braves' top brass unwilling to pay another year of the 40-year-old Home Run King's $165,000 salary—or actually make good on their ambiguous promises of a front office job upon his retirement—Hammerin' Hank was dispatched to finish out his illustrious career in Milwaukee with the Brewers, and the team was left without anyone of even remotely comparable marquee value.

What the Braves did have were workhorse pitchers Phil Niekro (15–15, 3.20 ERA) and Carl Morton (17–16, 3.50 ERA), who'd combined to pitch over a third of the team's innings in 1975, and a whole lot of holes in their bullpen and regular lineup. The "youth movement" that the Braves were pursuing in the post-Aaron era had thus far produced little in the way of offensive vitality, so they'd shipped their best young player—outfielder Dusty Baker, who'd hit .261 in 1975 with 19 home runs and 72 RBIs—off to Los Angeles in November in exchange for veteran slugger Jimmy "The Toy

Cannon" Wynn, in hopes that Wynn's declining bat might come alive again in the hitter-friendly park known as "The Launching Pad."

But even if the Toy Cannon managed to blast some life back into the Braves in 1976, there was no guarantee that the fans would return to Fulton County Stadium. Some pundits were questioning whether Atlanta was a major league city after all; the fall of 1975 had been rife with rumors that the Braves would soon be sold and relocated, maybe to Toronto or Denver. Others felt that Atlantans would be more likely to come out to the ballpark if the majority of their home games weren't already being broadcast on local TV station WTCG—not that most Atlanta households could actually pick up the low-powered UHF channel with decent reception.

Ted Turner didn't see it that way. For the 37-year-old media mogul, who'd bought the station back in 1970 and inked his broadcasting deal with the Braves three years later, the team and the station worked together as part of a bigger plan. With a few notable exceptions like *Future Shock*, the locally taped *Soul Train* knockoff produced and hosted by "Godfather of Soul" James Brown, WTCG mostly broadcast reruns of older shows like *Star Trek*, *Leave It to Beaver*, and *The Three Stooges*. These reruns were both cheap to program and enduringly popular with viewers, but WTCG's Braves broadcasts gave Turner's station greater commercial clout in the Atlanta area—and by beaming WTCG to various other Southern markets via microwave transmission, he also expanded the Braves' fan base.

Turner had plans to turn WTCG (named for his Turner Communications Group, but which he often claimed stood for "Watch This Channel Grow") into a cable "superstation" that would broadcast its transmissions nationwide via satellite, and knew that he needed something more than just *The Little Rascals* and forgotten

B-movies to anchor his programming. Keeping his Braves broadcasting arrangement intact was, therefore, of paramount importance—so on January 6, 1976, Turner solidified it further, surprising the baseball world by purchasing the financially ailing team for a reported $12 million, payable in installments over 10 years.

Turner had no prior background in baseball beyond his Braves broadcasts, and his knowledge about the game itself was cursory at best. ("Turner isn't sure if bulls are really kept in the bullpen," cracked *Atlanta Constitution* sportswriter Furman Bisher, exaggerating only slightly.) But the high-strung, hyperactive businessman was no stranger to competition, having raced yachts for over a decade, and he wasted no time throwing down the gauntlet on behalf of his latest purchase. "Getting into the World Series in five years is my objective," he told the press.

While former Braves owner Bill Bartholomay and former club president Dan Donohue would remain with the Braves as team directors, Turner announced that he was installing himself as both club president and general manager. "The millionaire yachtsman," as the sports pages were now calling Turner, immediately made it clear who was running the show: before the National League owners could even approve the team's sale, Turner was already filming TV ads in which he personally invited the people of Atlanta to buy tickets for the upcoming Braves season, and telling *Atlanta Constitution* sportswriter Wayne Minshew that he intended to change the name of the team from the Braves to the Eagles in honor of his favorite racing sailboat, the *American Eagle*.

Though initially taken aback when Minshew's subsequent name-change story generated a significantly larger stack of hate mail than his TV sales pitches garnered season ticket requests, Turner reveled in the sudden fame that major league ownership had brought him. He also instinctively grasped what old showmen like Bill Veeck and

Oakland A's owner Charlie Finley already knew: fielding a winning baseball team wasn't the only way to drum up fan interest and boost ticket sales.

Conceding that the Braves were going to be pretty bad for at least the next few seasons, Turner instructed Bob Hope to unleash a nonstop promotional barrage in 1976 that would compensate for (or at least distract from) the team's cruddy level of play. "I want this team to be like McDonald's," Turner raved. "I want an atmosphere built here that will make kids want to come to the games. I want it to be exciting. Excitement isn't the success of one individual promotion, it's the chemistry of everything combined." Turner greenlighted every promotional idea Hope threw at him, from building picnic areas along the baselines to "Halter Top Night," and demanded more, much more.

Though he quickly backed off his unpopular Atlanta Eagles idea, Turner continued to make provocative statements in the press and elsewhere. He told the Atlanta Chamber of Commerce that he intended to make the Fulton County Stadium parking lot safer by busing criminals from there to tonier neighborhoods, where their thievery would be considerably more lucrative. At the annual Braves Boosters Club banquet, he told the thousands of fans in attendance that he would call upon his Mafia connections to rough up opposing players if that was needed to help the team win. Was this guy for real? No one seemed to know for sure, though Turner's statement to the press regarding the NL owners' ratification of his Braves purchase displayed a touch of self-aware gallows humor. "We're not going to move the team, so there should be no problem," he said. "If we go broke, we're going to do it in Atlanta."

Turner received the league's approval on January 14, during a brief midwinter MLB meeting in Phoenix, Arizona. Now the city's most talked about individual, Turner's effervescent and eccentric quotes were plastered all over the local media, largely overshadowing some very pointed public comments from the man who, just a little over a year ago, had been Atlanta's most famous resident.

"I wish I could say I was happy with the progress of baseball," Hank Aaron revealed in the January 15 issue of the popular weekly black news magazine *JET*, "but I'm very disappointed in the relatively small progress Blacks have made in the sport. . . . [Blacks] who can afford it must continue to try to get in on the ownership level. That's where the real power is," he told the magazine. "People talk about owning a piece of the rock—well, Blacks must own their piece." Aaron had left Atlanta quietly in November 1974, but his words now betrayed a lingering bitterness and resentment over the shabby way he'd been treated by the Braves.

The *JET* piece also reported that Aaron would become vice president of the Milwaukee Brewers after playing for one more season. Nearly 30 years after Jackie Robinson had broken baseball's color line, there were currently only three African Americans in the management and executive levels of Major League Baseball: Cleveland Indians skipper Frank Robinson, White Sox co-owner (and *JET* publisher) John H. Johnson, and Bill Lucas, Aaron's former brother-in-law, who headed the Braves' farm system. As the *JET* article dryly noted, "the advances for Blacks [in baseball] have come in inches."

Minority advancement wasn't exactly a pressing concern for the owners and executives who convened for the January MLB meetings in Phoenix. More immediately troubling was the Seattle lawsuit, the Messersmith ruling, the fate of the San Francisco Giants, and the potentially far-reaching ramifications of all three.

The Giants had never drawn less than 1.2 million fans during their first decade in the Bay Area, but the arrival of the A's across the bay put a serious crimp in their gate receipts; since 1968, when Charlie

Finley moved the A's to Oakland from Kansas City, the Giants had only sold a million tickets once, in 1971. Without big-name stars or savvy promotions—Giants owner and president Horace Stoneham seemed oblivious to modern marketing methods, running his franchise (in the words of the *Sporting News*'s Wells Twombly) "like a mom-and-pop candy store"—the team struggled to attract fans to cold and cavernous Candlestick Park. It didn't help that the city of San Francisco had slapped a 50-cent tax on each Giants ticket to fund Candlestick improvements for the benefit of the 49ers, the NFL team that shared the stadium; even more off-putting was the ballpark's reputation for serving, literally, rotten food at the concession stands, and the fact that muggings and tire slashings were all too commonplace in the stadium's parking lot.

Having posted baseball's worst attendance figures in 1974 and 1975, the Giants had lost an estimated $3 million over the past two seasons; and Stoneham, who'd inherited the team from his father 40 years earlier, was nearly bankrupt, suffering from a heart ailment, and looking to sell his controlling share. Stoneham had fired manager Wes Westrum and his entire coaching staff right before Thanksgiving, hoping that cleaning house would somehow make the team more salable; he also slashed the salaries of all nonplaying personnel by 25 to 35 percent. "The atmosphere around here is very bad," one front office employee told Art Spander of the *Sporting News*. "We can't make plans. We can't sell tickets. There's nothing to do, no schedule."

A 72-year-old alcoholic prone to sudden mood swings and embarrassing displays of public intoxication, Stoneham now played the part of the indigent, dotty elder uncle, financially supported by his family while they tried to decide what exactly to "do" with him—Stoneham's family, in this case, being the National League. Led by Dodgers owner Walter O'Malley, who had lured Stoneham to the

West Coast in 1958, the other NL owners chipped in $400,000 to keep the Giants solvent enough to pay their players; the NL also appointed former Houston Astros general manager Spec Richardson to oversee the team's affairs while they looked for a buyer. "We could carry San Francisco for many years," O'Malley bragged to Art Spander in December 1975. But the Giants would still have to pay all that money back, as well as cover whatever debts the future would bring; in short, they needed new ownership and a major infusion of cash.

A Japanese firm had originally offered Stoneham $17 million for the club, its minor league franchises, and its spring training headquarters in Phoenix. That proposal evaporated before it got to the negotiating table, but a more concrete offer came in from another country: Canada. A syndicate headed by Labatt's, the largest brewery in Canada, bid $12.5 million to move the Giants to a new home in Toronto—$10 million for the team, and the $2.5 million to cover the expected litigation over breaking the team's lease at Candlestick, which ran through 1994.

Danny Kaye, still looking to buy a team and move it to Seattle, met with NL president Charles "Chub" Feeney to discuss the possibility of purchasing the Giants, but the Candlestick lease proved a major obstacle for Kaye and his partner, Seattle radio tycoon Lester Smith; they were prepared to offer $10 million for the team, but felt that it was up to MLB to deal with any legal issues resulting from the broken lease. Feeney told the press that while Kaye and Smith would be "acceptable owners," the NL was still intent on finding buyers who would keep the Giants in San Francisco. But during the last week of December, Labatt's officials met again with the Giants' front office, upping their offer to $13.25 million—and on January 9, Giants executive vice-president Charles Ruppert announced that the team had been sold to Toronto.

For new San Francisco mayor George Moscone, the timing of Ruppert's announcement couldn't have been worse. Inaugurated to his first term of office just a day earlier, Moscone feared that the loss of the city's baseball team would cast a dark shadow over his administration and hinder the liberal reforms that he'd planned to enact. Moscone obtained a temporary court order prohibiting the sale of the Giants, then flew to Phoenix on January 14 to meet with Feeney and the NL owners. The San Francisco mayor warned them that, if they approved the Giants' sale and move to Toronto, his city would slap a lawsuit on the league and the team to the tune of $10 million. Though the majority of NL owners felt that Moscone's efforts were coming too late to block the Labatt deal, they agreed to continue funneling cash to the Giants to keep the team afloat while the matter was resolved in a San Francisco court.

News of the Giants' sale and impending move to Toronto dashed the hopes of the many Seattleites who'd hoped that the Giants would be the team to fill their major league void. Ted Bowsfield, manager of the Kingdome, claimed that Kaye and Smith were not given an adequate chance to purchase the Giants. "Baseball is letting two fine owners get away," he said. "I think it is an unjust situation. All along, I felt the baseball solution here would be acquisition of the Giants."

King County executive John Spellman agreed, explaining that "It would be a little easier for the Giants to come to Seattle" than move to Toronto. And anyway, Spellman added, what sense did it make for America to be *losing* its baseball teams to other countries on the eve of its 200th birthday? "This is a Bicentennial year," he said. "The national pastime belongs here first."

The "bring baseball back to Seattle" faction was hardly mollified by the American League owners' January 14 vote to expand the junior circuit to Seattle in 1977; the city wanted an established franchise, and this new expansion resolution just sounded like another in a long string of empty promises they'd received from the league—especially since expanding the league to an uneven amount of franchises would cause numerous scheduling problems with no clear solution. For the American League to function effectively with thirteen teams, the National League would also have to add an expansion team, and then ratify interleague play.

Commissioner Kuhn announced himself strongly in favor of interleague play; and since he'd long promised to bring Major League Baseball back to Washington, D.C. (and was currently being pressured to keep his promise by a congressional committee led by Representative B. F. Sisk of California), the nation's capital seemed a likely candidate for National League expansion. But the NL owners were having none of it; theirs was the stronger of the two leagues, both at the box office and on the field, and they saw no reason to help bail their AL counterparts out of this mess. "I don't see why we have to go along with the American League," one unnamed NL official told a United Press International reporter. "Let them settle their own problems." "Expand we may, but interleague play is out," added another. "That's a dead horse, today, tomorrow and the day after that."

"The commissioner is not without his powers," responded Kuhn, ominously adding that "I have the authority to insist on agreement of a joint program by the two leagues." But despite Kuhn's posturing—which may have simply been for the benefit of the congressional committee breathing down his neck—the NL owners showed no sign of budging on interleague play; and if they wouldn't budge, then the AL owners' Seattle expansion promises amounted to little more than lip service.

In early 1976, there was no way to avoid the chatter of citizens band radio. The CB fad had begun in 1974, but didn't really reach critical mass until "Convoy," a hit novelty single by country singer C. W. McCall, topped the *Billboard* charts during the second week of January '76. McCall was actually an award-winning ad executive from Omaha, Nebraska, named William Dale Fries, Jr., but his throaty growl and encyclopedic grasp of CB slang (the distinctive truckers' argot that included several dozen code names for the police) convinced the American public that he was a real-deal truck-drivin' man with firsthand knowledge of white-line fever.

In "Convoy," a trucker going by the CB handle "Rubber Duck" leads an ever-expanding convoy of trucks and other vehicles (most notably "eleven longhaired friends of Jesus in a chartreuse micro-bus") on a high-speed cross-country journey, gleefully defying the speed limit and various Department of Transportation regulations, despite the best efforts of assorted "bears," "smokeys," toll collectors, and National Guardsmen to stop or slow them down. Though impossibly cheesy—the background singers sounded like they were recorded on day-release from a local production of *A Chorus Line*—the song's story of hardworking men challenging highfalutin authority resonated deeply with listeners in Bicentennial America, and triggered a massive spike in CB radio sales (not to mention sales of CB slang dictionaries) among the non-truck-driving populace. Whether you were avoiding highway speed traps, conversing with other CB aficionados, or just eavesdropping on real truckers as they bantered away the miles, the CB offered a new way to feel connected with your fellow Americans.

While "Convoy" was riding high on the pop charts, the King County lawsuit against the American League finally got under way in Everett, Washington—and what was happening in the Snohomish County Courthouse, as lead counsel Bill Dwyer faced down the AL on behalf of the people of Seattle, was far more revolutionary than any tale of rebellious truckers. Dwyer systematically dismantled the American League's defense, smashing his way through one attempted obfuscation after another with an unrelenting force that would have shamed the Rubber Duck and his army of a thousand screaming trucks. Journalist Fred Brack, who covered the trial for the *Seattle Post-Intelligencer*, later recalled that Dwyer "was so well-prepared that it was breathtaking."

Along with contending that there had been an "implied contract" between Seattle and the American League, which had lobbied the city to support the $40 million bond issue that funded the King-dome, Dwyer also argued that the AL had pulled the Pilots out of town not because of financial problems and poor fan support, as they'd claimed, but rather because of the league's illegal tying arrangement with a Minneapolis-based concessions company called Sportservice. The company had a history of extending credit to a number of MLB franchises in return for exclusive, long-term concession contracts at their ballparks; and in 1969, Sportservice gave $2 million to the Pilots' owners in exchange for the exclusive rights to sell hot dogs, beer, etc. at the privately owned Sick's Stadium. But since the King-dome was a publicly funded facility, any company that wanted to do business there would have been required by law to competitively bid for stadium concession rights. Milwaukee's County Stadium, where the Pilots moved in 1970 upon becoming the Brewers, just happened to be a privately owned ballpark—and Sportservice had just happened to follow the franchise to Milwaukee, where they set up shop without any competition.

Armed with several transcripts of private meetings and conversations between the AL owners revolving around the sale of the Pilots—Dwyer disclosed that the Pilots' owners had entered into secret negotiations with Bud Selig's Milwaukee group a month before the 1969 season had even ended—Dwyer knew just what questions to ask to make the witnesses sweat. After 18 days of testimony, the

American League's lawyers (who'd originally argued that the lawsuit was nothing more than a meritless multimillion-dollar shakedown) surrendered like the British at the Battle of Yorktown. They offered a settlement: in exchange for dropping the suit, Seattle would get an American League team in time for the 1977 season.

Dwyer countered by saying that his plaintiffs demanded substantial monetary compensation as well, but they'd be willing to forgo the compensation if the case was merely recessed (instead of closed) until Seattle's new team actually took the field at the Kingdome in April 1977. It was a sly move that effectively forced the AL to make good on their latest promise of a new franchise, regardless of whether the National League decided to expand as well.

If American League owners were unable to convince their National League counterparts to expand to 13 teams and join them in interleague matrimony, both circuits were well in agreement on how to deal with the Players Association. The owners had gone to court together in an effort to overthrow the Messersmith ruling; and since the outcome of that appeal would affect the content and wording of the new Basic Agreement, no progress had yet been made between players and management on that score.

Though most teams had already announced the dates that their spring training camps would open in late February, word began to circulate in January that the owners would attempt to force the Players Association's hand with a spring training lockout, refusing to open their camps until a new Basic Agreement was signed—one which would uphold the reserve clause that had just been gutted by the Seitz decision. "There are no definite dates for the start of spring training," said Kuhn. He still had hopes for a quick settlement with the players, he insisted, "but the matter is not resolved and I won't be satisfied until it is."

On January 31, Midwestern funkateers the Ohio Players topped the pop charts with "Love Rollercoaster," a hard-grooving dance track that spawned a grisly urban legend: the high-pitched scream that occurred during the song's instrumental breakdown was rumored to be the sound of a woman—some said it was the nude model from the cover of the band's *Honey* album—being stabbed to death in the studio. The tale was patently untrue, of course, but it spread like wildfire across American radio waves and schoolyards; the band intentionally kept mum and let the mystery boost their record sales. In any case, "Love Rollercoaster" could have easily served as the official MLB theme song for the first quarter of 1976; not only would February and March take baseball on a serious roller-coaster ride, but there would be times where you could almost swear that someone was trying to kill the game off.

3.

Tear the Roof off the Sucker
(February 1976)

For all the ominous rumblings within the baseball world regarding spring training, the Basic Agreement and the continuing Seattle/ San Francisco/Toronto conundrums, the casual fan was fairly oblivious to all the tension and tumult that swirled with increasing force around the National Pastime as January turned into February.

With Opening Day still two months away, there were plenty of other things to focus on besides baseball's growing pains—not the least of which were the XII Olympic Winter Games in Innsbruck, Austria, which kept a sizable portion of Americans glued to the boob tube for 12 days during the first half of February. Though the U.S. hadn't been expected to do particularly well in Innsbruck, the nation's athletes brought home 10 medals (three of them gold), their highest Winter Olympics total since 1932. The biggest winner among the Americans was 19-year-old Dorothy Hamill, who won the figure skating gold and became a pop culture icon in the process. Dubbed "America's Sweetheart" by the press, the pixielike Hamill not only parlayed her Olympic victory and wholesome good looks into deals for a network TV special, a headlining Ice Capades gig, and her own action figure, but her distinctively perky wedge hairdo was immediately copied by countless women and girls across the country.

There were also the ABA and NBA All-Star games, played a week apart at the end of January and beginning of February. Not only did both contests deliver genuinely exciting action that came down to the final minutes, but the ABA's halftime slam dunk contest also treated viewers to the mind-blowing spectacle of Julius "Dr. J" Erving sailing majestically from the free throw line to stuff a red-white-and-blue ABA ball through the hoop for the winning dunk. By June, the failing ABA would be history, with four of the league's remaining teams signing agreements to merge with the NBA. But Dr. J—along with other high-wattage ABA stars like Artis "The A-Train" Gilmore, David "Skywalker" Thompson, and George "The Ice Man" Gervin—would be a superstar fixture in the NBA for many seasons to come.

Even if you didn't care about basketball or the Olympics, there were dozens of other reasons to bask in February's warming cathode rays—including Pong, the Atari table tennis video game whose Sears-marketed home console version sold almost 150,000 units during the 1975 Christmas season (at the not inconsiderable sum of $98.95 apiece), inspiring several other electronics companies to jump into the home video game market with similar console systems before the end of 1976. ABC's *Rich Man, Poor Man*—based on Irwin Shaw's best-selling 1970 novel about impoverished German immigrant brothers finding their separate ways in America—did for the TV miniseries what Pong did for home video games; beginning on February 1, its seven-week, 12-episode run drew so many viewers that it would eventually end up as the year's second-highest-rated TV show (behind the CBS sitcom *All in the Family*), paving the way for decades of blockbuster miniseries to come. Popular sitcoms *Good*

Times, The Jeffersons, Sanford and Son, Barney Miller, Welcome Back, Kotter, and *Chico and the Man* all delivered the urban-oriented yuks, while the nostalgic '50s sitcom *Happy Days* spawned the even more popular *Laverne & Shirley,* which made its debut at the end of January.

It was a great season for gritty cop shows, too, with *Kojak, Baretta, Cannon, Starsky and Hutch, The Streets of San Francisco, Police Woman, Police Story, The Rookies,* and *The Rockford Files* all providing ample reason to pull up a beanbag chair and veg out in front of the tube. And if you wanted something even harder-edged, you could always venture out of the house to wherever *Taxi Driver*—the hottest and most controversial movie of the new year—was playing. Directed by Martin Scorsese, *Taxi Driver* starred Robert De Niro as a lonely and delusional Vietnam vet who takes it upon himself to wage a one-man war on the decadence and sleaze of mid-'70s Manhattan.

The decade had already produced numerous violent films set against the contemporary Big Apple's rotting core, including *The French Connection, Across 110th Street,* and *The Taking of Pelham One Two Three,* but *Taxi Driver* triggered a far greater public outcry, due to the unflinching brutality of the film's climactic shootout, as well as the unsettlingly adult performance of 13-year-old Jodie Foster as an adolescent streetwalker. Still, the controversy surrounding the film (which narrowly avoided an "X" rating only when Scorsese agreed to make the aforementioned shootout look less gory by desaturating the color of the film stock) helped boost *Taxi Driver*'s fortunes at the box office, where it eventually recouped over 20 times its original $1.3 million budget. De Niro's "You talkin' to me?" line quickly became one of the year's most oft-repeated catchphrases.

If the harsh post-'Nam reality of *Taxi Driver* wasn't quite your speed, *Frampton Comes Alive!* had the audio antidote. A double live album recorded at several 1975 concerts by hard-touring former

Humble Pie singer-guitarist Peter Frampton and released in January 1976, *Frampton Comes Alive!* oozed ingratiatingly mellow vibes across its four sides, making it the aural equivalent of a Maui Wowie–enhanced cruise along the California coastline in a Camaro. On the strength of sunshine-dappled hits like "Baby, I Love Your Way," "Show Me the Way," and "Do You Feel Like We Do" (all of which garnered considerably stronger radio airplay than their previously released studio versions), *Frampton Comes Alive!* reached gold-level sales figures of 500,000 by the end of February and would eventually go on to become the biggest album of 1976, selling over six million copies in the U.S. alone and transforming the shaggy-haired, bare-chested Frampton into a rock icon.

The affable serenity of *Frampton Comes Alive!* was unintentionally echoed in the political arena by Georgia governor Jimmy Carter, who'd shocked political analysts in January by considerably out-polling the other candidates in the Iowa Democratic caucuses, despite having been mostly unknown outside of his home state just a month earlier. Though Carter came in second behind "Uncommitted," the genial Georgian still received 27.57 percent of the vote, while heavily favored Arizona congressman Mo Udall trailed far behind with only 5.99 percent. The perpetually smiling Carter (who'd made his fortune as a peanut farmer) achieved his impressive showing via low-key, empathetic, and persistent campaigning among Iowa's blue-collar and farm workers, and he further strengthened his candidacy by using the same tactics to win the New Hampshire Democratic primary on February 24, a victory that upended the common perception that a Southern candidate would never be able to appeal to Northern voters. Meanwhile, the GOP race was already looking perilously tight for President Ford, who narrowly eked out a two-point victory over Ronald Reagan in the

Iowa Republican caucuses, then took New Hampshire from Reagan by only a single percentage point.

On February 5, a month before the presidential primaries reached Florida, a school election at Pensacola's Escambia High School ended in a race riot involving over 2,000 black and white students that injured 24 and resulted in considerable property damage to the school. The students had been voting on whether they wanted to revert to the school's "Rebels" nickname, which (along with its accompanying mascot, which distinctly resembled a Southern plantation owner) had been changed to "Raiders" in 1973, following a U.S. District Court decision banning the use of "racially irritating" Confederate names and symbols at the high school level. In the riot's aftermath, members of the Florida Highway Patrol and other law enforcement agencies were brought in to police the high school's halls, while the students eventually voted to change their nickname once again—this time to the more Bicentennially appropriate "Patriots."

On the same day as the Escambia riot, David Lewis—an Army private stationed at Fort Dix, New Jersey—collapsed and died after complaining of feeling weak and exhausted. Health officials announced two weeks later that his death had been caused by swine flu, a strain of influenza worryingly similar to the one that caused the 1918 flu pandemic that killed an estimated 50 to 100 million people worldwide, and that several hundred of Lewis's comrades had also been infected by the strain. Concerned that the country was looking down the barrel of another devastating epidemic, President Ford ordered a nationwide vaccination program at a cost of $135 million; the first swine flu vaccines were to be made available to the public on September 1, just in time for the next flu season.

In San Francisco, where the battle for the fate of the Giants was raging, Mayor Moscone's legal push to keep the team at Candlestick wasn't even the most high-profile court case in town: that honor belonged to the trial of Patty Hearst, which began at the city's Federal Building on February 4, two years to the day after the young publishing heiress had been kidnapped by members of the radical Bay Area group known as the Symbionese Liberation Army. Security cameras had captured images of Hearst participating in the SLA's April 1974 armed robbery of the Hibernia Bank in San Francisco's Sunset District, a crime she was eventually arrested for in September 1975. At the time of her capture, Hearst had defiantly claimed allegiance to the SLA; but now, with the infamously theatrical attorney F. Lee Bailey leading her defense, Hearst claimed to have been brainwashed by the revolutionaries into taking part in the holdup. Hearst's "trial of the century" would run for seven weeks; she was eventually found guilty of armed robbery and the use of a firearm to commit a felony, and sentenced to seven years in prison. Jurors would later reveal that Hearst's evasiveness on the witness stand made them doubt her claims of being brainwashed.

Many San Franciscans took a similarly skeptical view of Mayor Moscone's choice for a new Giants ownership group, an aggregation led by Bob Lurie and Bob Short. Both men had independently expressed interest in buying the team, but were brought together by Moscone when neither could raise sufficient funds on their own. Lurie, a San Francisco real estate magnate, was already a board member of the Giants' parent corporation, the National Exhibition Company, and was well respected in the Bay Area. But Short, who would be ponying up a significant chunk of the money needed to buy the beleaguered franchise, had already established a reputation for cheapness, duplicity, and general ineptitude during his six-year tenure as owner of the Washington Senators and (after he'd moved the Senators to Arlington following the 1971 season) the Texas Rangers.

On February 3, San Francisco city attorney Thomas O'Connor testified before Judge John Benson that Moscone was very close to being able to put an offer from Short and Lurie on the table: $8 million, with half a million in "good faith" cash up front. Giants attorneys Richard Murray and James Hunt countered that the Short-Lurie offer was far too low, and that the only acceptable bid—given the franchise's tenuous financial state—was the $13.25 million one from the Toronto group. NL president Chub Feeney further ratcheted up the pressure to seal the Toronto deal by declaring that the league would no longer be lending the Giants any additional money to cover their operating costs.

Even so, the judge's gavel came down hard on the side of Moscone and San Francisco, ruling that the city was entitled to do whatever it needed to protect its long-term investment in Major League Baseball. Don McDougall, president of Labatt's Breweries, continued to hold out hope that his group would still be able to buy the team and move it to Toronto, telling reporters that "logic is still on our side. Changing ownership is not going to put people in the ballpark [in San Francisco] and it's not going to pay the bills."

But McDougall had spoken too soon: Benson's ruling to keep the team in San Francisco was the best news Giants fans had received in years, and they responded by inundating the team with ticket requests, even though the sale of the franchise to Short and Lurie had yet to be consummated. Lurie announced to the press that he wanted to make Candlestick "a fun place" for the fans—a tall order indeed, given the stadium's frigid rep, though Short (no stranger to ballpark promotions) half-jokingly suggested that they could lure paying customers back to the 'Stick with a series of jacket and electric blanket nights. "If nothing else," cracked Art Spander in the *Sporting News*, the team's prospective new owners "came up with more ideas in a few minutes than the former Giants management did in years."

Still, when it came to creative promotional ideas, Lurie and Short had nothing on Ted Turner. Turner's campaign to woo the Atlanta fans and media took a literally ardent turn in February, when he instructed the Braves' front office to send Valentine's Day cards out to season ticket holders and local sportswriters. In a humorous nod to the fact that the '75 Braves finished 40½ games in back of the Cincinnati Reds—and would most likely fall far behind again once the upcoming season started—the card's rhyming inscription read:

> Rose is a Red, Morgan's one too.
> They finished first, like we wanted to.
> But last year's behind us, we're happy to say.
> Now we're tied for first, Happy Valentine's Day.

Several Braves players took part in a "Braves Blitz," the team's annual series of promotional appearances that crisscrossed the South, hitting shopping malls in cities like Chattanooga and Macon as well as Atlanta. Turner's marketing strategy of expanding the Braves' brand far beyond Atlanta city limits was already starting to pay dividends, as the fan turnout at these events was the largest and most enthusiastic the Braves had seen since they'd first moved to Atlanta.

Turner's efforts to woo his own players produced decidedly more mixed results. Shortly after purchasing the Braves, Turner invited the players to a party at his Atlanta home, where he attempted to impress upon them that he, too, was a successful athlete by screening home movies of his sailing exploits. Turner's plan fizzled when his malfunctioning projector chewed up the film, leaving him red-faced and his players bemused.

He tried a different tack a few weeks later, flying the entire team up the coast for dinner at the New York Yacht Club, where they toured the club's collection of trophies and model boats before sitting down to a prime rib feast. But the formality of the occasion was quickly breached by shortstop Darrel Chaney—a recent pickup from the

Reds, and an incorrigible prankster—who snuck a homemade fart machine (which he'd constructed from a wire hanger, a rubber band, and a metal washer) into the private dining room, and proceeded to let it rip. Chaney then surreptitiously passed the device under the table to other teammates, who did their best *Blazing Saddles* campfire imitations while the none-the-wiser Turner grew increasingly concerned and disgusted. "What's wrong with you guys?" he asked. "You sick or something?"

But if the Braves players didn't quite take Turner's buddy-buddy attempts seriously, they were at least impressed by his unbridled enthusiasm and energy, as well as his receptiveness to their input. Carl Morton, the team's player rep, described their new owner as "a revelation—he doesn't accept anything short of success and is the type of guy that when something isn't done correctly, he changes it right then, if possible."

Jimmy Wynn, the team's new left fielder, was so excited about Turner and his new team that he told Dodger General Manager Al Campanis—the man who'd recently traded him to Atlanta—"You guys will be lucky to finish third, because we are going to finish second."

Turner, however, was careful not to make any such grandiose predictions for the Braves' immediate future, preferring instead to humorously riff on his team's inept reputation. "If it gets as bad as it did last season, we'll just lock up the park and play in the afternoon," he told Furman Bisher. "That way we save on electricity and don't need any ticket takers. If people start bellyaching to me about losing, I'll say we're not losing, we're practicing on how to win."

On February 13, Seattle's reentry to the American League became official. Though the city received an expansion franchise rather than an established one, there was no longer any doubt that there would be a team playing at the Kingdome beginning in 1977. AL president Lee MacPhail said he still hoped to convince the NL to add an expansion team of its own and ratify interleague play for '77, but admitted to the press that, given the senior circuit's continued reluctance on the matter, the AL might have to add another new club.

Washington, D.C., was once again bandied about as a possible home for a new franchise. The Padres had almost been sold off and moved to the nation's capital for the 1974 season—the franchise's relocation seemed so imminent, the Topps Company actually printed cards of several Padres players that year with "Washington, Nat'l" listed as their team—but the prospective D.C. ownership group failed to meet the NL's financial requirements, leaving the door open for McDonald's mogul Ray Kroc to buy the team and keep it in San Diego. Now, with the National League owners seemingly uninterested in helping Commissioner Kuhn make good on his promise to bring his old hometown back into the major league fold, there were rumblings that the American League would now step up to the plate.

Still, the frustrating lack of progress on "the Washington problem" was but a minor headache for Kuhn, at least compared to the Leon Trotsky–grade migraine he must have experienced upon learning of Judge John Oliver's February 3 verdict, which upheld the right of arbitrator Peter Seitz to release Andy Messersmith and Dave McNally from their contracts. The ruling was a huge blow to the owners, whose lawyers had urged Oliver to consider the specifics of the contract dispute, arguing that the reserve system had always provided baseball with much needed stability, and that Seitz's decision would destroy the game. But the judge, who tartly responded that Congress did not enact legislation to make the federal courts "the protectors of the national pastime," refused to take the bait, ruling only on whether Seitz had acted within his jurisdiction as arbitrator.

Oliver's ruling was a Dr. J–worthy slam dunk in favor of the players, but the MLB owners stubbornly refused to acknowledge that they were teetering on the verge of total defeat. John Gaherin, the owners' chief representative at the Basic Agreement talks, reacted to the news of Oliver's verdict by telling Marvin Miller, "We must be realistic. We will proceed as though this decision does not exist." The owners promptly filed a second appeal, this time with the U.S. Eighth Circuit Court of Appeals in St. Louis. Kuhn, meanwhile, told the press that "positive" proposals would soon be presented to the players, but that "at this point, there is no decision at all about spring training."

On February 12, Marvin Miller met in New York City with player reps from all 24 clubs, who reaffirmed that the players wanted to report for spring training on March 1, and remained committed to bargaining in good faith on the Basic Agreement during the training period. As far as the players were concerned, the owners were merely cutting their own throats with their veiled threats of a spring training lockout. "We think the owners are playing a foolish game with these tactics," read the Players Association's statement to the press. "It is creating a bad image for baseball, but it is putting no pressure on us."

Several players, including Mets' player rep Tom Seaver, spoke of getting their spring conditioning regimens under way, despite the stalemated talks. "If the camps are not opened on time, as seems likely," Seaver told *Sports Illustrated*, "I'll go to Florida anyway and start my own training program. And I'll invite any player in the area to join me. Just because the negotiations are stalled, I see no reason for us to sit around and wait."

Seaver cut a highly visible figure in February, not only as a player spokesman, but also as a model in the Sears Spring/Summer 1976 catalogue. A full-page Sears Men's Store ad also ran in several national publications, featuring the 1975 NL Cy Young winner visually testifying to the versatility of Sears's new "Travelknit fourpiece." In the ad, Seaver sported four different leisure suit looks that ranged from boardroom exec to vaguely disreputable private investigator, while wearing a combination of items cut and constructed from a green double knit polyester fabric that wouldn't have looked out of place stretched across the Three Rivers or Riverfront stadium infields. "Everything about the Travelknit fourpiece says 'Style,' bragged the ad copy. "The $110 price speaks for itself."

Seaver wasn't the only major leaguer cashing in on a stellar 1975 season with a fashion endorsement deal: Fred Lynn, Boston's center field phenom, scored a $250,000, five-year contract with Botany 500, the same Philadelphia menswear company that provided the stylin' TV wardrobes of *Kojak*'s Telly Savalas, *The Jeffersons*' Sherman Hemsley, and comedian Bob Newhart. Lynn, however, had yet to ink a contract for 1976 with the Red Sox; having made only $38,000 during his rookie season—$18,000 plus a $20,000 signing bonus—the American League MVP/Rookie of the Year and his agent, Jerry Kapstein, were now holding out for a multiyear deal rumored to be worth upward of a million dollars. Catcher Carlton Fisk, Game Six hero of the '75 World Series, and shortstop Rick "The Rooster" Burleson were among other Red Sox stars who remained unsigned as spring training (or the spring training lockout) approached.

The AL champion Red Sox, who'd bolstered their rotation in the off-season by picking up former Cy Young winner Fergie Jenkins from Texas, were widely touted to take the AL East again in 1976; manager Darrell Johnson even went out of his way to assure Boston fans that they "should expect us to repeat." But Yankees manager Billy Martin had his own ideas on the subject. Speaking before an audience of over 500 Italian Americans at an early February dinner at the Lou Costello Tent of New Jersey, Martin said he believed that the Yankees had an exciting team that would be good enough to win the AL pennant. He added that he would be dedicating the 1976 season to his old mentor, the late Casey Stengel, and that he would attempt to resurrect the spirit and pride of the 1950s Bronx Bombers clubs that he'd played on and Stengel had managed.

"We'll hustle again," Martin said. "I promise you. I want the Yankee uniform to be a symbol of pride again. . . . I don't want players who worry about getting the hit to improve their average. I don't want players who think it's how you play the game, not whether you win. Anybody who thinks it's all right to lose as long as you try is full of it. If you come out there, I'll battle for you. And if you get mad at me and call me a Dago," he joked, "I'll beat the stuffing out of you."

Though star players going into spring training without signed contracts was practically a baseball tradition, the looming specter of the Messersmith ruling added a whole new level of uncertainty to contract talks in early 1976. If Seitz's decision held up successfully through another round of legal appeals, would MLB players decide to hold out en masse for big-money, multi-season deals? Should GMs lock their superstars down as soon as possible, before widespread free agency caused their salary demands to become significantly more inflated?

Cincinnati GM Bob Howsam was wrestling with these questions in triplicate. Joe Morgan (1975's NL MVP), Pete Rose, and Johnny Bench—his team's three best players, and arguably three of the biggest stars in baseball—were each demanding $200,000 contracts in the wake of the Reds' World Championship run; all three were already making over $100,000, as was Tony Perez, the team's All-Star first baseman. Shortstop Davey Concepcion, who'd made his second All-Star team and won his second Gold Glove in '75, was also asking for a substantial raise, as were outfielders George Foster and

Ken Griffey. "We have a budget and we must live within it," cautioned Reds administrative VP Dick Wagner—but Bench would become the team's first $200,000 player before the month was out, to be joined shortly thereafter at that plateau by Morgan. (Rose, the 1975 World Series MVP, would eventually settle for $180,000.)

Over in Oakland, you needed a scorecard to keep track of all the A's players who were demanding multiyear contracts, despite Charlie Finley's almost pathological aversion to such things. Jerry Kapstein, the agent who represented both hurler Ken Holtzman (who'd won 18 games for the A's in '75) and shortstop Bert Campaneris, sent Finley's blood pressure soaring with a phone call informing the A's owner of Holtzman's demand for a three-year, $480,000 deal. "I told him no way; I don't give multi-year contracts," Finley told Roger Williams of *The San Francisco Examiner*. "When he [asked for] $480,000 and three years, I said, 'You make me sick,' and I hung up on him."

Holtzman would have been surprised and a bit disappointed if Finley had actually considered his offer, since the reliable lefty (who'd won 77 games since coming to the A's in 1972) was really just looking for a way out of Oakland. "This is my one opportunity to play out my option and get away from Finley," he told reporters. A's slugger Reggie Jackson, on the other hand, was sending mixed messages through the media about his desire to stay in Oakland; the voluble All-Star, whose 36 homers had tied him for the 1975 AL crown with the Brewers' George "Boomer" Scott, had mentioned to at least one reporter over the winter that he wanted to be traded—but now, having recently purchased a stake in an Oakland limo company, Reggie sounded happy to stay put. "I feel like I'm part of the Oakland scene," he told Ron Bergman of the *Oakland Tribune*. "I'm not quite as much Oakland as Lake Merritt is, but I feel like an Oakland-grown boy. I really do. I have a home here. I have a great many friends here."

Much of the Oakland squad seemed considerably less copacetic than Jackson about remaining under the thumb of the cheap and combative Finley, who had made their lives miserable even as they were winning three straight World Series for him. The stack of unsigned Oakland contracts contrasted tellingly with the largely contented roster of the Kansas City Royals, who'd won 91 games in 1975 (finishing seven games in back of the A's) and now seemed potentially poised to unseat the A's from their five-year reign as AL West champs. With the exception of 22-year-old third baseman George Brett, who'd hit .308 in his second full season and was already inspiring Hall of Fame predictions, and slugging first baseman John Mayberry (who'd finished second in the AL MVP voting after hitting .291 with 34 homers and 106 RBIs), the entire Royals squad had already come to terms for the '76 season.

Chicago Cubs left fielder Jose Cardenal wasn't a superstar, but the 32-year-old Cuban was coming off one of the best years of his career, having hit .317 and stolen 34 bases for the Northsiders. In four seasons with the Cubs, Cardenal had firmly established himself as a fan favorite at Wrigley Field, thanks to his abundant afro ("With his huge puff of hair atop his slight frame," wrote *Chicago Sun-Times* columnist Mike Royko, "he looks like a skinny dandelion") and his colorful behavior, which included occasionally chewing on leaves from the ballpark's vines between pitches, and once begging out of the lineup because one of his eyes was mysteriously stuck shut. Cardenal told reporters that he was now holding out for a multiyear contract worth $140,000 per season from Cubs owner Phil Wrigley, which would make him the highest-paid player on the team. "I'd sign for five years if they'd let me," he said. "I like Chicago, and I am very grateful to Mr. Wrigley. But I no getting any younger and I got to make the big bread now."

Cardenal's teammate Geoff Zahn took a more spiritual approach to contract negotiations. The 30-year-old left-hander, an active participant in Baseball Chapel—an organization that provided Sunday services for all MLB teams—announced to the *Sporting News* that he was teaming with former Dodgers minor leaguer Bill Ralston to pen a series of negotiating guidelines (all backed by Bible verses) for Christian ballplayers. Among Zahn and Ralston's suggested tenets were, "We must ask ourselves whether we have ill feelings toward the general manager or owner," and, "We should never lose control of our tongues in negotiations."

But only a player of truly Christ-like demeanor would have been able to jettison his ill will and/or hold his tongue in the wake of the owners' February 23 announcement that they were officially delaying the opening of spring training until the players came to terms on the Basic Agreement. "We reluctantly but unanimously voted to delay the opening of spring training," said Chub Feeney. The verdict on the owners' second appeal of the Messersmith ruling wasn't due until early March, after the camps were due to open; as it stood, the owners were trying to force the players to sign a labor contract that would essentially void the rights that Messersmith and McNally had already won in arbitration.

The official announcement of the spring training lockout was a power play from a faction that had greatly misjudged its own power—or rather, its lack thereof. The statements from the owners' side of the table were almost absurdly paternalistic and condescending, painting the players as spoiled and unreasonable brats who needed a good spanking, and casting themselves as the stern but fair headmasters who were going to administer it for the players' own good. *Sports Illustrated*'s Doug Looney quoted one unnamed high-level exec as saying, "These doggone players have a misguided view of themselves because they've never lived in the real world. Of course, they are going to have to accept some restraints on their movement. And they had better learn quick that if you like scrambled eggs for breakfast, it's not a good idea to eat the chicken." John Gaherin, the owners' chief negotiator, didn't just ask that the players waive the rights granted them in the Messersmith case, but insisted that "they have a duty to do so." Charlie Finley, never at a loss for a zinger, declared, "The handwriting is on the wall, but these athletes can't read."

Marvin Miller could read just fine—and he understood quite clearly that it was the players, not the owners, who were coming from a strong negotiating position. "I'm bewildered," he told Looney. "Here these owners are with one hand in a vise and they're yelling at us, 'We're gonna fix you good.'" As Looney himself wrote, "The players are eager to go to spring training. And the owners would have to have a severe death wish to continue the torture much longer, partly because all the players are contracted to play this year, which means the teams are committed to pay them."

Robert Creamer, Looney's colleague at *Sports Illustrated*, lamented that the owners' spring training lockout would hurt the game and the fans, as well. "It would be a dreadful mistake for the owners to lock the players out of the training camps, as they are seriously threatening to do," he wrote. "After the upbeat note of last season, culminating in a splendid World Series, spring training this year is essential, as much for the continued goodwill of the fans as for the conditioning of the players. Neither side compromises itself by taking part in this warm, welcome rite of spring, and 'play ball' is not just an idle phrase."

But like a U.S. Army platoon bent on destroying a Vietnamese village in order to save it, the owners pushed ahead with the lockout, convinced that it was necessary for the greater good of the game—or at least necessary to preserve the game as they'd always known it. Only Bill Veeck refused to toe the ownership line, voting against the spring training lockout and announcing that he would still open the White Sox camp on March 1, at least for his minor leaguers. "We need spring training more than most of the clubs," Veeck explained. "We have an unusually young team with a lot of unknown players."

Veeck's fellow owners appeared unfazed by the dissenter in their midst. Minnesota Twins owner Clark Griffith responded to Veeck's announcement by chortling, "If we thought this was the act of a rational person, we'd worry about it."

4.

Let 'Em In

(March 1976)

Mike Marshall came by his "Iron Mike" nickname honestly. In 1973, while racking up 31 saves for the Montreal Expos, the indefatigable reliever set major league records for most appearances (92), games finished (73), and relief innings pitched (179) in a single season. Then, after coming to Los Angeles in an off-season trade, Marshall proceeded to break all of those records in 1974, appearing 106 times, finishing 83 games, and throwing a punishing 208.1 innings in relief, while winning 15 games and saving 21 more for the NL champion Dodgers—a herculean performance that earned him the first Cy Young Award ever won by a relief pitcher.

But Iron Mike's will was even steelier than his arm. A fiercely intelligent and often surly chap who spent his off-seasons pursuing a degree in kinesiology at Michigan State University, Marshall considered baseball a hobby—albeit a highly profitable one that allowed him to put his radical theories about physical conditioning to the test, such as his assertion that he was at his best when pitching four or five times a week. Flatly dismissive of those who put ballplayers on a pedestal (he notoriously refused to sign autographs for children, unless they could first produce an autograph of their schoolteacher), Marshall had equally little patience for anyone or anything that stood in his way. In March 1976, he further burnished his "Iron Mike" moniker by hacksawing his way into a batting cage in MSU's Intramural Building.

Marshall, who was employed in the off-season as a graduate assistant of MSU's physical education department, felt entitled to warm up for the upcoming season at the indoor batting cage of the school's Intramural Building. But the school's officials disagreed, banning Marshall from the AstroTurf-carpeted indoor facility in February after some of his batted balls landed too close to nearby tennis players for comfort. Undaunted, Marshall returned to the Intramural Building on March 3, having slyly reserved the cage under the name of a friend; but when the front desk refused to hand over the key, Marshall took matters into his own hands, gaining entry to the locked cage via the judicious use of a hacksaw and bolt-cutter.

"Before the police get here, let's get some throwing done," he barked to his accomplice, who squatted down behind the plate. With a crowd of MSU students watching—some took turns standing in the batter's box as he threw—Marshall managed to get about 120 pitches in before the arrival of East Lansing's finest. Speaking later to a reporter about his batting cage battle with MSU, Marshall compared the situation to MLB player-owner stalemate. "It's very similar to the baseball owners," he said. "If they're not willing to talk, then we must act."

With the owners' spring training lockout in effect at the beginning of March, Marshall was just one of hundreds of major leaguers conducting improvised preseason conditioning regimens. Unable to use their teams' stadiums, spring training, or minor league facilities, players worked out everywhere from home weight rooms to local high school gyms and even public parks. Whether out of habit or just plain restlessness, players began heading to Florida and Arizona despite the lockout, hoping to be ready to play when and if their teams' camps finally opened.

Phillies first baseman Dick Allen, who'd made headlines during the 1960s by showing up late to spring training, now made them by showing up early. "Here I am, and baseball is not ready." He grinned to reporters while working out with Phils teammate Tony Taylor near their team's complex in Dunedin, Florida. "If baseball wants to join me, that's okay." Tigers reliever John Hiller—newly bald after shaving his head in emulation of Telly Savalas—opened his own makeshift training camp, leading his Detroit teammates (most of them attired in T-shirts and cutoff shorts) through a hilariously anarchic series of pitching, hitting, and fielding drills at Lakeland's Henley Field, an ancient ballpark that hadn't been used by the Tigers since the mid-'60s. Hiller also tried exercising his arm one evening at the local county fair, where he won so many stuffed animals at the baseball-toss booths that the carneys banned him from the midway.

The lone major league training camp actually open at the beginning of March belonged, of course, to the White Sox. Though only nonroster players were eligible to participate, the fact that it was even open at all stuck in the craw of many owners. "I was afraid that things like this might happen," grumbled Angels owner Gene Autry. "That's why I definitely voted against Veeck when he was about to buy the White Sox."

On hand in Sarasota for the camp's opening, Veeck denied that this was another of his publicity stunts, though he admitted it made good copy for the baseball-hungry press and fans alike. "All I know is, at least we're getting some pictures in the papers of ballplayers hitting and throwing," he said. "It illustrates a very simple thing. Everybody except my peers recognizes that it's time to play ball."

Twins owner Calvin Griffith, a notorious skinflint, made no secret of where he stood on the subject of the ongoing labor negotiations. "We have the lowest payroll in baseball and I'm proud of it," he told the *Sporting News*. "I've felt all along the owners had to stand up to some of these demands the players have been making. Some of them are ridiculous. Players talk about owners being greedy; they're the ones who are being greedy. They want everything and care nothing about the game or its future."

It was no coincidence, then, that over half of the Twins' 40-man roster remained unsigned going into March, by far the largest percentage of spring holdouts; if the appeals court upheld the Seitz decision, the unsigned players would all be free to head for greener climes in 1977. Griffith's two highest-profile holdouts were second baseman Rod Carew and starting pitcher Bert Blyleven, both of whom were tipped to be future Hall of Famers, and both of whom were demanding healthy raises. The sweet-swinging Carew balked at Griffith's offer of a $10,000 raise from the $120,000 he'd made in '75, which seemed especially miserly considering that Carew was coming off a season wherein he'd hit .359 to win his fourth straight AL batting title. Blyleven, a hard-throwing righty whose vicious curve helped him compile 95 major league wins before his 25th birthday, was hoping to double his $65,000 salary after going 15-10 in '75 with a 3.00 ERA, 20 complete games, and 233 strikeouts in 275.2 innings.

Carew, who would later recall Griffith as a man trapped in "the Stone Age of baseball . . . when the owner was lord and master and the player a grubby peasant," eventually settled for a three-year contract—the lengthiest deal in Twins' history—good for $160,000 in 1976, with built-in $20,000 raises for the next two seasons. But

Blyleven, miffed at Griffith's offer of $85,000 for the coming year, remained resolutely unsigned.

The beginning of March brought glad tidings to one team owner: George Steinbrenner of the New York Yankees. Back in November 1974, Bowie Kuhn had banned Steinbrenner from participating in the day-to-day operations of the Yankees—a punishment handed down in response to his conviction for making illegal contributions to Richard Nixon's reelection campaign. But on March 1, 1976, Steinbrenner was officially reinstated by the commissioner. The suspension was originally supposed to last for two years, but Kuhn seemed inclined to give Steinbrenner time off for good behavior. Though it was hard for most people to believe that Yankees president Gabe Paul had actually been calling all the shots for the team in Steinbrenner's absence, the normally bellicose Steinbrenner had shown impressive restraint during his 15-month exile, keeping a low profile and staying out of both the commissioner's and his players' hair. "I think the purpose has been served," said Kuhn, upon lifting the ban.

Steinbrenner's reinstatement, however, likely had more to do with behind-the-scenes politics than any contrition on the Yankee owner's part. During the summer of '75, Steinbrenner had thwarted a "Dump Bowie" putsch led by A's owner Charlie Finley and Orioles owner Jerry Hoffberger, who mistakenly believed that Steinbrenner would align himself with them in an attempt to prevent the commissioner from serving a second term. Though there was certainly no love lost between Steinbrenner and Kuhn, Steinbrenner correctly surmised that he'd only dig himself a deeper hole by joining forces with Finley and Hoffberger; instead, he backed Kuhn for reelection, putting himself on the path to early reinstatement in the process.

The Yankee owner, if not exactly repentant, was at least publicly gracious about being allowed back into the game. "Naturally, I'm pleased," he told reporters. "As I said before, I have never agreed with the commissioner's original ruling. But I fully respect his right as commissioner to make it. I'm glad it's over." Yankee players, who had enjoyed a 1975 season blissfully free of what they termed "George's petty shit," were less than thrilled by the prospect of Steinbrenner resuming his meddlesome ways in 1976.

The day after Steinbrenner's return, Bob Lurie officially took control of the San Francisco Giants as co-owner and CEO. The purchase of the team from Horace Stoneham had finally been completed, but Bob Short, Lurie's nominal partner in the deal as recently as 48 hours earlier, had been ousted from the ownership equation at the behest of the other National League owners, who made it clear to NL president Chub Feeney that they didn't trust Short. In his place was Arthur "Bud" Herseth, owner of the largest cattle feeding and meatpacking company in Arizona, who just happened to be looking for a new investment after making millions on a recent cattle sale. San Francisco mayor George Moscone put Lurie and Herseth in touch with each other; in almost the blink of an eye, Short was out of the deal, and Herseth was in to the tune of $4 million.

The new owners announced that Bill Rigney, who had managed the Giants during their final years at New York's Polo Grounds and their first years in San Francisco, and later moved on to lengthy managerial stints with the Angels and Twins, would be returning as the team's new skipper. They also declared that the organization would be adopting a number of fan-friendly initiatives for the coming season—including more Bay Area–centric food options at the concession stands (egg rolls, bean burritos, and Napa wine would all be on sale), half-price "Bicentennial Family Night" promotions, and free shuttles from the city to Candlestick Point—all designed to goose attendance back up to the one million mark. Lurie also expressed interest in ripping up Candlestick's AstroTurf (which had been installed before the 1971 season) and replacing it with real sod, and said he was also investigating the possibility of installing an air-supported dome or roof on top of the ballpark, though it wasn't clear where the money for either of those projects would come from.

Relieved that they wouldn't have to decamp to another city for the coming season, the Giants' players allowed themselves to be cautiously optimistic about the prospect of playing for bigger crowds at Candlestick. "I'd like to see all kinds of people out at Candlestick actually making some noise," said Bobby Murcer. The gregarious right fielder had played his entire major league career with the Yankees prior to the 1975 season, and had been utterly unprepared for just how inhospitable Candlestick could be to fans and players alike. "You got no idea what a lot of silence a crowd of six hundred can make," he laughed.

The only Giant who seemed unabashedly pumped for the coming season was John "The Count" Montefusco, who'd won 15 games for the San Francisco Giants in '75, on his way to nabbing the NL Rookie of the Year award. A frizzy-haired right-hander whose live arm and even livelier mouth reminded old-timers of the great Dizzy Dean, Montefusco liked to brag to the press before a game about how many players he was going to strike out, and his predictions weren't usually too far off the mark. His 215 strikeouts in 1975 were the most by any rookie in Giants history; his 200th K of the season came at the expense of none other than Johnny Bench, the Reds' All-Star catcher, who bemusedly autographed the ball afterward at the Count's request.

After making ends meet during the off-season with a PR job at Bay Meadows racetrack in nearby San Mateo, Montefusco managed to pry a new contract rumored to be worth somewhere in the neighborhood of $60,000—the highest salary ever for a second-year pitcher—out of the Giants' new owners. He celebrated his new windfall with a March 11 party for himself and local sportswriters, organized by fellow Giants hurler John D'Acquisto, at the Playboy Club near San Francisco's Chinatown. Looking dapper in a three-piece suit with a "bunny" on each arm, the curly-haired Count radiated even more bravado than usual. "Next year after I win the Cy Young Award," he told the gathered reporters, "they'll have to pay me one hundred grand."

Bob Lurie may have talked a good game about removing the Candlestick AstroTurf, but over on Chicago's South Side, Bill Veeck was already well ahead of him. In 1969, the White Sox had become the first major league organization after the Houston Astros to adopt AstroTurf, though they'd inexplicably installed a layer of the newfangled artificial turf over their ballpark's infield, while keeping the outfield and foul territory natural. This horrifying horticultural hybrid was perpetuated through the 1975 season, and Veeck viewed it as an absolute abomination; besides, the artificial surface would get unbearably hot during summer day games, and players were constantly injuring their ankles and knees on it. From almost the very moment his ownership consortium solidified their purchase of the franchise, Veeck had set his sights on restoring the infield at White Sox Park to its original grassy glory.

Originally named White Sox Park when it opened in 1910, the South Side ballpark had been quickly rechristened Comiskey Park after Sox owner Charles Comiskey. Thus it remained until 1962 when, with the Comiskey family no longer involved in the team's business, the Allyn ownership group changed the name back to White Sox Park. When Veeck regained control of the franchise, one of his first orders of business was to reinstate Comiskey's name on the old ballpark. "Charley Comiskey was brave enough to build this thing," Veeck told the *Chicago Reader*. "I think he's entitled to have his name on it until the joint falls down."

On March 6, Veeck invited White Sox fans out to Comiskey to help him rip 8,000 or so square feet of "Sox Sod" from the infield. Despite gray skies and chilly temperatures, over a thousand Chicagoans enthusiastically pitched in, carting off everything from pocket-sized souvenir chunks of the plastic grass to room-sized rolls for home use. As with so many of Veeck's exploits, the removal of the artificial infield was either heroic or idiotic, depending on whom you talked to. At the time, the use of cheaply maintained artificial turf was nearing the height of its popularity; teams like the Reds, Phillies, Pirates, Cardinals, and Royals even built their rosters around it, stocking their lineups with speedy line-drive hitters who could use the hard carpet to their advantage. Yet here was Veeck, taking a revolutionary stance by becoming the first major league owner to banish the synthetic stuff from his ballpark.

"Those owners who attack me for usurping tradition are the same ones who put in artificial turf," Veeck told the *Chicago Reader*. "They put it in because they thought they could save some money. But in reality, they're taking an average of a year off a ballplayer's career because of increased problems with knee injuries. And they destroy the illusion they're trying to create—being outside and watching a game on natural grass." But even as Veeck was flying the flag for baseball tradition, he was preparing to unveil one of the most outrageous acts of his storied career: a radical redesign of the White Sox uniforms.

Veeck nearly let the cat out of the bag on March 4 when, surrounded by sportswriters and other drinking buddies at Miller's Pub, his favorite watering hole in downtown Chicago, he casually mentioned that the White Sox would be going for a new look in 1976. Over the previous five seasons, the team had worn some of the most distinctive uniforms in the majors, featuring bright red pinstripes on their white home jerseys and pants, with caps, undershirts, belts, stirrups, and shoes all in a matching shade of red. Their road uniforms were even gaudier, with the dominant red color scheme vibrating intensely against the shade of powder blue that many teams were now adopting in place of road grays. But the time had come, Veeck told his audience at Miller's, for the White Sox to break new sartorial ground.

"We are adding elegance to baseball styles," said Veeck. "We may not be the greatest team in baseball, at least not for a few years, but we'll immediately be the most stylish team in the game." Color television sets had only recently overtaken the number of black-and-white TVs in American households; and with teams like the Houston Astros (with their horizontally striped "tequila sunrise" jerseys) and Charlie Finley's Oakland A's (who wore various eye-popping combinations of what Finley called "Kelly Green, Fort Knox Gold, and Wedding Gown White") dressing to impress the folks tuning in at home, one could easily assume that Veeck would be cranking up the saturation knob for the new line of White Sox uniforms. But Veeck, unsurprisingly, had other ideas. "The White Sox are not going to be dressed like a bunch of peacocks," he insisted. "There is a difference between color and elegance, between style and class. You will be awed," he promised, with an unmistakable twinkle in his eye. "Comiskey Park will replace Paris and New York as the fashion center of the world."

On March 9, Veeck introduced the new White Sox uniforms with a fashion show so bizarre it bordered on Dada. Staged in the elegant drawing room of Chicago's tony Tremont Hotel, the presentation featured five grizzled former White Sox players from the '50s and '60s—Moe Drabowsky, Dave Nicholson, Dan Osinski, Bill "Moose" Skowron, and "Jungle" Jim Rivera—strutting their stuff, catwalk-style, as about a hundred journalists looked on. *Chicago Tribune* fashion columnist Maggie Daly served as the show's commentator, interspersing her running descriptions of the new uniforms they modeled with such cooed asides as, "This is sexy!" "Gorgeous!" and "Just look at those legs!"

Just look at those legs, indeed: not only did the new uniforms feature white-and-navy V-neck pullovers with Henley collars that split the difference between 1870s baseball tunic and 1970s leisure suit, but they also came with the option of a turtleneck undershirt and three different styles of pants: "Clamdiggers," which came down to just above the ankle; "Knickerbockers," which were worn tucked into knee-high socks; and "Hollywood shorts"—reminiscent of the Bermuda shorts worn by the Hollywood Stars of the Pacific Coast League in 1950—which left the players' knees fully exposed.

"It's comfortable," said Jungle Jim Rivera of the Hollywood shorts look. "But I'm afraid if you hit the dirt, you're going to tear up your legs. I sure wouldn't want to wear short pants sliding into third base." "You don't slide with your knees," Veeck interjected. "If you do, you shouldn't be sliding. Plus, the high socks have a roll top and a pad under them."

"I'm trying to put into practice what I've said about tradition," Veeck told the *Chicago Reader.* "I don't mean to say that things should stand still. But the lettering is from the 1903 Sox. The navy-blue came from the uniforms the Sox wore in the 20s and 30s. But the cut and the design and the fabric are all new. Without the fabric we couldn't use this kind of uniform. Yet it is more comfortable."

Though the current White Sox players had yet to don the new outfits, Veeck seemed certain that his team would enjoy the freedom that the shorts and jerseys (which were meant to be worn untucked) would provide. "These new uniforms are more practical and utilitarian," he enthused. "A guy who hasn't sweated as much may have that extra step on a hot day to help us win a game. Or a pitcher in the pullover shirt may have more freedom to throw than with the usual tucked-in shirt. Players should not worry about their vanity, but their comfort," he insisted. "If it's 95 degrees out, an athlete should be glad to put on short pants and forget his bony knees. Hell, I've got a worse-looking knee than any of my players. It's solid wood."

In a self-penned piece published that week in *Sports Illustrated*, Veeck wrote that the new uniforms were "perhaps my little way of hinting that strange and wondrous things are going to be happening at old Comiskey Park." Proudly noting in the piece that ticket sales were up 40 percent over where they'd been at the same time in 1975, Veeck expressed his gratitude to White Sox fans. "The fans don't owe me a thing, of course," he wrote. "I owe them. They have given a 62-year-old, one-legged, can't-see, can't-hear guy a chance for a last hurrah. . . . My own secret dream—and please don't tell anybody—is that as the season is coming to an end I will be able to mount the podium and say to the people of Chicago and its environs, 'I want to thank you for allowing me to smell the roses. I want you to come now and help us drink the champagne.'"

One person who wouldn't be sharing a beverage with Veeck in the near future was former White Sox manager Chuck Tanner, who still had three years left on his contract (at an annual salary of $60,000) when Veeck—having already promised the job to Paul Richards—gave him the boot in December. "I know what Paul can do," Veeck explained. "He knows the kind of ballclub that we have to have. I don't know Tanner that well. I don't know whether he's competent or incompetent or a great man. . . . I just don't know. So I didn't want to take a chance."

Charlie Finley, who'd fired Alvin Dark after the A's were swept by the Red Sox in the '75 ALCS—a devout Christian, Dark had angered and alienated Finley by publicly declaring that the A's owner was headed to hell unless he accepted Jesus as his personal savior—immediately swooped in and offered Tanner the job of Oakland skipper. Aware of Tanner's contractual situation with the Sox, Finley announced that he would only be paying Tanner $25,000 a year, and that Veeck and the White Sox would have to honor their prior deal with Tanner and make up the remaining $35,000. AL president Lee MacPhail, though initially unsure of how to handle the matter, approved the terms of Tanner's Oakland contract; but Veeck, refusing to pay Tanner a dime, appealed the decision to the league office.

Stuck in the middle of this battle of wills between baseball's two biggest eccentrics was the congenial Tanner. "Mr. Finley's been wonderful," he explained to journalist Jerome Holtzman. "His checks have come in on the first and 15th of each month. I don't know what Bill Veeck's waiting for. Maybe he's waiting until we come to Chicago and wants to give me a check at home plate."

Tanner petitioned MacPhail, advising him that the White Sox already owed him $7,500 in back pay through the end of February. Meanwhile, Finley and Veeck continued to take potshots at each other in the press, with Finley predicting failure for the White Sox ("You can't ballyhoo a funeral," he said, dismissing Veeck's promotional efforts), and Veeck accusing Finley—who'd lured fans to the Oakland Coliseum over the years with such events as "Hot Pants Day" and "Bald Headed Men Night"—of poaching his promotional concepts. "He's stolen all of his stuff," said Veeck, "and I won't complain if he continues stealing my ideas. After all, imitation is the most sincere form of flattery."

MacPhail, of course, had bigger problems on his plate—as did his NL counterpart, Chub Feeney, Commissioner Kuhn, and the major league owners. For on March 9, the same day as the White Sox fashion show, a three-judge panel of the U.S. Eighth Circuit Court of Appeals upheld the lower court ruling stating that arbitrator Peter Seitz had acted within his authority in finding that Andy Messersmith and Dave McNally had played out their options. Under the court's decision, all players who still hadn't signed a contract for 1976 by the March deadline would have the opportunity to become free agents in 1977. The owners had only one legal option left—appeal the decision via the U.S. Supreme Court—but that avenue didn't look particularly promising.

"There's no way to go now but to settle," said Tom Seaver. "Do they want to try going to the Supreme Court and meanwhile not play ball or pay salaries for two years? The Supreme Court wouldn't even hear their case." Judge Gerald W. Heaney, who wrote the appeals court opinion, expressed similar sentiments. The owners and players, he wrote, "certainly are in a better position to negotiate their differences than to have them decided in a series of arbitrations and court decisions. The time for plain talk and clear language has arrived. Baseball fans expect nothing less."

Basic Agreement talks between the two camps resumed almost immediately in New York City, but soon stalled over several obstacles, including the number of seasons that a player would be required to spend with a team before qualifying for free agency. (The owners wanted nine; the players insisted upon five.) In the meantime, the March 10 signing deadline passed with 162 players still unsigned for 1976. Among the players thus officially beginning their option year were Fred Lynn, Carlton Fisk, and shortstop Rick Burleson of the Red Sox, while the majority of the A's starting lineup—Reggie Jackson, outfielders Billy North and Joe Rudi, third baseman Sal Bando, shortstop Bert Campaneris, and catcher–first baseman Gene Tenace, along with pitchers Rollie Fingers, Ken Holtzman, and Vida

Blue—remained unsigned. Finley automatically renewed each of his players' contracts with a 20 percent pay cut, the most allowed by MLB rules.

Andy Messersmith, of course, was now free to field job offers for the coming season. "I'll return to the Dodgers," he said, "but only if they're the highest bidder." While Walter O'Malley expressed no interest in joining the bidding war, Bill Veeck did, offering Messersmith a two-year White Sox deal at $450,000. Messersmith's agent, knowing that far more lucrative offers for the star pitcher (who'd won 19 games for the Dodgers in '75 while leading the NL with seven shutouts and 19 complete games) would soon be coming over the transom, didn't even dignify Veeck's offer with a response.

Beginning to realize that the lockout wasn't working in baseball's favor, Commissioner Kuhn met with the owners' Player Relations Committee on March 16 and urged the teams to open their training camps, lest Opening Day (and its resultant profits) be interminably delayed. The response to Kuhn's plea was mixed; some owners, like the Cardinals' Gussie Busch, wanted to continue the lockout, mistakenly believing that the Players Association was just days away from caving to the owners' demands on the Basic Agreement talks. George Steinbrenner and Ted Turner, on the other hand, were very much in favor of letting the players into the camps. (Turner, following Veeck's lead, had opened the Braves' facility to nonroster invitees; WTCG even broadcast a few games between Braves and White Sox minor leaguers during the lockout.)

After canvassing the owners, Kuhn then called John Gaherin, the owners' chief representative, to get his perspective on the situation. "Commissioner," Gaherin told him, "I work for the PRC. If you quote me on this, I'll deny it. But if I were you, I would open the camps. We're not getting anywhere. Miller is laughing up his sleeve because he knows the clubs have got to open the camps."

On March 17, Commissioner Kuhn gave the official order to end the spring training lockout. "Because I think it is now vital that spring training get under way without further delay," he explained to the press, "I have directed that all camps be opened at the earliest possible time. While nobody is more disappointed than I that we do not have solid progress toward a final agreement, the fans are the most important people around and their interests now become paramount. Opening the camps and starting the season on time is what they want." The labor talks would continue, but depriving America of its National Pastime during the Bicentennial was simply not a viable option.

Within 48 hours of Kuhn's proclamation, all 24 major league training camps were open and buzzing with activity. Since there was little actual on-field action to write about, many of the initial press dispatches from Florida revolved around the players' appearance. Ted Simmons, the Cardinals catcher whose long black tresses were as impressive as his bat, came to Cards camp looking uncharacteristically clean-cut. Dick Young reported in the *Sporting News* that "Simba" had accidentally singed his hair while clearing brush on his property outside St. Louis, though some suspected that the freethinking switch-hitter—who'd been outspoken in his opposition to the Nixon administration and the Vietnam War, and who was known to engage in such distinctly nonjockish pursuits as art collecting—had actually been smoking weed rather than clearing it at the time of the hair-burning incident. Meanwhile, Red Sox ace Luis Tiant arrived at the Red Sox facility looking newly hirsute, thanks to his bespoke afro toupee. El Tiante had spent $750 of his World Series loser's share on the new 'do, which had been manufactured by Monsanto, the same company that developed and produced AstroTurf. Several members of the World Champion Reds, who were forbidden by team rules to wear hair past their collar or sport any facial hair other than short sideburns, were visibly delighted by the look of horror that flashed across manager Sparky Anderson's face when they showed up in camp looking like mountain men.

Impressed by the neatness of the '75 Reds as much as the all-conquering efficiency of their play, George Steinbrenner decided that the Yankees would sport a similarly businesslike look during the coming season. The Yankee owner instituted a new grooming policy for his team, one of the few ideas that he and manager Billy Martin would ever completely agree upon. "I don't want guys going on different trips by themselves," Martin told Gene Williams of *The Miami News*. "When we get where we're going, they can put a toilet seat on their head for all I care. But when we're together, I want them to be Yankees. I want them to look like Yankees and dress like Yankees. Beards and long hair aren't the New York Yankees."

It had only been a few years since the Oakland A's Mustache Gang had set the major league trend for long locks and facial hair in motion with their victory over the Reds in 1972's "Hair vs. Square" World Series, which emphatically proved that you could look like a bunch of scraggly hippies and still play championship baseball. But by now, most big leaguers were used to being able to groom themselves in accordance with the shaggy male hairstyles of the day, and there was no little amount of grumbling when Yankee players were greeted at the team's Fort Lauderdale complex by a missive from Steinbrenner and Martin reading, "No beards, no beads, no mutton chops, no long hair, no long stirrups." Catfish Hunter, Sparky Lyle, and Thurman Munson were at least allowed to keep their mustaches, but Lyle was deeply annoyed by the team's new "neatness counts" policy. "It cost me $50 to have my hair curled," the reliever complained, "and they said it was still too long."

The player with literally the most to lose under the new tonsorial tenets was off-season acquisition Oscar Gamble, who arrived at the Yankees' facility sporting the same hairdo he'd brought to Indians training camp the three previous seasons: namely, the biggest, funkiest afro ever seen on a major league diamond. Gamble's dynamic 'do stood an estimated 10 inches tall at its apex, and looked wide enough to simultaneously accommodate three baseball caps. While this copious coiffure would have simply marked Gamble as the hippest brother in any urban nightclub in America, it was way too hip for the still conservative world of major league baseball, where older coaches and sportswriters often assumed that large afros were synonymous with black rebelliousness and militancy. Still, the Indians had always let Gamble wear his hair however he wanted; Billy Martin, on the other hand, wouldn't give Gamble a uniform until he'd submitted to a serious shearing.

Though initially taken aback by Martin's refusal to even let him onto the practice field, the easygoing Gamble—who was also wearing what *The Miami News* described as a "Rip Van Winkle beard"—graciously acquiesced, making an impromptu visit to the barbershop at the Yankees' hotel. "I thought they'd let me work out," he told Gene Williams. "I mean, I played with long hair for four years. But that's the rule and if everybody else was going along with it, I wasn't going to rock the boat."

With his wife, Juanita, and Yankee coach Elston Howard along for moral support, Gamble spent an hour in the barber's chair, his cap size shrinking from 8 to 7½ in the process. Juanita wept at the sight of her husband's curls falling to the floor, but Howard kept the mood light. "They carted the hair away in bushel baskets," the coach claimed afterward. "There was so much of it, I'm making myself a wig out of it."

Gamble tried to be philosophical about the situation. "You know, I had an offer from Afro Sheen to do some commercials this summer," he said, "but now I don't have no hair. I'm losing a lot of money, but if I hadn't cut it, I might not have been on the team. And then I would have lost everything. I liked my hair long, but it'll grow back, I hope."

If George Steinbrenner (who eventually reimbursed Gamble for the fee he was due to receive for doing the ad) deprived the world of a truly righteous Afro Sheen commercial, the "before" version of Gamble's glorious growth would at least be forever immortalized by his 1976 Topps "Traded" card, where it was crowned with a crudely airbrushed ersatz Yankees cap that looked big enough to house a Chevy Vega. Gamble's card was part of a 44-card "Traded" subset issued by Topps and interspersed in their regular 10-card wax packs, which cost 15 cents apiece down at your local drugstore or news-stand. The purpose of these "Traded" cards—which Topps had first introduced in 1972, and also issued as part of their 1974 set—was to commemorate some of the bigger deals that had occurred during the off-season; but the Topps art department's inept attempts to "dress" the traded players in the uniforms of their new teams resulted in a surreal smorgasbord of crooked pinstripes (as on Gamble's card), puzzling color tints (former Braves reliever Tom House was pictured wearing a magenta Red Sox cap), and team logos that looked like they'd been on a week-long Boone's Farm bender.

Airbrushing antics aside, the 1976 Topps baseball set was among the company's most visually appealing series of the decade, featuring generally high-quality color player portraits and a simple-yet-striking layout. Along with the usual league leaders, rookie prospects, and postseason cards, the '76 set also included such unique subsets as "'75 Record Breaker" cards (with Hank Aaron's breaking of Babe Ruth's career RBI mark earning the pole position on the checklist), "Sporting News All-Time All-Stars" (featuring such legendary

Hall of Famers as Ruth, Ty Cobb, Ted Williams, and Honus Wagner), and "Father and Son" cards that paired photos of current major leaguers like Buddy Bell and Bob Boone with vintage baseball card images of their big leaguer dads.

But the most memorable oddity in the 660-card 1976 set was the one commemorating the victory of Milwaukee Brewers utility man Kurt Bevacqua in Joe Garagiola's 1975 Bazooka Bubble Gum Blowing Championship, an "annual" event that sadly lasted only one year. The front of the card pictured Bevacqua blowing the winning bubble, while a pair of bat-shaped calipers measured its prodigious 18½" diameter. The back of the card displayed the complete 22-player tournament bracket, listing several stars (Johnny Bench, Bill Madlock, Bert Blyleven, and George Brett) as participants, none of whom made it as far as the semifinals; apparently, part-time players like Bevacqua and his co-finalist, Phillies backup catcher Johnny Oates, had ample opportunity to perfect their bubble-blowing techniques while warming the bench.

Since 1966, when the Fleer chewing gum company sold off its player contracts to Topps and bowed out of the baseball card market, Topps had enjoyed the privilege of being the only company licensed by the Major League Baseball Players Association to sell nationally distributed baseball card sets. Other cards were still available as premiums in various products: kids could fish plastic 3-D cards out of specially marked boxes of Kellogg's Corn Flakes, and cut flimsy cardboard cards off boxes of Hostess snack cakes, but the Kellogg's and Hostess card sets were generally limited to star players, and their cards (much like the locally oriented sets given away by Cincinnati's Icee Drinks or A&P supermarkets in Kansas City and Milwaukee) weren't considered as legitimately collectible as those that Topps produced. In the spring of 1976, however, a small New York company called SSPC (for Sports Stars Publishing Company) attempted to challenge Topps's market dominance with its own 630-card set of contemporary players.

SSPC was an offshoot of TCMA, a "collector issues" company fronted by a card dealer named Mike Aronstein. TCMA had been in the baseball card business since 1972, mostly printing limited-run minor league sets and collections based around big leaguers from previous decades. These sets, which were sold by mail out of the back of TCMA's *Collectors Quarterly* magazine, all had what Aronstein called the "pure card" look—just a color photo surrounded by a white border, in the style of the classic 1953 Bowman set, without any words or graphics to complicate the visuals. Believing that Topps's baseball card designs had become too busy, Aronstein relegated all player information, including the player's name, to the back of his cards. (The copy on the back was penned by *Collectors Quarterly*'s editor, a precocious teenager named Keith Olbermann.)

TCMA's limited resources meant that the photography for the 1976 SSPC set had to be done primarily at Shea Stadium by amateur photographers, and many of the card photos were poorly lit, rushed-looking, or (as in the case of Phillies pitcher Joe Hoerner, who was depicted wearing a woman's large-brimmed straw sun hat) downright goofy. But though the SSPC set looked comparatively amateurish, the mail order cards still presented an exciting underground alternative to what Topps was doing at the time. Unfortunately, since the SSPC cards weren't actually licensed through the MLBPA, Topps was able to halt TCMA's manufacture of the set with a cease and desist order.

Topps would hang onto its monopoly until 1981, when the Fleer and Donruss companies—after considerable legal wrangling—began to license cards of their own through the MLBPA, and regained a share of the nationally distributed baseball card market. SSPC soldiered on, reappearing in 1978 with individual team sets included as tri-fold inserts in a magazine called *All Star Gallery*, but would never again attempt to compete in the baseball card big leagues.

On March 20, the same day Oscar Gamble bid farewell to his 'fro, a joint meeting of American League and National League owners was highlighted by the AL's announcement that it would be expanding to 14 teams for the 1977 season, with Toronto as its first choice for franchise number 14. Though AL president Lee MacPhail declared that there were two groups bidding for the franchise, it surprised no one when, a week later, the Labatt's Brewing Company group—which had been rebuffed in its attempt to buy the Giants—was awarded the team.

"We are very pleased, needless to say," said Labatt's president Don McDougall, who indicated that the company's first order of business—after working out a payment schedule for the $7 million cost of buying the franchise—would be to lock up a lease at Toronto's CNE Stadium. Recently enlarged at a cost of $15 million, the stadium (which was already home to the Toronto Argonauts of the Canadian Football League, and featured an AstroTurf playing surface) was capable of holding 40,000 baseball fans. The unnamed Toronto franchise would be added to the AL East, while its Seattle counterpart would join the AL West.

The American League's annexation of Toronto didn't sit well with some National League executives, like John McHale of the Montreal Expos, who'd gotten used to the idea of Toronto eventually becoming a National League outpost. (McHale felt that the addition of a NL team in Toronto would give his Expos a "natural rival.") But with a number of NL owners still opposed to expansion and/or interleague play, and the AL needing a 14th team to prevent outright scheduling chaos in 1977, the NL could hardly call "dibs" on Canada's biggest city. But shortly after the Labatt's group was given the thumbs-up from the AL, NL owners—suddenly changing their minds about expansion—voted 8–4 to send Commissioner Kuhn a resolution imploring him to intervene "in the best interests of baseball" and permit the National League to expand to Toronto and Washington for 1977.

Kuhn, much to the annoyance and consternation of the AL owners, then asked Toronto city officials and the prospective franchise owners to hold off on signing any legal paperwork for two weeks, in order to give the NL owners time to come to a unanimous consensus on expansion. Whether the commissioner was moved to act by behind-the-scenes pressure from Walter O'Malley and other NL owners (as was alleged by the AL), or simply because the NL resolution appealed to his long-standing desire to return baseball to Washington, his attempt to exert his authority on this matter quickly blew up in his face, and very nearly ignited a civil war between the two leagues.

"The American League vigorously disputes the authority of the commissioner to attempt to retroactively interfere with its expansion to Toronto," said AL president Lee MacPhail in an open letter to Kuhn. While AL teams had previously been open to the idea of playing "a significant number of regular season games" in D.C. for the 1977 season, MacPhail continued, that offer was now officially off the table. Meanwhile, the NL owners not only failed to come to a unanimous consensus on expansion, but wound up in further disarray, with nearly half of the teams voting against NL expansion of any sort.

The Toronto incident not only drove a stake into the heart of Kuhn's Washington baseball dream, but it also significantly strained his relationship with the American League. "He's not God," cracked Charlie Finley, reveling in the fact that his fellow AL owners were now almost as negatively disposed toward the commissioner as he was. "He can't just take anything and interpret it as in the best interests of baseball." In just a few months, however, Finley's words would come back to haunt him.

Basic Agreement talks had resumed between the owners and the Players Association, but were still going nowhere—in part because the owners were too busy squabbling about the addition of Toronto. "It's almost impossible to negotiate with them when the league presidents are running out the door every few minutes to settle the Toronto problem," Marvin Miller complained.

Tom Seaver was running into some negotiation difficulties of his own. Coming off his third Cy Young–winning season, "Tom Terrific" had been holding out for a three-year contract worth approximately $825,000, but Mets chairman M. Donald Grant was loudly dropping hints that the team would rather trade their star pitcher than meet his salary demands. As the Mets' union rep and one of the most respected players in the game, Seaver wielded a considerable amount of influence, and it gave Grant serious *agita* to read Seaver's staunchly pro-labor quotes in the paper each day. Upon pitching his first game of the 1976 season, Seaver would officially become a "10-and-5 man"—a 10-year major league veteran who'd spent five years with the same team, and thus would have the right to veto any prospective trade. But until then, Grant could still punish Seaver for his insolence by sending him elsewhere.

As Grant and the Mets dangled Seaver as trade bait, rumors swirled that Seaver might be swapped to Los Angeles for Don Sutton, who'd averaged 17 wins a season for the Dodgers since 1969. But Sutton, already a 10-and-5 man, found the idea of pitching in New York City profoundly unappealing. Grant, inundated by hate mail for even considering a trade of "The Franchise" (as Seaver was popularly known), wisely called off the deal and reopened contract negotiations. The pitcher eventually came away with an incentive-laden three-year deal with a base annual salary of $225,000, but his relationship with the Mets—the organization he'd signed with out of USC in 1966—was now permanently damaged.

Fans may well have wondered what Grant had been smoking to make him even consider dealing Seaver—and equally curious as to where they could obtain some of it for themselves—but it was the California Angels, not the New York Mets, who had the real marijuana problem. On March 21, rock superstars The Who played a concert (along with openers Rufus and Little Feat) at Anaheim Stadium in front of 55,000 fans, the largest show on the band's North American tour. A few days later, Angels groundskeepers discovered what turned out to be hundreds of marijuana plants growing robustly along the ballpark's left field line, and another lush patch in center field. These herbal invaders were presumably the result of pot seeds discarded during the concert, which were then inadvertently watered and fertilized by the ballpark's grounds crew. "At first we thought it was weeds," said stadium manager Tom Liegler. "Later we found out we were right."

Liegler initially attempted to eradicate the plants with heavy doses of herbicide, but his efforts produced little in the way of success; nor, once word spread about Anaheim Stadium's bumper crop, did he have an easy time dissuading volunteers from showing up to help with the harvest. Finally, someone figured out a way to clip the plants that caused them to die out quickly, and the "Big A" was declared cannabis-free—at least until Opening Day, since random clouds of pot smoke were not exactly an unusual sight at big league ballparks of the mid-'70s.

Anaheim mayor William J. Thom reacted to the agricultural anomaly with a commendable sense of humor, even if no one would ever accuse him of stealing his material from George Carlin or

Cheech & Chong. "The economic situation at the stadium has not reached such a perilous point that we have to resort to growing marijuana," Thom told reporters. "But they'll never be able to play 'Tea for Two' at Anaheim Stadium again."

5.

The Boys Are Back in Town

(April 1976)

"We got ourselves a nigger!" cried the white teenagers as they savagely attacked the black man who'd taken a wrong turn into their midst. The scene seemed like a flashback to 1962 Birmingham—but it was actually happening on April 5, 1976, at Boston's City Hall Plaza.

Ted Landsmark, a black attorney of some local prominence, was on his way to an affirmative action committee meeting with the Boston Redevelopment Authority when he ran into a mob of white youths leaving an antibusing rally. Taking their frustrations out on Landsmark, several of the teens kicked him, and another broke his nose with a punch. Joseph Rakes, a 17-year-old from South Boston, took a swing at Landsmark with the Stars 'n' Stripes–draped flagpole he'd brought with him to the demonstration.

Landsmark's beating was just one appalling example of the racial violence burning throughout Boston since September 1975, when the city had begun implementing the compulsory busing of black and white schoolchildren to each other's neighborhoods as part of a state-mandated public school desegregation plan. But the attack on

Landsmark, which was captured by *Boston Globe* photographer Stanley J. Forman in his Pulitzer Prize–winning photo *The Soiling of Old Glory*, brought Boston's long-simmering racial tensions to the attention of the rest of the nation, and did so with a visceral force that was impossible to ignore. Forman's photograph was like a perverse inversion of the flag raising at Iwo Jima; not only did Rakes desecrate the American flag by brandishing it as a weapon, but his use of it to attack a black man also seemed to repudiate everything (liberty, equality, the pursuit of happiness) that the flag and its country were supposed to stand for. That Landsmark was beaten mere blocks from the site of the Boston Massacre—where another black man, Crispus Attucks, became the first martyr of the American Revolution—was an irony not lost in this year of Bicentennial frivolity.

"Do the people of Boston," asked an editorial in *Ebony* magazine, "or the people of any other American city, understand what Bostonians were fighting for 200 years ago? Do they understand and believe in the Declaration of Independence? And if they don't believe in and understand the Declaration and the great dream it symbolizes, what, in God's name, are they celebrating?

"Crispus Attucks would have understood the racism," the editorial continued, "but it is doubtful whether he would have understood the insensitivity of public officials who are repeating the mistakes of the white Founding Fathers and subtly fanning the flames of discord with code words like 'forced busing' and 'Ethnic purity/heritage/ treasure.'"

The *Ebony* editorial's line about "ethnic purity" pointedly referenced the first major gaffe of Jimmy Carter's presidential campaign, which occurred just a few days before Landsmark was attacked. Asked to clarify his stance on neighborhood integration, the Georgia governor—who up until then had run a near-flawless campaign, and who'd already established a broad support base among both white liberal and black voters—said that while he supported open-housing laws that made it a crime to refuse to sell or rent houses and apartments based on race, color, or creed, he also opposed government programs that pushed integration for integration's sake. "I have nothing against a community that is made up of people who are Polish, or who are Czechoslovakians, or who are French Canadians or who are blacks trying to maintain the ethnic purity of their neighborhoods," he said.

Carter's comment was greeted with howls of derision and disappointment from opponents and supporters alike. Atlanta mayor Maynard Jackson, who'd intended to endorse Carter, reportedly responded to the governor's remarks by pounding his fist on his desk and shouting, "Is there no white politician I can trust?" After initially resisting pressure to retract his statement, Carter finally backed down at a press conference in Philadelphia. "I was careless in the words I used," he said, "and I apologized for it. It was a very serious mistake." Still, many felt that Carter had already done irreparable damage to his campaign—Mo Udall was now suddenly gaining on him in the polls—while others archly noted the location of his apologia: like Boston, Philadelphia was a former hotbed of the American Revolution that was now seething with racial tension, much of it fomented by Frank Rizzo, the city's embattled and divisive mayor.

On April 9, four days after Landsmark was attacked, Bill Veeck brought some much needed levity to the front pages of the nation's newspapers with some flag waving of his own. Shortly before the first pitch of Opening Day at Comiskey Park, Veeck, White Sox manager Paul Richards, and team business manager Rudie Schaffer donned powdered wigs and colonial gear, treating White Sox fans to a living re-creation of Archibald MacNeal Willard's iconic Revolutionary War painting, *The Spirit of '76*. The 40,318 fans in attendance (the team's largest crowd in over a year, and nearly twice the number who'd witnessed the previous year's Opening Day) went absolutely nuts as the three men marched out of the White Sox dugout and across the ballpark's new grass infield, giving Veeck a hero's welcome in his first regular season game as Sox owner since 1961.

Though the surprise reenactment had an undeniably comic element to it, there was also something sweet and poignant about watching Veeck—who'd lost his right limb as the result of a wound sustained in World War II—playing the peg-legged fifer as Schaffer beat a tattoo on the snare drum and Richards waved the Revolutionary army flag with its 13 stars. The normally reserved Richards was also called upon by Veeck to recite the little remembered fourth stanza of "The Star-Spangled Banner." "When I decided to work for Veeck," Richards said later, "I geared myself to expect almost anything."

Veeck had promised to turn Comiskey Park back into a fun and inviting place to watch a ballgame, and the Opening Day crowd saw that he'd been good to his word. Not only did the old ballpark look better than it had in ages, thanks to a new white and green paint job, but Veeck also ordered the exploding scoreboard he'd installed during his first tenure to be returned to its original potency—and it gave the fans a deafening display in the fifth inning, when off-season pickup Jim Spencer hammered a two-run homer off of Royals lefty Paul Splittorff. "Veeck's Wrecks," as local sportswriters dubbed the South Side assemblage of aging vets, untested rookies, and other spare parts, rose to the occasion by beating Kansas City 4–0 on the back of Spencer's three-hit, three-RBI day and a six-hit, seven-strikeout complete game performance by Wilbur Wood, the portly knuckleballer who'd been a fixture on the mound for the White Sox since 1967, longer than any current member of the team.

Wood wasn't the only veteran hurler in fine form that day. Jim Palmer and Tom Seaver, the respective AL and NL Cy Young winners from 1975, both appeared to still be in award-winning form, with Palmer scattering six hits in eight innings as he outdueled Fergie Jenkins for a 1–0 Orioles win over the Red Sox in Baltimore, and Seaver fanning eight Expos in seven innings as the Mets beat Montreal 3–2 at Shea Stadium. In Texas, President Ford—whose spirits were buoyed by his 11-point victory over Ronald Reagan in the Wisconsin primary three days earlier—threw out the first pitch for the Rangers' home opener at Arlington Stadium, then sat back and enjoyed a brilliant 11-inning complete game performance by 37-year-old spitball artist Gaylord Perry, who kept the Twins in check with pitches legal and otherwise until Rangers shortstop Toby Harrah gave Perry a 2–1 win by blooping a bases-loaded single in the bottom of the 11th.

The Orioles and Rangers games set Opening Day attendance marks for both teams, with 46,425 showing up to Baltimore's Memorial Stadium and 28,947 participating in the festivities at Arlington. In fact, overall Opening Day attendance showed an 18 percent spike in 1976, indicating that—for all the fans who wrote letters to the *Sporting News* and other periodicals during the spring training lockout threatening to boycott baseball unless the "greedy" players were put in their place—the spring's labor unrest had done little to dampen Americans' enthusiasm for their National Pastime. The Mets, on the other hand, drew just a hair over 17,000 for their first game of the season; though the chilly weather might have been more of a factor in keeping fans away from Shea than any lingering bad vibes over Seaver's contract holdout, the right-hander was still booed heavily during the pregame introductions. "I knew it was going to be like that," Seaver reflected afterward. "When you put yourself in an emotional situation you are going to hear from both ends of the spectrum."

In San Francisco, the 37,261 fans who made the scene at Candlestick Park gave the Giants their largest Opening Day crowd since 1966. "This is like the Second Coming of the Giants," enthused manager Bill Rigney before the game. "When was the last time you saw anybody sitting out there?" he asked, gesturing toward the ballpark's outfield seats. "Never is the answer. I tell you, it's a new show here. But the act better be good, too, or we'll lose the audience."

The act was indeed a good one, at least for a day. In his inimitably flamboyant way, John Montefusco had guaranteed Giants fans beforehand that he'd shut out the Dodgers in his Opening Day start. Though he blew that promise almost immediately by giving up a two-out solo home run to Dodger center fielder Dusty Baker in the first inning, the Count still notched his first W of the season as the Giants cruised to a 4–2 victory over their archrivals from Southern California. Montefusco's performance might have even been witnessed by a sellout crowd, if it hadn't been for a strike of city employees that curtailed bus service and—because most union vendors and concessionaires refused to cross the picket lines at the municipally owned stadium—kept all but four of the stadium's 30 food counters closed. But most of the fans who found their way to Candlestick on the unseasonably warm afternoon brought their own refreshments with them, as well as an audibly renewed enthusiasm for the team that almost got away. "There was a buzzing out there," said Gary Matthews, the Giants' left fielder, who put the home team up 3–1 in the fourth inning with a two-run shot off the Dodgers' Don Sutton. "It was the same kind you feel in places like Cincinnati." Matthews and his teammates were so excited about their Opening Day victory, they didn't even mind that there was no hot water in the shower room.

For the Dodgers, who chose to endure a fragrant bus ride back to their hotel over the added indignity of a frigid post-loss shower, the game was mostly notable for the fact that Ron "the Penguin" Cey had started his third straight season opener for them at third base—the first time in over 30 years that the team had enjoyed such stability at the hot corner. Cey, whose nickname derived from his squat build, stubby limbs, and waddling gait—"Looks like someone dropped a safe on him," noted a 1969 Dodger scouting report—had put up the best numbers of his career in 1975, hitting .283 and leading the team with 25 home runs, 101 RBIs, and a .372 on-base percentage; in order to stand a chance of catching the heavily favored Cincinnati Reds in the NL West, the Dodgers would need the Penguin to match or better that performance in '76.

If the World Champion Reds were the odds-on favorites to rack up another division title, the preseason jury seemed split on the question of whether the Pittsburgh Pirates would capture their sixth NL East flag in seven seasons, or the Philadelphia Phillies would finally make it to the postseason for the first time since 1950. "This could be the greatest year Philadelphia fans have enjoyed since the Whiz Kids won the pennant in 1950," wrote the UPI's Fred Down. "Or it could be a season of frustration capped by the fans making Manager Danny Ozark the guest of honor at a necktie party."

The two teams faced off in the Phillies' home opener on April 10, which began with a Bicentennial-oriented spectacle so over-the-top as to turn Bill Veeck's wooden leg green with envy. A colonial-garbed horseman named Russ Peterson, who'd ridden all the way from Boston in emulation of Paul Revere's 1774 "Suffolk Papers" ride, entered Veterans Stadium during the pregame festivities and circled the field on his steed. Upon Peterson's arrival at the Phillies' bullpen, which concluded his two-week, 318-mile ride, he handed a baseball to a man wearing a space suit, a crash helmet, and a Bell

Aerosystems Rocket Belt. Bill Suitor, aka Rocketman, then pro-pelled himself 150 feet into the air and made his own circle around the field before landing on the pitcher's mound and passing the ball to Phillies pitching legend Robin Roberts, who emerged from a gi-ant baseball-shaped float. Roberts, who'd recently been elected to the Hall of Fame, then threw out the game's ceremonial first pitch.

Both teams took the AstroTurf sporting striped, square-crowned 19th-century-style pillbox caps, designed in honor of the 100th an-niversary of the 1876 founding of the National League. Wearing the throwback pillboxes with modern polyester pullover jerseys didn't make much sense from a fashion standpoint; and yet, as with the pairing of a Paul Revere impersonator and Rocketman, the juxtapo-sition was not without its goofy charm. "They're giving me back the cap I started with," cracked Pirates manager Danny Murtaugh when the new hats were originally introduced to the media.

With the exception of the Expos, who wore a patch on their sleeves commemorating the upcoming 1976 Montreal Summer Olympics, all National League teams sported NL Centennial sleeve patches, which featured a stylized caricature of an old-time player with a handlebar mustache that would have given Rollie Fingers a run for his wax. (The Phillies also wore a special '76 Liberty Bell patch on their oppo-site sleeve.) But only half of the NL teams—the Cardinals (who also occasionally donned red batting helmets with white stripes painted on to match the pillbox caps), Mets, Reds, and Expos, in addition to the Phillies and Pirates—ever took the field in the unusual centennial brims, with the Bucs being the only team to adopt the pillboxes as full-time headwear.

The Phillies ditched the pillboxes soon after their opening series with Pittsburgh, possibly because their first two games of the year didn't go very well. With the Phillies up 4–3 going into the top of the ninth on Opening Day, the announced Vet crowd of 42,147 watched in horror as hulking Pirates right fielder Dave "the Cobra" Parker plowed into Phils catcher Johnny Oates while trying to score from third with two outs on a Bill Robinson fly ball. Left fielder Jerry Martin's throw beat Parker to the plate by a fraction of a second—Martin later called it "the throw of my life"—but the 6'5", 227-pound Cobra hit the catcher with such explosive force that he sent the ball bouncing out of Oates's mitt, and broke the catcher's collarbone in the process. "I'm sorry about Oates but I had to do it," Parker reflected later. "Either I jar the ball out of his grasp or the game is over." The Pirates went on to win 5–4 on a three-base error by Phils right fielder "Downtown" Ollie Brown in the top of the 11th, which was followed by light-hitting shortstop Mario Mendoza's RBI single off reliever Tug McGraw.

The next day at the Vet was even grimmer, with a 73-year-old Phillies fan named Joseph Corbett suffering a massive heart attack in the stands shortly before the Phils' 8–3 loss to the Pirates. Despite the ministrations of Pirates hurler Doc Medich, who jumped into the stands and attempted to save Corbett with CPR and mouth-to-mouth resuscitation, Corbett was pronounced dead on arrival at Methodist Hospital. "I just happened to be there," said Medich, who was soft-tossing in the Pirates' bullpen when he saw Corbett collapse. "There's nothing you can do but try to help."

Ted Turner undoubtedly gave his fellow owners a few coronaries of their own on April 10, when he announced that he'd signed Andy Messersmith to a lucrative deal with the Braves. Though no figures were disclosed, insiders reported that the deal was worth a cool $1 million over three seasons, with a $400,000 signing bonus tacked on. The contract also included a no-trade clause, leading Turner to characterize the arrangement as a "lifetime contract." "Andy will be a Brave as long as I am," Turner said. "And I plan to be around a long, long time."

Though Messersmith's salary fell short of the five-year, $3.75 million free agent contract that Catfish Hunter received from the Yankees in late 1974 when a contract loophole allowed him to escape Charlie Finley's A's, his new Braves deal served notice to owners and players alike that the economics of the game were about to shift dramatically in favor of the players. Even with rumors (most likely spread by the Dodgers) circulating about the questionable health of Messersmith's pitching arm, six teams had come forward with serious offers for the services of the newly free agent, all of which were for substantially more money than Messersmith had made with the Dodgers.

The weirdest aspect of Messersmith's Braves contract was that neither Turner nor any other Atlanta front office executive was involved in the final negotiations. After Turner's initial offer to the pitcher fell flat, Braves fan Larry Foster, the owner of an Atlanta heating and cooling company, rang Turner and asked permission to reopen negotiations with Messersmith. Turner, humoring Foster, jokingly told him to go ahead and call Herb Osmond, Messersmith's agent—and was pleasantly shocked when, 12 hours later, he received news from Osmond that Messersmith would be signing with the Braves. Foster hadn't actually been authorized by Turner to do anything except call Osmond, but he'd gotten carried away and offered Messersmith terms so good that Osmond couldn't refuse. After informing Osmond that Foster wasn't an official Braves representative, Turner agreed to honor the deal anyway, and he thanked Foster for his negotiating acumen with an autographed ball and a pair of Braves season tickets.

Turner's free-spending, seat-of-the-pants way of doing business didn't sit too well with some of the game's more established owners, but he was too busy reveling in the publicity onslaught generated by the Messersmith signing to care. On April 13, the new Braves owner got to bask in the love of Atlanta fans for the first time, when nearly 38,000 of them converged upon Atlanta Stadium for the team's Opening Night contest against the Reds. Though the home team lost 6–1, the largest Braves crowd in a year and a half left the ballpark thoroughly entertained, thanks to a circuslike evening that included a steady stream of marching bands, dancing girls, and other entertainers, including a guy in a gorilla suit who swept the bases between innings. When it came time for the seventh-inning stretch, Turner left his seat and took the field to lead the crowd in a raucous sing-along of "Take Me Out to the Ballgame." It was his second impromptu appearance on the field that night—in the second inning, when Ken Henderson rounded the bases after putting the Braves up 1–0 with a solo home run off Gary Nolan, the Braves right fielder was astonished to find an excited Turner waiting at home plate to offer his congratulations.

Though he also enjoyed injecting himself into the spotlight and staging outlandish promotions, A's owner Charlie Finley felt no kinship whatsoever with Ted Turner. The A's owner viewed the new Braves owner as a dangerous interloper who was willing to upset baseball's economic balance for the sake of his own self-aggrandizement—and as self-aggrandizing as Finley could be, paying top dollar for top talent was not his preferred method of making headlines. "People have only so much money for food, for rent, for entertainment," warned Finley, after Messersmith signed with the Braves. "Athletes are going to price themselves out of the market. I do not criticize the athletes, I criticize the owners for paying these unjustified, astronomical salaries."

Finley, who had already lost Catfish Hunter to free agency, saw the writing on the wall regarding the inflated salaries that full-scale free agency would bring, and knew that he would be sorely ill-equipped to compete in a new world where players were allowed to sell their services to the highest bidder. Not only was such a concept anathema to his parsimonious modus operandi, but Finley's insurance business was struggling in the wake of the recession, and he also happened to be looking down the barrel of an expensive divorce settlement. Strapped for cash and facing higher salary demands from his star players—most of whom would surely leave Oakland at the end of the season if they remained unsigned for 1976—Finley decided to cut his losses, even if it meant dismantling a team that had won five straight AL West titles and three World Series over the previous five seasons. He'd made his intentions clear on April 2, when he jolted the baseball world by trading Reggie Jackson, Ken Holtzman, and minor league hurler Bill VanBommel to the Orioles in exchange for outfielder Don Baylor and pitchers Mike Torrez and Paul Mitchell.

News of the trade caused more than a few sportswriters to hurriedly revise their predictions for the 1976 season: not only did the deal significantly improve the chances of the Kansas City Royals to end Oakland's dominance in the AL West, but it also made the Orioles suddenly look like the team to beat in the AL East. Earl Weaver's Birds had taken the division five times in the past seven years, and they'd finished only four and a half games behind the Red Sox in 1975, despite an aging lineup and poor performances at the plate from veterans Brooks Robinson, Mark Belanger, Bobby Grich, and Paul Blair. Adding a superstar slugger like Jackson—and a solid lefty like Holtzman—could only help their cause in '76. "I couldn't wait to get Reggie," Weaver later recalled in his autobiography. "[He was] a better outfielder with even more power than Baylor."

Reggie, however, was less than enthused about joining the Orioles. Shocked that Finley had actually made good on his threats to trade him from the only major league team he'd ever known, saddened at having to say good-bye to the teammates he'd won three rings with (including Joe Rudi and Rollie Fingers, whom he'd known since their days in the A's farm system), and furious about being exiled from his home and business interests so close to the start of the season, Reggie refused to report to Baltimore unless the Orioles agreed to pay him $200,000 for the coming season—a significant increase over the $112,000 he was due to make with Oakland. "If I'm going to get jerked around, then they're going to have to damn well pay me to get jerked around," Jackson privately told Gary Walker, his agent. "I think we can win a pennant in Baltimore, but it's going to cost them."

A proud and deeply sensitive man, Jackson spent the rest of April wandering bitterly between his home in Oakland, the Hilton Hawaiian Village in Honolulu, and Walker's home in Tempe, Arizona, brooding over the trade and fielding phone calls from Weaver, Orioles general manager Hank Peters, various O's players, and even Bowie Kuhn—all whom begged the superstar slugger to return to the game. But despite their appeals to his considerable ego ("The game needs you, Reggie," Kuhn insisted), Reggie remained unmoved. Either $200,000 for one season, or five years at $250,000 per, Walker told the Orioles; otherwise, his client was sitting out the season, and maybe even giving up baseball for good. "I have other alternatives," Jackson told reporters. "I have a real estate business, a Pontiac dealership, a television contract, and obligations to people who work with me. Life has more to offer than hitting a ball over a fence."

Earl Weaver tried to shrug off Jackson's holdout. "The way I look at it," he told the *Sporting News*, "this is just like having Reggie out with a pulled muscle or in bed with the flu. It's the manager's job to do what he can with the 25 players he has available. You can't worry about the ones that aren't here."

But other Orioles were singing a less tolerant tune. "Reggie not being here is psychologically destructive to the ball club," said Jim Palmer shortly before his Opening Day start. "We gave up three quality players to get him. If we have to start the season without him, the first inclination is to ask, why did we make the trade?"

"I'd like to think that Reggie has enough pride in himself and enough respect for the game to realize that if it weren't for baseball he wouldn't have these outside interests," said Hank Peters. "All players, no matter who they are, have a legal and moral obligation to perform."

Reggie refused to budge. "I was giving them a take-it-or-leave-it offer," he later recalled in his autobiography. "All the years of working for Charlie Finley had taught me a rock-hard stance. I was giving the Orioles a taste of *his* medicine. I had been taken away from my home, I had been taken away from the West, I had been taken away from my team and my friends. I hadn't even gotten a phone call from Finley. I couldn't make him pay, but *someone* was going to have to pay."

Jackson's absence also left a giant, star-shaped hole in the Oakland lineup and clubhouse. "Without Reggie, this is a different club," A's center fielder Bill North told the *Oakland Tribune*'s Ed Levitt before Opening Day at the Oakland Coliseum. "I'm talking about the personality of the team. When Reggie left, a lot of the flair and flamboyancy left with him. Look around. Don't you miss it?" But if the Jackson trade seemed destined to cut the heart out of the Swingin' A's, it didn't diminish their fight. Even with Baylor hitting only .129 during his first month in Oakland, the A's still scrapped their way to a 9–8 record—ending April a game behind the first-place Rangers and two and a half games up on the Royals and White Sox.

New skipper Chuck Tanner's emphasis on the running game resulted in the A's stealing 33 bases in those first 17 games, while new pitcher Mike Torrez won three games and posted a 2.88 ERA in his first six starts, but Charlie Finley was even more excited about his latest addition to the organization, a Chicago-based astrologer named Laurie Brady. Brady, an attractive Irish American lass who lived in the same Chicago apartment building as Finley, wasn't a baseball fan, but she'd previously predicted that the '75 A's would win their division but fail to make the World Series. Impressed with her prophetic accuracy, Finley hired Brady in early April to help Tanner make astrologically advantageous decisions regarding his lineup and pitching rotation. Brady announced that the stars were aligned to allow the A's to go all the way in 1976.

The addition of a team astrologer officially gave the A's the most bizarre front office in the majors, with Brady joining ranks that already included a 14-year-old Oakland kid named Stanley Burrell, who'd been discovered by Finley dancing for change in the Coliseum parking lot. Originally hired by Finley as a batboy—the A's players dubbed him "Little Hammer" due to his striking facial resemblance to Hank Aaron—Burrell was soon promoted to executive vice president, though "team narc" might have been a more appropriate title. Since Finley lived in Chicago, he relied on Burrell to be his "eyes and ears" in the A's clubhouse; the players, upon getting wise to Burrell's true role, soon changed his nickname to "Pipeline" and would clam up whenever the kid was around. (A decade later, Burrell would reclaim his original nickname and enjoy a lucrative career in music as MC Hammer.)

The Orioles didn't need an astrologer—they needed Reggie Jackson. Without a bat in the lineup comparable to his or Baylor's, the punchless O's scored only 36 runs in April, going 6–9 in their first 15 games. The Red Sox started off almost as badly, going 6–7 for April, though their problems were mostly weather-related, with a string of rainouts and travel delays preventing their starting pitching from finding anything approximating a steady groove; at one point, postponements caused Fergie Jenkins to go 10 games between starts, the longest idle period the former Cy Young winner had ever experienced during the regular season. Stumbling out of the gate, the Orioles and Red Sox quickly found themselves left in the dust by the New York Yankees and Milwaukee Brewers, both of whom got off to hot starts in April (10–3 and 9–3, respectively) after facing each other in a pair of hotly contested games at Milwaukee's County Stadium.

Before Opening Day in Milwaukee on April 8, Yankee skipper Billy Martin called a team meeting and told his players, "You know, we're going to win this thing this year. You're all good enough to win. The only way you won't win is if you don't listen to me and do what I tell you. . . . Anyone who doesn't think so can leave now, no hard feelings. I might be rough, but I'm going to treat you like men until you act different. I'm not a guy checking curfews; just be ready when the bell rings."

The Yankees responded to Martin's fiery pep talk by losing 5–0 to the Brewers. Milwaukee righty Jim Slaton breezed through a four-hit shutout, while Yankee ace Catfish Hunter struggled and gave up five runs—three on a pair of RBI singles by Hank Aaron—in the first two innings. Afterward, the ever-combative Martin filed an official protest of the game, claiming that the County Stadium pitching mound was illegally steep and had contributed to Hunter's control problems. Umpiring supervisor John Stevens measured the mound the following day and overruled Martin's protest, stating that he found nothing irregular. "They worked all night grading it," Martin shot back.

The Yankees made Martin proud in the second game, digging their way out from a six-run deficit and scoring five runs in the top of the ninth to go up 9–6. But Sparky Lyle failed to close out the contest, allowing the first two Brewers batters to reach base in the bottom of the ninth before Martin pulled him in favor of Dave Pagan. Bobby Darwin, the first batter Pagan faced, then reached first on an error by third baseman Graig Nettles. With the bases loaded and Don Money at the plate, Martin screamed at Pagan to pitch from a full windup instead of a stretch. Pagan didn't hear him, but first baseman Chris Chambliss did, and asked first base umpire Jim McKean to call time out. As McKean raised his hand to do so, an oblivious Pagan pitched to Money, and the Brewers' third baseman promptly deposited the ball in the left field stands for a game-winning grand slam.

Watching a TV broadcast of the game from his office at Yankee Stadium, George Steinbrenner was so enraged by Money's homer that he kicked the TV screen, sending a shower of glass and sparks into the air, and causing panicked Yankees staffers to wonder if a bomb had gone off in their boss's lair. Billy Martin was even hotter; as Money rounded the bases, the Brewers ran out of the dugout to congratulate him and County Stadium erupted into joyful chaos, a red-faced Martin buttonholed McKean and insisted he nullify the home run. "You called time out!" he screamed. "You have to back it up!"

Much to the surprise of the Yankee players—most of whom were already trudging back to the visitors' clubhouse—and to the immense dismay of the Milwaukee players and fans, McKean sheepishly admitted that he had indeed called time. The home run was disallowed, the players were ordered back onto the field, and three outs later, the Yankees emerged victorious by a 9–7 score. Brewers owner Bud Selig immediately filed an appeal with the league office, telling MacPhail that, "If I ever see Jim McKean or [home plate umpire] George Maloney again, it'll be too soon." Selig's appeal, like Martin's earlier one about the height of the mound, was quickly overruled.

Martin, meanwhile, rejoiced in the Yankees' first victory of the season, as well as in the knowledge that his tenacity had won the game and inspired a new level of respect from his players. "I got these guys now," he bragged to Yankees traveling secretary Bill Kane as the team flew east to Baltimore. "They'll do whatever I tell 'em. We'll win this easy. You watch."

Though Martin had originally rejoined the Yankees as their manager in August 1975, his true homecoming as a Yankee occurred on April 15, 1976, the day Yankee Stadium reopened its doors to the public after two years of extensive renovations. Martin was the third Yankee great introduced during the Opening Day festivities, which also included appearances by Whitey Ford, Mickey Mantle, Joe DiMaggio, Elston Howard (the first black Yankee player, and now the Bronx Bombers' first black coach), Yogi Berra (also a member of Martin's coaching staff), and several members of the 1923 Yankees, the first team to play in the original "House That Ruth Built." Bob Shawkey, the Yankees' starting pitcher for their 1923 opener, threw out the first ball.

Once the most popular baseball team in America, the Yankees could now no longer even boast of being the most popular team in the New York metropolitan area. That title had been usurped by the upstart Mets, who'd outdrawn their venerable Bronx neighbors in every season since 1964, when the modern and colorful Shea Stadium opened for business in Flushing Meadows, Queens. The lovable Mets had won the 1969 World Series and very nearly taken another from the A's in 1973, while the Yankees had only come within striking distance of the playoffs once after their loss to the St. Louis Cardinals in the 1964 World Series.

When the aging Yankee Stadium closed for much needed repairs following the 1973 season, the Bronx Bombers had been forced to play their 1974 and 1975 home games in Queens, sharing Shea Stadium with the Mets in an awkward arrangement that both underscored the Yankees' diminished NYC standing and contributed to the sudden decline of Yankee outfielders Bobby Murcer and Elliott Maddox. Murcer, a left-handed slugger once touted as the second coming of Mickey Mantle, hit 19 homers at Yankee Stadium in 1973; in '74, without a short porch in right field to aim for, he hit only two round-trippers while playing at "home." Maddox, perhaps the team's best player in 1974, got stuck in the mud of Shea's poorly tended outfield during a game in June 1975, and injured his right knee so badly that his doctors initially thought he'd be in a leg brace for the rest of his life.

Now, with the $100 million modernization of their old baseball palace completed, the Yankees were ready to reclaim their crown as New York City's premier ball club. But for Yankee veterans like Roy White, who'd patrolled the Bronx outfield since the mid-'60s, the newly rehabbed digs took a little getting used to. The pitcher's mound seemed lower than anyone remembered, and there were odd slopes on the new playing surface. While the ballpark would never be confused with the symmetrical concrete donuts of the modern era, its once eccentric outfield dimensions had been reined in somewhat: the park's left-center "Death Valley" wall now resided 430 feet from home plate instead of 457, while straightaway center field was now only 417 feet from home instead of 461, and the right field foul pole had been moved back from its temptingly close 296-foot mark to a more respectable 310. The ballpark's granite monuments to Miller Huggins, Babe Ruth, and Lou Gehrig, once the bane of innumerable center fielders, were now positioned out of play in the new "Monument Park" built behind the center field wall.

The place had changed outside the lines, as well—and not just in terms of the Yankees' new fuchsia-carpeted clubhouse. The copper latticework that once famously ringed the top of the grandstand was sold off and melted down; but since the team wanted the ballpark's new look to retain some classic elements, a new concrete frieze with a similar lattice pattern was placed atop the bleachers. A $3 million electronic scoreboard now stood at the back of the right-center bleachers; the first of its kind in the majors, this "telescreen" offered instant replays to the fans, as well as team lineups and scores from other games. Modern architectural advances allowed the organization to remove all 118 of the view-blocking steel girders that formerly held up the roof and upper decks, while the ever-enlarging modern American waistline necessitated the replacement of the original 18-inch-wide wooden seats with 22-inch-wide molded plastic ones. Between the larger seats, and roughly a third of the bleachers being blacked out for the "batter's eye" in center, the park's official seating capacity was reduced from 65,010 to 54,028.

During the early hours of April 14, shortly after returning from Baltimore, where the Yankees had taken two games from the Orioles, Yankee pitcher Rudy May got his first real look at his team's new home. Inspecting the field by the light of the full moon, the left-handed hurler thought that, despite the recent modifications, Yankee Stadium's left field was still dauntingly expansive. "It looked like Yellowstone Park," he told reporters, while preparing to take the mound for his Opening Day start against the Minnesota Twins. "We'll see which hitters reach out there." It didn't take May long to find out—after walking Twins leadoff man Jerry Terrell in the top of the first, Dan Ford rocketed a May pitch over the left-center wall, just a few feet from the 430 mark.

Ford, nicknamed "Disco Dan" for his love of the Minneapolis nightlife, had just hit the first home run in "new" Yankee Stadium history, but the Yankees weren't about to let Ford and the Twins hijack their party. After a lengthy break in the action caused by a mischievous fan releasing a live piglet onto the field ("Go Yogi!" was painted on its sides), the New Yorkers bounced back with a 14-hit attack and romped to an 11–4 victory. The $3 million scoreboard malfunctioned during the game, leading some wags to theorize that the Babe's spirit was less than pleased with the renovations to his old stomping grounds. Right fielder Oscar Gamble, one of the game's heroes (going 3-for-4 with a double, a triple, and two RBIs), was informed afterward by a reporter that Babe Ruth had been in right field the last time Yankee Stadium opened. "After today," the writer joked, "should we start calling this 'The House that Oscar Rebuilt?'" Gamble just looked at him quizzically. "What are you talking about?" he replied.

Two days later, during a 10–0 rout of the Twins, Thurman Munson became the first Yankee to homer at the newly refurbished ballpark. During the postgame press conference, Martin announced that he'd named Munson the team's first captain since Lou Gehrig in 1939. "He waited until I had a good day before announcing it," the gruff catcher joked.

Eight days after the Yankees' home opener ushered in a new era for Yankee Stadium, New York punks the Ramones marked the emergence of a new era in American music with the release of their self-titled debut album. Blindingly fast (at least by 'luded-out mid-'70s standards), blazingly loud, and brutally simple—and recorded in just seven days on a shockingly tight budget of $6,400—the compact three- and four-chord anthems cranked out by these leather-jacketed reprobates from Forest Hills, Queens, bore little resemblance to the highly polished music of Fleetwood Mac, Aerosmith, Queen, or Thin Lizzy, to name some of the bigger rock acts of the moment; ditto for their lyrics, which referenced such taboo topics as slasher films, drug abuse, Nazism, and male prostitution. But the Ramones' sound, look, attitude, and lyrical worldview meshed perfectly with the vibrant scene that had sprung up in recent years around New York's CBGB and Max's Kansas City clubs, where the band quickly established itself as one of the leading progenitors of what local scenesters and journalists were now calling "punk rock." Though it wasn't the first New York punk album—the Dictators and Patti Smith had released long-players in 1975—the Ramones' debut LP would prove the most influential; despite rising no higher than Number 111 on the *Billboard* album charts, *Ramones* paved the way for the greater success of local bands like Blondie and Talking Heads, while igniting countless musical revolutions (and plenty of imitators) abroad. "If that Ramones record hadn't existed, I don't know that we could have built a scene here," Joe Strummer of U.K. punk pioneers The Clash would later reflect.

It would be a few more years before punk music reached the U.S. mainstream in the guise of "New Wave," but another underground musical movement announced its commercial ascendance in April '76, when Johnnie Taylor's "Disco Lady" topped *Billboard*'s Pop and R&B singles charts. Once strictly the province of young black, Latino, and gay club-goers, disco music had risen exponentially in mainstream popularity since November 1974, when DJ Steve Andrews launched a four-hour Saturday night disco show on New York's WPIX-FM. Andrews's show, *Disco 102*, marked the first time that a commercial American radio station had devoted a specific time slot to this funky-yet-streamlined brand of dance music. Now, 17 months later, what was formerly a trend centered around NYC and Philadelphia nightlife had spread nationwide, with an estimated 10,000 discotheques—just some of the places where Americans were beginning to take Coca-Cola's ad slogan "Coke adds life" a bit too literally—pumping out the jams across the continental United States. Taylor, a veteran soul singer in his early 40s, cashed in by slobbering lasciviously over his sexy "Disco Lady" while grooving to a gloriously slinky backing track that featured contributions from P-Funkateers Bootsy Collins, Glenn Goins, and Bernie Worrell. The first single to sell two million copies in the United States, "Disco Lady" served four-on-the-floor notice that disco was no longer just the music of a select minority. (Further proof that disco had officially made it would come in October, when Memphis DJ Rick Dees hit Number One with a novelty song called "Disco Duck.")

That the Yankees got off to their hottest April start since 1958 wasn't a complete surprise, given their lineup's abundance of talent. In addition to their All-Star captain, and reliable veterans like left fielder Roy White, third baseman Graig Nettles, first baseman Chris Chambliss, and designated hitter Lou Piniella, the Bombers now boasted two potent sparkplugs in off-season pickups Mickey Rivers and Willie Randolph. "Mick the Quick," who walked like a stooped old man yet ran like a deer, hit .317 for the month with eight stolen bases, scoring 11 runs and knocking in 12 from the leadoff spot, while rookie Randolph hit .400 and scored 10 times in April while swiping five bags of his own.

The Yankees' crosstown counterparts weren't starting off the season too badly, either. Despite their impressive pitching staff, few expected the offensively challenged Mets, under the guidance of rookie manager Joe Frazier, to be much of a factor in the NL East. And yet, they played 13–7 ball in April, thanks in part to the bat of their one major offensive weapon, right fielder Dave "Kong" Kingman. Kong—or "Sky King," as Kingman preferred to be called—hit 36 homers for the Mets in 1975, and appeared to be on track for even more in '76. The free-swinging Kingman rarely walked, and struck out around four times for every home run he hit; yet, despite an ungainly swing that *Sports Illustrated*'s Larry Keith likened to "a very tall man falling from a very short tree," the 6'6" slugger specialized in gargantuan rainbow shots that seemed to pierce the very atmosphere before returning to earth. "Dave's style is to swing hard in case he hits it," said veteran Mets first baseman Ed Kranepool. "When he's connecting, the only way to defense him is to sit in the upper deck. I've never seen anybody hit the ball farther."

Nor had too many other people. On April 14, with the wind blowing out at Wrigley Field, Kingman launched a moon shot off of Cubs reliever Tom Dettore that sailed over the left field bleachers, carried across Waveland Avenue, and headed up Kenmore Avenue, where it finally caromed off the air-conditioning unit of a residence three houses up from the corner. Variously estimated at traveling between 530 and 630 feet, Sky King's blast was widely adjudged to have been the longest home run ever hit at Wrigley. Though the Mets lost that game 6–5, Kingman came back the next day and sent two more baseballs flying out of the park and clanging off building facades along Waveland, with his second of the game plating three runs to give the Mets an eventual 10–8 victory. The three tape-measure blasts in Chicago came as part of a spree that saw Kingman hammer seven homers in seven days.

With his jaw-dropping power—even his infield pop-ups were awe-inspiring—and angular good looks, Kingman could have been a major New York celebrity, but the only swinging this bachelor ever did was *on* the field. A moody introvert, Kingman preferred to lead a solitary existence at his four-bedroom home in rural Cos Cob, Connecticut, where he spent his downtime building furniture in his garage. "I prefer a private life of my own. I like to live quietly," he told sportswriter Jack Lang. "I enjoy playing in New York, but I don't enjoy living in the city. I like peace and quiet. I like to get away from it all. I enjoy woodworking. I enjoy making things."

Mike Schmidt, who'd bested Kingman in the 1975 NL home run race with 38, was doing some woodworking of his own in the first month of the 1976 season. Like Kingman, Schmidt had a tendency to whiff mightily—he'd led the majors in 1975 with 180 strikeouts—though Schmidt's eye for the strike zone was good enough that he'd also walked 101 times that same year. "You can set Kingman up to swing at bad pitches," testified Cardinals reliever Al "The Mad Hungarian" Hrabosky, perhaps the most confrontational pitcher in the game, "but you have to throw strikes to Schmidt."

For the extremely self-critical Schmidt, each strikeout was like another thorn in his side. "One hundred eighty strikeouts is a ridiculous number," he told Larry Keith. "No one with good hand-eye coordination like mine should strike out that much. This is what makes them so hard to take. I do so many things well that I can't understand why hitting a baseball is so difficult."

Dick Allen had a pretty good idea of what was missing from his teammate's game. On April 17, two days after Kingman and the Mets left town, the Phillies rolled into Wrigley for a pair of games against the Cubs. Schmidt had begun the season 3-for-18 with nine strikeouts, causing Phils skipper Danny Ozark to drop him to sixth in the lineup until he got his swing straightened out. "Mike, you've got to relax," said Allen, pulling Schmidt aside before the first contest. "Remember when you were a kid and you'd skip supper to play ball? You were having fun. Hey, with all that talent you've got, baseball ought to be fun. Enjoy it. Be a kid again."

With the wind once again blowing out of Wrigley, the Cubs had plenty of fun of their own in the early innings of the game, chasing Steve Carlton in the second inning with a seven-run barrage and putting five more runs on the board in the third. With the Phillies down 13–2 going into the top of the fifth, Schmidt figured he might as well heed Allen's advice. Using a shorter, lighter bat borrowed from backup infielder Tony Taylor, Schmidt hit a two-run homer off the Cubs' Rick "The Whale" Reuschel, then followed it with a solo shot off Reuschel in the seventh, and (following a bases-loaded single by Allen) a three-run blast off Mike Garman in the eighth inning that landed deep in the center field bleachers.

Even after Schmidt's third homer of the day, the Phillies still trailed 13–12—but catcher Bob Boone tied it up in the top of the ninth with a solo homer off Darold Knowles, and the Phillies took a 15–13 lead on an RBI triple by shortstop Larry Bowa and a squeeze bunt by right fielder Jay Johnstone. Unfortunately, Phillies reliever Tug McGraw blew the save in the bottom of the ninth by serving up a two-out, two-run single to Cubs catcher Steve Swisher, which sent the game into extra innings and set up Schmidt's date with destiny. With Allen on first and nobody out in the top of the 10th, Paul Reuschel (Rick's even more portly brother) came inside on Schmidt with a high fastball. "I was just trying to hit a single," Schmidt would later claim, but his swing launched Reuschel's pitch into the left-center-field basket.

The blow put the Phillies up 17–15 on the way to a 18–16 10-inning victory, and put Schmidt in the record books. Just the 10th player in history to hit four home runs in a major league game, he also became the first NL player since Bobby Lowe in 1894 to homer in four consecutive plate appearances. "I guess it is just a case of being a little overdue," said Schmidt, who drove in eight runs and (thanks to a fourth-inning single) racked up 17 total bases in the game. The next day at Wrigley, Schmidt laughed while posing with four bats for photographers before the game, then proceeded to hit another bomb off Paul Reuschel during the afternoon's contest, which the Phillies won 8–5. Schmidt also homered in his next two games, which saw the Phillies defeating the Pirates twice in Pittsburgh.

Frustrated by those losses to the Phillies—part of a 3–8 slide after winning their first five games of the season—and by the "Pittsburgh Lumber Company's" apparent inability to swing their wood well enough to give their shaky pitching staff a consistent chance to win, Pirates right fielder Dave Parker called upon the power of funk to put things right, showing up to the Bucs' clubhouse wearing a custom-printed T-shirt that read, "If You Hear Any Noise It's Just Me and the Boys Boppin'." The line was cribbed from the title track of Parliament's *Mothership Connection*, one of the biggest and funkiest R&B albums of early '76, but the Cobra's T-shirt unfortunately failed to ignite much in the way of steady bopping. Having come into the season with nothing less than a World Series appearance as their stated goal, the Pirates were now causing many to wonder if they even had enough gas to win their division again. "We've been through good and bad days before," said team captain Willie Stargell, attempting to shrug off the cold spell. "We were aiming for a good start this year, but what's to be will be."

Not that things were running particularly smoothly for the Phillies, either. Despite Schmidt's home run heroics, and a collective team batting average of .303 for the month, the team was also struggling to establish a winning rhythm. In late April, after losing two out of three games to the Braves by a single run, the normally mild-mannered Danny Ozark had to be restrained from punching out Associated Press reporter Ralph Bernstein, after Bernstein and several other journalists annoyed the Phillies skipper with repeated queries about Dick Allen's absence from the lineup during the third Braves game. "He didn't play because I didn't think he was right to play," said Ozark of Allen, who'd injured his shoulder while sliding two games earlier. "It's a stupid fucking question. I won't answer stupid fucking questions."

The Big Red Machine also got off to an uncharacteristically

creaky start, going 5–7 after winning their first four games. But Reds skipper Sparky Anderson seemed none too concerned about it, what with third baseman Pete Rose hitting a scorching .466 for April and scoring 21 runs from the leadoff slot, and right fielder Ken Griffey and second baseman Joe Morgan hitting .365 and .364, respectively. First baseman Tony Perez and Johnny Bench struggled for much of April (the recent breakup of Bench's year-long marriage to model Vickie Chesser may have been weighing heavily on the All-Star catcher's mind), but the defending World Series champs still hit well enough to stay atop the NL West for most of the month. When Bench finally appeared to break out of his slump by homering twice in an April 30 game against the Expos, Anderson didn't bat an eye. "When a guy hits 20 to 30 homers every year and drives home 100 or more runs," he laughed, "you just don't worry about him. Because you always know that sooner or later he's gonna begin hitting."

Reliable pitching was in shorter supply for the Reds—as was solid defense, with four of the team's first seven losses decided by unearned runs. Even stranger than the uncharacteristically sloppy Reds glove work was a Reds-Giants game at Riverfront Stadium on April 17, which came close to being preempted by a giant swarm of bees. The beginning of the contest was delayed 35 minutes as an estimated 10,000 of the little buzzers invaded the ballpark, terrorizing the visitors' dugout and the box seats along the third base line. With the game about to be shown nationally on NBC's *Game of the Week*, Reds assistant general manager Dick Wagner tried to avoid any postponement of the broadcast by rousting the bees with a fire extinguisher; but the bees quickly returned, sending Sparky Anderson and Reds coach Ted Kluszewski (the latter of whom was allergic to bee stings) running for cover. NBC announcer Tony Kubek, who kept bees on his property, tried to convince the players that the bees wouldn't bother them if they stood still. Fred Norman, the

Reds' 5' 8" lefty, who was scheduled to take the mound for Cincinnati that afternoon, skeptically asked Kubek if he would guarantee his safety.

The Cincinnati swarming incident occurred in the midst of the "killer bees" panic that had been buzzing for years: any day now, or so the oft-repeated rumors went, Africanized bees were going fly up from Mexico and mercilessly sting to death every unfortunate American in their path, just as they'd done in the 1974 Gloria Swanson "beesploitation" vehicle *Killer Bees*—or in *The Squage Bees*, a made-for-TV movie that would run on NBC in November. The Riverfront bees, however, were just plain old nonlethal honeybees; and, by a bizarre stroke of luck, there turned out to be a couple of amateur beekeepers in attendance at the game, who used their skills to lure the critters into a makeshift cardboard hive. Once the disruptive insects were removed from the field, Norman finally took the mound and pitched a four-hit shutout as the Big Red Machine savagely stung the Giants by an 11–0 score.

Eight days later at Dodger Stadium, Cubs center fielder Rick Monday encountered some field invaders of a different sort. While warming up before the bottom of the fourth inning on a beautiful Sunday afternoon, Monday and Cubs left fielder Jose Cardenal saw two figures jump out of the left field pavilion and land on the outfield grass. Cardenal let them pass; since streakers and other rowdy miscreants regularly disrupted ballgames, the bushy-haired outfielder figured that the pair—37-year-old William Errol Thomas and his 11-year-old son (whose name would go unreported due to his juvenile status)—were just a couple of freaks looking for a bit of attention. But when the Thomases knelt down in left center and began unfolding an American flag on the outfield grass, Cardenal and Monday understood that something darker was about to occur. "I didn't know what the hell they were doing there and suddenly they're laying out the flag like a picnic blanket," Monday told reporters afterward. "My first thought was to run 'em over."

Monday was already running toward them at a full sprint when he saw the man douse the flag with lighter fluid and reach into his pocket for matches. While dashing past the two intruders, Monday deftly snatched the flag away before Thomas could set it ablaze. Thomas chucked the can of lighter fluid at the center fielder in frustration, but Monday kept running until he reached the Dodgers' dugout, where he handed the flag to pitcher Doug Rau for safekeeping.

The affable Cardenal attempted to calm the elder Thomas down as security apprehended him and his son. "He was sick," Cardenal later testified. "You look at his eyes and you knew he was on something—not grass, worse stuff. I didn't know whether he would pull a gun or what. But that kid, he was the one that surprised me. Just a fat little boy, 11, maybe 12 years old. What the hell was he doing there?"

"Rick Monday . . . You Made A Great Play," flashed the Dodger Stadium message board as Monday returned to his position in center, and the 25,167 Dodger fans in attendance gave him a standing ovation; several sections of the stadium even burst into a spontaneous a cappella rendition of "God Bless America." "They weren't clapping for me," Monday said of the crowd's reaction, "but for what the flag means to them."

While the burning of the American flag had been a common occurrence at anti–Vietnam War rallies and other antigovernment demonstrations, Thomas—a Native American who hailed from Eldon, Missouri—had apparently intended to burn the flag in protest of his wife's incarceration in a Missouri mental hospital. Why Thomas (who was fined $60 and given a year's probation for his actions) had chosen to stage his protest in Los Angeles was never made entirely clear.

Not that Thomas's motives mattered at all to former Marine

Corps reservist Monday. "I don't know what those clowns were trying to demonstrate and frankly I don't care," said the Cubs center
fielder. Nor did it matter to the many people throughout the country who were touched by Monday's actions. Armand Schneider of
the *Chicago Daily News* called Monday's patriotic intervention "the
Rick Monday Bicentennial Minute," and it certainly struck a chord
in the Bicentennial year, perhaps because—unlike so many of the
activities centered around the nation's 200th birthday—it was such
a spontaneous and unscripted demonstration of American pride.

Monday, a solid but unflashy player, was off to one of the best starts
of his career, hitting .369 with five homers and 18 RBIs for April; but
the mountains of fan mail and personal appearance invitations he
received over the rest of the season—including one from Chicago
mayor Richard Daley, asking Monday to be the grand marshal of the
Windy City's annual Flag Day parade—were largely inspired by his
flag-saving heroics. "Now we got three patriots," said Cardenal.
"Abraham Lincoln, George Washington, and Rick Monday."

ABOVE: Chicago White Sox owner Bill Veeck unveils his team's new uniforms at a "fashion show" starring former players. Veeck's return to Chicago's South Side significantly boosted attendance at Comiskey Park, but the team's Bermuda shorts (modeled here by Jim Rivera) provoked mostly horror and derision. (*Associated Press/LO. Courtesy of Corbis Images*)

LEFT: San Francisco Giants pitcher John "The Count" Montefusco, 1975's NL Rookie of the Year, arrives at San Francisco's Playboy Club for a party celebrating his lucrative new contract. The Count received what was at that point the largest raise ever given to a second-year player. (*Bettman Archive. Courtesy of Corbis Images*)

LEFT: Oscar Gamble's 1976 Topps "Traded" card, complete with ineptly airbrushed cap and jersey. The Yankees forced Gamble to shear off most of his legendary 'do before allowing him to don actual pinstripes, thus costing the outfielder a potentially lucrative Afro Sheen endorsement. (*Baseball card courtesy of Topps Company, Inc.*)

BELOW: Several of the special uniform patches worn during the 1976 season. Clockwise from top left: Oakland A's; Cleveland Indians; Chicago Cubs (franchise centennial); New York Mets (with black armband in memory of Mets owner Joan Payson and original Mets skipper Casey Stengel); Boston Red Sox; Philadelphia Phillies; Detroit Tigers; Montreal Expos (Summer Olympics); and National League Centennial patch (worn by all NL teams except the Expos). (*Courtesy LTC(R) Dave Grob/Mears Museum*)

Tatum O'Neal takes the mound as Amanda Whurlitzer, iron-armed ace of the Bad News Bears. A surprise box office smash in the spring of 1976, the tartly hilarious film seemed to foreshadow the brawling, antagonistic tone of the early months of the '76 season. (*Bettman Archive. Courtesy of Corbis Images*)

Rick Monday receives a Good Citizenship medal and scroll from the Daughters of the American Revolution before a June 16 Cubs-Dodgers contest in Los Angeles. Monday's rescue of an American flag from being burned during an April 25 game at Dodger Stadium transformed the Cubs outfielder into a Bicentennial hero. (*Associated Press. Courtesy of AP Images*)

LEFT: Curly-topped soft-tosser Randy "The Junkman" Jones spent much of the 1976 season on pace for 30 victories, despite pitching for a truly lousy San Diego Padres ballclub. Jones wound up with "only" 22 wins, but that — along with a 2.74 ERA and a league-leading 25 complete games in 40 starts — was still good enough to nab him the NL Cy Young Award. (*SSPC baseball card courtesy of Mike Aronstein*)

BELOW: Mark "The Bird" Fidrych interacts with fans before an August game at Yankee Stadium. As "Birdmania" swept the nation, opposing teams' general managers begged Detroit Tigers skipper Ralph Houk to reconfigure his rotation so that the charismatic rookie could pitch in their ballparks. (*Bettman Archive. Courtesy of Corbis Images*)

BELOW: Phillies slugger Dick Allen wields his mammoth 42-ounce bat during a 1976 game at Veterans Stadium. The mercurial first baseman helped power his team to its first postseason appearance since 1950, but he was also a lightning rod for controversy. (*From the collection of Andrew Woolley*)

BELOW: Greg "The Bull" Luzinski, Dave Cash, Garry Maddox, Larry Bowa, and Mike Schmidt goof around on the picture sleeve of their "Phillies Fever" single. Harold Melvin and the Blue Notes and other Philly Soul acts didn't lose any sleep over the quintet's lone attempt at chart success. (*From the collection of Tom Underwood. Courtesy of Altra Moda Music*)

Temporary Oriole Reggie Jackson scores against Carlton Fisk and the Red Sox during a June 28 game at Fenway Park. Both players made headlines throughout the season with their contract demands; Fisk eventually re-signed with Boston, while Jackson rode the free agency train to a five-year deal with the New York Yankees. (*Bettman Archive. Courtesy of Corbis Images*)

Atlanta Braves owner Ted Turner rolls a baseball with his nose during a pregame race against Phillies reliever Tug McGraw. Like Bill Veeck, Turner used a wide variety of oddball stunts (including ostrich races, cash grabs, and the infamous "Headlock and Wedlock" promotion) to increase attendance because of his team's poor performance. (*Bettman Archive. Courtesy of Corbis Images*)

589. George Brett & Al Cowans

Kansas City Royals third baseman George Brett and outfielder Al Cowens demonstrate their game faces on this misspelled SSPC card. Brett won his first American League batting title in 1976, but his bid for the crown against teammate Hal McRae ended with a racially charged dispute. (*SSPC baseball card courtesy of Mike Aronstein*)

Yankees first baseman Chris Chambliss tries to outrun a mob of jubilant New Yorkers after homering to send the Bronx Bombers to their first World Series since 1964. Royals shortstop Freddie Patek (top center) walks dazedly into the visitors' dugout. (*Bettman Archive. Courtesy of Corbis Images*)

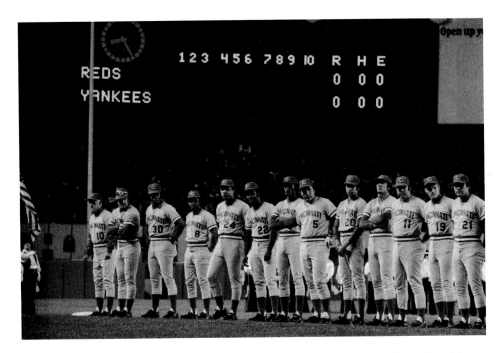

The Big Red Machine lines up for introductions before Game 4 of the 1976 World Series. From left: Sparky Anderson, Pete Rose, Ken Griffey, Joe Morgan, Tony Perez, Dan Dreissen, George Foster, Johnny, Bench, Cesar Geronimo, Dave Concepcion, Bob Bailey, Joel Youngblood, and Mike Lum. (*Bettman Archive. Courtesy of Corbis Images*)

Yankee captain Thurman Munson slides home against Johnny Bench and the Cincinnati Reds during Game 4 of the 1976 World Series. Both catchers performed brilliantly throughout the Fall Classic, but it was Bench who walked away with the World Series MVP. (*Bettman Archive. Courtesy of Corbis Images*)

6.

More, More, More

(May 1976)

Film critic Roger Ebert called it "an unblinking, scathing look at competition in American society." Jay Cocks of *Time* described it as "a fracturing comedy of honor, victory and defeat." *Sports Illustrated*'s Martha Smilgis characterized it as "a cross between *The Dirty Dozen* and *Lilies of the Field*." But Little Leaguers everywhere simply thought *The Bad News Bears* was the coolest baseball movie they'd ever seen.

A tartly scripted comic saga about a no-hope Little League team from L.A.'s San Fernando Valley, whose roster is comprised largely of "a bunch of Jews, spics, niggers, pansies and a booger-eating moron," and who are reluctantly coached by alcoholic former minor leaguer Morris Buttermaker (played with hangdog magnificence by Walter Matthau), the film shocked and amused audiences with its unrestrained vulgarity, as well as its unflinching portrayal of the ugly competitiveness lurking at the dark heart of Little League baseball—and, by extension, America. Refreshingly free of sentimentality or happy endings (unlike so many baseball films before and after), *The Bad News Bears* follows the kids as they ascend against all odds to the climactic championship game, only to lose to their arch-nemesis Yankees on the final play.

Though ostensibly a kids' film, *The Bad News Bears* was actually closer in tone and spirit to such classic 1970s anti-hero-oriented ensemble flicks as *M.A.S.H.* and *One Flew Over the Cuckoo's Nest* than, say, *The Apple Dumpling Gang* or *Escape to Witch Mountain*. Under the assured direction of Michael Ritchie (who'd previously directed the 1975 teen beauty pageant comedy-drama *Smile*), the young actors in *The Bad News Bears* came across not like blandly adorable Hollywood moppets, but like actual mid-'70s kids—unwashed, obnoxious, mean-spirited, gleefully profane, unrepentantly juvenile, yet also far more worldly than their counterparts from a decade or two earlier would have been. (In one memorable scene, local minibike-riding adolescent delinquent Kelly Leak, played by Jackie Earle Haley, brashly informs 11-year-old Tatum O'Neal that he hangs out at the league field because of the abundance of "nice ass" there.)

The adults in the film, of course, behave even worse. Matthau teaches his Bears to mix martinis and presses them into pool-cleaning duty, while uptight, win-at-all-costs Yankees coach Vic Morrow strides to the mound and slaps his own son for disobeying his pitching instructions. And the preseason league meeting scene, which takes place at the local Pizza Hut, may be the most accurate portrayal of banal '70s suburban existence ever committed to celluloid.

While there are positive messages subtly interwoven throughout Bill (son of actor Burt) Lancaster's script—O'Neal's Amanda Whurlitzer proves that girls can be just as tough and competitive as boys, Buttermaker informs his frustrated charges that quitting is "a hard habit to break once you start," and the motley squad of Chico's Bail Bonds–sponsored losers eventually gains some collective self-respect—*The Bad News Bears* isn't a feel-good film in any traditional sense of the term. In the end, Buttermaker is the only one who really grows up; the kids are all too busy dousing each other in Budweiser.

Released during the second week of April, *The Bad News Bears* was a surprise box office smash, grossing $2.4 million in its first week; it would wind up the 11th-highest-grossing film of 1976. And with its scrappy, brawling ballpark scenes, the film seemed to presciently foreshadow the antagonistic tone of the first few months of the 1976 season. For while the American airwaves in the spring of '76 were filled with such feel-good dance jams as the Sylvers' "Boogie Fever" and Silver Convention's "Get Up and Boogie"—not to mention sleek and mellow rockers like Gary Wright's "Dream Weaver," Peter Frampton's "Show Me the Way," and Fleetwood Mac's "Rhiannon"— the general vibe on major league diamonds was anything but feel-good or mellow.

Though he wouldn't turn 23 until July, California Angels left-hander Frank Tanana was already considered one of the elite pitchers in the American League. He'd led the junior circuit with 269 strikeouts in 1975, his second full season in the bigs, while posting a 16–9 record and a 2.62 ERA, and the excellence of Tanana and his fireballing California compadre Nolan Ryan, combined with the predictable awfulness of the rest of the Angels' rotation, would soon inspire the popular sportswriter couplet "Tanana and Ryan, and two days of cryin'."

The son of a Detroit policeman, Tanana had matinee-idol looks, shaggy dirty-blond surfer hair, and plenty of down-to-earth charm, all of which allowed him to fit right in with the singles scene in his new home of Newport Beach, California, where he quickly acquired a playboy image to rival that of '60s Angels pitching phenom Bo Belinsky. "I'm out chasing women, partying, trying to get in a little education, trying to find out what makes Frank Tanana go," he breezily informed Dick Miller of the *Sporting News*.

But despite his sunbaked beach boy facade, Tanana wasn't the sort of cat who was inclined to flash a peace sign when things got heated. On April 19, during an Orioles-Angels game at Anaheim Stadium, Tanana avenged the earlier plunking of his catcher Andy Etchebarren by O's reliever Wayne Garland with a nasty inside pitch that sent Baltimore's wiry shortstop Mark Belanger sprawling in the dirt. Both dugouts and bullpens emptied, but the players mostly just shouted and glowered at each other. After Baltimore skipper Earl Weaver was tossed for insisting that Tanana be given a warning, both sides cooled off sufficiently to allow the game to resume, and Tanana fanned Belanger (his 11th strikeout of a 12-K performance), then set down five of the next six Orioles he faced to record his first W of the season in the Angels' 9–4 victory.

Things got even more heated the next night in St. Louis, when a beanball war between Mets lefty Jon Matlack and Cardinals righty Lynn "Big Mac" McGlothen climaxed with Dave Kingman leading his New York teammates in a San Juan Hill–style charge to the mound. Cards first baseman Keith Hernandez and utility infielder Lee "Bee Bee" Richard managed to intercept and tackle Kong before he could take a swing at Big Mac, though aging Mets third baseman Joe Torre, who'd won the NL batting crown five years earlier, showed he still had some pop by sucker-punching McGlothen from behind as they both went down in a surge of home whites and road grays.

The Orioles-Angels and Mets-Cardinals fracases were ugly enough to prompt Los Angeles sportswriter Melvin Durslag to call for the outright outlawing of "duster" pitches, but the A's and Indians apparently didn't read Durslag's column in the *Sporting News*. On April 25, an A's-Indians game at Cleveland Municipal Stadium degenerated into a full-scale brawl when Oakland shortstop Bert Campaneris—who'd already been fastballed in the rib cage by Cleveland reliever Jim Kern in the top of the fifth—pegged Tribe third sacker Buddy Bell in the forehead with his double-play relay throw in the bottom of the sixth. Both benches cleared; Campy stepped on Bell's face in the ensuing melee, and hulking Indians first baseman Boog Powell—who'd hit the ground ball that started the whole affair—wound up on the 21-day disabled list after teammate Rick Manning accidentally stepped on his ankle and sprained it. Bell was taken to Lutheran Medical Center for X rays (which thankfully proved negative), while A's manager Chuck Tanner pulled his short-stop out of the game, which the A's eventually won by a score of 9–1.

"They can't hide him forever," warned Indians player-manager Frank Robinson, intimating that his pitchers would retaliate against Campaneris at some point during the nine upcoming contests sched-uled between the two teams. Campy, for his part, claimed that his Bell beaning was an accident. "I play good clean baseball," he in-sisted, adding, "If it was Frank Robinson coming into second I'd put it between his eyes."

Such *Bad News Bears*–worthy mayhem spilled into the second month of the season, with the Cubs and Giants going at it hard during the third inning of a May 1 game at Candlestick. Cubs left fielder Jose Cardenal, who just a few days earlier in San Diego had dodged several bottles and oranges tossed at him by Padres fans, thought a brushback pitch from Giants hurler Jim Barr was one in-dignity too many; the two exchanged colorful insults, whereupon Cardenal lifted his batting helmet off his voluminous afro and whipped it at the pitcher. Cardenal was ejected from the game, and Pete LaCock (best known for being the son of *Hollywood Squares* host Peter Marshall) was sent up to finish his at-bat. But after LaCock struck out looking, Cubs third baseman Bill "Mad Dog"

Madlock stepped in and "accidentally" let his bat slip from his hands while swinging at Barr's first pitch, sending it sailing toward the mound. Barr then drilled him in the shoulder with his next pitch, and all hell broke loose. It finally took eight uniformed San Francisco cops to break up the fight and restore order on the diamond, whereupon the umpires initially awarded Madlock first base before deciding to eject him for charging the mound. This ruling set off another protracted howl from the Mad Dog, who left the field under protest while furiously pointing to the spot on his shoulder where Barr's pitch had hit him.

The Giants won the game 3–1, but their celebration was short-lived; having already lost their five previous games, they would go on to lose their next six and 17 out of their next 21, at one point going 35⅓ innings without scoring a single run. San Francisco's initial excitement over their team's new lease on life was dissipating quicker than a homegrown weed buzz: the May 1 game against the Cubs was played on a sunny Saturday afternoon with the temperatures in the low 70s, yet barely 4,700 fans made it out to the 'Stick to witness the win. On May 17, when the Giants returned to Candlestick following a two-week road trip, they were greeted by only 2,226 fans, who witnessed the home team getting pummeled 12–2 by the lowly Padres. Less than 1,700 even bothered to show up the next afternoon.

The new White Sox regime was experiencing attendance woes of its own, though the chief culprit was lousy weather, rather than the team's equally lousy play. A deeply soggy Chicago spring had forced the Sox to cancel all but six home games during April, and Bill Veeck estimated that the rainouts cost him around $750,000 in lost fan revenue. There was, however, one spot of sunshine for the White Sox as April turned into May: the return to form of Wilbur Wood, the team's paunchy left-handed knuckleballer.

Wood, who'd been tutored in the mysterious art of the knuckler by no less than future Hall of Famer Hoyt Wilhelm, could eat innings like French fries; from 1971 through 1975, he averaged a deadball era–worthy 44.8 starts and 336 innings pitched per season while racking up 96 wins. Wood had slipped a little in 1975, with his ERA ballooning to an ungainly 4.11; but in the first few weeks of the 1976 campaign, he seemed like his old potbellied self again, starting six of the team's first 14 games, pitching five to their completion, and winning three while posting a 2.49 ERA. And for five and two-thirds innings on May 9, his seventh start of the season, it looked like he was well on his way to hurling a complete game shutout at Tiger Stadium—at least until Tigers center fielder Ron LeFlore lined a single off Wood's left knee.

Just three years earlier, LeFlore had been doing time at Michigan's Jackson State Prison on an armed robbery charge—just the latest mark on a criminal rap sheet that extended back to 1963. Billy Martin, the Tigers' manager at the time, had heard via one of his bartender friends about the blazing speed and outstanding baseball skills that LeFlore displayed on the prison diamond, where the Jackson State team competed against visiting semipro and amateur teams. A tryout was arranged at Tiger Stadium, and LeFlore impressed the team enough that they offered him a minor league contract upon his release from prison in July '73. The reformed LeFlore hit exceedingly well in the minors, and earned a promotion to the parent club in August '74. But he had trouble finding his groove in the majors, hitting only .258 as the starting center fielder in '75; LeFlore's 28 stolen bases were the highest by any Tiger since Jake Wood in 1961, but he was also caught 20 times.

Nineteen seventy-six started roughly for LeFlore, who hit poorly in spring training and had to field endless questions from the press about his age: already 25 years old when he'd signed his initial deal with the Tigers, he'd chopped four years off his age, fearing that the team wouldn't want to take a chance on such an "old" prospect. But now his secret was out, thanks to some investigative reporting by the *Detroit Free Press*, which revealed that LeFlore would be turning 28 in June, as opposed to 24; and reporters wouldn't let up about it, even though the Tigers claimed they had no issue with LeFlore's ruse. "I don't give a damn if he's 58, as long as he can run and hit and throw," insisted Tigers manager Ralph Houk.

Worse for LeFlore, Houk announced during the spring that longtime Detroit fan favorite Mickey Stanley would be in competition with LeFlore for the center field gig. The Tigers were loaded in the outfield for '76, what with the presence of redheaded slugger Rusty Staub (picked up in the off-season from the Mets), former AL batting champ Alex Johnson and left-handed-hitting Ben Oglivie, and veteran slugger (and former left fielder) Willie Horton holding down the full-time DH spot. Still, LeFlore thought he'd already earned the starting job for '76, and was dismayed to find himself on the bench during the first four games of the season.

Houk later admitted that all his talk about Stanley (a versatile but aging player who hadn't spent a full season in the lineup since 1973) and his benching of LeFlore were simply intended to motivate the promising outfielder. Having never actually played organized baseball until his incarceration at Jackson State, LeFlore was still incredibly undisciplined at the plate and in the field, though he was able to get by on his more than ample natural abilities. "I wanted to make him realize there were other things he had to work on if he was ever going to be the player he could be," Houk explained.

The Detroit skipper's strategy eventually paid off. "In 1975 I counted my games before they were played and my at-bats before they came," LeFlore later recalled in his autobiography. "In 1976 I was determined to take my at-bats as my name was called. I cut down on my jiving in the clubhouse, too; I made up my mind to be more serious about the game." When LeFlore finally found himself in the starting lineup on April 17, he responded by doubling in his first at-bat, and just kept hitting from there. By May 9, the day the Tigers faced Wood, LeFlore had already hit safely in 12 straight games and raised his batting average to .358, earning himself a permanent spot in center field and as the Tigers' leadoff man.

LeFlore's inspiring personal story would later form the basis of a best-selling autobiography, *Breakout: From Prison to the Big Leagues*, which would be adapted into a made-for-TV movie starring actor LeVar Burton. Later retitled *One in a Million*, *Breakout* would scar an entire generation of young baseball fans with LeFlore's graphic descriptions of fellow inmates furtively engaging in anal sex under the prison yard bleachers; on May 9, though, the only thing he scarred was Wood's left patella, which was badly fractured by LeFlore's line drive. "I thought I was shot," said Wood, who rolled on the ground in agony while LeFlore scampered to first. The Sox held on to win 4–2, giving Wood his fourth victory of the year, but the 34-year-old knuckleballer was done for the season—and without their ace, the Sox were likely done, too. Veeck, as always, tried to inject some gallows humor into the situation. "If it was the other one," he told Wood, "I could have given you one of my wooden legs."

LeFlore continued to torch American League pitching, hitting .398 for the month, but it took until May 22, when he hit safely in his 24th straight contest—the longest single-season Tiger hitting streak since 1937—for the press to perk up and take notice. The center fielder's drug-addicted younger brother Gerald had been killed on April 23 in what was ruled an accidental shooting; this unfortunately made for a far juicier story than LeFlore's steady hitting, and he was now forced to answer endless questions about his brother's tragic death. Also, the Tigers were already in free fall, and their express trip to the AL East cellar helped keep LeFlore's lengthening streak under the radar, as did the sudden emergence of a Tigers rookie who would make an indelible mark on the 1976 baseball season.

Mark Fidrych was a gangly, frizzy-haired 21-year-old right-hander out of Northboro, Massachusetts, who'd joined the Tigers organization just two years earlier. After rising rapidly from Class A to AAA ball during 1975—he'd picked up the name "The Bird" in the minors, thanks to his resemblance to Big Bird from the PBS children's show *Sesame Street*—Fidrych made the parent club out of spring training as a nonroster invitee, even though Ralph Houk didn't seem entirely clear on how he'd use him. Fidrych spent the first five weeks of the season on the bench and in the bullpen, taking the mound only twice in brief relief appearances. "I wasn't really involved in the team at the beginning of this year," he told writer Tom Clark. "I was just sittin' there watchin' everything happen." But on May 15, Detroit starter Dave Roberts was sick with flu and unable to make his scheduled start, so Houk gave Fidrych the ball—and the rookie responded with a masterful complete game performance, no-hitting the Cleveland Indians through six innings before giving up his only two hits in the seventh, walking one batter, striking out five, and giving up only one run as the Tigers beat the Tribe 2–1 at Tiger Stadium.

The rookie's impressive poise and control weren't the only memorable aspects of his pitching performance on this gray and drizzly May afternoon. The 14,583 Detroit fans in attendance got their first real look at The Bird in full flight, and they instantly loved what they saw. On the mound, Fidrych was an almost comical figure; the lanky lad worked quickly, jabbering away to himself, agitatedly chewing gum and tugging the bill of his cap, pacing in circles after each out, wildly applauding his fielders after good plays, and dropping to his knees on several occasions to mold the dirt on the pitching mound to his personal specifications. George Kell, who was calling the game's TV broadcast for the Tigers on local station WWJ, summed it up when he turned to his color man, Al Kaline, and drawled, "You know, Al, that guy is kind of goofy out there."

Oddest of all, Fidrych seemed to be talking to the ball between each pitch, giving it instructions on how to behave and where to go; and, given that the Indians didn't even manage to put a hit on the board until the seventh inning, the ball actually seemed to be listening. With his shaggy hair, fidgety mannerisms, and bubble-blowing sangfroid, Fidrych could have been an elongated funhouse-mirror reflection of one of the Bad News Bears—only this kid could actually *play*.

"He had us psyched out with all that stuff he does on the mound," lamented Indians DH Rico Carty, who came into the game batting a league-leading .402, but couldn't buy a hit off the Bird in three tries. "The more he does, the more you want to hit him. And the more you want to hit him, the worse you get. . . . It was like he was trying to hypnotize us. I said, 'Just throw the ball.' Then he did—and I couldn't hit it."

It was almost as if Fidrych was the one in the hypnotic trance. "I really don't know what I do out there," he admitted afterward, when reporters pressed him for details on his mound antics. "That's just my way of concentrating and keeping my head in the game." But despite his laserlike focus on the mitt of catcher Bruce Kimm—Houk paired the young backup backstop with Fidrych because they'd already worked together in the minors—The Bird was still well aware of the bigger picture. In the sixth inning, when the Tiger Stadium grounds crew tried to neaten up the pitching mound, Fidrych chased them away, grabbed a handful of sand from their wheelbarrow, and took care of business himself. "Why should I let them mess up the mound when I had a no-hitter going?" he reasoned.

Fidrych didn't pitch again until May 25, when he took the mound at Fenway Park to face off against Luis Tiant, whose extensive array of whirling windups and gravity-defying deliveries had made him the most entertaining pitcher in the game—at least before the Bird came along. Despite the pressure of pitching in front of a Boston crowd that included hundreds of his friends, acquaintances, and family members who'd made the 40-minute trip from Northboro to see their hometown boy make good, the animated young rookie held his own against the ageless Cuban, giving up six hits to El Tiante's seven. The Bird's only real mistakes against the Red Sox came in the fourth inning, with a walk to Carlton Fisk and an outside pitch to Carl Yastrzemski that Yaz golfed high into the screen over Fenway's "Green Monster" in left. LeFlore doubled in the top of the fifth, running his hit streak to 27 games (it would eventually reach 30, the longest in the AL since Dom DiMaggio's 34 in 1949), but El Tiante still managed to blank the Tigers 2–0.

The Bird's Fenway outing earned him a regular spot in the Tigers' rotation, and he faced the Milwaukee Brewers in his next start, a May 31 night game at Tiger Stadium. Fidrych's already surging adrenaline got an extra boost in the first inning, when he faced Hank Aaron with a man on first and two outs. Aaron, the reigning all-time major league home run and RBI king, was playing out his final major league season as the Brewers' full-time designated hitter. Though he was only hitting .250 with two homers and 10 RBIs going into the game, the 42-year-old Aaron still cut a cool and imposing figure at the plate. Fidrych was both confident enough in his own abilities to blow an inside fastball by Hammerin' Hank for strike three, and awed enough by the encounter to exult "Whoa, I struck out Hank Aaron!" to anyone who would listen upon his return to the dugout.

Fidrych gave up four runs in the contest, including a three-run homer to Milwaukee third baseman Don Money, but still hung on for 11 long innings to record his second complete game victory, radiating a joyful and infectious exuberance the entire way. The Monday night crowd of 17,894 Tiger fans roundly cheered Fidrych's mound antics throughout the 5–4 win, and George "Boomer" Scott, the most feared hitter in the Milwaukee lineup, gave the young pitcher high marks for his performance. "I like him," said Scott, who singled and walked twice in the game before Fidrych got him to hit into an inning-ending double play in the top of the 10th. "That's confidence. A lot of people call it flaky and a lot of people call it looney, but I like it. His ball really moved. The ball exploded. I asked the man to check the ball one time because I thought he was throwing a spitter. This guy could be a goodie."

The seeds of "Birdmania"—a fever which would first sweep Detroit, and then consume the rest of the country as the star-spangled summer progressed—had been planted. But for now, another shaggy-haired pitcher with an unusual mound approach was soaking up all the column ink. Randy Jones, the Padres' mild-mannered six-foot, 172-pound ace, had a big blond perm that stuck out from under his cap and gave him more than a passing resemblance to the popular koala bears at the San Diego Zoo. The left-hander's "super sinker," a sinking fastball that topped out on a good day at somewhere around 73 miles per hour, appeared equally mild-mannered, yet major league batters were losing their minds trying to hit it out of the infield. During the month of May, Jones made seven starts—six of which were complete game victories where he allowed two earned runs or less, and four of which came against some of the most formidable lineups the National League had to offer: the Pirates, the Phillies, the Reds, and the Dodgers.

Jones, who'd posted a 20–12 record in 1975 with a NL-leading 2.24 ERA, accounted for nearly half of the Padres' victories in the first two months of the season, going 10–2 with a 2.11 ERA; in his first 98 and a third innings, he gave up only 79 hits and 15 walks, and only nine of those hits were for extra bases. If Jones's arm (and control) held out through September, there was the distinct possibility of him attaining the lofty 30-win plateau last reached in 1968 by Denny McLain. In the meantime, "The Junkman," as Jones was known, was starting to surpass the San Diego Chicken as the team's primary gate attraction. Padres general manager Peter Bavasi estimated that each Jones start drew about 6,000 more fans than usual for a Padres game—though thanks to Jones's remarkably efficient delivery and pinpoint control, they rarely had time to get comfortable in their seats before the game ended. "I hate a three-hour game," laughed Jones, who rarely took longer than two hours or required more than 100 pitches to finish nine innings of work.

"He's the exact opposite of Tom Seaver, but he gets the same results," marveled Joe Morgan, following the Reds' 4–2 loss to the Padres on May 21, in which Jones needed only 87 pitches and 99 minutes to complete the victory. "I think the next time I face him I'll go up without a bat," added Pete Rose, who went hitless in four tries. "Maybe it'll confuse him and he'll walk me."

Chasing Jones in the NL victories column was veteran Phillies right-hander Jim Lonborg. An AL Cy Young winner with the 1967 "Impossible Dream" Red Sox, the 34-year-old Lonborg had been repeatedly beset by injuries since then, including a strained rotator cuff that prematurely ended his 1975 season and caused him to seriously consider retirement. But between special stretching exercises and Transcendental Meditation—which he'd begun practicing in 1974, at the surprisingly enlightened behest of team president Ruly Carpenter, who also convinced several other Phillies to practice the meditation technique developed by Maharishi Mahesh Yogi—Lonborg now felt good enough again to take the ball every five days, and he rode his expertly controlled slider to an 8–0 record by the end of May.

Lonborg's win streak was just one of the many factors behind the Phils' explosive May, which saw them go 22–5 and surge to a six-and-a-half-game lead in the NL East over the Pirates. The team hit .285 for the month, with most of their starting lineup (including shortstop Larry Bowa, first baseman Dick Allen, center fielder Garry Maddox, and third baseman Mike Schmidt, whose 15 home runs by the end of May were second in the league only to Dave Kingman's 17) hitting at a .300 or better clip. The pitching staff, led by Lonborg, fellow TM practitioner Steve Carlton (who won five games in May after a winless April), and young righty Larry Christenson (who also notched five wins in May) posted a collective 2.39 ERA for the month, while holding opponent bats to a cool .234 average. And with the exception of the lumbering Greg Luzinski in left, the Philadelphia defense was stellar; during a mid-May series at the Houston Astrodome, where the balls were ricocheting around the AstroTurf with such speed that Jim Kaat likened playing there to "shooting marbles in a bathtub," the Phils' outstanding glove work made the difference in two of the team's three victories. "We've got the pitching, the power, and the defense," exulted Bowa. "We can throw every phase of the game at the opposition. Heck, we can steal bases, too, and we haven't even gotten into that part of it yet."

Phillies manager Danny Ozark also had a number of talented role players his disposal, including the right field platoon of Jay Johnstone and "Downtown" Ollie Brown, sure-handed outfielder Jerry Martin (whom Ozark usually brought in during the late innings as a defensive substitute for Luzinski), and backup catcher Tim McCarver. Bob Boone, who'd primarily been platooned with the left-handed-hitting Johnny Oates in 1975, was promoted to full-time catcher in the wake of Oates's injury, but McCarver—the team's third-string catcher before Oates got hurt—was now catching Carlton every time "Lefty" took the mound. The pairing was initially suggested by Ozark, in light of the fact that Carlton and McCarver had worked together well during their late-'60s days with the Cardinals, and it seemed to be paying off. "Lefty has been trying too damn hard for his own good," McCarver told Philadelphia sportswriter Ray Kelly, "but now he's starting to relax out there and acting like himself. He's snapping that slider again and taking charge."

Second baseman Dave Cash, who'd been a member of the 1971 World Champion Pirates, and whose speed and battle cry of "Yes we can!" energized the Phillies when he joined the team in time for 1974 season, was especially appreciative of the way the Bicentennial squad was gelling. "It's very important for people to know their roles," he told *Sports Illustrated*'s Ron Fimrite. "My main job is to get on base for the guys who hit behind me. . . . I'd say I also have a responsibility to keep morale high, but this team is about as close as any I've been on. I can't really compare us with the '71 Pirates because we haven't done anything yet, but potentially we're as good as anyone. Instead of talking about what we're going to do, we do it. We don't get emotionally high winning or low losing. That's good, because it's too early to get excited. The real test will come when we lose a few in a row."

After weathering somewhat shaky Aprils, the Cincinnati Reds and Los Angeles Dodgers spent May battling each other for control of the NL West. Pete Rose cooled off at the plate after his torrid start, a sore left shoulder limited Johnny Bench's production at the plate (he hit only .225 with three homers for the month, but still drove in 14 runs), and shortstop Davey Concepcion started the month slumping so badly at the plate that he tried showering *before* a game in order to "wash away the bad luck"—it apparently worked, since he wound up hitting .320 in May—but the Big Red Machine still got plenty of production from their loaded lineup. Left fielder

George Foster and his black bat led the way, hitting .360 for the month with seven home runs and driving in a whopping 31 runs.

The Reds' arms warmed up considerably in May, posting a 2.81 staff ERA that was far more appetizing than their 4.65 April mark, but manager Sparky Anderson—nicknamed "Captain Hook" for his tendency to pull pitchers at the first sign of trouble—found himself sticking with his starters longer than usual, mostly because his normally reliable relief trio of Pedro Borbon, Will McEnaney, and Rawly Eastwick were horribly erratic during the first two months of the season. When some rough outings by Pat Darcy and a pinched nerve in Don Gullett's neck also forced Anderson to slot Pat Zachry and Santo Alcala into the Reds' rotation for May, the two rookie righties came through with flying colors, combining for nine wins over the course of the month.

The Dodgers' feeble 5–9 start during the first two weeks of April had many Los Angeles fans and sportswriters calling for the head of Walter Alston, the 64-year-old skipper who'd helmed the team for 22 seasons dating back to their final years in Brooklyn. And then, during the last week of April, the Dodgers suddenly woke up, rattling off a 12-game winning streak that lasted through the first week of May. Ron Cey hit safely in all 12 games, driving in the game-winning run in four of them—including a May 7 game at the Vet against the Phillies where he homered and racked up five RBIs in the Dodgers' 10–8 win. The Penguin continued to power the Dodger offense throughout May, hitting .323 for the month with five doubles, six homers, and 21 RBIs; first baseman Steve Garvey, the team's other main offensive weapon, hit .336 for the month with six doubles, three home runs, and 17 RBIs.

The Dodgers' 12-game win streak ended on May 8 with a 6–4 loss to the Phillies, who also beat them 10–3 the next day. But then the Dodgers took off again, winning 11 of their next 13; overall, from April 23 on, the team won 23 out of 27—"the best stretch of baseball since the Dodgers of 1955," as the beaming Alston proclaimed. The last win of that roll took place on May 23, when 38-year-old pinch-hitting specialist Manny Mota drove in the winning run in the bottom of the 11th to give the Dodgers a 6–5 victory over the Astros, and put the team on top of the NL West by two and a half games over the Reds. "We're just playing our own game and we're not worrying about the Reds or anyone else," Cey told Gordon Verrell of the *Sporting News*. "We're piling up wins that we can take into September with us."

But September was still a long way off. An ugly road trip during the last week of the month saw the Dodgers drop two of three to the Padres and three of four to the Reds—the latter series opening with a 9–0 Cincinnati blowout marked by a stellar five-hit, nine-strikeout performance from Pat Zachry, who notched the first complete game shutout of his career. The next day, May 29, Mike Marshall came into the game in the bottom of the ninth with Dave Concepcion on first, nobody out, and a 5–3 Dodger lead. After giving up a single to center fielder Cesar Geronimo and a sacrifice bunt to Ed Armbrister, Iron Mike got Pete Rose to ground out to first; Concepcion scored, but the Dodgers were still up by a run, and Marshall only needed one more out to nail down his ninth save of the season.

He never got it. Ken Griffey tripled home Geronimo, and then Joe Morgan stroked a single to center that ended the game and pulled the Reds into a first-place tie with the Dodgers. With the Big Red Machine just starting to fire on all cylinders, the Dodgers' time at the top of the NL West was growing short; they would have to enjoy the view while it lasted.

The Atlanta Braves had spent six days in April tied for first place in the NL West, but those memories of glory were now fading fast, thanks to a 13-game losing streak that began April 26 and bled well into the second week of May. Ted Turner had reportedly put an incentive deal in place for his players, wherein each Brave would receive $500 at the end of the season for every win over 81, as well as additional bonuses if attendance at Atlanta–Fulton County Stadium surpassed 900,000 for the year. Many observers questioned the legality of such an arrangement; but with the team going 8–21 for May while batting only .228 and averaging a paltry 3.3 runs per game to their opponents' 4.7, the chances of the Braves winning 81 games in 1976 looked about as likely as the Ramones selling a million copies of their debut album. Turner's megabucks signing of Andy Messersmith wasn't paying off yet, either. Without the benefit of spring training, it took a while for Messersmith to shake the rust out of his right arm, and it wasn't until his seventh start—a 3–2 complete game victory over Houston at the Astrodome on May 17—that he looked anything like his dominating former self.

Despite his team's losing ways, Turner was determined to make baseball in Atlanta as entertaining as possible. During one game in early May, Turner startled fans at Atlanta–Fulton County Stadium when he left his seat beside the Braves' dugout to run the bases with Susie Sweeper (the hot-pants-clad young woman who swept the infield in the middle of the fifth inning) and Bleacher Creature, the team's fuzzy green mascot; when the trio approached third base, Turner performed a somersault that ended with him kissing the bag. "I felt like I was in *The Wizard of Oz* out there," he gushed afterward. "Dorothy, me—the tin man, the straw man and that monster, the cowardly lion."

There was truly "no place like home" for Braves fans in 1976, as Turner and his promotions man Bob Hope did their damnedest to pack the team's home schedule with one alluring promotion after another. Turner himself even got in on the action, participating in such pregame shenanigans as bathtub and ostrich races, and besting

Phillies pitcher Tug McGraw in a contest to see who could roll a baseball to home plate faster using only their nose.

In addition to typical ballpark giveaways like Jacket Night and Cushion Night, May witnessed the first of several Cash Scramble Nights at Fulton County Stadium, in which $25,000 in crumpled dollar bills was strewn about the field, and six "lucky fans"—most of whom just happened to be attractive young women in shorts and halter tops—were given two minutes to stuff as many of the bills into their clothes as possible. The promotion proved so popular with the fans (and, more importantly, garnered so much press coverage), that Turner and Hope decided to repeat it several times over the course of the season, even ratcheting up the spectacle by having the crumpled bills delivered via Brinks truck.

Turner and Hope's creative touch also extended to the Braves' uniforms. In 1960, Bill Veeck made baseball history by putting the last names of White Sox players on the backs of their jerseys; it seemed a radical idea at the time, but most MLB teams had followed suit by the '70s. Now, Turner and Hope decided to go Veeck one better by replacing the last names on the backs of the team's red-pin-striped home jerseys with *nicknames*, a move they felt would further endear the players to Atlanta fans. Some of the nicknames sewn onto the Braves' jerseys were obvious: catcher Biff Pocoroba wore "Poco" across his shoulder blades, while outfielder Rowland Office sported "Row"; Jimmy Wynn, the Toy Cannon, wore "Cannon," and knuckleballer Phil Niekro wore "Knucksie." Then there were the ones that weren't so obvious, like the "Nort" on shortstop Darrel Chaney's back (because of his resemblance to Art Carney's Ed Norton character on TV's *The Honeymooners*), the "Heavy" on Earl Williams (self-chosen, apparently, because the moody catcher and first baseman considered himself to be one bad dude), or the "Taco" on Marty Perez—a nickname that could have easily been misinterpreted as a racial slur, but actually originated in the fact that the Mexican American second baseman really, *really* liked tacos.

And then there was the "Channel" emblazoned across Messersmith's back, which made absolutely no sense at all—at least until you noticed that he also wore number 17, and remembered that Turner's TV station WTCG was located at Channel 17 on the Atlanta UHF dial. Messersmith didn't wear "Channel" for long, however; Chub Feeney called Turner on the carpet over Messersmith's jersey, which the NL president considered an illegal advertising ploy. Feeney also gave Turner a disapproving earful about his bonus incentive plan, his propensity for jumping onto the field, and reports that Turner often played poker with his players. Turner backed down on most of the issues—Messersmith would soon adopt his college nickname "Bluto" in place of "Channel"—but demanded to know why he couldn't enjoy a friendly penny-ante card game with his players. "You might win money from them," said Feeney. "So what?" Turner retorted. "They can afford it."

As feisty as Turner could be, even his spirit was dampened at times by the Braves' ineptitude. On May 31, already steamed about placing second in a pregame race of motorized bathtubs, Turner grabbed the stadium's PA microphone after a Marty Perez error led to six runs in the eighth inning of the Braves' 10–7 loss to the Padres. "Nobody is going to leave here a loser tonight," he announced to the sparse Memorial Day evening crowd of 2,994. "If the Braves don't win, I want you people to come back tomorrow night as my guests. We are going to be in big league baseball for a long, long time, and we appreciate your support. . . . Soon, we're going to beat the hell out of these teams who have been beating the hell out of us." Over a thousand fans accepted Turner's invitation, returning the following night to see the Braves beat the hell out of the Padres by a 9–1 score.

———

As odd as it was to see nicknames on the back of the Braves' jerseys, there was perhaps no more jarring a sight on a major league diamond in May 1976 than that of Reggie Jackson in an Orioles uniform. Reggie finally ended his holdout in late April, when the Orioles' front office finally agreed to pay him $200,000 for the season; but after playing eight straight seasons (and slugging 254 home runs) in A's green-and-gold, he just looked wrong in the orange-and-black of the O's.

Reggie thought so, too, though he didn't openly admit it at the time. "I showed up thinking of myself as an interim Oriole," he later recalled. "That didn't mean I wasn't going to play hard. I had tremendous respect for the Oriole organization. . . . But in the back of my mind, I always knew it would only be for one season. I was going to become a free agent. I was going to find myself a windfall." Rather than rent an apartment in Baltimore, Jackson simply booked a hotel room at the local Cross Keys Inn for the season; even though the Orioles had already given him an unsigned contract for 1977, guaranteeing him another season at $200,000, putting down roots in Baltimore was never on the Reggie agenda.

Ironically, Jackson's first game as an Oriole came against the Oakland A's, in the second half of a May 2 doubleheader in Baltimore. Orioles fans greeted their new cleanup hitter with a minute-long standing ovation, which took Jackson by surprise. "I expected to hear more boos, but that ovation felt damn good," he said after the game. "They let me know that they appreciate me being here." Jackson went hitless for the day, but still managed to drive in a key run in the Orioles' 4–3 victory with a hot grounder to first. He also provided the crowd with some light entertainment in the bottom of the eighth, when he flamboyantly danced out of the way of a low and tight slider from his old friend Rollie Fingers. Jackson claimed the ball had hit him on his left toe, and beckoned Earl Weaver out of the dugout to help him plead his case to home plate umpire Joe Brinkman, who finally waved the slugger to first.

Jackson's unusual deal with the Orioles—which essentially gave him a hefty raise for 1976 while also allowing him to walk at the end of the season—didn't sit well with the team's nine unsigned players (including star second baseman Bobby Grich and Jackson's former A's teammate Ken Holtzman), all of whom had taken 20 percent pay cuts to play the 1976 season without a contract. The players didn't take it out on Jackson, though, and most went out of their way to make him feel welcome. Earl Weaver was another story; though happy to finally have Reggie in his lineup, he also wanted to make damn sure that Reggie played by *his* rules.

The inevitable showdown between the fiery manager and the self-centered superstar took place on May 11, at the beginning of Jackson's first road trip with the team. Weaver demanded that his players wear sports jackets and ties on all team flights; and when Reggie showed up for the team's United Airlines charter flight to Milwaukee in a leather jacket, crewneck sweater, and designer jeans, Weaver wouldn't let him on the plane. "If you don't put on a tie, you can't make the trip," the manager calmly yet firmly informed him. Jackson just as calmly turned around and went back into the airport to reconsider his travel options; he was about to head to the ticket counter to buy a ticket on a commercial carrier, when Brooks Robinson intercepted him. The veteran third baseman handed Jackson a tie he'd borrowed from the team's United Airlines rep, and gently coaxed him into putting it on. "Everything will be fine, Reggie," Robinson said. "Just be part of the team. Earl has a certain way of doing things, and we're all pretty much used to them."

Reggie reboarded the plane wearing the tie, though he left it mockingly draped over his sweater. Neither he nor Weaver said anything to each other on the plane; but when the Orioles arrived at

Milwaukee's Pfister Hotel, Weaver let him have it in front of the entire team, as well as anyone else who happened to be in the hotel lobby at the time. In his nicotine-burnished rasp, Weaver told Jackson in no uncertain terms that he was happy to have him on the team, but—and he raised his voice a couple of octaves and stabbed the air with his index finger for emphasis—"I can't have you shitting in my face!" Restraining himself from laughing, Jackson quickly smoothed things over by assuring Weaver that he respected him and that he'd wear a tie for all future flights.

Jackson hit his first home run for the Orioles the following night, a second-inning grand slam off Jim Slaton of the Brewers in an 8–6 victory at County Stadium; two nights later, he hit his second round-tripper of the season, a two-run shot off of former teammate Catfish Hunter in a 6–2 win over the Yankees in the Bronx. By the time the Orioles returned to Baltimore on May 17, they'd won five of their six road games, regaining a .500 record for the first time in a month. Jackson found two dozen neckties—gifts from O's fans—waiting in his mailbox upon his return.

Reggie's former team struggled in May, winning only 12 games and losing 17, with only the lowly Angels standing between the A's and the dirt floor of the AL West cellar. They did kick up some dust on the base paths, however, stealing 77 bases in 29 games, which gave the team 110 swipes in two months and put them on a pace to steal nearly 390 for the season, which would break the 1911 New York Giants' 20th-century record of 347. "I like our running game," raved Oakland captain Sal Bando. "It's like a double every time we get a guy to first."

On May 24, the A's broke an eight-game losing streak with a 12–7 win over the Minnesota Twins that saw Bert Campaneris steal five bases—and Campy would have tied Eddie Collins's single-game AL record of six swipes if highly touted Twins rookie catcher

Butch Wynegar hadn't gunned him down in the third inning. Twins pitcher Steve Luebber caved under the pressure put on him by the A's running game, uncorking three straight wild pitches in the bottom of the fifth, two of which scored runs.

Oakland's thievery didn't always win games, but it certainly made them some enemies. The night after Campy's five-base feat, Don Baylor stole his 19th base of the season with the A's already up by six runs over the Twins—swiping third in the fourth inning off reliever Joe Decker and veteran catcher Phil Roof—leading Minnesota first baseman Rod Carew to blow his top. "It's chicken-shit baseball," Carew groused to reporters afterward. "If we get ahead of them 20–0 someday," added Roof, "I hope we try to make it 40–0." "Our goal is to try to win," Oakland skipper Chuck Tanner insisted. "I don't try to steal bases for any record. I just try to steal bases to win ballgames. What good does a record do if you don't win?"

While the A's were struggling to regain their familiar footing at the top of the AL West, the Kansas City Royals made their move. Following a dreary 5–7 April, the team played .667 ball in May, winning 20 and losing just 10 as they elbowed the Texas Rangers out of the way to grab hold of the division lead. The Royals batted a collective .309 for the month, leading the league in practically every offensive category other than home runs and stolen bases, thanks to a lineup that consisted mostly of speedy line drive hitters who could turn the AstroTurf of Royals Stadium into a bright green nightmare for opposing pitchers and fielders. "I inherited a good young team that was just getting ready to blossom," Royals manager Whitey Herzog would later reflect, "a team that played in a big, AstroTurf ballpark which was made to order for the way I like to play baseball."

Amply muttonchopped Royals centerfielder Amos Otis had nearly been traded to the Pirates in the off-season for center fielder Al Oliver and infielder Art Howe, but the transaction fell through at the last minute when veteran Royals second baseman Cookie Rojas, whom the Bucs also wanted included in the deal, scotched it by invoking his 10-and-5 status. Though Rojas was no longer playing regularly in 1976, having lost the starting second base gig to the slick-fielding Frank White, the Royals owed much of their success in May to him—or at least to his blocking of the Oliver-Otis deal, since Otis hit .322 for the month while leading the team in home runs (eight), RBIs (25), and runs scored (25). Diminutive shortstop Freddie Patek (who hit .316 while stealing 17 bases in 20 attempts) and designated hitter Hal McRae (.325 with 11 doubles) also played significant roles in the team's surge, but third baseman George Brett was the one getting the most attention.

Brett, the younger brother of pitcher Ken (who was traded in May from the Yankees to the White Sox in exchange for outfielder Carlos May), was still just 22 years of age when the season started. But after hitting only .261 in April, Brett spent May reminding AL pitchers why he was being touted as perhaps the best young hitter in the league. He batted .384 for the month, scoring 20 times, driving in 11 runs, and setting a major league record by logging six straight three-hit games. His bat was so dangerous in May, it even put Royals coach Galen Cisco in the hospital; Cisco had the misfortune to take a Brett liner in the ribs while pitching batting practice.

Off the field, Brett enjoyed a laid-back lifestyle, cruising around in his Porsche and cranking Beach Boys tapes. He was all business on the diamond, though, hustling as aggressively as Pete Rose on the base paths while drawing comparisons to perennial Gold Glover Brooks Robinson at third and five-time AL batting king Rod Carew at the plate—though, as Kansas City batting coach Charlie Lau pointed out, "George is going to hit more home runs than Carew ever thought about." Brett told Sid Bordman of the *Sporting News* that his goals for the 1976 season were to "Make the All-Star team and play in the World Series." The way he and his Kansas City teammates were playing, Brett seemed to have a pretty decent chance of both.

"I knew we had a hell of a shot at our division," Herzog would later recall. "The players seemed to know it, too. Finley's run was just about over in Oakland." It wasn't going to be easy, though. A rash of injuries forced Herzog to shuffle and reshuffle his lineup, rotation, and bullpen throughout the first two months of the season. Dave Nelson, who was supposed to open the season as the team's DH, pulled a leg muscle in spring training; Herzog moved McRae, originally slated to be his starting left fielder, into the DH slot, and stationed backup outfielder Jim Wohlford in left. Then, when Wohlford got hit by a Bill Lee pitch in early May and had to miss a few weeks, rookie Tom Poquette took his place and hit .341 for the rest of the month with eight doubles, three triples, and 13 RBIs. "We've got talent and we've got depth," Herzog told reporters. "Nothing this team does surprises me."

It would be harder to replace Steve Busby, the two-time All-Star who'd won 40 games for the Royals over the past two seasons. The 26-year-old righty hurt his shoulder in spring training, then pulled a muscle in his back shortly after returning from the disabled list. Busby's fragile health forced Herzog to go with a four-man rotation of Dennis Leonard, Al Fitzmorris, Paul Splittorff, and Doug Bird—in Herzog's words, "The damnedest bunch of no-name pitchers you ever saw"—for the second half of May. The Royals tried and failed to make a deal for disgruntled Twins hurler Bert Blyleven, but did manage to shore up their bullpen with the addition of left-handers Tom Hall, whom they obtained from the Mets for minor leaguer Bryan Jones, and Larry Gura, shipped to Kansas City from the Yankees in exchange for catcher Fran Healy. Buck Martinez had won the Royals' starting backstop gig in spring training, and they already had veteran Bob Stinson in place as his backup, so Healy was deemed expendable.

Just three days after Healy was dealt to New York, however, Martinez badly hurt himself while trying to stretch a single into a double during a game against the A's; sliding hard into second base, Martinez—who had just extended his hitting streak to a career-best 11 games—somehow spiked his own left hand, cutting it deeply enough that he could see the bones and tendons within. Onto the 15-day disabled list Martinez went, and up came rookie John Wathan from the Triple-A farm team in Omaha to serve as Stinson's backup.

The Boston Red Sox were in relatively good health during the first weeks of May, but you wouldn't have known it from the standings. The defending AL champs spent two weeks in May at the bottom of the Eastern Division, after opening the month with a 10-game losing streak, the team's longest since 1960. The Boston media heaped blame for the slide upon the contentious contract talks between the team and holdouts Fred Lynn, Carlton Fisk, and Rick Burleson—though Lynn, unlike the slumping Fisk, was hitting well enough to keep his name in the AL batting leaders column. Jim Rice, Lynn's partner in terrorizing pitchers the previous season, was doing so poorly at the plate that manager Darrell Johnson actually benched him for several games. Also receiving his share of flak was Bill Lee; the eccentric Red Sox lefty had won 17 games for Boston in each of his last three seasons, but now he couldn't seem to get past the fifth inning. Always a lightning rod for controversy and criticism even when he was pitching well, the voluble "Spaceman"— who could eloquently and hilariously hold forth on everything from busing to Buddhism—was now practically on the verge of being burned at the stake.

"I know I'm pitching well, but it's because I'm not using my head properly," he tried to explain after giving up six earned runs in five innings to the Royals on May 4. "A lot of what I do is mental, and right now I'm not thinking right. I'm not using my mind the way I should when I'm on the mound. . . . I'm not walking as many and I'm throwing strikes. The only thing is that they're still hitting them."

Things were looking so bleak for the Red Sox that, following their 10th straight loss on May 11, a Boston radio station flew a genuine Salem witch to Cleveland in an attempt to snap the losing streak. Laurie Cabot, a 42-year-old teacher of "Witchcraft as a Science" at Massachusetts's Salem State College, had been similarly pressed into Sox service the previous season, when she'd been brought in to dispel a curse supposedly placed upon the team by a Kenyan witch doctor employed by the Orioles. Now, on May 12, Cabot took the field in a flowing black gown before the Red Sox–Indians game at Cleveland Stadium, intending to "examine the auras" of the Boston players and help them "unify their energy." Bernie Carbo, a self-described "flower child" who'd broken out of a slump in 1975 with Cabot's help, didn't think twice about asking the witch to touch his bat for luck, but Carlton Fisk reacted to her appearance with a disdain that would have done his New England Puritan forefathers proud.

"This is a rap against the players," the catcher growled. "It makes us look unprofessional. This is business not a sideshow." Indians television announcer and former big league hurler Jim "Mudcat" Grant got into the spirit of the occasion, trying to nullify Ms. Cabot's magic with a little homebrew voodoo of his own. Mudcat, who hailed from Lacoochee, Mississippi, gave Cabot a big kiss before the game and informed her, "That's the Lacoochee whammy, and it renders you powerless." But after the Indians drove Boston starter Rick Wise to the showers with a four-run outburst in the third inning ("Take That, Witch!" flashed the Cleveland Stadium center field scoreboard), the Red Sox battled back to tie it 4–4 on a double off Carbo's newly enchanted bat, and eventually won the game 6–4 in

12 innings. "It wasn't the witch," insisted Indians first baseman John Lowenstein, who committed three errors in the game. "It was simply a matter of incompetence."

"Whatever did it for us, I'm happy about it," said a visibly relieved Red Sox manager Darrell Johnson afterward. "We definitely needed this. . . . It'll take us some time now—you can't do it overnight— but we're a strong team and we'll catch up to those other clubs."

For the following evening's rematch, the Indians tried to counter-act Cabot's witchcraft with the surprise appearance of their "fairy godmother," who was actually former ball girl Debbie Berndt in a white wig and matching gown. But the "magic dust" that Berndt sprinkled on Rick Manning's glove brought only bad juju to the Tribe center fielder; the normally sure-handed Manning misplayed a Carl Yastrzemski line drive into an RBI triple, allowed another run to score with an error, and also went 0-for-5 in the 7–5 loss to the Red Sox. Advantage: Witch.

True to Johnson's prediction, the Red Sox won six out of their next seven games, and fought their way up to third place in the division behind the Orioles and the Yankees. But perhaps the Red Sox should have considered taking the witch with them to New York City for their four-game series with the Yankees that began on May 20. Earlier in the month, the Houston Astros—in town to play a series with the Mets—had left New York City over $2,000 lighter after someone robbed the hotel rooms of shortstop Roger Metzger, catcher Skip Jutze, and second baseman Larry Milbourne. (The fashion-conscious Milbourne, who lost 17 shirts and nine lei-sure suits in the robbery, grumbled that he'd "bring nothing but jeans to New York next trip.") The Red Sox, on the other hand, would leave the Big Apple with their personal possessions intact . . . but with Bill Lee's shoulder in tatters.

Though the Yankees had stumbled somewhat during the second

week of May, losing five of seven games at one point, they still had a three-and-a-half-game lead heading into the Boston series, not to mention a six-game advantage over the Red Sox. "If we do worse than break even, we might never catch up," said Carl Yastrzemski of the four game series. "I know it's early, but eight or 10 games is a lot of ground to cover. The Orioles fell way behind like that last year, and it killed them."

But the Yankees were going to be difficult to catch, what with six of their regulars hitting .300 or close to it, Mickey Rivers and Willie Randolph leading the league in steals, team captain Thurman Munson driving in runs on an almost daily basis, Catfish Hunter, Ed Figueroa, and Dock Ellis all pitching more or less up to pre-season expectations, and the consistently solid performance of a relief corps led by Sparky Lyle, who'd already saved seven games and won three others by the time the Red Sox rolled into town. With the Yankees playing the sort of cocky, aggressive baseball that Billy Martin lived for, and the Red Sox already feeling tense about their prospects of repeating as AL East winners (much less league champs), the first series of the season between these bitter rivals promised to be nothing less than combustible.

Suitably pumped up for the confrontation, Lee took the mound at Yankee Stadium on the night of May 20 and pitched like the Spaceman of old, holding the Yankees to one unearned run over the first five and two-thirds innings. Then, in the bottom of the sixth with two out, Lee gave up back-to-back singles to Lou Piniella and Graig Nettles. When the next batter, Otto Velez, singled to right, Piniella tried to score from second. Red Sox right fielder Dwight Evans, who possessed one of the best arms in the game, threw a perfect strike to the plate that arrived well in advance of the slow-moving Piniella—a man who, in Lee's words, ran like he was wearing "tight high-heeled shoes." Seeing that he'd be out by a mile unless he forced the issue, the hard-nosed DH tried to steamroll Carlton Fisk, who was patiently awaiting his arrival at the plate.

The two men collided with a mighty bang; as they went rolling in the dirt, Piniella tried to kick the ball loose from Fisk's glove. Fisk held on to the ball, and attempted to make Piniella eat it—whereupon players from both teams surged out onto the field. "See ya in there, kid," said Catfish Hunter, courteously holding the stadium's shared bullpen gate open for Red Sox reliever Tom House. Billy Martin, in an uncharacteristic moment of good judgment, restrained Willie Randolph from leaving the Yankee dugout with a bat in his hand.

The biggest brawl of the season was on. Lee, who was backing up the play behind home plate, saw Velez steaming toward Fisk with murder in his eyes; as the pitcher was trying to tackle Velez, Mickey Rivers ran up and sucker-punched him in the back of the head. Yankee third baseman Graig Nettles attempted to pull Lee off of Velez—Nettles later claimed that he only meant to extract the pitcher from the progressively populous pile of bodies, but he somehow wound up dropping Lee on his pitching shoulder.

Lee stood up and stomped around in a blind rage for a few seconds, then suddenly discovered that his arm was dead. "My first thought was, 'I don't think I can finish this game,'" he later recalled. "Then, realizing how badly I was hurt, my brain screamed, 'I have no fucking feeling in my arm!'" Lee lit into Nettles, yelling, "You son of a bitch! How could you do this to me? I played ball with your brother Jimmy in Alaska, you no-good prick! How could you be such an asshole?" Nettles responded with a hard right to Lee's jaw. Both players were ejected, but their teammates continued to wrestle, punch, and kick each other for a full 20 minutes before order was finally restored. The Bad News Bears would've loved every second of it.

The Red Sox came back to win the game 8–2, thanks to an unexpected meltdown by the Yankee bullpen, but the damage was done.

Carl Yastrzemski's thigh was so badly bruised in the fight that he could barely walk—though he still managed to homer twice in the ballgame—and Lee was out for six weeks with a torn ligament in his left shoulder. The Red Sox hoped that their post-fight comeback might give them some momentum, but they dropped the next two games in heartbreaking extra-inning fashion before eking out a 7–6 win in the final contest.

When the two teams met up again eight days later, 35,939 Boston fans—the largest Red Sox crowd in 20 years—packed Fenway and bayed lustily for Yankee blood. "If any fans come over the top of the dugout," Martin told his players beforehand, "pick up your bats and be ready to take them apart. I'll be right with you." While things didn't escalate to the level of mayhem that Martin had witnessed in 1974, when his Texas Rangers were attacked by fans at Cleveland Stadium during the Indians' ill-fated "10 Cent Beer Night" promotion, Mickey Rivers still had to wear a batting helmet in center field to protect him from the deluge of coins, batteries, golf balls, beer bottles, cherry bombs, and other objects that rained down upon him throughout the game. In the bottom of the eighth, with the Yankees up 8–2, a firecracker exploded at Rivers's feet, and the Red Sox public address announcer informed the crowd that Boston would forfeit the game if any further objects were tossed on the field. The Red Sox lost anyway, by a score of 8–3; the next night's game was rained out, and the teams split the following two games before a more subdued gathering of the Fenway faithful.

On the evening of May 31, while Rivers was ducking cherry bombs in Boston, Twins pitcher Bert Blyleven was subjected to a memorable razzing from Minnesota fans. The 25-year-old righty took the hill that night against the Angels looking for the 100th victory of his career, but everyone at Metropolitan Stadium knew that it was most likely his final game in a Twins uniform. The still unsigned Blyleven was demanding a $1.2 million, four-year contract from Calvin Griffith, who refused to give him anything of the sort. But rather than let his star pitcher become a free agent at the end of the season, Griffith decided to cut his losses by trading him to whichever team could provide the richest package in return. A deal was already in the works to send Blyleven to the Rangers in exchange for infielders Mike Cubbage and Roy Smalley, veteran pitcher Bill Singer, pitching prospect Jim Gideon, and $250,000 in cash; but since the terms wouldn't be finalized until the next day, Minnesota skipper Gene Mauch decided to run Blyleven out there one more time.

Blyleven pitched well against the Angels that night, whiffing nine and walking only three, while allowing three runs on six hits in a complete game effort. But Angels hurler Frank Tanana fanned 12 Twins, walked none, and allowed only two runs, racking up his seventh win of the season while handing Blyleven his fifth loss. In the eighth inning, a group of about 20 Twins fans began taunting Blyleven with a chorus of "Bye, Bye, Bertie," which was then picked up and parroted by many of the other 8,379 fans in attendance. Walking off the mound after the top of the ninth, Blyleven issued a Bad News Bears–worthy response, bidding farewell to his hecklers with an emphatic middle finger salute.

7.

Strange Magic

(June 1976)

American Motors touted it as "the first wide small car," *Motor Trend* raved that it was "the freshest, most creative, most people-oriented auto to be born in the U.S. in 15 years," while *Car and Driver* magazine snidely christened it "The Flying Fishbowl." Whatever you wanted to call it, there was no question that the AMC Pacer was the most unique-looking new mass-production car on the road in 1976. Short as a Volkswagen Dasher, wide as a Cadillac Coupe de Ville, with huge rear, front, and side windows that made it look like a soap bubble on wheels, the Pacer was introduced in 1975 and reached its sales and production peak in 1976, when AMC rolled out nearly 120,000 of the low-slung hatchbacks—available in such quintessentially mid-'70s colors as Mellow Yellow, Caramel Tan, and Aztec Copper.

AMC's attempt to crack the compact car market while still ac-commodating American drivers' unquenchable desire for comfort, the Pacer was ultimately doomed by its distinctive design and its compromising nature, since its 3,200-pound body (over 12 percent heavier than the Gremlin, AMC's other eye-catching compact) resulted in both inferior gas mileage and a frustrating lack of get-up-and-go from its six-cylinder engine. But there were other issues as well: the Pacer's odd shape made parking difficult; the door windows were actually bigger than the panels below them, which meant they couldn't roll down all the way; and riding in the backseat under its wraparound rear windows often felt like sitting in a rolling terrarium. Pacer sales started slowing halfway through 1976 as word of its shortcomings spread, and subsequent improvements to the line (including a station wagon edition and a more powerful V-8 engine in the hatchback) failed to reignite consumer interest. By 1980, the most futuristic car of the 1970s would be out of production, fated to be remembered chiefly as an anachronistic punch line.

Cut from a similarly futuristic mold in the mid-'60s, the Houston Astrodome circa 1976 still seemed like a "state of the art" indoor stadium. With a $4.5 million air-conditioning system that kept temperatures inside at a perpetual 73 degrees, a rainproof roof with 4,596 skylights that were specially treated to repel both light and sound, and (of course) its synthetic, AstroTurf-carpeted playing surface, the "Eighth Wonder of the World" was a 45,101-capacity monument to man's triumph over nature. Players and fans alike could enjoy each game in hermetically sealed comfort, oblivious to whatever storms, winds, or insect plagues raged outside. But on June 15, 1976, the Astrodome experienced the only weather-related cancellation in its vaunted, vaulted history.

On the evening of June 14, dependable Pittsburgh lefty Jerry Reuss outdueled Houston righty James Rodney "J.R." Richard—a 6'8" intimidation machine pitching in his second full season, who finally seemed on the verge of gaining control over his terrifying 98 mph fastball—to an uneventful 2–1 Pirates victory at the Astrodome. The second game in the series was slated for the following evening, with Doc Medich scheduled to take the mound for the Pirates, who were currently sitting six and a half games behind the Phillies in the NL East with a 33–25 record. The Astros, who at 29–33 were already 10 games behind the Reds in the NL West, planned to send rookie Gil Rondon out to face the Pittsburgh Lumber Company. First pitch was scheduled for 7:35.

But on the morning of the 15th, torrential rains began soaking the city of Houston, and continued to fall well into the afternoon. Players from both teams began arriving at the Astrodome around 1 p.m., in order to be dressed and on the field by 3:30. But by 5 p.m., the rain was coming down so viciously that the streets surrounding the stadium were flooded and all but impassable—as were the Astrodome's lower entrances and ramps. The field, of course, was still dry as a plastic-wrapped bone, and the players were ready to play; however, with most Astros fans and stadium workers unable to reach the park, the Astros' front office decided to call off the contest. "We could have played the game," said Astros GM Tal Smith. "But if we had announced it was on, we would have been inviting misfortune. Many would have tried to make it and would have become stranded. We just felt it was best to postpone it." Normally, the umpires would have had a say in the matter—but their rental car had stalled out in high water on the way to the 'Dome, forcing them to wade back to their hotel.

With nothing left to do but wait out the storm, the small percentage of concession workers who'd successfully made it inside the stadium's doors set up banquet tables in the infield and served the players and coaches a buffet dinner. Both teams chowed down while still attired in their uniforms—the Pirates in their road grays, the Astros in their tequila sunrise rainbow stripes—though many of the players exchanged their cleats for more casual and comfortable flip-flops. After dinner, several Astros players, led by pitcher Larry

Dierker, killed time by climbing to the top of the 'Dome and crawling along the catwalks that hung suspended from the roof. The 20 or so diehard fans that actually showed up for the game (they'd literally canoed their way to the stadium) were treated to dinner on the Astros as well, though they were served in the Astrodome's cafeteria.

The rain subsided in the early evening, and the waters eventually receded enough to allow the players to return to their hotels and homes. The third game of the series was played as planned on June 16, and the postponed game was rescheduled as part of an August series in Pittsburgh. The "rain-in" would be forever recalled as one of the strangest occasions in Astrodome history—and yet, it wasn't even the weirdest thing to go down during the often gloomy, occasionally glorious baseball month of June 1976.

"The nation is running pretty well by itself right now," wrote journalist Hugh Sidey in the June 14 issue of *Time* magazine. "There is no major crisis at home or abroad." Since, in Sidey's words, the U.S. now had "only muted adversaries in the Communist world, quiet ghettos and more food than we can eat," it surely followed that Americans were, by and large, experiencing a far greater degree of contentment than they had during the last presidential election. Yes, busing was still an intensely heated subject in Boston, people were still getting mugged in New York's Central Park (and just about everywhere else in "Fun City") and choking on smog in Los Angeles, and there was a grassroots campaign under way in Philadelphia to recall Mayor Frank Rizzo in the wake of his bid to raise city property taxes (which broke a promise from his recent reelection campaign) and his unpopular decision to close Philadelphia General Hospital. Gerald Ford and Ronald Reagan continued to slug it out in the GOP primaries, though the main issue between them now seemed to be who could best defeat Jimmy Carter in November, since the Georgia governor had already wrapped up the Democratic nomination by dominating his party's primaries in May. Meanwhile, a breaking Washington sex scandal involving Representative Wayne Hays (D-Ohio), chairman of the House Administration Committee, provoked as much hilarity as outrage when Elizabeth Ray, a busty 27-year-old member of Hays's staff, revealed that she was being paid $14,000 a year to be his mistress. "I can't type. I can't file," Ray told reporters. "I can't even answer the phone."

But with unemployment down a full percentage point from where it had been a year earlier, inflation at its lowest level since July 1973, and Detroit's automakers on track for their third-highest sales year in history—thanks in part to the success of such popular mid-sized luxury models as the Ford Granada and the Chrysler Cordoba (whose "soft Corinthian leather" was rapturously exalted by actor Ricardo Montalban in a memorable series of TV commercials)—there was no denying that the country now appeared a happier, more optimistic, more relaxed place on the whole than it had in years, at least on the surface. It was no coincidence that Paul McCartney's band Wings scored June's biggest pop hit with the summery, Al Green–quoting "Silly Love Songs," or that "Happy Days"—the upbeat, doo wop–tinged theme song from ABC's nostalgic '50s sitcom of the same name, sung by L.A. studio duo Pratt & McLain—had been firmly nestled in the Top Five for the first two weeks of the month.

You weren't likely to hear the lords of baseball joining in on a gang chorus of either song, however. As May turned to June, no real progress had been made on the Basic Agreement talks, and rumors (albeit largely unfounded) persisted that the players would sit out July's All-Star Game if their demands weren't met. American League owners, still bristling over Bowie Kuhn's attempted intercession into their annexation of Toronto, were reportedly preparing to pressure the commissioner to allow the use of the designated hitter in both the All-Star Game and the upcoming World Series. Charlie Finley and Bill Veeck were still quarreling over who was supposed to pay how much of Chuck Tanner's salary. And with 54 players still unsigned at the beginning of June—16 in the NL, and 38 in the AL—it was anyone's guess as to what kind of chaos the June 15 trading deadline might bring.

Tim Foli wasn't an unsigned player, but he was definitely an unhappy one. The slick-fielding shortstop, who back in April had become the first Expos player to hit for the cycle in a single game, started June on the bench, thanks to an increasingly ugly feud brewing between him and Montreal's first-year manager Karl Kuehl. Other Expos had already locked horns with Kuehl in 1976; catcher Barry Foote repeatedly voiced his displeasure about the amount of playing time he was losing to Gary Carter (Foote would see more action behind the plate in June, but only because Carter broke his left thumb in a collision with teammate Pepe Mangual), and several players clashed with Kuehl over his "no facial hair" policy—including pitcher Steve Renko, who bitched so vociferously (and so defiantly sported a mustache) that the team finally traded him to the Cubs in May, along with outfielder Larry Biittner, in exchange for Cubs first baseman Andre Thornton.

But Foli, whose tendency to go off on his own abrasive tangents earned him the nickname "Crazy Horse," elevated Kuehl-baiting to a new extreme. During a late-May game against the Phillies, Foli took issue with the manager's decision to have pitcher Fred Scherman intentionally walk "Downtown" Ollie Brown; after Scherman's first ball to Brown, Foli visited the mound and tried to talk the hurler into throwing strikes. When Kuehl told Foli to leave the managing to him, the shortstop responded by calling an impromptu press conference after the game to disparage his skipper.

"He's not capable of managing the club right now," Foli told reporters. "He wants me to sit down and say nothing. I won't do that when I know he can't do the job. He might be trying very hard but he's still a rookie. . . . He does things that there is no justification for and then refuses to explain them. All he's trying to do is prove he's the manager."

Kuehl responded to Foli's tirade by benching him and starting backup infielder Pepe Frias in his place. But when Frias bobbled two grounders and made a third error on a throw to first in the team's 6–2 loss to the Cardinals at Parc Jarry—the outmoded minor league park the Expos were occupying until they could move into Montreal's new Stade Olympique in 1977—on June 1, Expos president John McHale insisted that Foli be reinstated in the lineup. Kuehl's days as Montreal's manager were clearly numbered; the Expos would go on an 8–20 slide in June, with injuries, morale problems, and the league's worst offense and pitching all contributing to their woes.

While Brewers skipper Alex Grammas had technically managed in the majors before—he'd helmed the Pirates for the last five games of the 1969 season—he was, for all intents and purposes, another rookie manager in 1976. As with Kuehl, Grammas was faced with the challenge of turning around the fortunes of an awful team; and, like Kuehl, he attempted to do so by imposing the sort of discipline that didn't sit very well with mid-'70s ballplayers: Grammas (formerly one of Sparky Anderson's coaches on the Reds, a team with extremely conservative grooming guidelines) banned his players from wearing mustaches, beards, or long hair, an unpopular move on a team that practically led the league in Fu Manchus during the previous season. He also wasn't shy about berating the team's lackadaisical play to reporters. "It's about as bad as a team can look," was how Grammas described the Brewers in June, a month where they went 9–21 and effectively cemented themselves to the bottom of the

AL East. "I get tired of looking at it myself. They're falling asleep out there."

Grammas also ran afoul of George "Boomer" Scott, the team's Gold Glove first baseman, when he moved him from third to sixth in the lineup. Boomer, who'd tied Reggie Jackson for the AL home run title in 1975 with 36 and led the league with 109 RBIs, was experiencing a serious power outage, hitting .255 with only seven homers and 35 RBIs through the first three months of the season. Doubly stung by his lineup demotion and Milwaukee GM Jim Baumer's public criticism of his and catcher Darrell Porter's run production, an irate Scott lashed out at Grammas and Baumer in the press. "Quote me as saying that [Baumer] can get on a uniform and come down here and play himself," he fumed. "Two guys can't make you win. Four guys can't make you win. It takes 25 guys. . . .

"Alex Grammas apparently doesn't know anything about me," Scott continued. "He better go check the record books. My thing is driving in runs. My thing is being left alone. . . . I think my talent enables me to play baseball anywhere in America or anywhere out of America. If you don't like the way I'm producing, then, hey, get rid of me."

Scott would get his wish, but not until after the season. His frustrations with Grammas and Baumer aside, Boomer would chiefly remember 1976 for the pleasure of being able to play with Hank Aaron on a daily basis. "I knew I was playing with one of baseball's all-time greats," he would later reflect. "The way he carried himself made me a better individual, a better player. He carried himself so professionally that I never thought about him being diminished as a player. Not once. He wasn't sad. I was sad for myself that I wasn't going to get to play with this man anymore."

At the age of 42, Aaron was no longer playing like one of the all-time greats—or even like the man who, just two years earlier, had hit 20 round-trippers in 382 plate appearances for the Atlanta Braves. The all-time Home Run King had returned to Milwaukee a year earlier, expecting to play out his career under friend and former Braves teammate Del Crandall, and he found little common ground with Grammas, Crandall's replacement. Though Grammas typically penciled Hank into the cleanup spot, one sensed it was mostly out of deference and respect for the fearsome hitter Hank had been, as opposed to the aging DH he was now. "I'd be lying if I denied some adrenaline hasn't diminished," Aaron admitted to reporters. "But once I get to the plate, I have an awful lot of pride, and the desire to do well is still the same. I still enjoy playing baseball."

The cheerless trek of Aaron's early-1976 campaign indicated otherwise; through June 13, he was hitting only .238 with only a pair of home runs and 12 RBIs. And then, on June 14, he suddenly started hitting like the Hammerin' Hank of yore, cracking five home runs in eight games, including a solo shot off A's reliever Jim Todd in the top of the ninth on June 18 that gave Aaron his 750th career homer and lifted the Brewers to a 3–2 victory. "I got a big kick out of that, doing what I can to help the team win," said Aaron, who revealed that he'd hit four of those five home runs using Scott's weighty 37-ounce bat.

Like Aaron, Frank Robinson was a future first-ballot Hall of Famer whose glory days were well behind him; though unlike Aaron, who spent most of his games silently smoking cigarettes and drinking coffee in the Brewers' clubhouse between turns at the plate, Robby now had his hands full as the Cleveland Indians' player-manager. Led by a solid pitching staff that included veteran starter Pat Dobson, charismatic young fireballer Dennis Eckersley, and gangly reliever Jim Kern (dubbed "The Amazing Emu" by Dobson and Eckersley), and bolstered by hot hitting from third baseman Buddy Bell and DH Rico Carty, the Tribe played 15–12 ball in June, which was good enough to put them in second place in the AL East for most of the month, though not good enough to keep them from continuously losing ground to the first-place Yankees. It also wasn't good enough to bring a smile to Robinson's perpetually scowling mug.

Robinson felt he had ample reason to fume, especially when it came to dealing with the AL umpiring crew of Lou DiMuro, Richie Garcia, Bill Kunkel, and David Phillips. Through the first week of June, Indians players and coaches had been ejected 13 times in 1976—and the DiMuro-led crew had been responsible for 12 of them. "Not one of those ejections would have happened with another crew," claimed Robinson, who was tossed (along with two of his coaches) by Garcia during the second game of a June 6 doubleheader against the White Sox at Comiskey Park; Garcia took offense to Robinson's kicking of a towel, which had somehow ended up on the roof of the Indians' dugout. "There is no doubt in my mind they have a psychological malice against our team," said Indians president Ted Bonda, who asked Lee MacPhail to prevent DiMuro's crew from working any further Indians games.

MacPhail granted the Indians' request, up to a point—Dick Butler, the AL supervisor of umpires, wouldn't be able to rearrange the crew's schedule until after July 1, which meant that they would still cross paths with the Cleveland club during a mid-June series against the Rangers. Robinson responded by implementing a team-wide "gag rule" forbidding his players from communicating with DiMuro or the rest of his crew. "I told them I didn't even want them to say hello to the umpires," said Robinson, who threatened a $100-a-word fine to any player who defied his edict. The games passed without incident; the Indians kept quiet, even when Garcia made a bad call that many on the team believed was intentional.

Robinson also clashed with Bill Veeck during the June 6 twin bill at Comiskey, initially refusing to allow Veeck sufficient time between games to conduct his lavish "Salute to Mexico" promotion, which involved Mexican cowboys on horseback, mariachi bands, and a children's parade; fans were treated to the additional comic spectacle of White Sox first base coach Minnie Minoso dressed as a toreador and doing battle with a man in a bull costume. (White Sox players also took the field for the second game wearing large sombreros, though these were thankfully discarded before the contest actually began.) Robinson only relented after being informed that Veeck would retaliate by canceling his upcoming trip to Cleveland, where the former Indians owner was scheduled to appear as part of a "Welcome Back Veeck Night" promotion before a June 11 White Sox–Indians game at Cleveland Stadium; even though it had been decades since Veeck owned the Tribe, he was still a popular figure in Cleveland, and the Indians' front office was counting on him on to lure a few thousand extra fans to the cold and rickety "Mistake by the Lake." Robinson ultimately got the last word on June 11, welcoming Veeck back to town with a two-run pinch home run off Terry Forster in the bottom of the 13th that gave the Indians a 5–4 win. It was the 584th homer of Robinson's career, and the last game-winning blast he'd ever hit.

The Indians' player-manager did land another memorable blow on June 30, though it was during an exhibition game against the Indians' Toledo Mudhens farm club—and it didn't involve the use of a bat. In the fifth inning, Robinson stepped to the plate against "Bullet" Bob Reynolds, a former Indians pitcher who'd been demoted to the minors by Robinson at the end of spring training. Reynolds threw his first pitch over Robinson's head; "I was trying to throw a fastball, and my spikes were cluttered with mud," he insisted later. Then, when Robinson jogged by the mound after flying out, Reynolds loudly demanded to know why he'd been cut from the Indians. Robinson objected to Reynolds's line of questioning, and responded by decking the hurler with the second of two sharp rights. Robinson was ejected from the game, though this time he left without a protest. Reynolds never pitched in the majors again.

Joe Frazier of the Mets was another manager feeling the June chill—both from angry players and the Mets' ice-cold bats. Though blessed with one of the best rotations in the majors, the Mets were nearly lifeless at the plate; "new guy" Mickey Lolich (the former Tigers hurler who'd come to New York in the off-season in exchange for Rusty Staub) was particularly hamstrung by the lack of offense, going 4–9 through the end of June despite posting a more than respectable 2.96 ERA in his starts. Not that Mets fans were particularly sympathetic to his plight; the *Sporting News* reported that "vandals" spat and threw stones at Lolich's car one June evening, as the portly pitcher and his wife attempted to exit the Shea Stadium parking lot following a loss. The good-natured Lolich, who would later entertain the Shea faithful on "Camera Day" by circling the field on his Kawasaki motorcycle with teammate Joe Torre in the "bitch" seat, merely shrugged off the ugly incident. But he and his staff-mates clearly deserved better support—from the team's starting lineup as well as the fans.

"We can't knock the fuzz off peaches the way we're swinging," Frazier moaned during one particularly dismal stretch. With no help in sight from their farm system, the Mets' front office kept trying to make deals for solid bats, only to find that every team they spoke to wanted Jon Matlack in return—and Matlack, 9–2 with a 2.81 ERA with three shutouts and 10 complete games through the end of the June, was simply not on the trading block.

Desperate for runs, Frazier attempted to shake some action out of his offense by frantically shuffling his lineup each day, an approach that rankled a considerable portion of the Mets' roster. "It isn't just the fact that you never know when you're playing, one anonymous Mets veteran told sportswriter Jack Lang. "It's that when you are playing, you never know where you're hitting. One day it's second, next day sixth, next day fifth. What kind of sense does that make?"

Dave Kingman, the team's lone reliable power source—though he whiffed far more reliably than he clubbed home runs—cast an especially moody shadow over the Mets' clubhouse. On the afternoon of June 3, a frustrated Kingman went into King Kong mode after striking out with two on and two out to end the Mets' 2–1 loss to the Cubs at Shea; he smashed a bottle of hair tonic, destroyed his hair dryer, and sent coat hangers sailing through the locker room. The next day in L.A., Kingman had a chat with his old USC baseball coach Rod Dedeaux, who told him to change his approach by hitting the first good pitch he saw. Kingman followed Dedeaux's instructions that evening, swinging at first pitches from Dodger starter Burt Hooton in the fourth and fifth innings, and the first pitch he saw from reliever Al Downing in the seventh—all three of which sailed over the fence at Dodger Stadium, plating eight runs (breaking Donn Clendenon's single-game franchise record) in the Mets' 11–0 victory, Tom Seaver's second shutout of the season.

Kingman hit 10 of the Mets' 24 home runs in June—giving him an almost Roger Maris–esque 27 round-trippers on the year—and drove in 24 of the Mets' 94 runs. Thanks to Sky King's bombs and a Mets staff that held opponents to a .221 batting average, the team was able to bounce back from a 11–17 May with a 15–13 June that put them back above the .500 mark for the year; only, with the Phillies already ahead of them by 14 games in the NL East, the prospects of another "Miracle Mets"–style surge looked fairly dim, indeed.

The Mets' Bronx counterparts didn't have much to complain about, hustling along at a 17–11 pace for the month that kept them sitting comfortably in the soft Corinthian leather of the AL East driver's seat. The only odd aspect of the Yankees' 43–26 record through June was that they were playing over .700 ball on the road, while barely breaking even at their newly renovated home. "What difference does it make where you win your games?" asked Billy Martin. "As long as you win them, that's all that counts. I don't know why we're having trouble playing .500 at home and at this point I don't really care."

But Yankee fans cared, all right. On June 5, the Yankees—who had already lost all of two games in a row—blew a sloppy 7–6 game to the A's in the Bronx. Fans booed loudly when catcher Thurman Munson unleashed an uncharacteristically errant throw on a Don Baylor steal of second, an error that allowed Baylor to score the go-ahead run in the top of the ninth; they booed even louder when Rollie Fingers struck Munson out in the bottom of the ninth for the penultimate out of the game. The Yankee captain responded in typically blunt fashion by giving the finger to the stands.

While another Yankee player might have been crucified in the New York media for such a gesture, several local writers actually jumped to Munson's defense, scolding the fans for behaving in such a spoiled manner. New York *Daily News* sportswriter Phil Pepe wrote that, while Munson could indeed be a difficult and abrasive individual at times, "the fans were being totally unfair, and picking on the wrong man. Nobody plays harder than Thurman, nobody has contributed more to the Yankees over the past few years. And nobody was more responsible for their fast start this season and their standing on top of the American League East." Munson, who was hitting .316 at the time with a team-leading 37 RBIs, agreed.

"I just felt that considering the season I've been having, they should have shown a little more appreciation," he grumbled to reporters after the game. "New York is like that. They want you to hit a home run every time, or be a complete bum so they can boo you."

But New York City wasn't the only town where boo-birds roosted, as Reggie Jackson could corroborate. Baltimore fans had hoped that the arrival of Jackson would turn the Orioles' season around; but on June 4, with the team still four and a half games behind the Yankees with a 23–22 record, and their new superstar slugger batting only .225 with three home runs in 28 games, they expressed their disappointment with a torrent of abuse after Jackson grounded into two rally-killing double plays in an 8–6, 10-inning loss to the Twins at Memorial Stadium. "That's the first time I've ever been booed by my hometown fans," he lamented after the game, but it wouldn't be the last. Boos rained down the next day when Jackson muffed an easy fly in center, and again the following afternoon, when Jackson—whose batting average had now dipped to .211—grounded into two more double plays during the second game of a doubleheader.

Worse than the booing was the news Reggie received on June 20, when his friend Everett Moss called to tell him that a fire of unknown origin had burned through his Oakland condominium, causing an estimated $70,000 in damages. Reggie was crushed. "That was my A's house, paid for with my A's money, filled with emotional bits and pieces of the glory years," he would later reflect. "It was if the fates were saying, 'Okay, kid. Close the chapter on the A's years, as painful as that may be. Let's get on with it.'"

The O's went 12–16 in June, including a disastrous 10-game losing streak. It wasn't all Jackson's fault, however, as most of Baltimore's bats were colder than a fridge full of Natty Boh. Lee May, who alternated hitting in the cleanup and fifth slots with Jackson, had 13 home runs and 45 RBIs through June, but was hitting only .230. Outfielder/DH Ken Singleton batted .303 in June, but hit only two homers and drove in a mere five runs all month. Speedy leadoff hitter Al Bumbry struggled to get his average above .250. Perhaps the most depressing development was that perennial Gold Glove third baseman and Baltimore fan favorite Brooks Robinson, who'd turned 39 in May, was playing so poorly that Earl Weaver had no choice but to bench him; unfortunately, Doug DeCinces, his 25-year-old replacement, hit so feebly that Weaver was soon forced to reinstate Robinson.

The Orioles' pitching staff, the best in the AL for so many years, also now appeared to be a shadow of its former self, posting a 3.80 ERA for June while giving up 71 extra-base hits in 28 games. Staff ace Jim Palmer had been uneven all season, winning nine games but also demonstrating a sudden inability to locate his pitches. Ken Holtzman was pitching well, but wasn't getting run support; Doyle Alexander and Ross Grimsley were inconsistent as starters; and Mike Cuellar, the 39-year-old Cuban palm-baller who'd averaged nearly 20 wins per season for the O's over the last seven years, looked all but finished. After going 2–7 with a 7.00 ERA in his first 11 starts, Cuellar was briefly demoted to the bullpen; when he complained bitterly to Weaver about his treatment, the diminutive skipper blew a gasket. "If you don't think I've been fair with you," he yelled, "then get on the phone and call some other clubs. If you can find a team that will promise you 11 starts, we'll give you to them free."

Weaver soon returned Cuellar to the rotation, telling the press, "I feel I've stayed with Mike Cuellar longer than I did my first wife. At least, I've given him more chances." The veteran lefty responded by pitching his two best games of the season, including a three-hit, six-strikeout blanking of Texas on June 20; it would be the 36th and final shutout of Cuellar's career. Cuellar's gem was immediately followed by a two-hit, 10-strikeout shutout of the Red Sox, courtesy of Wayne Garland, a 25-year-old reliever whom Weaver had pressed into service as a starting pitcher in late May. Garland, whose bushy mustache and dirty-blond perm made him look more like a member of the Eagles than a professional ballplayer, ended June with the best record on the staff: 8–1 with a 2.16 ERA. But the Orioles would need a full-team effort in order to pull themselves out of fifth place in the AL East, which is where they stood as June came to a close, a distant 10 games behind the self-assured Yankees.

"Write this down and file it," Red Sox skipper Darrell Johnson boasted to Associated Press reporter Dave O'Hara on June 8, shortly after the Bostonians fell six and a half games behind the New Yorkers with a 6–5 loss to the A's. "We'll catch the Yankees in six weeks. It might take seven, that depends on how they play, but we'll get our nose up soon and we'll catch up. We're doing everything better now, and there's no way to go but up. We're about ready to put things together."

These were brave words coming from the manager of a 22–25 ball club, especially a club whose low-grade discord hung tangibly in the air like a Fenway fog. Cecil Cooper, a talented hitter and first baseman, seethed at Johnson using him primarily as a left-handed platoon DH. Trade rumors continued to swirl around the still unsigned Carlton Fisk, Fred Lynn, and Rick Burleson, and Johnson briefly benched Fisk following a dugout shouting match triggered by Fisk missing a team bus and showing up late to the ballpark. Bill Lee, who wouldn't return to action until the middle of July, had the sneaking suspicion that his team had already quit for the season after the Yankees had handed them back-to-back extra inning losses in the same late-May series where Graig Nettles injured Lee's shoulder. "We were still in the pennant race," he'd write later, "but, when the Yankees won [those games] in extra innings, they soared and we packed it in. I'm certain [those games] convinced the Yankees that they were going to do it that year. Just as it convinced us that we weren't."

Lynn and Burleson, for their part, seemed to accept the possibility that they might be shipped out of Boston before the June 15 deadline. On the evening of June 10, as the Sox were leaving Boston for a 13-game road trip following another loss to Oakland, the star center fielder and hot-tempered shortstop sarcastically chanted "Goodbye, Fenway" from their seats on the team bus, an outburst that one appalled Red Sox official described to the press as "simply bush." "I think this unsigned situation and the fact that the trading deadline is coming up is responsible for a lot of this," Johnson told reporters. "Everybody's on edge. On the field and off it. It certainly has affected the play of the team—anybody can see that. I think once [the trading deadline] passes, things will be better."

Johnson's prediction couldn't have been more off; things would only get more complicated for the Red Sox (and the Yankees, and especially the A's) in the immediate wake of the trading deadline. For in the waning hours of June 15, A's owner Charlie Finley set baseball on its ear by enacting what quickly became immortalized as the "Tuesday Night Massacre": the multimillion-dollar sale of three of his biggest names—outfielder Joe Rudi, reliever Rollie Fingers, and starting pitcher Vida Blue—to the Red Sox and Yankees.

With seven A's stars still holding out as the trade deadline approached, Finley had been burning up the phone lines trying to arrange one blockbuster trade after another, desperate to get something in return for them before they left as free agents at the end of the year. Unable to find any takers for his outlandish offers (like the one where he wanted to trade Rudi, Fingers, Blue, Gene Tenace, and Sal Bando to the Red Sox in exchange for Lynn, Fisk, and several lesser lights), Finley opted to market his stars on a cash-and-carry basis. "I'm offering Rudi, Blue, Baylor, or Tenace for a million apiece and Sal Bando for half a million," he barked down the phone to Red Sox GM Dick O'Connell, two days before the trade deadline. "Are you interested?"

Finley's sales query set off a frenzied chain of events that would reverberate throughout the rest of the season and beyond. O'Connell was indeed interested in Blue and Fingers, feeling that the Red Sox would need additional pitching to have any hope of overtaking the Yankees in the AL East. His manager, however, wanted Rudi instead of Blue; unable to convince Johnson of Blue's value as the deadline neared, O'Connell told Finley he'd take Rudi and Fingers at a million apiece. O'Connell then put a call in to Tigers GM Jim Campbell, strongly encouraging the Tigers to offer Finley $1 million for Blue before the Yankees—who'd already expressed interest in the former Cy Young winner—could close a deal with Finley. Campbell, a conservative man who generally frowned on Finley's antics (and lavish expenditures in general) was swept up by O'Connell's enthusiasm and made a million-dollar offer to bring Blue to Detroit. Finley then called Yankees GM Gabe Paul and demanded $1.5 million for Blue, only to be informed that the Yankees weren't going to pay that much for Blue without a signed contract in place.

Not wanting to leave an extra $500,000 on the table, Finley hurriedly initiated a new round of contract talks with Blue and his agent Chris Daniel—only, in typical underhanded Finley fashion, the A's owner neglected to inform either man that there was a pending transaction to send Blue to the Yankees. A deal was finally agreed upon that would pay Blue $485,000 over three years; but when the Yankees prematurely announced their purchase of the southpaw, Blue belatedly realized that he'd once again been bamboozled by slick ol' Charlie O. Still, he was happy to get out of Oakland. "The Yankees are a first-class organization and they are in first place now," Blue told reporters. "It will be a relief to go out and do my job without having to worry about Charlie Finley."

News of Finley's sales hit the wire services around 5:50 p.m. Oakland time, just a little more than an hour before the A's were due to take on the Red Sox at the Coliseum. Having yet to inform anyone on the A's, including manager Chuck Tanner, of what was going on, Finley called the Oakland clubhouse from his office in Chicago in an attempt to do some cursory damage control. "We'll rebuild, Chuck," he told his skipper. "I'm sorry we had to do this today." To Tanner and the press, Finley blamed agent Jerry Kapstein, who represented many of the unsigned A's, for making astronomical contract demands that forced him to sell off his stars. Finley gave a similar spiel to Blue, adding, "I love you buddy and believe me when I tell you that." The fact that Finley let several members of the press eavesdrop on his end of the conversation rather belied the sincerity of his words.

Since the Red Sox were already in Oakland for a three-game series, Rudi and Fingers simply had to walk over to the visitors' clubhouse at the Coliseum in order to suit up for their new team. Darrell Johnson gave them the night of June 15 off, however, feeling that they'd probably need a day or two to recover from the shock of being shopped to a new team for the first time in their respective careers. Both players had come up through the A's farm system, and both had been instrumental in bringing three straight championship trophies to Oakland. Now, suddenly, they were members of the Red Sox, a much different organization located over 3,000 miles away. "Hey, I'm worth a million dollars," laughed Fingers. "Somehow that just doesn't sound right." Rudi seemed to take it harder, bidding lengthy and tearful farewells to his brothers in the green-and-gold. "I'm both happy and sad about this deal," said Rudi, who reportedly wept for half an hour after receiving news of the sale. "I'm happy that I'm going to a good club and sad because I'm leaving the A's."

Their former teammates, who were 27–31 going into the June 15 game, which put them fifth in the AL West and 10 and a half games behind the division-leading Royals, were understandably less sanguine about the whole thing. "I can't believe that it was just a cash deal," lamented team captain Sal Bando. "We can't win without these guys. The way it stands we're battling the California Angels for last place in the American League West." Designated hitter Billy Williams, who'd toiled for 14 frustrating seasons with the Cubs before finally reaching the postseason with the A's in 1975, was completely puzzled by Finley's dismantling of a once great team. "I can't figure these deals out," he said, "unless they mean Finley doesn't want a team anymore. As long as I have been in baseball, I've never seen a deal like this—three key guys gone in a matter of minutes."

Reaction from the Red Sox clubhouse was mixed—Darrell Johnson told reporters, "I think we'll catch the Yankees now," but pitcher Rick Wise revealed that the Sox players were confused by the purchase of Rudi, since the addition of the left fielder would make Jim Rice the team's full-time DH, and result in the benching of Cecil Cooper, who was currently batting .292 and had driven in 13 runs in his past 12 games. "We'll have guys on the bench who should be playing every day," said Wise.

Oakland's designated astrologer Laurie Brady had predicted that the A's would take the first two games of their mid-June series against the Red Sox. Brady's astrological forecast proved correct, with Gene Tenace breaking a 2–2 tie on June 15 with a solo homer off Fergie Jenkins in the bottom of the ninth, and Paul Lindblad outdueling Luis Tiant for a 4–1 victory the following night. But Finley somehow neglected to have Brady consult the stars regarding his sale of Rudi, Fingers, and Blue. Perhaps this was for the best, since—as Brady confessed to *Time* magazine—"When I tell him negative things, he gets angry." And Finley would soon have plenty to be angry about.

Commissioner Bowie Kuhn was watching an Orioles–White Sox game at Comiskey Park on the evening of June 15 when he first got word of Finley's wheeling and dealing; he left his seat in the sixth inning looking "visibly distressed." "I won't believe it until I see it on paper," he said, before calling O'Connell to express his displeasure with the sale of Rudi and Fingers to the Red Sox. Kuhn placed a similar call to Gabe Paul regarding the Blue deal, then dialed Finley and announced, "I don't like the look of these sales at all. I'm putting everything on hold until I can decide whether or not to stop them." Finley was furious. "Commissioner, it's none of your damn business," he raged. "You can't stop me from selling players. Guys have been selling players forever and no commissioner has ever stopped them."

Finley had a point. There was already a long, if not exactly glorious, tradition of baseball owners selling off their star players, dating at least as far back as 1915, when cash-strapped Philadelphia A's owner and manager Connie Mack sold off a significant chunk of his roster. No players had ever changed hands for this kind of money, however; and by selling his stars to the Yankees and Red Sox, Finley hit a nerve with Kuhn, who had already expressed deep concerns that the new economic era ushered in by the Messersmith decision would lead to the wealthier teams cornering the market on the best players.

Still, there were no laws on the books preventing owners from selling players for whatever prices the market would bear, and Finley remained certain that his sales would eventually go through. Following a 90-minute hearing with the commissioner on June 17, which also included George Steinbrenner, Marvin Miller, John Gaherin, Gabe Paul, Dick O'Connell, Lee MacPhail, and 10 attorneys, Finley—who was jauntily attired in a gray plaid sports jacket with canary yellow shirt and hat—seemed positively cheerful. "I think the commissioner called the meeting because he wanted to know how we went about making the sales," he jovially told report-ers. "I think he was happy with the presentation." Kuhn had told the assembled parties that he would make his final ruling on the transactions the next day, and Steinbrenner seconded Finley's sunny take on the matter by flashing the assembled newsmen a thumbs-up as he left the meeting.

Steinbrenner had an additional reason to be cheerful: the same evening the Yankees purchased Blue, Gabe Paul also pulled off a 10-player deal with the Orioles that brought pitchers Ken Holtzman, Doyle Alexander, and Grant Jackson to New York, along with backup catcher Elrod "Ellie" Hendricks and minor league hurler Jimmy Freeman, in exchange for pitchers Rudy May, Tippy Martinez, Dave Pagan, backup catcher Rick Dempsey, and minor league hurler Scott McGregor. "This trade just won you a pennant," Steinbrenner crowed to Billy Martin. "You now have the best team on paper, and now you're just a push-button manager."

Though Martin was unhappy with the trade (and doubly unhappy about Steinbrenner downplaying his role in the team's four-and-a-half-game lead in the AL East over second-place Cleveland), the mega-swap did unload a couple of disgruntled players from the Yan-kee roster. May, a big lefty known to his teammates as "The Dude," had thrown some solid starts for the Yankees in 1976, including a four-hit shutout in Detroit on May 30, but he'd also been visibly alien-ated by Martin's daily outpouring of racial slurs. ("I might be black, and [Yankees utility man] Sandy Alomar might be Puerto Rican, but I'm not a 'fuckin' nigger,' and he's not a 'fuckin' Puerto Rican,'" was how May succinctly put it.) Dempsey, arguably a better defensive catcher than Munson—though nowhere near his equal with a bat or at handling pitchers—resented his long-running role as a backup back-stop, and was happy to move to a team where he'd be in the starting lineup more than once a week.

More importantly, it looked like the A's and Orioles deals were going to reunite three main cogs of the A's 1972–74 starting rotation—Holtzman, Blue, and Catfish Hunter—in pinstripes. Though none of the three pitchers was enjoying an outstanding season thus far (Holtzman was currently 5–4 with a 2.86 ERA, despite walking more batters than he struck out; Blue was 6–6 with a 3.09 ERA; and Hunter was 7–6 with a 3.69 ERA), it had only been three years since the trio had all been 20-game winners on the World Champion '73 A's. With Ed Figueroa (6–4, 3.47 ERA as of June 15) and the unexpectedly serene Dock Ellis (6–4, 3.78 ERA) already on board, the reunion of Holtzman, Blue, and Hunter would give the Yankees the most formidable rotation in the American League. Unfortunately for the Yankees, Blue, and Finley, Kuhn announced on the afternoon of June 18 that he was voiding the sale of Blue, Rudi, and Fingers, and ordering the three players to return to Oakland, effective immediately.

"[I cannot] persuade myself that the spectacle of the Yankees and the Red Sox buying contracts of star players in the prime of their careers for cash sums totaling $3.5 million is anything but devastating to baseball's reputation for integrity and to public confidence in the game," wrote Kuhn in his statement. "If such transactions now and in the future were permitted, the door would be opened wide to the buying of success by the more affluent clubs, public suspicion would be aroused, traditional and sound methods of player development and acquisition would be undermined, and our efforts to preserve competitive balance would be greatly impaired."

Kuhn's voiding of Finley's sale "in the best interests of the game" was the weightiest ruling to come down from a baseball commissioner since Kenesaw Mountain Landis banned "Shoeless" Joe Jackson and seven other "Black Sox" players from the game in 1921 for their alleged involvement in throwing the 1919 World Series, or at least since Happy Chandler's year-long suspension of Brooklyn

Dodgers manager Leo Durocher in 1947 for "associating with known gamblers." Unsurprisingly, Finley took Kuhn's decision as a personal attack. "The man has been out to get me for some time," he railed. "This is just another attempt. I think it's a personal vendetta on his part against me. This guy really sounds like the village idiot. He acts and talks like it."

Though an immensely unpopular man in the world of baseball, Finley suddenly found himself with a whole new circle of allies, including Marvin Miller. "The commissioner has single-handedly plunged baseball into the biggest mess it has ever seen," said the Players Association leader. "I consider it sheer insanity. It's raised the potential for litigation which would last for years. He is asserting a right to end all club owners' rights with regard to all transactions. Whenever there's a trade made, he can decide that one team did not get enough value and veto that deal."

"Suppose we want to buy a player," asked O'Connell. "Do we check to see if his batting average is low enough? If his price is low enough? Who are we supposed to check with? Those were the questions I asked Bowie Kuhn. And he said he couldn't answer them."

"What he's trying to be is another Judge Landis," Billy Martin fumed. "He has opened a big can of worms. Is this decision in the best interests of baseball, having lawsuits all over the country?" A *Sporting News* poll revealed that only 12.7 percent of the paper's readership agreed with Kuhn's decision, while sports columnists throughout the country excoriated the commissioner for overstepping the bounds of his office. "Baseball in Chaos: Bowie Kuhn Jolts the System," trumpeted the cover of the June 26 issue of *Sports Illustrated*.

The commissioner was not without his defenders: Walter O'Malley, who many felt was behind Kuhn's initial "investigation" of Finley's player sale, opined that Kuhn's ruling "probably was right," and Brewers GM Jim Baumer said he agreed "wholeheartedly with what the commissioner is attempting to do." Tigers owner John Fetzer also supported Kuhn, saying, "I feel that the present situation, if allowed to continue, will alienate the fans of the game and bring about a material deterioration of their confidence in the integrity of baseball." Fetzer's GM, Jim Campbell, mostly seemed embarrassed by his involvement in the whole fiasco. "To be honest with you, we really couldn't afford the million dollars," he told writer Jim Hawkins. "But we figured we had to get into the crap game or get out."

Campbell added that he believed "the elimination of the reserve clause is going to ruin the competitive balance of baseball. Everyone said it wouldn't happen, but here we have the first example. The players are calling the shots. And most of them would prefer to play in the same few cities." Campbell's rhetoric may have played well with his boss and the rest of the game's conservative factions, but it conveniently ignored the fact that the players involved in Finley's deals were merely along for the (increasingly confusing) ride. Or, as *Sports Illustrated*'s Ron Fimrite put it, "It does seem apparent now that the owners have been wrong about one thing: their real enemies in an open market will not be the venal players. No, the enemy is within, and it is just possible that one of their more enlightened number will paraphrase the Bard and advise his embattled commissioner, 'The fault, dear Bowie, is not in our stars, but in ourselves.'"

Finley announced that he was seeking an immediate restraining order to block Kuhn's ruling, and would be filing a $10 million federal lawsuit against the commissioner's office; the Yankees were considering legal action, as well. In the meantime, Finley said he intended to bar Rudi, Fingers, and Blue from taking the field with the A's, so as not to run the risk of them getting injured—and thus becoming "damaged goods" in the eyes of their new teams—while he awaited the court's decision on his lawsuit. When Rudi and Fingers phoned him to protest, Finley agreed to let the players dress, work out, and sit in the dugout with the team; but he still refused to allow them to play in any actual games, which meant that Chuck Tanner was stuck for the foreseeable future with a 22-man roster. Kuhn ordered Finley and Tanner to use Rudi, Fingers, and Blue "in a normal way," threatening them with unnamed "grave penalties" if they refused. Dick Moss, legal counsel for the Players Association, warned Finley that the three players could become free agents if they weren't used in within 10 days of Kuhn's order.

Finley didn't seem moved by Kuhn or Moss's threats, so the A's players decided to take matters into their own hands, voting to strike unless Rudi, Fingers, and Blue were allowed to play ball. Finley initially threatened to bring up the Tucson Toros, the A's Pacific Coast League affiliate, to replace his striking players, but backed down when the owner of the PCL's Salt Lake City Gulls threatened to sue Finley if any upcoming Gulls-Toros games had to be canceled because Finley was using the Toros as replacement players. On the afternoon of June 27, with his players on the verge of walking out, Tanner made the announcement that Rudi would be batting sixth and playing left field in that evening's game against the Twins. The announcement triggered a raucous celebration in the clubhouse. "It was like mass hysteria," said Sal Bando. "It was like the World Series around here. We weren't even listening to who was batting where when Chuck was reading the lineup. All we wanted to hear was whether Rudi's name was in there. Before that, it was the saddest clubhouse I'd ever seen. Some of us had begun to take off our uniforms."

Rudi went hitless that night, but the A's won the game 5–3, and Fingers—despite the two-week layoff—pitched three and a third innings of shutout ball, striking out five while only allowing two hits and two walks, to earn his ninth save of the year. "All I wanted to do was get back to playing baseball," the mustachioed reliever said afterward. "For the past two weeks, I'd been reading my name in the papers everywhere but the box scores, and that's the only place I wanted to see it."

What this all meant for Rudi, Fingers, and Blue in the long term was still unclear, though it now seemed like they all would remain active members of the A's until at least August 2, when U.S. District Court Judge Frank McGarr was scheduled to rule on Finley's lawsuit. Finley released a statement to the press on June 28, which read in part, "Since all members of the American League have agreed not to protest any of the games in which these players will appear, I have decided to acquiesce to Commissioner Kuhn's directive regarding the playing of the three players already sold by the Athletics. At the same time, however, I strongly dispute and protest his decision that his actions are in the best interest of baseball."

It was Blue who got off the best line, however. "Maybe if Oakland and the Yankees meet in the playoffs," the left-hander told reporters, "I'll just stay on the mound and pitch for both teams."

The Royals watched the A's situation with great interest. Turbulent as things appeared in Oakland, Whitey Herzog was well aware that the A's had a history of thriving on drama; even with their roster weakened by Finley's transactions, they were still a far more talented club than their 36–38 record at the end of June seemed to attest, and it was still far too early in the season to count them out. Herzog's team managed to retain sole possession of first place in the AL West throughout the month, pushing their record to 44–27 despite injuries to shortstop Fred Patek, second baseman Frank White, outfielder Tom Poquette, and hurlers Larry Gura and Doug Bird, a six-game losing streak in late June, and the steadfast refusal of the second-place Texas Rangers to exit the race. Thankfully, the Royals still had some hot bats to lean on: Big John Mayberry launched seven home runs in June and drove in 24 runs, while George Brett (who raised his batting average to a league-leading .361 by the end of June) and Hal McRae (whose .336 mark was third only to Brett and the Tigers' Ron LeFlore, who was batting .351) continued to outhit just about everyone in the American League.

"There are two teams competing in the AL West," observed Angels skipper Dick Williams. "Between Kansas City and Texas, it all boils down to pitching. If Whitey's pitching is healthy I like his chances. I think he also has more consistent punch. Some people say Brett can't keep going the way he is. Well, he's been doing it for two and a half years."

Williams's last-place Angels were so desperate for offense that they lured Tommy Davis out of retirement. Davis, a two-time NL batting champ with the Dodgers in the early '60s whose potential Hall of Fame career was repeatedly derailed by injuries, had spent the three previous seasons as the full-time DH for the Baltimore Orioles. After being released by the O's in February 1976 (then being briefly picked up and released by the Yankees), the 37-year-old Davis left baseball and started a new life and career for himself as a promotions man—and softball team manager—for Casablanca Records, the Hollywood-based label that was currently minting money via the success of *Destroyer*, the platinum-selling KISS album featuring "Beth," the band's breakthrough ballad, and whose roster also included Parliament and disco diva Donna Summer.

By the time the Angels came calling in early June, Davis "just wasn't thinking about baseball anymore," he told the *Long Beach Press-Telegram*. "I thought it was all behind me. I was just getting used to this new life." But the lure of the game was too strong—and the first night Davis suited up for the Angels, he drove in two runs with a pinch-hit bases-loaded single. "As soon as I hit the park and put on that uniform, I got that old feeling," he laughed.

———

Nearly lost in the furor over Finley's fire sale was the news of two big Dodger deals: one bringing four-time All-Star Reggie Smith to Los Angeles, and the other sending former Cy Young winner Mike Marshall to Atlanta. Smith, a 31-year-old switch-hitting outfielder with a cannon arm, who'd averaged .305 with 21 home runs over the last three years, blasted three home runs for the Cardinals against the Phillies in a game on May 22, but had otherwise been mired in a disappointing season, hitting .218 with only eight homers for a lackluster Cardinals team that never seemed able to rise above fourth place in the NL East. Most frustrating for Smith was the fact that—despite his considerable talents as an outfielder—he'd become a glorified utility man under Cards manager Red Schoendienst, who played him at third and first more often than he put him in right field or center, areas that were generally occupied by comparative youngsters Jerry Mumphrey, Willie Crawford, and Bake McBride.

With the Dodgers, however, Smith was assured of a regular gig in right field, since they'd just traded their regular right fielder Joe Ferguson (plus two minor leaguers) to St. Louis in exchange for Smith. A better catcher than outfielder, Ferguson had been bumped from the Dodger backstop gig in 1975 by Steve Yeager, who'd emerged as one of the top fielding catchers in the majors. Though the Cardinals already had Ted Simmons behind the plate, Simba's declining batting average (.261 as of June 15, after hitting .332 in 1975) had triggered talk of moving him to first base—and since the Cards' highly touted 22-year-old first baseman Keith Hernandez was only hitting .194 halfway through his first full major league season, Schoendienst was ready to experiment with Ferguson behind the plate and Simmons at first. The Smith-for-Ferguson deal would go down as one of the Dodgers' biggest steals of the '70s, though Smith's value to them wouldn't truly become apparent until 1977.

Mike Marshall, on the other hand, was way past his Dodger sell-by date. Iron Mike's MSU break-in and subsequent misdemeanor charges (for which he was scheduled to stand trial in the fall) had already caused considerable molar grinding in the Dodgers' front office; but Marshall had further worn out his welcome by pitching with maddening inconsistency on the mound while deflecting much of the blame to his teammates. "I haven't been able to pitch in a relaxed and comfortable fashion," he told reporters after giving up the final run in an 8–6 loss to the Phillies on June 6. "It goes back to early May. We have won some games since then, but we haven't played with the same aggressiveness. I'm the type of guy who tries to do too much himself and that's exactly what I've been trying to do when I walk into a game and see no life, when I look around and see four infielders resembling cigar store Indians."

Marshall later claimed he was simply referring to the demoralizing effects of the booing at Dodger Stadium (which just coincidentally happened whenever Marshall, never a Dodger fan favorite, took the mound), but his fellow Dodgers took it personally. On June 9, shortstop Bill Russell singled twice and hit an RBI triple in the Dodgers' 3–2 win over the Phillies. "That was for the Indians," he grunted afterward, loud enough that the whole clubhouse could hear him. "Mike would tell a Persian how to make a rug," one unnamed Dodger told L.A. sportswriter Jim Murray. "Or Betsy Ross how to make a flag."

Unable to deal Marshall by the June 15 trade deadline, the Dodgers put Marshall on waivers, where he was claimed for a $20,000 fee by the Atlanta Braves on June 23. The Dodgers then purchased the contracts of infielder Lee Lacy and reliever Elias Sosa from Atlanta; knuckleballer Charlie Hough, who'd been splitting closing duties with Marshall, was anointed the Dodgers' top fireman. "I see it one way as a vote of confidence," said Hough, whose sunny and genial personality made him the polar opposite of the perpetually brusque Marshall. "But it's probably more of the Dodgers being down on Mike than being wild about me."

While he was no longer the same Iron Mike of his record-setting 1973 and 1974 seasons, Marshall's arrival brought some much needed respectability to an Atlanta relief staff that'd blown so many games local sportswriter Wayne Minshew likened a call to the Braves' bullpen to "bringing in a time bomb." But despite their reliever woes, the Braves suddenly got on a roll, winning more games in June (18) than in April and May combined. Andy Messersmith performed like he was worth every penny Ted Turner paid him, throwing five straight complete game victories—including a near-no-hitter against the Expos on June 4, which was broken up by a Pepe Mangual single with one out in the bottom of the ninth—posting a 1.51 ERA for the month, and holding opposing hitters to a .178 batting average. Phil Niekro went 5–0 (including a 10-strikeout shutout against Montreal on June 23) for June with a 2.84 ERA. Rowland Office, the team's slap-hitting centerfielder, began a hitting streak on May 23 that ran to 29 games before Don Stanhouse of the Expos finally shut him down on June 24. Overall, Office hit .375 for the month with 13 doubles, 19 RBIs, and 21 runs scored. "I'm over my head," the leadoff hitter said during the streak, a grin spreading across his narrow visage. "I'm getting hits by the threes and fours. . . . I'm usually happy to get them two at a time."

The Braves' sudden success coincided with their decision to stop wearing the nickname jerseys, which came about after the players realized that they'd gone 3–13 at home since donning the controversial new lettering. Jinxed or not, the team went on to win seven of their next nine home games after reverting to name-free home uniforms. With the exception of high-wire artist Karl Wallenda's death-defying walk across the top of Atlanta–Fulton County Stadium between games of a June 19 doubleheader (the German-born daredevil had accomplished a similar feat at Veterans Stadium in May), Bob Hope's promotions were, for the time being, actually being overshadowed by Braves home victories.

Along with Marshall from the Dodgers, the Braves acquired first baseman Willie Montanez and infielder Craig Robinson from the Giants in June, in exchange for first baseman Darrell Evans and second baseman Marty Perez. Montanez was hitting .309 when the trade went down, but the Giants were more than happy to get rid of the flamboyant first-sacker—about whom Dick Young famously wrote, "Willie Montanez is such a hot dog that it takes a quart of mustard to cover him"—having grown weary of his one-handed "snap catches" and his constant complaints about how cold it was at Candlestick.

Montanez wasn't the only unhappy Giant; the San Francisco squad, who followed up an 11–20 May with a 13–17 June, was showing serious signs of a morale problem. Fed up with his team's rampant negativity, Giants manager Bill Rigney called a meeting on June 29, in which he ordered "an end to all this bitching and groaning, moaning and complaining, about Candlestick Park, the weather, the long waits at airports and everything. I've had it." Rigney also dictated that all player beards must be shaved off immediately. "I don't think making them shave the beards will have anything to do with the way they play baseball," explained the skipper, who noted that mustaches were still allowed. "But if they want to act like boys, griping and complaining all the time, then I'll treat them like boys. If they act like men, maybe they'll get treated like men."

The Giants ended June in the same place they ended May—the cellar of the NL West—though they were now 16 and a half games behind the first-place Cincinnati Reds, who solidified their grip on the division by playing .600 ball for the month, improving their record to 46–29 while the Dodgers slipped to four and a half games back at 42–34.

Nagging injuries to Joe Morgan (who hit seven home runs and knocked in 23 runs despite missing over a week with a pulled hamstring), Tony Perez, Johnny Bench, Ken Griffey, and Cesar Geronimo forced Reds skipper Sparky Anderson to repeatedly juggle his lineup throughout the month, calling upon bench players like Dan Driessen, Bill Plummer, Doug Flynn, Mike Lum, and Bob Bailey to plug the holes when needed. "I really wish I could have a lineup card mimeographed with the names of the same eight players I'd like to use every day and then use that card for at least 30 straight days," Anderson grumbled. "Even though a lot of fans might think I do, I don't make all these lineup changes for kicks."

The way the Reds were playing, Anderson could have penciled the names of the Bay City Rollers on his lineup card and achieved practically the same results. Left fielder George Foster, a quiet, clean-living Christian who studied karate to improve his reflexes, continued to make deafening noise with his black bats—"I'm integrating the bat rack," he said of the custom-stained Louisville Sluggers— upping his home runs for the year to 16 and his league-leading RBIs to 62 as he (.337), Morgan (.335), Pete Rose (.327), Griffey (.319), and Geronimo (.314) kept their names among the NL batting leaders; only the Pirates' Al Oliver (.357) and the Cardinals' Bake McBride (.338) were ahead of Foster as June rolled to a close. Perez was only hitting .269, but the "Big Doggie" still managed to place third in the NL RBI column with 54, and he slugged some key home runs in June, including a three-run blast off the fearsomely Fu Manchu'd Al Hrabosky that beat the Cardinals 8–7 in the bottom of the ninth on June 11.

Johnny Bench, continuing to struggle with a bad back, an aching right shoulder, and a cold bat, went so far as to give the popular "pyramid power" fad a try, hanging an aluminum pyramid above his locker in order to harness some of the dynamic energies purportedly radiated by the mystical geometric shape. Bench wasn't the first professional athlete to try this New Age technique—on February 7, Toronto Maple Leafs center Darryl Sittler recorded an NHL record 10 points in a game after putting his hockey sticks under a pyramid—but Bench's slump seemed immune to supernatural intervention; by the end of June, he was only hitting .244 with eight home runs and 37 RBIs for the year.

"Is your first name Elmer?" Phillies shortstop Larry Bowa asked his Reds counterpart Dave Concepcion before their teams faced off at Veterans Stadium on June 19. "Why you ask that?" replied an annoyed Concepcion. "Because every time I look at the box score it says 'E-Concepcion,'" cackled Bowa. Two of the slickest-fielding shortstops in the league, both men had mastered the art of playing deep on the artificial turf, and winging the ball to first on a hop. Concepcion was indeed more error-prone than Bowa but had better range in the field and considerably more power at the plate. That afternoon, the Reds beat the Phils 4–3, as Concepcion went 3-for-4 with an RBI double, a stolen base, and a couple of key defensive plays, including one that robbed Bowa of a single. "Elmer's glue," Concepcion taunted Bowa. "That's me!"

That would be the only game the Reds took from the Phillies in June, however; of their five meetings over the course of the month, the Phils walked away victorious from four, as they continued to put distance between themselves and the rest of the NL East. Winning 20 games in June, the Phils became the first team in the majors to reach the 50-win mark. Despite losing six of the Reds' eight games against the Phillies thus far, Sparky Anderson wasn't concerned about facing them in October. "There are a lot of games left," he said. "Pittsburgh will be heard from before it's all over." But the Pirates, even with a 16–10 June, still found themselves slipping to nine and a half games behind the Phillies, who were leaving quite a few believers in their burgundy, white, and powder-blue wake. "I think the Phillies have reached a point where they are now better than Cincinnati," said Dodgers hurler Tommy John, who was battered by the Phillies in a 14–2 loss on June 8. "But that's like comparing the atom bomb to the hydrogen bomb. They both kill you."

And if the Phillies didn't kill you with their bats, they'd murder you with their singing: in late June, the Phillies—or rather, the recording group Cash & Bowa & Schmidt & Luzinski & Maddox—released a seven-inch single called "Phillies Fever" on the local Grand Prix label, which featured the five Phillies stars attempting to "get on down" to a Philly disco groove, replete with funky wah-wah guitars and cut-rate "Sound of Philadelphia" soul strings. "Veterans Stadium is the hippest place in town," they sang in less-than-tuneful unison, before breaking into some CB radio–style banter. "What's the hottest thing in Philadelphia?" asked Maddox. "It's got to be the Phillies, good buddy," replied Cash. "That's a big 10-4!" Maddox agreed. Though undeniably goofy, and hardly destined to go down as one of the great soul (or even novelty) singles of the '70s, "Phillies Fever" effectively captured the good vibes and relaxed chemistry that seemed to be fueling the club's success.

(Seemingly taking a cue from the Phillies, Dodgers third baseman Ron Cey also entered the recording studio in 1976 to wax the country-tinged single "Third Base Bag," with "One Game at a Time" on the flip. Released on Long Ball Records, the Penguin's risible musical efforts made "Phillies Fever" sound like Queen's "Bohemian Rhapsody," but still managed to achieve some occasional airplay via Dr. Demento's syndicated novelty music radio show.)

The Phillies slugged 22 home runs in June, including six by

Schmidt—who raised his total on the year to 21—and five by Luzinski. But the team's big bopper for the month was none other than
Philadelphia prodigal son Dick Allen, who blasted seven round-
trippers and knocked in 20 runs. With his batting average hovering
around .300, Allen was producing like the '72 AL MVP who'd
nearly carried the White Sox to a division flag, as opposed to the
aging, struggling vet of 1975. Best of all, the Philly fans (who'd
abused Allen so badly during his first Phillies tenure that he'd taken
to wearing a batting helmet while playing first base) were now ef-
fusive in their appreciation of his contributions. On June 25, Allen
crunched two home runs during a 12–4 romp over the Cardinals at
the Vet; when his second blast left the park, some 38,000 fans rose to
their feet and gave him a thunderous standing ovation. The cheering
continued well into Ollie Brown's at-bat, to such deafening degree
that home plate umpire Nick Colosi had to call time and signal Allen to come out and take a curtain call. Allen stepped out in front of
the dugout, doffed his ever-present helmet, and bowed to the roaring
crowd.

"It was one of the most exciting things I ever saw," said Garry
Maddox after the game. "I was so proud of Dick, I felt like crying."
"Hard to believe something like that could happen to me in Philly,"
marveled Allen. "It was a wonderful thing for me, considering what
happened before."

But even the Phils' ferocious offense was no match for the Padres'
Randy Jones, who breezed almost effortlessly through their lineup
on June 15, shutting them out 5–0 on six hits for his 12th win of the
year. "If I were a pitcher, I'd be embarrassed to go out to the mound
with that kind of stuff," carped Mike Schmidt afterward, but the
shutout marked the second time in 1976 that the soft-tossing lefty
had nullified the Philly bats. Jones also ran his walk-less streak to
55 consecutive innings in the game, and kept the streak going until

June 22, when—having just tied Christy Mathewson's 63-year-old record of 68 straight innings without giving up a base on balls—he served up a ball four to Giants catcher Marc Hill. Jones still won that game, though, then beat the Reds 3–1 on June 30 to run his record to 14–3. Pete Rose was driven to such distraction by Jones's super sinker that the switch-hitter decided to try hitting left-handed against him for a change; he ended up grounding out twice, whiffing once, and drawing a walk. "Left-handed, right-handed, cross-handed, he still gets you out," testified an admiring Rose.

Ultimately, Major League Baseball in June '76 belonged to one man . . . or rather, one Bird. Mark Fidrych began the month as a rookie whose eccentric mannerisms weren't even mentioned in wire service reports of the games he pitched; six consecutive wins later, he'd become a full-blown American folk hero.

Fidrych's first start of the month came in Texas against Bert Blyleven, who was making his debut appearance for the Rangers and another bid for his 100th career victory. Despite giving up two runs in the third inning (and being spiked while covering first base on a play in the seventh), Fidrych thwarted Blyleven's quest, holding the Rangers hitters at bay until the Tigers finally parlayed an 11th-inning error by Texas third baseman Roy Howell into a 3–2 victory. Fidrych made quick work of Mike Hargrove, Toby Harrah, and Jeff Burroughs—the heart of the Rangers' lineup—for the game's last three outs. "Far out," exulted Fidrych, when asked by reporters about his eight-strikeout, seven-hit performance. "What else can I say? I don't know what to think. This is a rush."

The rush would get more intense on June 11, when the Tigers returned to the Motor City and sent Fidrych to the mound against Nolan Ryan and the Angels. By now, word of the Bird had spread, thanks in part to some amusing profile pieces in *The Detroit News* and *Detroit Free Press* that played up Fidrych's goofy and unaffected personality, and the old ballpark at Michigan and Trumbull creaked under the weight of 36,377 Friday night ticket holders (the Tigers' third-largest home turnout of the season to date) who'd shown up to get a good look at this *rara avis* in action. Fidrych didn't let them down, giving them the full range of crowd-pleasing mound movements while scattering nine hits and walking none in nine innings to earn the 4–3 win, which the Tigers eventually pulled out in the bottom of the ninth on a two-out Alex Johnson single that scored Ron LeFlore from second.

On June 16, an atypically large Wednesday night crowd of 21,659 showed up at Tiger Stadium to catch a Bird versus Bird matchup: Fidrych against Doug Bird of the Kansas City Royals. The Royals had put a 21–7 hurting on the Tigers the night before, but Fidrych delivered the payback, holding the Royals to three runs (two earned) on five hits, and blanking George Brett, John Mayberry, and Hal McRae in the Tigers' 4–3 victory. (The "real" Bird gave up two solo homers to rookie Tigers first baseman Jason Thompson, and was gone by the sixth inning.) Fidrych once again went the distance, then hollered happily from the dugout as his teammates found a way to win it in their final frame. This time, Alex Johnson tied it up with a two-out single off reliever Marty Pattin that scored Dan Meyer, then stole second and scored the winning run on a Mickey Stanley single. It was Fidrych's sixth straight complete game and fourth straight victory; his record now stood at 5–1 with a 1.86 ERA.

Tigers skipper Ralph Houk announced that he was going with a four-man rotation of Fidrych, Vern Ruhle, Dave Roberts, and rookie Frank MacCormack for the immediate future, which meant that the Bird was back on the mound on June 20 in Minneapolis. While he once again "talked" to the ball (though his repeated mantras of "gotta flow," "keep it down," and "let it fly" were really directed more at himself than at the horsehide orb in his hand) and dropped to his knees to manicure the mound, Fidrych was unusually wild against the Twins, walking six while giving up nine hits and three earned runs. Houk finally pulled him in the eighth, breaking the Bird's string of complete games; but he still got the W, thanks in part to a three-run homer from Jason Thompson off Twins' starter Bill Singer. "I walked six guys and was lucky to get away with it," the Bird reflected after the 7–3 victory. "I didn't feel the same, but don't ask me why."

June 24 saw Fidrych return to Fenway for a rematch with the Red Sox. He blew through nine batters in the first three innings, then suddenly unraveled in the fourth, giving up a screaming line drive triple to Cecil Cooper, followed by back-to-back home runs to Fred Lynn and Carl Yastrzemski. "I got in a real rut," Fidrych explained later. "They started digging in on me, and all of a sudden it was Rocket City. I just said to myself, 'Put it all aside and start over again.'" He calmed down and held the Red Sox to just three hits the rest of the way, as the Tigers took the lead on yet another Jason Thompson homer (this time off Rick Wise) and rolled to a 6–3 win.

Fidrych further endeared himself to his teammates and fans in the bottom of the ninth when, with two outs, the normally sure-handed Tigers third baseman Aurelio Rodriguez muffed a Dwight Evans pop-up that should have ended the game. Rather than curse or pound his mitt in frustration, Fidrych ran over to sweetly console his third baseman with a few calming words and a pat on the back, then returned to the mound and threw three straight strikes to Rico Petrocelli to clinch his seventh win. "Right now this is a dream," Fidrych told reporters, before heading home to Northboro for a celebratory hang with family and friends at a local bar. "I don't want to spoil it by thinking about the future." But the future had big plans for the Bird.

On the afternoon of Monday, June 28, Fidrych hitched a ride to Tiger Stadium with Tom Veryzer, his neighbor and teammate—and the only Tiger with longer hair than the Bird's. As they approached "The Corner," Fidrych was stunned to see thousands of fans already in front of the ballpark, four hours before first pitch. "Mark," Veryzer laughed, "these people aren't here to see Tommy Veryzer play shortstop." He was right—the 47,855 fans who packed the park that night were there to see the Bird take on the New York Yankees in a game broadcast nationally on ABC's *Monday Night Baseball*.

The popular weekly baseball telecast had switched over from NBC for the 1976 season, and the new *MNB* broadcast team of former Pirates broadcaster Bob Prince, Brewers broadcaster Bob Uecker, and Washington, D.C., sports anchorman Warner Wolf had thus far received less-than-stellar reviews. The *MNB* matchup of the first-place Yankees with the fourth-place, sub-.500 Tigers normally wouldn't have been anyone's idea of mandatory viewing, save for the presence of Fidrych, who was quickly becoming the most talked about young player in the country. Only a small percentage of baseball fans had actually seen him do his funky thing, but now millions of them would get to see him in action—and by the next morning, he'd be a household name. Even Wolf, who referred to the pitcher throughout much of the *MNB* broadcast as "Mark Feed-rich" (as opposed to the proper "FID-rich") would learn how to pronounce it correctly.

From the pregame warm-ups on, the electric atmosphere in Tiger Stadium was closer to a rock concert than a ballgame, with the fans—many of them kids who'd brought homemade bedsheet banners bearing slogans like "Give Them The Bird"—cheering Fidrych's every move. From his first delivery to Yankee leadoff man Mickey Rivers (who'd come into the night toting a 20-game hitting streak),

Fidrych seemed be feeding off the crowd's vibrant energy, working even faster than usual from pitch to pitch. "He's talking, telling the ball where he wants it to go," Uecker explained to the viewers at home. "If that ball starts talking back, he's in trouble!"

Like Randy Jones, Fidrych was a control pitcher, but he threw much harder than his San Diego counterpart; twice during the broadcast, the announcers mentioned that he was winging it in there at 93 miles per hour. With the exception of a second-inning solo shot by Yankees backup catcher Elrod Hendricks—filling in for Thurman Munson, who'd been recently injured in a home plate collision with Cleveland's aptly named Charlie Spikes—the Yankees couldn't do much with the Bird's pitches. Fidrych scattered seven hits in all, most of them weak singles, and didn't walk a single batter. A case study in hyperkinetic energy, the young hurler did deep knee bends between pitches and darted to and from the mound between innings; in the seventh, he even chased a Graig Nettles slow-roller nearly all the way out of the infield, and had to hurdle over second baseman Pedro Garcia (a veteran infielder who'd recently been traded to the Tigers from Milwaukee, in part because he wouldn't trim his sideburns neatly enough for Alex Grammas's liking) in order to narrowly avoid an ugly collision.

Ken Holtzman, pitching in his third start for the Yankees, spotted the Tigers a 2–0 lead in the first when Rusty Staub blasted a two-run homer off the ancient ballpark's right field overhang. The Tigers added another run in the seventh and two more in the eighth, but the Bird—who was moving through the Yankee lineup with a productive efficiency that would have impressed Henry Ford—already had the game well in hand by then. In the top of the eighth, he got Rivers to ground out to Veryzer, ending the speedy center fielder's hitting streak.

Smelling victory, Fidrych opened the top of the ninth by fanning Chris Chambliss on three straight pitches for his second strikeout of the game. Chattering excitedly to himself, he then got Nettles to ground out to Garcia; the ABC cameras captured him enthusiastically shouting "Nice play, Pedro!" "Boy, this guy's higher than a kite," laughed Uecker, though—the young pitcher's shaggy post-hippie looks and Uecker's unintentional double-entendre aside—adrenaline was the only thing the Bird was flying on. The Tiger Stadium crowd, just as pumped up as he was, thunderously chanted "Go Bird Go!" between every pitch.

Oscar Gamble, determined to not be the Yankees' final out, singled to right-center. Hendricks, who'd homered earlier, was up next. After running the count on him to 3–0, Fidrych told the ball (and himself) to settle down, then got the catcher to ground out to Garcia. Just an hour and 51 minutes after it had begun, the game was over. The Bird practically flew over to second base to congratulate Garcia, then spun around and ran to hug his catcher, Bruce Kimm, as Tiger Stadium erupted around them.

"The Tigers act like Fidrych has just won the seventh game of the World Series!" cried Uecker. "He's thanking his teammates! He's thanking the umpire!" "I've been in baseball 35 years," added a slightly soused-sounding Prince, "and I've never seen anything like this!"

It was the most exciting night Tiger Stadium had witnessed in years, and the fans refused to leave, sending up lusty chants of "We want the Bird! We want the Bird!" that were practically loud enough to chip the green lead paint from the ballpark's steel girders. In the Tigers' clubhouse, Rusty Staub found Fidrych, who was already partially undressed, and urged him to suit up and return to the field; the game had been over for a good fifteen minutes, and the grounds crew was already rolling out the tarp, but the fans were clamoring louder than ever for a Bird curtain call. "You gotta come with me," a panicked Fidrych begged Staub. "You hit a home run!" "They're not saying 'We want Rusty,'" Staub replied. "They're saying, 'We want the Bird!'"

Fidrych finally did as he was told, sprinting out of the dugout in his stocking feet for the first Tiger Stadium curtain call since Denny McLain won his 30th game of the 1968 season. When the Bird emerged, the ensuing roar from the Detroit fans was so forceful, it seemed to briefly knock him off his stride. Visibly teary-eyed, Fidrych waved his cap and shook the hands of several fans (and at least one security guard) standing atop the dugout roof, but he was so overwhelmed by the outpouring of Motor City affection that he could barely stand up straight. "Mark, I know this is a very emotional moment for you," said Bob Uecker, pulling him into microphone range for the *Monday Night Baseball* postgame interview. "Hell yeah!" blurted the Bird, blissfully unaware that his words were going out live on national television.

Back in the clubhouse, Fidrych enjoyed some celebratory beverages—a paper cup of milk on the rocks, followed by four cans of beer—while conducting several interviews. "I couldn't ask for anything better," he told one reporter. "The only other job I could have is working in a gas station back home."

"He's the most exciting thing I've seen in any city I've been in," raved Staub. "I've never seen a city turn on like this. I've seen Tom Seaver go out and mow them down, but I've never seen anybody electrify the fans like this. And the best part of it is that none of it is contrived."

Just how completely uncontrived became apparent when a New York reporter asked Fidrych for a response to comments made by

Thurman Munson, who called the Bird a "fly-by-night" and a "showboat," and warned him not to try his ball-talking routine at Yankee Stadium. Fidrych looked taken aback. "Who's Thurman Munson?" he asked.

8.

Afternoon Delight

(July 1976)

After years of buildup, hype, and anticipation, there was no way that America's 200th birthday party was going to be anything less than a gloriously, gaudily, ridiculously over-the-top affair. President Ford urged Americans everywhere to "break out the flag, strike up the band, light up the sky" for the star-spangled occasion. But from Mars Hill, Maine—where the first rays of dawn's early light hit the continental U.S. at 4:31 a.m. Eastern Daylight Time—to the harbor village of Pago Pago in American Samoa, flag-waving, marching bands, and fireworks constituted just a fraction of the festive fun on the agenda for July 4, 1976.

The marquee event of the nationwide celebration (or at least the one that presented the most impressive visual spectacle to the many millions watching it in person and on television) was Operation Sail, which featured the arrival of 212 sailing vessels from around the world (including a full-scale model of Christopher Columbus's *Santa María*) in New York Harbor. The Tall Ships were met by an estimated 30,000 smaller crafts ranging from yachts to kayaks—as well as the 80,000-ton aircraft carrier *USS Forrestal*, which served as both host ship to the flotilla and viewing station for some 3,000 dignitaries—including President Ford (who'd already made appearances in Valley Forge and Philadelphia earlier in the day) and most of his cabinet, various members of Congress, and Prince Rainier and Princess Grace of Monaco—before sailing majestically up the Hudson River.

In Boston, two replicas of lanterns used to signal Paul Revere's midnight ride of 1775 were lit using an electrical impulse generated from the light of the star Epsilon Lyrae, which scientists believed to be positioned exactly 200 light-years from Earth. (The light currently seen from the star would therefore have been generated around the time that John Hancock put his "John Hancock" on the Declaration of Independence.) Some 400,000 Bostonians gathered along the banks of the Charles River on the evening of the Fourth to hear a Boston Pops concert; in nearby Foxboro, another 60,000 turned out to see British pop star Elton John—whose new duet with Kiki Dee, "Don't Go Breaking My Heart," was rocketing up the pop charts—perform at Schaefer Stadium. John, whose appreciation for his sizable American audience was surpassed only by his love for all things camp, appeared onstage as a silver-robed Statue of Liberty. Some 3,000 miles away, the Ramones returned the cultural exchange, playing the first overseas gig of their career supporting the Flamin' Groovies at London's Roundhouse, where they served up their stripped-down, speeded-up brand of New York punk rock (as well as dozens of promotional plastic baseball bats, in reference to their anthem "Beat on the Brat") to a crowd comprising a substantial segment of London's burgeoning punk scene.

Every municipality in America, large and small, seemed to have something extravagant planned for the Fourth. Washington, D.C., lit up the night with the largest fireworks display in U.S. history, a

33-and-a-half-ton affair detonated by Etablissements Ruggieri, the venerable French fireworks firm that had once designed a display that entertained Thomas Jefferson during his 1786 Paris visit. In Los Angeles, county officials staged an "All Nations, All Peoples" Bicentennial parade, whose 10.8-mile route was billed as the longest in the nation. Seven thousand one hundred forty-one new U.S. citizens were sworn in simultaneously in Miami, while another 1,776 were naturalized in Chicago, along with still another 1,100 in Detroit. Italian Americans in Rome, New York, celebrated Italian contributions to American culture by throwing a spaghetti dinner for 3,000 attendees, involving 600 pounds of pasta and another 600 pounds of sausage. Residents of George, Washington, gorged themselves on the world's largest cherry pie, a 60-square-foot behemoth, while Minneapolis staged the world's largest ice-cream social. And every single event of the gigantic birthday celebration—every time capsule burial, every historic battle reenactment, every watermelon-eating contest—was thoroughly swathed in the Stars and Stripes, signifying (at least for a day) a unified patriotism and unabashed optimism that would have been unthinkable in America just a few years earlier. As Louis Tucker, executive director of the New York State Bicentennial Commission, told *Time* magazine, "The Bicentennial is acting as a kind of catharsis. It's become a way of clearing the American soul in a very positive way."

Not that the celebration was completely free of glitches or bad vibes. The *ARC Gloria*, the three-masted flagship of the Colombian navy, was rejected from Operation Sail after it was discovered that the vessel was carrying six kilos of cocaine in its hold en route to Miami, its first stop before New York City. The ships that did sail into New York harbor were supposed to be greeted by the world's largest American flag, hung from the Verrazano-Narrows Bridge; unfortunately, strong wind gusts cut the flag—which was the size of one and a half football fields—to ribbons several days before the flotilla arrived. Plans to write "1776–1976 HAPPY BIRTHDAY AMERICA" across the sky with a laser beam during the D.C. fireworks display had to be shelved due to an elevator malfunction at the Washington Monument, which prevented the necessary gear from reaching the top of the world's tallest obelisk. And the much ballyhooed Mars landing of NASA's Viking 1 spacecraft, originally scheduled to coincide with the Bicentennial celebrations, had to be postponed until scientists could pinpoint a surface on the planet smooth enough for the craft to touch down upon.

But the blue ribbon for the most embarrassingly botched Bicentennial plan went to the city of Baltimore, which commissioned the baking of a record-breaking 35-ton birthday cake to serve as the centerpiece of *The Great American Celebration*, a syndicated 12-hour variety pageant broadcast live from Baltimore's Fort McHenry beginning on the evening of July 3, which would be hosted by *The Tonight Show*'s Ed McMahon and feature performances from Lynn Anderson, Roger Miller, Dinah Shore, Jonathan Winters, Mary Tyler Moore, and more. Unfortunately, the cake—which was constructed aboard a 120-foot barge moored in the city's harbor—had to be completely refrosted at the last minute following a massive July 1 thunderstorm that washed away 3,000 pounds of red, white, and blue buttercream icing. The cake was then successfully towed to Fort McHenry, where its 200 candles were lit on national television, but the city's plan to subsequently recoup its expenditures by selling 153,000 individually boxed slices of the confection at $2.25 apiece failed to pan out; not even a 10th of the pieces were sold, and rats and rain soon did enough damage to the cake that the rest of it had to be thrown out. The frosted fiasco eventually cost the city around $70,000.

Not everyone was in the mood to party, either. "If the Bicentennial is some kind of self-congratulatory celebration, it is frivolous and meaningless to the black community," remarked Charles Rangel, a black congressman from New York. There were other disenfranchised segments of American society who weren't buying into the feel-good spirit of the Bicentennial, either—and, much to Mayor Frank Rizzo's dismay, many of them were planning to march on Philadelphia for the Fourth. The July 4th Coalition, made up of 130 radical, left-wing, pacifist, and civil rights groups (including the American Indian Movement, the National Coalition of Gay Activists, the Puerto Rican Socialist Party, Vietnam Veterans Against the War, and whatever remained of the Black Panther Party) announced that they planned to send some 60,000 protesters to Philadelphia on the Fourth. "We're not going [to Philadelphia] to celebrate a flawed and incomplete American Revolution," peace activist David Dellinger told *The Washington Post*, "but to join in aspirations for equality. We're going to expose the terrorism of the government."

Less than sympathetic to the coalition's cause, Mayor Rizzo petitioned the Feds to dispatch 15,000 National Guardsmen to Philadelphia to help prevent the dissidents from crashing his party. His request was eventually refused, but rumors of an impending 1968 Chicago Democratic Convention–style showdown between Philly cops and radical protesters were daunting enough to keep a substantial number of tourists away from Philadelphia during the holiday weekend. So were reports that the city lacked sufficient hotel space, public toilets, parking, or transportation to handle the deluge of visitors that the endless Bicentennial hype would surely generate. Rather than risk getting tear-gassed or stranded without lodging, many families opted to stay home and enjoy their local celebrations instead. Though over one million people did attend Philadelphia's reenactment of the signing of the Declaration of Independence, the Bicentennial weekend wasn't quite the financial boon to the City of

Brotherly Love's tourism industry that had been imagined. In the end, some 10 million visitors would make the pilgrimage to Philadelphia during 1976, only about half the number predicted.

The Phillies, ironically enough, were away from Philadelphia for most of the Bicentennial weekend, having already been scheduled for a three-day stay in Pittsburgh, where they split a four-game series with the Pirates at Three Rivers. The Phils' most memorable moment of the road trip occurred in the first game of their July 4 doubleheader, when Phils catcher Tim McCarver launched a pitch from Bucs hurler Larry Demery over the right field wall with the bases loaded. Unfortunately, Garry Maddox, who was standing on first at the time, held up for a few seconds to make sure that the ball wasn't caught; McCarver, who was also keeping his eye on the flight of the ball, made it about four strides past Maddox when he suddenly realized his mistake. Second base umpire Ed Vargo called McCarver out for passing the runner, but the first three runs of the grand slam were allowed to score, and the play went down in the books as a three-RBI single. "That was the longest single I ever hit," McCarver laughed afterward. The Phillies wound up winning the game 10–5, earning Steve Carlton his eighth victory of the season and absolving McCarver of his base-running gaffe. "It wouldn't have been quite as funny in a 5–4 loss," cracked Phillies first base coach Carroll Beringer.

Likewise, the Phillies' 6–0 loss to the Dodgers on July 5 at Veterans Stadium—where a record crowd of 60,942 enjoyed a festive Monday evening that included a massive postgame fireworks display—might have been more of a bummer if the team wasn't already enjoying a nine-game lead in their division. The Phils managed only two hits against perpetually gloomy-looking Dodger righty Burt "Happy" Hooton, while Philadelphia starter Jim Lonborg gave up home runs to Steve Garvey and Bill Russell, but no one in the Phillies' clubhouse seemed particularly disturbed by the game's outcome. "I don't see anybody panicking," said Dave Cash, who pointedly noted that the second-place Pirates had also lost that day. "Our record stands for itself coast-to-coast. We just have to hang in there, show up tomorrow. This one is history."

Astros right-hander Larry Dierker made history four days later on July 9, when he pitched the first no-hitter of 1976 against the Expos at the Houston Astrodome. The 29-year-old Dierker, who allowed only four base runners while cruising to a 6–0 victory, had come close to throwing no-nos on four previous occasions during his 12 seasons in the majors, including two where he lost his bids in the ninth. The fifth time was the charm, however, thanks to Dierker's self-described "nasty" fastball, which he blew past the hapless Montreal hitters for eight strikeouts. "It was really sailing and I was too keyed-up to try anything else," said Dierker, who helped his cause by driving in the game's second run with a second-inning sacrifice fly off Don Stanhouse. "I wanted to keep the ball in the upper part of the strike zone and make 'em pop it up." Having pitched at the Astrodome since the stadium opened, Dierker was well versed in the hazards of pitching on artificial turf. "The one thing I didn't want was ground balls," he explained. "Anything can happen when they hit into the dirt." Dierker's no-hitter, the fifth in Astros history (and the first since Don Wilson's in 1969), also marked the first time that an Expos team had ever been no-hit.

Additionally thrilling for the Astros fans in attendance was the fact that Dierker's feat occurred during "Foamer Night," an Astros promotion in which free beer was provided whenever a pitcher struck out a batter while a red "foamer light" was illuminated on the Astrodome scoreboard. The foamer light flashed on in the top of the seventh while Dierker was facing Expos second baseman Pete

Mackanin; Mackanin whiffed, triggering an excited exodus toward the refreshment stands.

July 9, 1976, was a far more somber day in Red Sox history. Tom Yawkey, the man who'd owned the franchise since 1933, succumbed to leukemia after months of intermittent hospitalization; he was 73. With the American flag (and the team's 1975 AL pennant) lowered to half-staff at Fenway in Yawkey's honor, the struggling Sox—who had finally climbed above the .500 mark for first time all season just three days earlier—lost 8–6 to the Twins.

Unlike so many baseball owners, Yawkey was generally popular with his players, even Bill Lee. Despite their diametrically opposed political and philosophical viewpoints, Yawkey and Lee had formed something of a bond over their mutual love of *National Geographic*, debating whether mankind was responsible for the vanishing species and ecological damage that regularly appeared in the magazine. Several months after Yawkey's death, Lee witnessed a pigeon flying headfirst into a bleacher seat at Fenway, killing itself. "I knew it was the late Mr. Yawkey," wrote Lee, a firm believer in reincarnation. "He had been sent back as a pigeon with instructions to get a firsthand knowledge of the dangers of pesticides. Having done that, he was now simply shedding his skin so he could assume another form. I wish they had let him come back as our owner again."

Yawkey's passing further darkened the clouds that were already hovering over the Red Sox and their skipper, Darrell Johnson, whose head was now widely rumored to be on the chopping block. Managing the American League team at the All-Star Game in Philadelphia on July 12 should have provided a nice respite from the misery; but even there Johnson took flak, this time from Jim Palmer. The Orioles righty, who'd won the AL Cy Young two of the last three years and was leading the league with 11 victories at the All-Star break, was incensed that Johnson ignored him and rotation mate

Wayne Garland (who was 10–1 at the break with a 2.37 ERA) when putting together his staff for the Midsummer Classic. "He picked the team the way he managed last year," Palmer griped. "He showed what kind of manager he was in the seventh game of the World Series when he took out his best reliever and brought in a rookie in a tie game."

Though Palmer and Garland certainly deserved All-Star consideration, Johnson clearly had no shortage of quality pitchers to choose from. Frank Tanana (10–6, 2.91) led the AL in complete games (13), and was second in the strikeout leaders column with 130; Catfish Hunter (10–8, 3.34) was leading the league in innings pitched (175) and had thrown 12 complete games for the Yankees thus far. Boston's Luis Tiant (10–6, 2.92), Milwaukee's Bill Travers (10–6, 1.91), and relievers Sparky Lyle (6–5, 2.20 with a league-leading 17 saves), Rollie Fingers (5–5, 2.62, 12 saves), and Cleveland's Dave LaRoche (0–2, 1.56, 10 saves), and Chicago's Goose Gossage (who posted a 2.91 ERA as a starter in the first half, pitching better than his 5–7 record indicated) were all worthy picks. And then, of course, there was Mark Fidrych.

The Bird's national debut on *Monday Night Baseball* had unleashed a torrent of Fidrych profile pieces in the print media, all of which further stoked the public's rapidly intensifying crush on the charismatic young man from Massachusetts. A feature in the July 19 issue of *People* magazine included photos of him excitedly stomping around the mound at Tiger Stadium, blowing a gigantic bubblegum bubble between innings, and crashing out in his boxers in his Southgate, Michigan, apartment (which could have easily passed for a college dorm, complete with a sheet over the window substituting for actual curtains). "Sometimes I get lazy and let the dishes stack up," Fidrych confessed to the *People* writer. "But they don't stack too high. I've only got four dishes."

Though initially hooked by his mound antics, fans everywhere were further charmed by the Bird's down-to-earth attitude and his fun-loving approach to baseball and life. As *New York Times* columnist Dave Anderson wrote, "Part of the chemistry of Mark Fidrych's appeal might be that he's making only $16,000, the major-league minimum. People not only can identify with him easier than they can with the millionaire athletes, but people also *want* to identify with a ballplayer who is driving a Dodge Colt instead of a Rolls-Royce." The identification was especially intense in Detroit, where working-class fans readily embraced the Bird as one of their own.

Fidrych made his first post–*Monday Night Baseball* start on the night of July 3, when 51,032 fans packed Tiger Stadium to see if he could duplicate his *Monday Night* magic against Reggie Jackson and the visiting Orioles. The Bird soared even higher this time out, allowing only four hits and three walks while pitching the first shutout of his career. Once again, Rusty Staub helped out with an early home run—a three-run round-tripper off Mike Cuellar—and Fidrych cruised easily to a 4–0 victory. Once again, despite the mound-molding and ball-talking interludes, Fidrych worked so efficiently that he finished the game in a hair under two hours; and once again, the old ballpark rocked with cries of "Go Bird Go!" in the final inning, and an ecstatic curtain call chant of "We Want the Bird!" once the game was over.

While some of the Yankees had taken umbrage at Fidrych's mannerisms, the Orioles were nothing but complimentary about his pitching and his attitude. "This kid really enjoys the game, doesn't he?" O's first baseman Lee May—who struck out twice—marveled to Tigers first base coach Dick Tracewski. "He's got excellent concentration," said Reggie Jackson, who like May went 0-for-4 against the rookie phenom. "He didn't overpower you. He didn't try to get cute. He pitched. This is not a boy's game. It's a man's game and I respect the job he did." Cuellar, who lost his ninth game of the season as

Fidrych was earning his ninth win and eighth straight victory, joked to the press afterward that "I talked to the ball in Spanish, but I found out it was an American ball."

"These people don't just come out to see me," Fidrych modestly told reporters after the game, "they come out to see the Detroit Tigers." But in just two nights, Fidrych had drawn nearly 100,000 fans to Tiger Stadium—or roughly one-tenth of the Tigers' entire home attendance from 1975. Clearly, these people *were* coming out to see Fidrych. The amount of money the Bird was making rapidly became a source of controversy; in a year where fans and sportswriters were decrying the rampant greed of modern ballplayers, both factions now expressed genuine concern that the Bird was being underpaid at best, and exploited at worst. Michigan state representative Dan Angel, a Republican from Battle Creek, even authored a resolution recommending that the Tigers raise Fidrych's salary; the matter was tabled in favor of more pressing legislation.

Though Fidrych mostly appeared to be dealing well with his initial burst of fame, the questions about money seemed to both annoy and embarrass him. "Hell no," he told Associated Press sportswriter Larry Paladino, when asked if he thought he should get a raise from Tiger GM Jim Campbell. "This is the most I've ever made in my life. What happens if he did give me a raise? It might go to my head and I'd start losing." Campbell, for his part, told Paladino that the Tigers were not in the practice of giving midseason raises, but hinted that the organization would reward their prize pitcher come season's end.

Fidrych made his final start before the All-Star break on July 9, once again attracting one of the largest Tiger Stadium crowds of the season. Fifty-one thousand forty-one fans paid to see the Bird battle Dennis Leonard and the Kansas City Royals—"an audience," as AP sportswriter Ken Rappoport put it, "that provided a World

Series aura to crusty Tiger Stadium." But while Fidrych only allowed a single run (George Brett scored from third on a fourth-inning base-knock by Hal McRae), the Tigers failed to score at all against Leonard. The brilliant pitcher's duel ended with the Royals winning 1–0. Leonard notched his ninth win of the season, and the Bird's eight-game winning streak was history.

Though disappointed by the game's outcome, the Tiger Stadium crowd was having too much fun to leave. "We Want the Bird! We Want the Bird!" they chanted. In a surreal twist on the *Monday Night Baseball* finale, someone—this time, a Tiger Stadium security guard—once again ventured into the Tigers' clubhouse to inform an already undressed Fidrych that he needed to put on some clothes and return to the field; only now, the Bird was getting a curtain call as the game's *losing* pitcher. "There has never been a love affair in our city to match what's happened around here in the past month," wrote *Detroit Free Press* columnist Joe Falls. Even the Tigers' World Champion squad of 1968 hadn't captured the hearts and imaginations of Detroit quite like Fidrych had in just a couple of months.

During the next day's game at Tiger Stadium, the public address announcer informed the crowd that the Bird had been selected by Darrell Johnson to be the AL's starting pitcher in the All-Star Game, making him the second-youngest pitcher (behind Jerry Walker of the 1959 Orioles) to receive such an honor. The crowd's reaction to the announcement was so jubilant and protracted, Royals starter Al Fitzmorris finally had to step off the mound for several minutes and let the fans cheer themselves out; a grinning, moist-eyed Fidrych emerged from the dugout to gratefully acknowledge the ovation. Asked by reporters if he was surprised by the All-Star honor, Fidrych responded in his usual filter-free fashion. "Was I surprised?" he laughed. "Fuckin' ay, I was surprised!"

The Bird got an even bigger surprise the following night, when he attended Elton John's show at the Pontiac Silverdome. Taken backstage for a preshow audience with John, Fidrych was stunned to discover that the biggest pop star in the world actually knew who *he* was. "Oh, Mark Fidrych, how are you?" John warmly greeted him. "How's Thurman Munson?" The two shared some wine and exchanged gifts—John receiving a "Bird" T-shirt, and Fidrych leaving with a signed pair of Elton's gym shorts.

The national buzz over the Bird's All-Star selection largely obscured one of Bob Hope's most creative (if downright bizarre) Braves promotions: "Headlock and Wedlock Day," which was held at Atlanta-Fulton County Stadium on July 11, the day before the All-Star break. The promotion was originally billed as "Home Plate Wedding Day," in which couples would tie the knot on the field before a Mets-Braves game. But while Hope and his staff were busy rounding up willing brides and grooms, Ted Turner went and promised the July 11 date to Jim Barnett, owner of Georgia Championship Wrestling, whose bouts were a popular fixture on WTCG. With the date double-booked, and not wanting to disappoint either the happy couples or one of Turner's most important clients, Hope came up with the "Headlock and Wedlock" concept.

When the blessed day finally arrived, 10 players from each team lined up on the field before the game, raising their bats to form a makeshift archway under which nine happy couples and their groomsmen and bridesmaids paraded to the sound of the ballpark organ. Once the couples were gathered at home plate, they were joined in holy matrimony in a single ceremony conducted by a local justice of the peace. Then, after an eighth-inning bases-loaded double by Willie Montanez off Mets reliever Bob Apodaca that gave the Braves a 9–8 comeback victory, a wrestling rink was set up in the stadium's picnic area along first base line, where four matches of no-holds-barred rasslin' action—including a headlining bout between the masked Mr. Wrestling II (who no less than Jimmy Carter had name-checked as his favorite wrestler) and the corpulent heel Abdullah the Butcher, aka "The Madman from the Sudan"—were staged for the delight of the remaining fans.

While the final results of the epic battle between Mr. Wrestling II and Abdullah the Butcher failed to make the papers, news from a much longer-running conflict hit the wire services on July 12, when it was revealed that major league players and owners had finally come to tentative terms on a new labor contract. It would be another week before the new Basic Agreement was ratified—with 17 of the 24 owners approving the pact—and it wouldn't officially go into effect until August 9, but the players could start celebrating now: the reserve clause was now officially dead and gone, and the new Basic Agreement would serve as its headstone.

The final pact was so complex and convoluted it was almost comical to call it a Basic Agreement—but the essential details stood out: in addition to raising the minimum player salary to $19,000 for 1976 and '77 (and to $21,000 for '78 and '79), the contract stipulated that all signed players would be eligible for free agency after six years of service with the same team, and that all currently unsigned players who remained so through the end of the season would automatically become free agents in October. Clubs would not receive any financial compensation for losing players to free agency, though teams would be permitted to sign as many free agents as they'd lost in November's inaugural free agent reentry draft. (Designed to keep free agency from becoming a free-for-all, as well as to limit the players' bargaining leverage, the draft rules stipulated that no more than twelve teams would be allowed to draft a particular player, and that the players would only be allowed to negotiate and sign with teams that drafted them.)

Thanks to the new Basic Agreement, the players would now have greater control of their own destinies than ever before; at the same time, there were enough provisions in place regarding the drafting and signing of free agents that the oft-repeated owners' nightmare of the wealthiest teams stockpiling all the top-echelon talent seemed less likely to come true. Of course, many players believed that such fears were unwarranted to begin with. "There won't be many guys jumping around [to other teams]," Royals shortstop Freddie Patek assured *Sports Illustrated*'s Robert Creamer. "Too many are happy where they are. As long as they can get their maximum value, most will stay."

Earl Weaver wasn't so sure about that, but he also wasn't buying the notion that increased player mobility would be bad for the game. "Once the World Series is over, we don't get much ink [on baseball] through the winter except for the trades that are made at the meetings," Weaver told *Detroit Free Press* columnist Joe Falls. "Now can you imagine how many words are going to be written when these players start switching teams?

"The smartest owners will get the best players," the Orioles skipper assured Falls, reasoning that free agency would force owners to become more involved in building their teams, rather than just operating on autopilot. "I guarantee it's not always going to be the owner with the most dough that gets the best players. I think the fun is only beginning in baseball."

Mark Fidrych found himself in familiar company on his trip to Philadelphia for the All-Star Game. Ron LeFlore (hitting .330 at the break with 29 stolen bases) and Rusty Staub (hitting .310 with six homers and 48 RBIs) had both been voted in as starting outfielders for the AL, making this the first time since 1966 that three Tigers were in the starting lineup of a Midsummer Classic. Boston's Fred Lynn (.324 with six home runs and 34 RBIs), the AL's top vote-getter with over 2.95 million ballots, would be joining LeFlore and Staub in the outfield. Minnesota first baseman Rod Carew (.326, six HRs, 47 RBIs, 35 stolen bases), Baltimore second-sacker Bobby Grich (.295, seven HRs, 23 RBIs), Texas shortstop Toby Harrah (.278, eight HRs, 43 RBIs), Kansas City third baseman George Brett (hitting a league-leading .365 with four HRs and 34 RBIs), and New York catcher Thurman Munson (.319, eight HRs, 50 RBIs) comprised the rest of the AL starters. Though Munson had uttered some tart words about Fidrych in June, the irascible Yankee captain now took it upon himself to greet the young pitcher in the AL clubhouse, jovially informing him that he'd gotten a good chuckle out of the Bird's "Who's Munson?" quote. The ice broken, the new battery mates exchanged signed baseballs.

In what was surely the first pairing of Harpo Marx look-alikes in All-Star Game history, Fidrych's mound counterpart would be Randy Jones, whose 16–3 record and 2.53 ERA marked him as the obvious choice to start the game for the National League. John Montefusco (the Giants' lone All-Star representative, despite having racked up a rather un-"Count"-like record of 7–8 with a 3.13 ERA during the first half of the season), was so annoyed by the endless attention the press devoted to Fidrych—who inadvertently burnished his down-to-earth image by showing up at the All-Star Game press conference in blue jeans and a flower-patterned shirt—that he convinced Jones to help him play a practical joke on the Bird, wherein the Count introduced himself as Jones, and the Junkman introduced himself as Montefusco. When it came time for the press photographers to take a photo of the two starting pitchers posing together, Fidrych sought out Montefusco. "Come on, Randy, they want us," he said. "You don't even know who you're pitching against, do you?" Montefusco laughed.

Cincinnati second baseman Joe Morgan (currently hitting .330

with 14 HRs, 62 RBIs, and 23 stolen bases) was the top vote-getter
in the overall balloting, receiving over three million votes from the
fans, and he was joined in the NL starting lineup by four other
Reds: left fielder George Foster (.327 with 17 HRs and a league-
leading 72 RBIs), catcher Johnny Bench (who received nearly 2.7
million votes despite hitting .234 with nine HRs and 45 RBIs in
what was beginning to look like the worst season of his career), shortstop Dave Concepcion (.263, six HRs, 33 RBIs), and third baseman
Pete Rose (.335, six HRs, 38 RBIs). Since NL manager Sparky Anderson also named first baseman Tony Perez and right fielder Ken
Griffey to the NL roster as subs, it meant that the entire Reds'
starting lineup save center fielder Cesar Geronimo was represented
at the All-Star Game. Dodgers first baseman Steve Garvey (.300,
seven HRs, 45 RBIs) would be the lone non-Red in the NL infield.

The heavy percentage of Reds in the NL lineup didn't sit well
with Phillies fans, who felt that Bob Boone (.309, four HRs, 40
RBIs) was far more deserving of the starting catching honors than
Bench. Still, Philadelphians could be consoled by the presence of
Greg Luzinski (.307, 12 HRs, 57 RBIs), who'd been elected to the
third starting spot in the outfield, where he joined Foster and NL
home run leader Dave Kingman (.234, 30 HRs, 69 RBIs). The Bull
and Kong participated in a pregame home run contest, wowing the
early arrivals with some of the most prodigious clouts ever seen at
Veterans Stadium, including a blast by the Bull that landed halfway
up the second deck in left-center.

Though the 1976 All-Star Game was played at the Vet on July 13,
the pregame festivities were essentially a starred and striped extension of the Bicentennial pageantry witnessed in Philadelphia and
elsewhere nine days earlier, complete with a colonial-costumed color
guard flying the flags of the 13 original colonies. "Happy Birthday"
read the light-up lettering along the left field wall; "America" read

the light-up lettering in right. A giant five-pointed star with "76" in the center had been painted onto the artificial grass in center field, while the Phillies' '76 Liberty Bell logo was likewise rendered behind home plate.

President Ford was on hand to ambidextrously toss out the first balls to Bench and Munson. Before the game, Ford (surrounded by a posse of Secret Service agents) paid a visit to the NL and AL clubhouses, schmoozing awkwardly with players from both teams. "My hat size depends on how the polls are going," he joked to Steve Garvey, who offered him a Dodgers cap. "Right now I'll take 7½." Like the 200-plus journalists in town for the event, Ford made a point of seeking out Mark Fidrych, who seemed exasperated by the approach of his latest visitors—"I thought we had a game to play," he complained—until he realized that the president was among them. Though initially shocked by his unexpected meeting with the Leader of the Free World, Fidrych was really more interested in whether Ford's 19year-old son, Jack, was at the game, because he wanted to ask him what it was like to date a celebrity like tennis star Chris Evert.

Fidrych was one of the few American League players to get a rousing ovation from the 63,974 in attendance, the third largest crowd in All-Star Game history. Brewers third baseman Don Money, who'd played several seasons with the Phillies (and knocked the first homer in Veterans Stadium), also received a warm welcome from the Philly fans, but the loudest cheers were predictably reserved for the Phillies players—and manager Danny Ozark, who was one of Sparky Anderson's coaches for the game—while the loudest jeers were directed at the Reds, all of whom seemed to take the booing in humorous stride. There was also clearly no affection in the City of Brotherly Love for Twins manager Gene Mauch, who'd been named to the AL coaching squad by Darrell Johnson, and who would be forever associated with mismanaging the 1964 Phillies to a stunning September collapse. Mauch's introduction was met with a volley of abuse so vociferous that it was practically comical; at least, Mauch and fellow AL coach Frank Robinson seemed to think so, since the ABC cameras captured them sharing a belly laugh as the boos cascaded down onto the field.

As with every All-Star Game of the 1970s, the 1976 contest was a colorful affair, showcasing an eye-popping variety of polyester double-knits ranging from the orange and yellow horizontal stripes worn by Houston Astros Cesar Cedeno and Ken Forsch, to the collared White Sox tunic sported by Goose Gossage, to the maroon pinstripes of the host team. Phil Garner and Rollie Fingers, the A's two representatives, each donned different Oakland uniforms—Garner wearing a gold jersey with green sleeves, and Rollie Fingers sporting a green jersey with gold sleeves. Al Oliver and Bake McBride respectively sported Pirates and Cardinals pillbox caps; the entire National League squad actually posed for photos together before the game wearing special white NL centennial pillbox caps with blue stripes and a blue "N" logo, but the players swapped them out for their regular headgear at game time.

Out of uniform for the occasion was Hank Aaron, who could be seen in the commissioner's box wearing a conservative suit and tie. This was the first time since his rookie season of 1954 that Hammerin' Hank, who was hitting .255 with nine home runs and 27 RBIs for the season, hadn't taken the field at the All-Star Game. Bowie Kuhn had suggested making a special dispensation to allow Aaron to appear in what would be his record 25th consecutive All-Star Game—the commissioner had issued a similar edict in 1973 on behalf of Willie Mays—but baseball's reigning Home Run King declined, not wanting to make the AL squad as a charity case. There were a couple of other noticeable absences, as well: Willie Randolph, the Yankees' sparkling rookie second baseman, was there in uniform, but couldn't play because of a knee injury. Andy Messersmith, the highest-paid hurler in the National League, had begged off the trip to Philadelphia altogether, citing a pulled hamstring; Atlanta hurler Dick Ruthven (also a former Phillie) was added to the NL roster in his place.

The game itself began with Jones giving up a quick leadoff single to LeFlore. After erasing the Tiger from the base paths by inducing Carew to hit into a 4-6-3 double play, Jones—who was uncharacteristically nervous about his All-Star start—walked George Brett with a fastball he later deemed to be "the hardest I've thrown in three or four years. . . . I was just so pumped up to be out there, I just couldn't smooth it out." Jones then got Munson to ground to short for a force-out, and left the mound to his curly-haired AL counterpart.

Fidrych was even more nervous than Jones, who at least had previous All-Star Game experience. It was as if the Bird had suddenly awakened from a dream to find 63,000 people staring at him, and he struggled to regain his famed concentration and keep the ball low in the strike zone. Pete Rose, who'd faced Fidrych during spring training and took offense at Fidrych's habit of talking to the baseball, promised Larry Bowa before the game that he would hit a liner back through the box his first time up; sure enough, Rose took the second pitch he saw from Fidrych and drove it up the middle. Steve Garvey, the second NL batter of the night, drove a high and outside pitch on a line to right field, where Rusty Staub attempted to play the ball on a hop, then stumbled on the AstroTurf as it skipped past him to the wall. Staub's return throw to the infield arced high like a softball pitch, and Rose scored standing up while Garvey took third. It was the first time Fidrych had given up a first-inning run since entering the majors.

Though his mound antics were comparatively muted, Fidrych

looked a little more like the Bird of legend while facing the next three batters. Joe Morgan—who habitually pumped his left arm while waiting on a pitch, a "funky chicken"–like motion meant to remind himself to keep his elbow away from his body—flailed wildly at Fidrych's first offering before popping to short right; George Foster grounded weakly to second, scoring Garvey; and Greg Luzinski popped the first pitch he saw to Carew in foul territory. But despite regaining his poise, Fidrych left the mound with the AL squad sitting in a 2–0 hole.

Staub attempted to make up for his fielding gaffe with a two-out single to right off Jones in the top of the second. Staub's hit brought Bobby Grich to the plate, and—since the designated hitter hadn't yet been approved for All-Star action—brought Fidrych to the on-deck circle, where ABC cameras caught him enthusiastically swinging the bat with his warm-up jacket half on. Grich grounded out to short, however, depriving Fidrych (who often hopped into the cage during batting practice at Tiger Stadium) of the chance to face Jones.

The NL bats continued to peck away at the Bird in the bottom of the second, when he gave up singles to Johnny Bench and Dave Concepcion. With runners on first and third and one out, Jones stepped to the plate. Fidrych handcuffed Munson with a sinking fastball, and Concepcion advanced to second on the passed ball. Fidrych struck out Jones, then got Rose to hit a grounder to the right side, and gave the Veterans Stadium crowd a glimpse of his impressive athleticism when he ran to first to take the toss from Carew. After recording the final out of the inning, the Bird dashed excitedly to the dugout and grabbed a bat, only to learn that Darrell Johnson was sending Hal McRae up to pinch-hit for him. Fidrych begged Johnson to allow him to go up to the plate and see just one pitch. "No," answered Johnson, "because I know you'll swing at it."

Later in the game, ABC's Warner Wolf cornered Fidrych in the clubhouse and asked him about his first All-Star Game outing. "Life," the obviously disappointed pitcher smiled, shaking his head. "I don't know, man. . . . I was happy to be here. . . . I'm happy to have my teammates here that helped me get here. . . . But damn, I didn't show what I could do, though!"

Then again, not too many of his fellow AL All-Stars showed what they could do that night, either. After Jones settled down in the third and held the AL bats hitless, Catfish Hunter—who replaced Fidrych on the mound—gave up a two-run 'tater to George Foster, who crushed it over the "Happy Birthday" in left center to make it 4–0. Fred Lynn hammered a Tom Seaver pitch over the right field wall for a solo homer in the top of the fourth inning, but the AL bats only managed two more hits over the next five innings (singles from Staub and Mickey Rivers), while the NL hitters put three more runs on the board off Frank Tanana in the eighth.

As the 13th NL victory in the last 14 Midsummer Classics became an increasingly foregone conclusion, ABC began cutting away to the Democratic National Convention at New York City's Madison Square Garden, where the likes of Senator Hubert Humphrey and Chicago Mayor Richard Daley were among the evening's speakers. Jimmy Carter would be officially nominated for president the following night, with Minnesota senator Walter Mondale receiving the vice presidential nod the night after. A record 60 million people tuned in that evening to watch the All-Star Game, giving the contest a significantly higher Nielsen rating than the CBS or NBC broadcasts of the convention; but the fact that ABC deemed snippets of platform-related speeches more interesting than the game at hand pretty much said it all

Three days after the All-Star Game, American moviegoers got to enjoy some additional all-star action, courtesy of *The Bingo Long Traveling All-Stars & Motor Kings*, which was released in theaters nationwide on July 16. Coproduced by Motown Records mogul Berry Gordy and Rob Cohen of Universal Pictures, the film—loosely adapted from William Brashler's novel of the same name—was Hollywood's first attempt at depicting the experience of life in the Negro Leagues. Billy Dee Williams starred as Bingo Long, a charismatic, Satchel Paige–like pitcher who, fed up with the Negro League owners' tight-fisted ways, joins forces with a Josh Gibson-esque slugger played by James Earl Jones to form an independent barnstorming team.

The film debut of TV director John Badham, who had previously helmed several *Night Gallery* episodes, *Bingo Long* suffered from some serious tone issues; as with many comedies of the blaxploitation era (such as *Black Shampoo* and *Cooley High*) it veered awkwardly between lighthearted slapstick and deeply disturbing moments of violence. The racism of pre–World War II America received only a cursory nod in the script, making the attempts of outfielder Charlie Snow (Richard Pryor) to pass himself off as Cuban or Native American so that he can play in a "white" league seem more comic than poignant.

Still, whatever the film's faults, *Bingo Long*'s baseball scenes—mostly filmed in such venerable Georgia minor league parks as Macon's Luther Williams Field and Savannah's William L. Grayson Stadium—were a blast. It also featured former Angels star Leon "Daddy Wags" Wagner in a supporting role, and its theme of players rising up to take control of their own destinies had an added resonance in a year where the reserve clause was finally overthrown. Though *Bingo Long* didn't match the box office performance of such summer blockbusters as the Gregory Peck–Lee Remick horror film *The Omen*, the Clint Eastwood western *The Outlaw Josey Wales*, or the Sensurround-assisted World War II battle epic *Midway*, it was enough of a success that Badham was able to parlay it into his next directorial gig: a little slice-of-disco-life called *Saturday Night Fe-*

ver, based on a June 1976 *New Yorker* article by British journalist Nik Cohn about the Italian American denizens of a Brooklyn discotheque.

In the two weeks following the All-Star Game, baseball was largely upstaged by the events of the XXI Olympiad in Montreal, including Romanian gymnast Nadia Comaneci's seven perfect 10.0 scores, Bruce Jenner's record-setting decathlon triumph, and the five gold medals won by U.S. boxers Howard Davis Jr., Sugar Ray Leonard, Leo Randolph, and brothers Leon and Michael Spinks—the mightiest performance of any American boxing team in Olympic history.

Comaneci's record-setting performance captured the imagination of the American public in a manner similar to Dorothy Hamill's Winter Olympics triumph—though since the 14-year-old gymnast hailed from behind the Iron Curtain, she was unable to capitalize on her Olympic success the way Hamill had. But others found a way to profit off of it, most notably composers Barry De Vorzon and Perry Botkin Jr., who renamed their wistful instrumental "Cotton's Dream" (originally featured in the 1971 film *Bless the Beasts and Children*, and later used as the theme music for the CBS soap opera *The Young and the Restless*) as "Nadia's Theme" after ABC's *Wide World of Sports* used it as a musical bed for slow-motion montages of Comaneci's Olympic highlights. An elongated version of the renamed piece would become a Top 10 single later in the year, and take up residence on the *Billboard* pop charts for 22 weeks.

Anyone who'd taken a two-week vacation from the baseball box scores wouldn't have noticed much of a difference in the pennant races at the end of July: the Yankees, nine and a half games up on the second-place Red Sox at the All-Star break, were now 10 and a half ahead of the second-place Orioles in the AL East; the Royals, previously seven games up over the second-place Rangers in the AL

West, were now nine games up on the second-place A's. In the NL East, the Phillies—thanks in part to a late-July series where they wrested four out of five games from the visiting Pirates—extended their lead over the Bucs to 11 and a half games, while the Reds widened their margin over the Dodgers to nine and a half.

Still, it was an eventful couple of weeks. Just five days after the AL's humiliating All-Star Game loss, Darrell Johnson was fired by the Boston Red Sox, taking the fall for his players' flat and uninspired play. "We know the ball club has not played up to its capabilities this year," said Boston General Manager Dick O'Connell in a written statement to the press. "Therefore, a change at this time, we hope, will make for improvement. . . . We cannot blame everything on Darrell Johnson, but it's easier to change managers than the team, which would be practically impossible."

Team captain Carl Yastrzemski echoed O'Connell's frustration. "Just two days before he was fired," Yaz told Larry Whiteside of the *Sporting News*, "[Johnson] called me and Rico Petrocelli into his office and asked us if we had any thoughts as to what we could have done to stop what was happening to our club. We couldn't. There are a lot of reasons besides Darrell Johnson why we haven't done well this year, and everybody knows what some of them are. The biggest thing lacking on this club is pride."

Though there were ample ways to apportion the blame, contract holdouts Carlton Fisk, Fred Lynn, and Rick Burleson remained the primary Red Sox scapegoats. "Our failures this year can be blamed directly to a lack of concentration on the field," said Yaz, and it was clear whom he was referring to, especially since Lynn's misplays in center field had become nearly as commonplace as his acrobatic catches. "I get hate mail a lot," Lynn admitted to Whiteside. "I get letters from fans who think it's wrong that I held out. You think it was wrong when Joe DiMaggio held out for as long as he could under the old system? What about some of the other stars from years ago? I think, given the same circumstances I have today, they'd have done the same thing."

The Red Sox initially tapped third base coach Don Zimmer as a temporary replacement for Johnson. But after the team went 5–9 during Zim's first 14 games at the helm, the organization signed him to a contract for the 1977 season, feeling that his aggressive style of managing had already made a marked difference in the team's attitude, if not their record. "I like the way he manages," Yaz told the press. "He's daring and not afraid to make a move."

Dick Williams was the second manager to lose his job in July, getting axed by the California Angels on July 23. Just a few days earlier, Angels owner Gene Autry had told the press, "I'm satisfied with Manager Dick Williams. I'm not satisfied with the way some of the players are playing." But after Williams got into it with third baseman Bill Melton on July 22, Autry and general manager Harry Dalton concluded that they'd be better off with a new skipper.

Beltin' Bill had held a grudge against Williams dating back to 1973, when the skipper (then with the A's) had left Melton (then with the White Sox) off the All-Star roster. So on the night of the 22nd, when Williams upbraided Melton and several other Angels for singing and laughing on the back of the bus following yet another loss, the veteran third baseman didn't mince words. "Fuck you," he growled.

"Who said that?" Williams shouted. "I did, you cocksucker!" Melton responded, making his way along the bus aisle toward the skipper. Williams angrily suspended Melton on the spot. "This is the happiest day of my life," retorted the third baseman, whereupon Williams challenged him to a fight. The two men had to be separated by the Angel coaches, while the players demonstrated their solidarity with Melton by blasting their portable tape decks at top volume and yelling obscenities at Williams. "I knew my career as a California

Angels manager was over," Williams would later reflect, perhaps with some degree of understatement.

Morale on the Angels had been on a downward slide since early April, when Bobby Bonds broke his hand while sliding home in an exhibition game against the Dodgers. Bonds insisted on returning to the lineup almost immediately, but Williams felt that many of the Angels became demoralized once they realized that their star slugger was hurt and couldn't carry the team. "And not just the kids," Williams bitterly recounted in his autobiography. "Except for [Nolan] Ryan, most of the veteran leaders quit too."

Tommy Davis, picked up in early June from Casablanca Records, failed to provide the veteran leadership Williams was hoping for. In one game shortly after Davis joined the Angels, Williams caught the DH shaving in the clubhouse bathroom between at-bats. "Another time I found him using the telephone in my office between innings," he recalled. "That was bad enough, but did he also have to give the operator my credit card number?"

The Angels replaced Williams with third base coach Norm Sherry, a more easygoing sort who'd already managed several of the club's younger players in the minors. Though he was a first-time big league manager inheriting a team that was currently in last place in the AL West with a 39–57 record, 20 games behind the first-place Royals, Sherry put a brave face on the unenviable task at hand. "I hope I'm the Walter Alston of the '70s, '80s and '90s," he said, referring to the venerable Dodger manager, who, on July 17, had become just the sixth manager in major league history to win 2,000 games.

"Why don't I want to talk about home runs?" Dave Kingman rhetorically asked a reporter in July. "Because the more I talk about them, the more I think about them." The less he thought about them, apparently, the more of them he was likely to hit; and Kong, who'd parked three round-trippers right before the All-Star break following a nine-game homerless drought, picked up where he left off on July 15, crushing a two-run bomb off J. R. Richard that gave the Mets a 3–1 win (and Jerry Koosman his 10th victory of the season) at Shea Stadium. Kong hit a solo shot three days later off Carl Morton, which smacked the back of the bullpen fence and padded the lead for Mickey Lolich's 2–0 shutout victory over the Braves at Shea. Morton's gopher ball gave Kingman 32 homers for the season; if the Mets' slugger wasn't quite on pace to break Roger Maris's single-season mark, he still had a good shot at surpassing Hack Wilson's NL mark of 56—and he seemed like a lock to become the first player to hit 50 in a season since Willie Mays launched 52 in 1965.

But on July 19, Kingman tore a ligament in his left thumb while diving for a down-the-line double off the bat of Braves pitcher Phil Niekro, an injury that required immediate surgery and a six-week stay on the disabled list. "I'm really worried about our offense now," moaned Jon Matlack, who went 1–4 in seven July starts, four of which saw his team scoring less than two runs. But the Mets' front office was also concerned about their ticket sales—and with the exception of Tom Seaver, who could usually be counted on to pull in above-average crowds for his starts, Sky King was the Mets' lone gate attraction; even as the Phillies were running away with the NL East, Mets fans were still drawn to Shea by the possibility that they might get to see him hit another colossal moon shot.

With Kingman out, the Mets traded third baseman Wayne Garrett and outfielder Del Unser to the Expos for outfielders Jim Dwyer and Pepe Mangual. The Mets' front office hoped that Mangual, a speedy 24-year-old from Ponce, Puerto Rico, would enable them to market the team to New York's sizable Puerto Rican population. Unfortunately, Mangual would hit only .186 for his new team, striking out at an even higher rate than Kingman while stealing only seven bases and bumbling so badly in center field that he inspired *Long Island Press* sportswriter Jack Lang to write, "Pepe Mangual can drop anything he gets his hands on." New York baseball fans, Puerto Rican or otherwise, were not impressed.

On July 20, Henry Aaron hit the 755th homer of his career, following George Scott's three-run blast off Angels reliever Dick Drago with a blow of his own during the Brewers' 6–2 victory at County Stadium. While each homer Hank hammered was officially historic at this point, no one realized at the time just how significant this one was; though Hank still had another 10 weeks to play, the solo shot off Drago would be the last round-tripper of his remarkable career.

Hank's 755th home run ball was retrieved from an empty seat in the left field stands at County Stadium by Dick Arndt, a part-time member of the Brewers' grounds crew, whose main duties involved opening and closing the left field gate for the bullpen cart. Harry Gill, the team's head groundskeeper, asked Arndt to hand over the ball; in exchange for it, the Brewers offered to give Arndt a photo of him returning it to Aaron, as well as a different ball autographed by the Home Run King and one of his bats. Arndt said he wanted to think about it overnight, and left County Stadium without returning the ball. He was fired the next day for taking Brewers property; the club also deducted the $5 cost of the ball from his paycheck. Despite Aaron's subsequent requests for the ball's return, Arndt chose to hold on to it; the Home Run King would never get his final home run ball back.

Reggie Jackson made some home run history of his own in July, homering in an AL record-tying six straight games from July 18 to July 24. Jackson's clout on the 24th gave him 16 homers for the year, putting him just three behind former teammate Sal Bando, who was currently leading the league with 19. "I've got my bloodhounds out," Jackson joked with reporters. "Before, the leaders were a couple of hills away. But now I can see them. Park it, Sal—you're cluttering up the highway!"

Always a man in the center of the action, Jackson found himself in the middle of a beanball war between the Yankees and Orioles in Baltimore on July 27—in fact, he basically provoked it. Dock Ellis was on the mound for the Yankees that evening; despite preseason concerns over how a man of his headstrong nature would fare on a team run by Billy Martin, Dock had thus far enjoyed a successful and controversy-free season with the Yankees, going 11–4 with a 3.22 ERA. Dock enjoyed the rough-and-tumble camaraderie of Martin's Yankees, which he felt was considerably stronger than those of the Pirates teams he'd previously played on. "The difference was that on the Yankees, the white boys knew how to party," he'd later recall. "It was kick ass and take names, led by Billy Martin. Billy would say to us, 'Do whatever the fuck you want to do, but give me one hundred and twenty-five percent.'"

In the July 27 game against Baltimore, Ellis accidentally came close to hitting Mark Belanger with a ball while tossing it to home plate umpire Bill Deegan. Ellis warned Belanger to duck; but to Jackson, sitting in the Orioles' dugout, it looked like the pitcher had buzzed the spindly shortstop intentionally. "Why don't you hit a big motherfucker like me?" Jackson shouted at the pitcher.

Ellis, by his own admission, was "high as a Georgia pine" on greenies at the time. While many baseball players of the era indulged in amphetamines as a way to keep their energy and focus up during the long season, Ellis had an appetite for uppers (and downers) that far surpassed that of most of his colleagues. "I'd take fifteen Dexamyls just to get ready to start thinking about pitching," he'd later admit. "Then, after the game, I'd want to do some cocaine, smoke some weed and drink some Courvoisier." Ellis's teammates (some of whom would join him in his postgame excesses) never expressed any concern about his drug use, even though it was blatant enough that even fans in the Yankee Stadium bleachers were hip to his habits. "Kids threw me drugs on the field, because they'd heard I was a head, a get-high, a doper," Ellis recalled. "That was a big, beautiful playpen for me, New York. I had all the drugs I wanted."

Jackson had just picked a fight with the wrong dude. When he stepped to the plate in the bottom of the eighth inning with the Orioles leading 4–0, Munson walked to the mound for a conference with Ellis. "Did you hear your brother-man over there?" Munson goaded him. "Your brother-man says why don't you hit a big motherfucker like him? What are you going to do, Babe?" "Get your ass back there behind home plate," Ellis spat, "and don't give me no signals."

Through his amphetamine haze, Ellis recalled the towering home run Jackson had hit off him in the 1971 All-Star Game, and the showboating way in which Jackson stopped to admire the flight of the ball, which would have flown clear out of Tiger Stadium if it hadn't crashed into one of the giant light standards atop the ballpark's right field roof. "I owe him one," thought Dock, starting Jackson off with an outside sinker, which the slugger swung at and missed. Dock then threw two pitches inside, in order to back Jackson off the plate; Jackson swung at the second one and missed. The next pitch came in high and tight, as well—but Ellis had thrown it knowing that Jackson was fully expecting him to dangle a third strike on the outside corner. The pitch hit Jackson square on the right cheekbone, shattering his aviator shades and dropping him into the dirt, unconscious.

Ellis wandered toward home plate to inspect the damage. "Did I kill him?" he playfully asked to no one in particular. Deegan ordered the pitcher back to the mound, and Jackson was rushed to the hospital for X rays.

Jim Palmer, who was in the process of racking up his 14th victory of the season, retaliated by plunking Mickey Rivers, the sparkplug of the Yankee offense, in the back with a medium-speed fastball during the top of the ninth. Though Rivers was uninjured, Billy Martin was furious and threatened to escalate the feud at a future date. "I'm sure [Palmer] was ordered to do it," he raged after the game. But most of the Yankee players were more amused than angered by the pitch that hit Rivers. "The big joke," Ellis later recalled, "is that I tried to kill Reggie and Palmer hit our guy with a change-up. So there was no real retaliation."

Despite the frightening force of the impact, Jackson somehow sustained nothing worse than a badly bruised cheekbone, which kept him out of action for only a couple of days—though he did admit that his feelings were hurt when Ellis didn't reach out to him afterward to see how he was doing. Then again, Ellis was probably too busy counting the twenty-dollar bills that some of his teammates had surreptitiously stuffed in his locker as a thank-you for the Jackson beaning. "Somebody didn't like him," an amused Ellis would later reflect. "He was *supposed* to get hit!"

Back on June 12, 1970, Ellis had thrown one of the sloppiest no-hitters of all time, walking eight Padres and hitting another while (as he would reveal many years later) buzzing hard on a winning combination of LSD, Benzedrine, and Dexamyl. On July 28, White Sox pitchers John "Blue Moon" Odom and Francisco Barrios combined for a no-hit performance against the A's that was even more erratic than Ellis's—only this time, presumably, no hallucinogenic drugs were involved.

Odom, a former A's star who'd pitched for all three of Oakland's World Championship squads, had recently fallen on hard times, splitting 1975 among the A's, the Indians, and the Braves while posting a horrific combined ERA of 7.22 over 77 and a third innings. Odom had opened the 1976 season with the Richmond Braves of the

International League, but Bill Veeck, thinking there might still be life in the 31-year-old pitcher's arm, traded White Sox catcher Pete Varney for him in June. Odom made his first start for the White Sox on July 22, and performed well enough to earn another start for the pitching-depleted Sox.

On July 28, Odom took the mound against his former team at the Oakland Coliseum. He struck out A's center fielder Bill North, the first batter he faced, but his control quickly deserted him. "I had a pretty good idea about the second inning that Odom wasn't going to last the whole game," admitted White Sox manager Paul Richards afterward. And yet, despite walking a batter in the first, another in the second, and three in the third, Odom kept extricating himself from trouble as the A's hit one grounder after another directly at his infielders.

In the bottom of the fourth, however, Odom's wildness finally came back to haunt him. With the White Sox up 1–0, Odom walked Billy Williams and Gene Tenace; Tenace was forced at second by a Claudell Washington grounder, but the A's tied the score when Washington stole second and the throw from White Sox catcher Jim Essian sailed into the outfield, allowing Williams to come home. The White Sox took a 2–1 lead in the top of the sixth on a Jim Spencer home run off A's reliever Paul Lindblad, and Odom returned to the mound in the bottom of the frame; but when he walked Williams again for his ninth free pass of the game, then missed the strike zone on his first pitch to Sal Bando, Richards decided he'd seen enough.

In came Barrios, a barrel-shaped 23-year-old rookie from Mexico, who promptly threw three more balls to Bando, but got Tenace to pop out to Essian for the first out of the inning. Washington, up next, hit a grounder back to the mound. Barrios tossed the ball to shortstop Bucky Dent at second to force Bando, but Larry Lintz (one of Finley's "designated runners," who'd been brought in to pinch-run for Williams) rounded third and kept on running; seeing Lintz heading home, Dent threw to Essian, who ran Lintz back toward third before tossing the ball to third baseman Bill Stein. Stein noticed the fleet Washington loitering between first and second, and whipped the ball to Spencer at first; Washington took off for second, so Spencer threw the ball to Dent, who slapped a tag on Washington a second before Lintz could cross the plate. Just your average inning-ending 1-6-2-5-3-6 double play, in other words.

Barrios cruised easily through the next two innings. Incredibly, the rookie had no idea that he and Odom had a combined no-hitter going until he looked up at the scoreboard while heading to the mound in the bottom of the ninth; since there were runners on base while he was warming up in the bullpen, Barrios just automatically assumed that hits had been involved. Bando, the first hitter in the ninth, almost broke up the no-no with a slow roller to the right side, but second baseman Jack Brohamer charged in and flipped it to Spencer in time to nip Bando at first—or so ruled first base umpire George Maloney, much to Bando's annoyance. "I was safe," the A's captain grumbled after the game, "but I knew Maloney wouldn't call it because he can't see anyway."

Barrios, his adrenaline surging, struck out Tenace, then walked Washington, the 11th free pass the A's had received in the ballgame. With the fleet Washington dancing off first, Barrios got Ken McMullen to hit a routine grounder to Dent, and the Odom-Barrios no-no—only the fourth combined no-hitter in major league history, and the first to involve a record 11 walks—was in the books in all its messy glory.

"I couldn't take it, man," whooped a visibly relieved Odom in the clubhouse, as he and Barrios posed for photos together with the final ball of the game. "I was in here pacing. This was like the World Series. This is the greatest experience I've ever had. It tops them all!" It would be the final victory of Odom's major league career.

A's manager Chuck Tanner had a different take on the momentous occasion. "It was the most tainted no-hitter I've ever seen," he laughed. "Or maybe I should call it the funniest."

9.

You Should Be Dancing

(August 1976)

Making a quick spin through the AM radio dial on any day of August '76, it was almost as if you were privy to a scientific laboratory experiment bent on concocting the most perfect summer pop hit ever recorded. From the polished post-folk harmonies of the Starland Vocal Band's "Afternoon Delight" and England Dan and John Ford Coley's "I'd Really Love to See You Tonight," to the infectious disco grooves of the Bee Gees' "You Should Be Dancing" and Walter Murphy's "A Fifth of Beethoven" to the silky-smooth R&B of the Brothers Johnson's "I'll Be Good to You" and Lou Rawls's "You'll Never Find Another Love Like Mine," practically everything wafting out of the speakers sounded backlit by afternoon sunshine and caressed by gentle ocean breezes.

But the sunniest, breeziest, most intrinsically summery song of 1976 had to be "Summer," the new single by multiracial L.A. funk band War, which sang of stickball games and open fire hydrants, rhymed "Disneyland" with "rappin' on the CB radio in the van," and meandered up the *Billboard* charts with the same happily unhurried groove that the musicians laid down on the recording. It sounded blissful, stoned, and several galaxies removed from the Legionnaires' disease hysteria that seemed to be dominating every radio station newsbreak.

No one seemed to know what this new disease actually was—only that, of the 2,000 veterans who'd attended a Pennsylvania American Legion convention held July 21–24 at Philadelphia's Bellevue-Stratford Hotel, over 130 had been hospitalized with similar symptoms: headaches, fatigue, chest pains, high fevers, and serious lung congestion. By the first week of August, 25 of them were dead.

Swine flu? Bird flu? Typhoid fever? Epidemiologists quickly ruled out all of those possibilities, but that did little to ease the nation's already heightened anxiety over the possibility of a massive influenza outbreak; if anything, the mysterious nature of this new affliction—which killed some convention goers, yet somehow completely spared many of the people they ate, drank, and shared hotel rooms with—just ratcheted the panic and paranoia up even higher. In the towns were the Legionnaires were buried, some acquaintances of the deceased avoided their funerals for fear of contagion, while an information hotline set up by Philadelphia city officials received up to 400 calls an hour from concerned citizens. Philly tourism took another unexpected hit in the midst of what was supposed to be a banner summer, as frightened tourists canceled their plans to visit the city. The Bellevue-Stratford was temporarily closed while health officials conducted an investigation; since visiting baseball clubs often stayed at the hotel (the All-Star Game press conference had even been held there just a little over a week before the Legion convention), travel directors of the Phillies' August opponents worked frantically to rearrange their lodgings, discovering too late in some cases that their backup hotels had also played host to some of the late Legionnaires.

The Phillies remained untouched by the new disease—as did most Americans, since the total number of reported cases eventually only came to 221, with 34 related fatalities. (It would be another six months before scientists identified the cause of the disease: a strain of bacteria, dubbed *Legionella pneumophilia*, carried by amoebae that thrive in stagnant water, which had apparently been spread via the Bellevue-Stratford's air-conditioning system.) In fact, the Phillies jogged into August in rude good health, exemplified by the colossal grand slam Greg Luzinski crushed off of Mets starter Bob Apodaca at Shea Stadium on August 1. The Bull's blast, his 16th of the year, came in the top of the fifth with Jim Kaat, Larry Bowa, and Mike Schmidt on base, giving the Phils a 6–4 lead in the first game of a Sunday doubleheader; the ball sailed over the left field bullpen, then cleared a city bus before landing in the parking lot and bouncing into the street. While the Mets tied the game in the ninth on an RBI single from John "The Hammer" Milner—tagging former Met hero Tug McGraw with his fourth blown save of the year—the Phillies eventually came back to win it in the 11th, thanks to a Garry Maddox RBI single and two innings of scoreless relief from Gene Garber, who racked up his sixth win.

Garber, McGraw, Ron Reed, and Ron Schueler made up one of the most formidable bullpens in the NL, and could usually be counted upon to nail down a victory when their colleagues in the starting rotation fell short. Wayne Twitchell, another esteemed member of the Phillies' relief corps, was given his first start of the season in the second half of the August 1 doubleheader, and struck out seven Mets over seven scoreless innings; Mike Schmidt plated all the runs the team needed for their 2–0 victory with a sixth-inning shot off of Nino Espinosa, his 27th round-tripper of the season. Schmidt finally caught up with the still injured Dave Kingman in the NL home run race on August 19 when he went deep off Astros rookie Joaquin

Andujar for his 32nd of the season; the game, which the Phillies won 7–1, not only gave Steve Carlton his 15th victory of the year, but it also drew a Thursday night crowd of 35,605, which put the Phillies' season attendance over two million for the first time in franchise history.

The only thing really missing for the Phillies was the presence of Dick Allen in the lineup. The veteran first baseman had been out of action since July 25 when he injured his back and shoulder in a collision at first base with Pirates pitcher John Candelaria. Though Allen had maintained a relatively positive relationship with the Philadelphia media for most of the season, things went sour when he took it upon himself to take a few days off after the collision without asking Danny Ozark's permission. Ozark was initially angry about Allen's desertion, but the two men sorted things out. "I know how he is," said Ozark, who assured reporters that Allen would be back in the lineup in time for the September stretch run. "He didn't want to go out there and play knowing he had no chance to perform reasonably close to his capabilities." But the local press, recalling some of Allen's late '60s walkouts, wasn't giving the moody slugger any benefit of the doubt.

With Allen out for the month—he was hitting .289 with 13 home runs and 41 RBIs at the time he went on the disabled list—first base became home to a revolving cast of Phillies, including catcher Bob Boone (who'd been freed to move to first by Johnny Oates's return from the DL), veteran outfielder Bobby Tolan, backup 1B/OF Tommy Hutton, and right fielder Jay Johnstone. Johnstone, whom Ozark primarily started against right-handed hitters (while putting "Downtown" Ollie Brown out there against lefties), was on fire, hitting nearly .390 over the course of July and August. The team's biggest practical joker, Johnstone was also partly in charge of boosting team morale via "cold duck parties," the monthly bull sessions that he and Tony Taylor threw when the team was on the road. Johnstone and Taylor would commandeer a hotel suite, pick up a case of sparkling wine, and invite their teammates to come in, kick back, and clear the air.

"Somebody would pop a cork, stand in front of the room, and say, 'OK, any bitches? Any gripes?'" Johnstone would later recall. "If some outfielder was getting a little tired of the same infielder blowing the cutoff throw, he'd let him have it, right there. You play six to eight months a year with the same people and personality conflicts can really develop . . . so we would let it rip and throw it all out for discussion. Play a little music, tell a few jokes, maybe even hire a dancer or two, and, above all, have some laughs. It helped us become a team."

Of course, it was easy to maintain morale while being in first place by as much as 15 and a half games, which is what the Phillies' lead reached on August 24, when they trounced Andy Messersmith and the Braves 14–3 at Atlanta. But as the Pirates were learning, it was much harder to keep the good vibes pumping on the other side of that margin. The Pirates hadn't looked up at first place from so vast a distance since August 1969, when they slipped to 14 and a half behind the Cubs; there were just a handful of Bucs left, like 36-year-old first baseman Willie Stargell, who even remembered that season.

"I'm not happy about the fact we're so far behind," Stargell told *Sports Illustrated*'s Ron Fimrite. "Nobody likes to lose, but what do you do? Do you just tuck in your tail, or is it worthwhile to grind? I know it's worthwhile to grind. When you come up short it shouldn't be because you didn't give your best. It's like a guy trapped in a mine. When he finally sees that light, does he stop digging?"

Stargell, the team's de facto leader (Dave Parker nicknamed him "Pops" in honor of his paternal gravitas), had been distracted for much of the season by the ill health of his wife, Dolores, who'd nearly died in late May from the combined effects of a blood clot, an aneurysm, and a stroke. "It was something I had never had to deal with before," he reflected. "I came close to losing my wife. I haven't been producing this season—I've got to be man enough to admit that—because I've had to make myself think about doing things that I had always done naturally. The other day I dropped a ball at first base because I didn't think that ball into the mitt."

But even at his most preoccupied, Pops was more diligent in his day-to-day approach to the game than many of his teammates. Jim Rooker, the oldest member of the Bucs' rotation at 33, admitted to Fimrite that he was angered by the attitude he'd noticed in the Pirates' clubhouse. "[The Phillies] are not uncatchable," he said. "And yet I've heard other players around here saying, 'The season's over, let's play for ourselves.' That's selfish, and I don't believe it's fair. It's disappointing, discouraging, and frustrating—yes, all of those things—to be on a team with so much talent and be so far out. I just don't believe the Phillies are 13 games better than we are. But they're playing fundamental baseball, and we haven't been."

The Pirates' biggest problem was that they weren't producing at the plate in a manner befitting a team nicknamed "The Pittsburgh Lumber Company." Left fielder Richie Zisk (who was hitting in the .290s while leading the team in RBIs) and center fielder Al Oliver (who'd entered August hitting a league-leading .340) were performing consistently well at the plate, but almost everyone else in the regular lineup was having an off year. Dave Parker, who'd boasted at the start of the season that he would hit 35 homers, had actually hit only seven through July, though his batting average continued to hover around .300. Manny Sanguillen, the gap-toothed veteran catcher who would usually swing at just about anything, was once again hitting in the .290s, but wasn't coming through with men on base like he'd done in 1975. Frank Taveras, the team's new shortstop, was leading the league with 37 stolen bases when he injured his knee in early August; but since Tavaras wasn't much of a hitter, rarely walked, and had no power, he wasn't supplying the offensive spark the Pirates needed, either. Bill Robinson, the 33-year-old "super utility man" who regularly shuttled between third, first, and all three outfield positions just so that manager Danny Murtaugh could fit his hot bat into the lineup, unexpectedly led the team in home runs for much of the summer, hitting his 19th on August 10 against the Dodgers, who were experiencing some morale issues of their own.

On August 5, the Dodgers went into a four-game series with the Reds at Dodger Stadium, knowing that it was their best (and possibly last) chance to take a serious bite out of Cincinnati's nine-game lead. But it wasn't to be: Fred Norman outdueled Don Sutton on August 5; Tony Perez hit his 12th home run of the year to give the Reds a 3–2 victory, and Norman notched his 11th win against only two losses. "Norman is the best pitcher in the National League," bragged Sparky Anderson. "Look at his stats, his strikeouts, everything. He's better, per inning, than Randy Jones." The next night, Rick Rhoden—who'd won nine straight decisions dating back to the beginning of the season—endured his first loss of the year after Joe Morgan broke a tie game open in the ninth with a solo homer to send the Reds on their way to a 7–4 win. Rookie Pat Zachry notched his 10th win of the season on August 7, beating Tommy John 4–1; and Jack Billingham, despite giving up solo shots to Ron Cey and Dusty Baker, completed the sweep the next night with a 3–2 victory over Burt Hooton. The Dodgers were now 13 back, and the NL West race looked all but over. "They should have a funeral before the body decomposes," cracked Reds reliever Rawly Eastwick, who collected his 14th save of the season in the final game of the sweep.

Don Sutton disagreed. "You know why this series became so important?" asked the veteran right-hander as the team flew east for a series in Pittsburgh. "Because we screwed up earlier. I really object to placing so much value on one four-game series. The games you win and lose in April are as important as those in September. But a lot of things can happen with 50 or so games to play. It's not time for us to pack up and plan our winter vacations yet." Davey Lopes, who was in the process of challenging Frank Tavaras for the NL stolen base lead, despite missing all of April and much of June with injuries, sang a more pragmatic tune. "The minimum we wanted was three wins," said the second baseman. "You have to beat the team you're chasing. It's that simple."

But the team they were chasing was just too damn strong: even Dodger manager Walter Alston was forced to cop to the fact that the Reds were simply a deeper squad. "If they have one or two guys go into in a slump, it's not a big problem," said Alston, following the Reds' sweep. "The men they have on their bench can step right in and do the job. As for us, well, if Garvey and Cey stop hitting, we just don't seem to score runs."

Oozing with confidence, the Big Red Machine vowed to keep rolling to the finish line at the same unstoppable rate. "Foster wants that league RBI title," said Sparky Anderson of his left fielder, who upped his RBI total to 98 during the Dodgers series. "I don't think you'll see him letting up any, no matter how big a lead we take." "Batting titles, runs-scored titles, RBI titles—that's all that's left," seconded Pete Rose, who was in the hunt for two of those three crowns, hitting .333 and having already scored 98 runs, while Foster, Morgan, Ken Griffey, and Cesar Geronimo were all also in contention for the NL batting title.

With the Dodgers running a distant second in the NL West for the second year in a row, murmurs that it was time for Walter Alston to retire became increasingly audible. The morning after the sweep by the Reds, the *Los Angeles Herald Examiner*'s Allan Malamud ran a column titled, "It's Time for a Change," which called in no uncertain terms for the retirement (or firing) of the only manager the Dodgers had known in Los Angeles, and pushed for third base coach Tommy Lasorda as his replacement. The 64-year-old Alston was so incensed by Malamud's column that he challenged the 34-year-old journalist to a fight, calling the rotund scribe "an over-stuffed pig" and offering to "settle this in my office." Malamud declined, and Alston eventually apologized—but not before threatening to break a tape recorder over the head of another writer who asked him about the confrontation.

Malamud wasn't the only one criticizing Alston in the press. Bill Buckner, the Dodgers' sweet-swinging left fielder, was angry about Alston batting him second in the lineup behind Lopes, and wasn't shy about mentioning it to local sportswriters. With his bushy mustache and caterpillar eyebrows, Buckner was a dead-ringer for Harry Reems, the porn actor who'd just been convicted in Tennessee in April for conspiracy to distribute obscenity across state lines, thanks to his appearance in 1972's massively popular *Deep Throat*; and just like Reems, Buckner felt he was being prevented from making full professional use of his stick. "By taking a lot of good pitches so Davey can steal, I waste my aggressiveness," Buckner complained. "Then I have to waste my consistency by trying to pull to the right side of the infield so he can go to third."

Hoping for a fresh start after the Reds' sweep, the Dodgers landed in Pittsburgh, and were promptly no-hit their first night there by Pirates lefty John Candelaria. A lanky 6′7″ 22-year-old from Brooklyn with scraggly locks, a heavy-lidded smile, and Cantinflas-style mustache wisps, "The Candy Man" looked more like the sort of college kid you'd see smoking a jay upstairs in the cheap seats at Three Rivers Stadium than a top-notch pitcher capable of dominating major league offenses. In fact, Candelaria had reportedly blown a tryout with the Dodgers several years earlier when he showed up wearing a

T-shirt emblazoned with a pot leaf and bearing the caption, "Try some, you'll like it." But on the evening of August 9, Candelaria gave the Dodgers ample reason to regret not signing him.

Each one of the 15,131 fans who attended that night's game—including 5,271 youngsters who were members of the Pirates' "Knothole Gang"—received a free candy bar as part of the team's "Candy Night" promotion, but the Candy Man delivered an even sweeter treat, striking out seven Dodgers and walking just one on only 101 pitches, and not allowing a single hit. It wasn't an effortless performance, however; Candelaria had to pitch out of a jam in the third after a walk to Steve Yeager and back-to-back errors by Frank Taveras and Bill Robinson loaded the bases, and sparkling defensive plays (including two running catches by right fielder Dave Parker) were required to keep his no-no intact. Dodger left fielder Lee Lacy almost broke it up in the top of the eighth when he led off the inning with a line drive back to the mound; Candelaria stopped it with his foot, then threw to first for the out. "Candy's size 13s saved him," Pirates catcher Duffy Dyer laughed afterward. "If he wears a size nine or 10, it might have gone right past him."

Candelaria later admitted that his legs were shaking when, with two outs in the ninth, Dodger shortstop Bill Russell popped one to short left-center. "I thought Russell's ball was going to fall in," he said. "I thought, 'What a way to lose it—on a bloop single!'" But Al Oliver, who'd made a tough play on a deep Davey Lopes fly to start the game, raced in to snare the ball just a fraction of a second before Frank Taveras could get there. "That's the fastest I've run all year," said Oliver. "It's lucky we didn't collide or somebody might have been killed."

The Pirates mobbed Candelaria on the mound, their striped gold pillbox hats bouncing up and down like giddy stacks of pancakes. It was only the fifth no-hitter in Bucs history, and the first scoreless no-hitter ever pitched by a Pirate in Pittsburgh; the last Buc to throw a no-hitter at home was Nick Maddox in 1907, but he'd allowed a run.

"This is something I've been dreaming about since I was five years old," admitted Candelaria, who seemed simultaneously overjoyed and freaked out by his feat. "I don't know if I'll come down. It's going to take a while to realize what happened." The pitcher immediately called his mom, who'd been watching the *Monday Night Baseball* broadcast from her Brooklyn home. "I'm sure my mother is drunk by now," he told reporters while dialing the phone, only to have her correct him— she was so nervous during the game's final innings, she'd been pounding Bromo-Seltzer instead. Candelaria's teammates gave him a champagne shower, but the Candy Man's celebration was just beginning. "I am going to go out and drink beer all night." He grinned. "I don't think anybody can blame me, either."

"We're at rock bottom now, I guess," said Steve Garvey after the Dodgers skulked off the field. "You can't do much worse than to be shut out and no-hit." Twelve nights later in Los Angeles, Don Sutton tried to return the favor, throwing seven and a third perfect innings against the Pirates before Dave Parker boomed a cannon shot into Dodger Stadium's right field pavilion. Manny Sanguillen doubled two batters later, but Sutton was able to wrap up his 15th victory of the season without further difficulty. "I never pitched a game in which I made more pitches in a good location as I did tonight," Sutton said afterward. "But I figured if I was going to get it, I had two awfully tough guys to get out—Dave Parker and Manny Sanguillen."

Candelaria's beer-drinking comment could have just as easily tumbled out of the mouth of Mark Fidrych—one could only imagine the trouble the Bird and the Candy Man might have gotten into as teammates—except that Fidrych wasn't able to pop a few cold ones in public anymore. Despite his stumbles in the All-Star Game, he emerged from the Midsummer Classic an even bigger star than before.

The last baseball player to capture the public imagination in a similar manner was Vida Blue during his Cy Young/MVP season in 1971; but as a moody, intimidating-looking black man, Blue's opportunities to cash in on his popularity were fairly limited. Fidrych, on the other hand, was white, with quirky charisma and cuddly charm to spare, and his appeal resonated well beyond the baseball world and across multiple generations, turning him into a pop-culture icon to rival Peter Frampton, John Travolta, and the Fonz.

By August, the Bird was mobbed every time he ventured out in public; even just stepping out the door of his apartment in Southgate, a bland and faceless Detroit suburb, he could easily draw a crowd. Fidrych was besieged by personal appearance requests and offers ranging from endorsements to TV cameos, which led to him inking a deal with the prestigious William Morris Agency, who would represent him in all non-baseball-related endeavors. In August, he filmed a small bit for an upcoming episode of Bill Cosby's ABC variety series, *Cos*, wherein he was featured alongside such special guests as Betty White, *Welcome Back, Kotter*'s Gabe Kaplan, and character actor Ted Cassidy, who appeared in the guise of "Bionic Bigfoot" from *The Six Million Dollar Man*. During the *Cos* shoot, Fidrych got into a shouting match with the show's director, who was critical of his line-reading abilities. "Hey man," Fidrych retorted, "this isn't my field. I'm a baseball player!"

On August 11, Fidrych and the Tigers beat Gaylord Perry and the Rangers 4–3, lifting his record to 13–4 (and leveling his ERA out at a league-leading 1.97). The same day, a short United Press International article titled "Will 'Bird' Fly Off to Hollywood?" ran in newspapers across the country, informing their readers that high-powered Hollywood producer and talent agent Allan Carr wanted Fidrych to play a supporting role in his upcoming film adaptation of *Grease*, the long-running Broadway musical. "If he can fill stadiums, he can fill theaters," drooled Carr, who insisted that he wasn't concerned about Fidrych's star dimming in the time it would take to complete and release the film. "He's got at least a two-year run," Carr predicted. Though he failed to sign Fidrych up for *Grease*, Carr managed to nab another big sports star of 1976 for his next project: Olympic decathlon gold medalist Bruce Jenner would make his silver screen debut as the male lead of *Can't Stop the Music*, a big-budget musical comedy featuring gay disco group the Village People.

In mid-August, the Beach Boys—currently riding high on the charts with their "oldies" album *15 Big Ones*—rolled into the Detroit area to play the Pine Knob Amphitheater, and invited Fidrych to one of their shows. The pitcher, whose listening habits tended to lean more toward the likes of the Grateful Dead, Peter Frampton, and Bad Company, accepted the invitation and shared a limo to the venue with Beach Boys front man Mike Love, who lectured him on the benefits of Transcendental Meditation. ("I could *see* it," Fidrych reflected later on the popular practice, "but I just, I'm not *into* it, y'know?") The Bird had his photo taken with the group for a spread in *CREEM*, the influential Detroit-based music magazine, and Beach Boys drummer Dennis Wilson invited him to come out onstage at the beginning of the concert and introduce them. Fidrych declined, opting instead to watch the show from the privacy of the lighting rig catwalk, with only a six-pack for company.

Fidrych hadn't even been in the big leagues for a full year, and already he was hobnobbing with rock stars and being considered for film roles. ABC even wanted to mic him up while he sat on the bench during a game telecast, just so the folks at home could hear the wacky impromptu things that emerged from the mouth of the

Bird. (Tigers skipper Ralph Houk, mindful of Fidrych's tendency to inadvertently pepper his conversation with obscenities even when he was being interviewed on camera, wisely nixed the idea.) Throw in the avalanche of "Bird" merchandising (T-shirts, buttons, iron-ons, posters, etc.), multiple musical tributes—including "The Bird," a lightly funky ditty by Canadian pop-rock duo Fanz, which included lines like "He really is different/And he talks with the ball"—and it was enough to make anyone's head spin.

And yet, Fidrych, who turned 22 on August 14, still seemed largely unfazed by the attention and adulation, and continued to pitch extremely well amid all of the insanity, even if he occasionally showed signs of mortality on the mound—like his 10th-inning meltdown against the Twins on August 21, when he hit "Disco" Dan Ford with the bases loaded, and then proceeded to give up three more runs on back-to-back hits by the Twins' two rising stars, catcher Butch Wynegar and center fielder Lyman Bostock. The loss brought Fidrych's record to 14–5, and elevated his ERA to a somewhat more mortal 2.22. But most of the time, he continued to live up to his reputation as the best and most exciting young pitcher in the game—like in his August 17 performance against the Angels, where he dueled Frank Tanana to a 3–2 win. Despite the fact that the Tigers were playing sub-.500 ball and sat a lowly 14 and a half games out of first place, 51,822 "Birdmania"-crazed fans showed up that night to watch the Bird soar, the largest Tiger Stadium crowd since 1970.

Most of Fidrych's starts had fallen on home games, but with Birdmania taking hold coast-to-coast, opposing general managers clamored for the Bird to bestow his personal brand of box-office magic upon their ballparks, as well. When Ralph Houk refused to reconfigure his rotation to accommodate their requests, some of the teams found other ways to capitalize on his fame. Though Fidrych wasn't scheduled to pitch in a late-August series against the Angels in Anaheim, the Angels organization attempted to boost their ticket sales by asking him to sign pregame autographs at Anaheim Stadium while sitting in a temporary "bird cage" erected to keep balls from hitting him during infield practice. Good-natured as ever, Fidrych went along with the scheme. "It ain't gonna hurt me," he reasoned. "What am I gonna be doin'? I'm just sittin' around. Maybe I'll get lucky and find a lady that comes through, you know?" But Fidrych's teammates were once again concerned that he was being exploited. "They said, you better not be doin' it for nothin'," he recalled later. "Because you're takin' *your* time . . . make sure you get somethin' out of it." The Angels gave Fidrych a small TV set in return for his signing services, and he pronounced himself satisfied with the arrangement.

In all, Fidrych would make 18 of his 29 starts in 1976 at Tiger Stadium, where 605,677 fans came to see him pitch. This meant that the Tigers averaged 33,649 per game when the Bird was perched on the mound, as opposed to 13,893 when he wasn't. In all, the Tigers would draw nearly 1.5 million fans for the season, good enough for the fourth-highest attendance figure in the league, and a sales jump of over 400,000 tickets from 1975. There was no question that Birdmania was largely responsible for the attendance boost, as well as for the extra money the Tigers were making in concessions when he pitched. Every time Fidrych took the mound at Tiger Stadium, it wasn't just a ballgame—it was a party, and a roof-raising one at that.

The celebratory mood surrounding Fidrych's starts at Tiger Stadium contrasted markedly with the despair that gripped the rest of Detroit's decaying East Side, where a vicious turf war between local gangs the Black Killers and the Errol Flynns was making life increasingly miserable for an already stressed populace. The situation came to an ugly head on August 15, when an estimated 200 members of both gangs crashed a Kool & The Gang concert at Cobo Arena and proceeded to rob concertgoers and beat them with umbrellas and the venue's folding chairs. The violence then spread outside, where several other victims were beaten and robbed, one woman was gang-raped, and at least two neighboring stores were vandalized. Sixty policemen were eventually called to quell the "mini-riot," as the papers described it, and 28 people were arrested and charged. The melee prompted Mayor Coleman Young to rehire 450 of the 913 city police officers who'd been recently laid off due to budget constraints; most of the rehired officers were to be redeployed as part of a special gang-fighting task force. The city also put a new curfew into place, which prohibited any youths 17 or younger from being on the streets after 10 p.m.

The violence on the Motor City's streets lent an undercurrent of poignancy to the jubilant lovefest vibe of Fidrych's Tiger Stadium starts. "I don't think it is Mark Fidrych the fans are cheering for so much," wrote *Detroit Free Press* columnist Joe Falls in an op-ed piece for the *Sporting News*. "I get the overpowering feeling the fans are really cheering for themselves. They see in this young man something that is good and exciting and alive. . . . These people are crying out for a better life, and at the moment they are getting it, vicariously, through the exploits of one young ballplayer." Falls pondered why Detroiters couldn't derive similar pleasure from the city's streets, parks, and cultural institutions, and suggested that "the answer is because none of these things are safe now; it is safe to come to the ballpark because of the numbers and . . . because everyone leaves at the same time.

"Detroit is no different than your city," Falls concluded. "We want all the good things here, too. It bothers me that we have to get it from such a strange source—a 22-year-old rookie pitcher. It's really all we have, though."

Like his curly-haired counterpart in Detroit, Randy Jones also came back to earth somewhat following the All-Star Game—most frighteningly on the night of August 4 when his car slammed into a telephone pole near his home in Poway, California. Jones and the rest of the Padres had just returned from a road trip through Houston, Cincinnati, and Atlanta, and the pitcher was driving home from the San Diego airport at the time of the accident. "Randy lost control of his car on a curve and the next thing he knew the telephone pole was sitting in the front seat," Randy's wife, Marie, told reporters the following day. "He has some minor glass cuts on his face and had stitches for a cut chin and two cuts on this neck."

Jones had gone 1–2 on the journey, including a heartbreaking 1–0 loss to the Braves on August 4, wherein he and Dick Ruthven matched scoreless inning for scoreless inning until the bottom of the ninth, when Jones gave up a run-scoring double to Jimmy Wynn. The loss put the Junkman's record at 18–6, and the prospects of him winning 30 games in 1976 were beginning to dim—all the more so after he lost the next four of his five starts following the accident. Jones finally notched his 20th win on August 27 at San Diego Stadium, where 21,301 fans watched him shut out the woeful Expos on six hits; with his pinpoint control recovered, Jones walked only one batter, needing just 92 pitches and 98 minutes to finish the deed. The first pitcher in either league to reach 20 victories, Jones was currently the odds-on favorite to win the NL Cy Young Award, an honor for which he'd been beaten out by Tom Seaver in 1975. "I'm not thinking about the Cy Young," he insisted after the game. "I've got at least 10 starts left and I'm planning on going out there and see if I can win all of them until I lose one."

In the middle of August, the Republican National Convention rolled into Kansas City. While the Democratic National Convention in July had chiefly functioned as both a coronation of nominee Jimmy

Carter and a chance for the Dems to demonstrate a renewed sense of purpose and unity after their fractious conventions of 1968 and 1972, the GOP gathering was essentially the final round in a months-long bare-knuckle brawl between Gerald Ford and Ronald Reagan.

Ford came into the convention having won 27 states and 53.3 percent of the popular vote in a grueling primary campaign, but he was still short of the 1,130 delegates he needed in order to carry the nomination. Reagan, meanwhile, had won impressively in several key states, most notably Texas and his home state of California; he could also boast staunch support from the GOP's conservative wing, which Ford had effectively alienated with his efforts to thaw the Cold War between the U.S. and the Soviet Union. Buttons bearing cartoon caricatures of the two candidates in Western wear and quick-draw holsters (along with the legend, "Shoot Out at Kansas City, Republican National Convention, 1976") were handed out to attendees; there were two versions—one for Ford supporters, showing the president in a white cowboy hat and Reagan in a black one, and the other for Reagan supporters with the hat coloring reversed.

More than a shootout, the convention almost turned into a full-scale civil war between the moderate and conservative Republicans, with Reagan supporters literally trying to drown out the other side with deafening blasts from their plastic horns. The matter of the nomination wasn't fully settled until the wee hours of August 19, when West Virginia governor Arch Alfred Moore Jr. crisply announced to the crowd at Kemper Arena that 20 of his state delegates had voted for Ford, as opposed to just eight for Reagan, a tally that put the president over the top with 1,135 delegate votes. For all his perceived clumsiness, Ford had run a more organized campaign than his challenger, while Reagan was widely judged to have hurt his shot at the nomination by announcing in advance that he'd chosen Pennsylvania senator Richard Schweiker as his prospective running mate; though the choice of the more moderate Schweiker was Reagan's attempt to curry favor with the party's moderate wing, it only succeeded in infuriating archconservatives like North Carolina senator Jesse Helms, who launched a last-minute campaign to draft conservative New York senator James L. Buckley as the presidential nominee.

Reagan's managers then further bungled his shot at the GOP nomination when they tried to enact a change in the convention rules that would have forced Ford (who'd thus far remained mum on the subject) to reveal his choice of running mate before the presidential balloting. The controversial rules change proposal was defeated by a vote of 1,180 to 1,069, giving the Ford campaign the additional momentum he needed with the delegates; upon receiving the GOP nomination, Ford announced that he'd chosen Kansas senator Bob Dole to replace departing Vice President Nelson Rockefeller. Reagan and Helms did leave a decidedly conservative mark on the party platform, however, managing to insert several planks that openly conflicted with Ford's stated policies—including a "Morality in Foreign Policy" provision which asserted that the U.S. had the moral obligation to secure and protect the God-given "unalienable rights" mentioned in the Declaration of Independence (such as "Life, Liberty and the pursuit of Happiness") in other nations.

Commissioner Bowie Kuhn was doing some frantic politicking of his own in August, spending a substantial amount of time testifying in Washington before the House Select Committee on Professional Sports, where he once again insisted that it was necessary for the health of the sport to keep baseball's antitrust exemption intact. The National League's refusal to follow the lead of the American League in terms of expansion had raised some congressional eyebrows, since it flew in the face of Kuhn's previous pledge to bring baseball back to the nation's capital. Kuhn reassured the congressmen that it was only a matter of time before the National League expanded to 14 teams, one of which would of course be placed in the nation's capital. (Neither Kuhn nor congress could have guessed at the time that it would be nearly another 30 years before major league baseball returned to the District of Columbia.)

In the meantime, the AL's two expansion teams were beginning to forge their respective identities. On August 12, the new Toronto franchise announced that their team had officially been named the Blue Jays, following a name-the-team contest that ran for five weeks and drew more than 30,000 entries, with suggestions for more than 4,000 different names. A panel of 14 judges, including 10 members of the local media, reduced the list to 10 names, and then turned it over to the team's board of directors for the final decision. "The Blue Jays was felt to be the most appropriate of the final ten names submitted," said the club's press release. "The blue jay is a North American bird. . . . It is strong, aggressive, and inquisitive. It dares to take on all comers yet is down-to-earth, gutsy, and good looking." More cynical observers believed that the name was chosen due to its implied connection with Labatt's Blue, the popular beer manufactured by the team's owners.

Two weeks later, the Seattle franchise announced that they'd be known henceforth as the Mariners, a name chosen by the club's directors from the results of a similar contest. The two teams would build their rosters in a November expansion draft, choosing five players apiece from each of the other AL teams' 40-man rosters; since each established club would only be allowed to protect 15 players, there was ample speculation about which players would be made available for the Blue Jays and Mariners to choose from.

Just days after vacating the hot seat in Washington, Kuhn placed himself in another uncomfortable position by casting a tie-breaking vote in favor of using the designated hitter in the upcoming World Series. The American League had adopted the DH in 1973, in a desperate bid to boost their teams' offensive output; but the senior circuit, which was in fine shape offensively, had shown no interest in adding the position. The three World Series played since then had been business as usual, with AL pitchers batting—and in some cases, like Ken Holtzman's 4-for-7 performance with three doubles over the 1973 and 1974 Fall Classics, actually hitting. But on August 12, with the two sides deadlocked on the issue during a meeting of major league owners in Phoenix, Kuhn settled the matter (at least for the time being) with a pro-DH vote. The designated hitter would be used in all games of the 1976 World Series, and in alternate years thereafter; in the meantime, Kuhn asked the major league presidents to appoint a six-member committee, three from each league, to find a permanent solution on the issue.

NL president Chub Feeney insisted that his league was "unanimously opposed" to the DH in any form, and that the commissioner had "forced the issue." Though there were rumors that two or three NL owners were leaning toward the use of the DH, the Reds and the Phillies—the two NL clubs that looked most likely to make it to the World Series—made it quite clear that they were unhappy with the ruling. "To me, it isn't baseball," declared Sparky Anderson. "If they're going to have designated hitters, why not go all the way [and] have offensive and defensive specialists and players who do nothing but pinch-run?" "All [Kuhn and the AL owners] think about is putting more offense in the game," complained Reds starting pitcher Gary Nolan. "Everything they do seems to favor the hitters." Joe Morgan acerbically commented that major leaguers should be "complete players," and cited the most controversial play of the 1975 World Series as an example of what the Fall Classic would lose if the DH was employed.

"What's the play everybody remembers?" he asked. "That's right, the Ed Armbrister bunt, when he and Carlton Fisk collided. If the DH rule had been in effect, Armbrister never would have gotten into the Series as a pinch-hitter for the pitcher."

Danny Ozark's discomfort with the DH addition was more pragmatic. "The National League is at a disadvantage with the DH because we haven't used one," he protested. "My fear is that our players won't be able to adjust to being DHs. It's a lot easier to come to bat when you've been in the field, been involved in the game situation. If you're the DH you have to know when to start getting prepared for your time at bat. I talked to Henry Aaron, and he said that it takes him 12 or 13 minutes to get ready, but that each hitter is different. I might wind up using Ollie Brown," he added. "At least he's used to pinch-hitting."

The Royals and Yankees, the two front-runners in the American League, were of course far more positively disposed to the change. When Kuhn cast his deciding vote on the issue, Hal McRae, the Royals' full-time DH, was in the midst of a seven-game hitting streak that boosted his average to a league-leading .358. Carlos May, the left-handed hitter Billy Martin generally alternated in the Yankees' DH slot with Lou Piniella, was positively overjoyed by the news. Having spent his entire career on the White Sox—despite accidentally blowing off part of his right thumb in 1969 while serving in the Marine Corps Reserve—the 28-year-old May was looking forward to finally playing October baseball; and now, thanks to the addition of the DH, there would be a place for him in the Yankees' starting World Series lineup. "That is the best news I've heard since May 18," said May, referring to the day he'd been traded to the Yankees for Ken Brett.

The Yankees entered August with a double-digit lead in the AL East, despite being in the midst of their first real skid of the season, which saw them go 4–11 from July 26 to August 9. The team's lead over the second-place Orioles never slipped below eight and a half games, however, and a 15–6 run from August 10 to the end of the month increased that margin to 11 and a half. Each victory seemed to produce a different hero: on August 10, Dock Ellis pitched 10 strong innings for his 12th victory of the year (and Sparky Lyle nabbed his 19th save) in an 11-inning 2–1 win over the Royals at Kansas City. Mickey Rivers hit the first inside-the-park home run in "new" Yankee Stadium history on August 16 in a 5–1 victory over Gaylord Perry and the Rangers, while Fred "Chicken" Stanley added a fence-clearer of his own off Perry—the first time the slap-hitting shortstop had homered in the big leagues since 1973. Two nights later, switch-hitting left fielder Roy White homered from both sides of the plate against the Rangers, with the second blast winning the game in the bottom of the ninth.

On August 25, when the Yankees came back from a 4–0 deficit to beat the Twins 5–4 in a 19-inning marathon in the Bronx, there were almost too many heroes to mention: Willie Randolph set an AL record for second basemen with 20 total chances in a game, while getting three hits, stealing two bases, scoring a run, and laying down a smooth sacrifice bunt in the bottom of the 19th that put Oscar Gamble in scoring position for Mickey Rivers's game-winning single off Tom Burgmeier. Dick "Dirt" Tidrow, the Yanks' gritty right-handed reliever, gave a whole new meaning to "long relief" by throwing 10 and two-thirds scoreless innings (and allowing only four singles) after starter Ed Figueroa left the game in the seventh. And Graig Nettles, the Yankees' power-hitting third baseman, crushed his 22nd round-tripper of the year, thus surpassing his entire home run total of 1975. After going into June hitting only .181 with just four homers and 13 RBIs, Nettles had caught fire; by the end of August, he had amassed 23 homers and 70 RBIs for the season, while raising his average to .244. He was also making great play after great play at the hot corner, bolstering his burgeoning reputation as one of the AL's best third basemen.

"I had more fun playing baseball than any time before or since," Nettles would recall of the summer of '76. "We had a set lineup, everyone knew what his role was, Billy was clearly in charge, and everything clicked like it was supposed to, and there were no roadblocks or distractions. . . . We were back in the Stadium, we had our fans back, and they were behind us all the way. We had a lot of laughs and the players were very close. We had a clique of Piniella, Munson, Catfish, Rivers, Randolph, Fred Stanley, Oscar Gamble, Carlos May, and myself, and Billy got along great with everybody."

Everybody, that is, except George Steinbrenner. Though their love-hate relationship wasn't yet as operatic as it would become, the two men constantly battled for control of the team, actively trying to demonstrate—to each other as well as the outside world—who was *really* responsible for the team's success. Martin and Steinbrenner fought over which light-hitting shortstop should be in the starting lineup (Martin liked Stanley, while Steinbrenner pushed for Jim Mason), which relievers Martin should use, what the batting order should be, and just about everything else.

"George was always calling the dugout," recalled Ed Figueroa, who beat Oakland 5–2 on August 30 to run his record to 16–7 with a 2.94 ERA. "He wanted to tell Billy what to do. But Billy always said that he's the manager and he's going to do whatever he wants." Martin became so infuriated during one call that he tore the phone off the dugout wall and slammed it to the floor, much to the amusement of his players. Undaunted, Steinbrenner simply rang for him on the trainer's office line instead.

The owner and the manager even clashed over the organ music at Yankee Stadium: Steinbrenner wanted ballpark organist Toby Wright to provide a steady stream of tuneful jollity throughout the game, while Martin was deeply annoyed by what he felt was a sonic intrusion upon the sanctity of the game's natural sounds and rhythms. Martin would often call upstairs to Wright and tell him to stop playing; but almost as soon as he stopped, Wright would get a phone call from Steinbrenner, ordering him to rev up the organ again.

Martin was in the process of negotiating a multiyear contract with Steinbrenner, and attempting to use the team's success as leverage for a better deal. But during an early August visit from the Tigers, Steinbrenner demonstrated a stronger negotiating hand by inviting the newly unemployed Dick Williams to share the owner's box at Yankee Stadium. Though Williams had just been fired by the Angels, he still had three American League pennants and two World Series championships on his managerial résumé, and Martin was well aware that Steinbrenner had already tried to hire him once before. "That was his way of trying to intimidate me, to let me know if I didn't do the job, someone else was waiting in the wings," Martin recounted in his autobiography. "It's the way he does business. It didn't intimidate me, but it sure made me madder than hell."

The stress of the situation caused Martin to drop 20 pounds from his already scrawny physique, and he began drinking even more than usual. He also began to panic, reacting to the team's late-July/early-August slump by shifting to a four-man rotation of Ellis, Doyle Alexander, Catfish Hunter, and either Figueroa or Holtzman for a few weeks. "Because George was beating on him, Billy wanted us to pitch on three days' rest instead of four," Ellis recalled. "I told him, 'I've never done that and never will.'" But when Catfish Hunter, the spiritual leader of the Yankees' staff, made it clear that he was okay with it, the other pitchers grudgingly agreed to go along with Martin's new rotation concept.

If life at the top of the AL East was one antacid tablet and glass of scotch after another for Martin, life at the top of the AL West seemed a relative breeze for Whitey Herzog. "The White Rat," as the genial Herzog was known (a reference to his shock of light blond hair, as opposed to any rodent-like personal qualities) led the Royals into August with a nine-game lead over the second-place A's; despite closing the month with a 6–8 road trip, his team still finished the month eight games up in the division. A combustible collection of what sportswriter Jim Kaplan termed "disgruntled veterans and confused younger players" when Herzog took the reins in mid-1975—"I held more meetings than Henry Kissinger my first month here," the skipper joked to Kaplan—the Royals had been transformed into a harmonious and hard-playing outfit. "This is a happy place to be," said George Brett of the Kansas City clubhouse.

Brett and McRae were clearly the heart of the offense. "Two guys you never have to worry about," said Herzog. "If McRae and Brett aren't too banged up to play, you put their names in the lineup and go from there." Though McRae wasn't running well, thanks to a deep pull of his thigh muscle suffered while stealing a base in mid-July, the injury actually seemed to improve his hitting, prompting Herzog to call the 31-year-old DH "the best one-legged hitter I've ever seen." With McRae's batting average hovering in the .350s throughout August and Brett hitting in the .340s, there was much talk of the two teammates competing for the AL batting crown, though that wasn't a subject either man wanted to dwell on. "George and I aren't in a contest," McRae insisted. "We pull for each other. This kind of talk about titles doesn't help either one of us. It would be stupid for me to not pull for George. I'm an RBI man. I want to see George get on ahead of me. I'd rather get a World Series check than the batting title." Brett agreed. "Why should I be concerned about anything except us winning?" asked the 23-year-old third baseman.

"I'd rather have Mac drive me in and win games. Our objective is to win the pennant for Kansas City."

Brett hit third in the Royals lineup and McRae hit fifth, sandwiching Big John Mayberry in the cleanup spot. Though Mayberry was in the midst of a disappointing year—the man who'd crushed 34 homers in 1975 only had 13 to his credit through the end of August—he was still among the team leaders in runs batted in. In fact, the Royals almost seemed to take pride in winning despite their lack of power. As of August 31, the team was on pace to finish the season with 71 homers in 162 games; the legendarily light-hitting AL champion "Go-Go" White Sox, by comparison, had poled 97 in 154.

"We have to scratch for everything we can get," said Herzog, but the Royals were good at scratching, thanks to a lineup that largely consisted of contact hitters who had enough speed to take an extra base and enough savvy to know how to steal one. Well on their way to setting a franchise record for swipes with 218 (though they would also set a franchise mark by getting caught 106 times), Herzog's players relished their ability to break a game open with their speed and aggressiveness. On August 17, with the Royals and Indians tied 3–3 in the bottom of the 10th, Brett stroked a one-out single to left off Tribe reliever Dave LaRoche. LaRoche got Mayberry, the next batter, to go down swinging—but Brett stole second on strike three, then advanced to third when the throw from catcher Rick Cerone sailed into center field. Dave Nelson, who'd come into the game in the eighth inning as a pinch-runner for the still gimpy McRae, stepped into the right-hand batter's box against LaRoche. Brett watched the lefty deliver two pitches to Nelson; then, on the third, he took off running.

"After the first pitch I knew I could steal home because [Laroche] wasn't looking at me," said Brett, after he slid safely across the plate to win the game. "On the next pitch I checked things out a little more, and then I took off." "I was going to get the game-winning hit, but George took care of that," laughed Nelson, who'd just stolen home nine days earlier against Blue Moon Odom and the White Sox. "We didn't get to first place by standing around," said Herzog.

The A's hadn't been doing much standing around either, but Chuck Tanner's speed-crazy Oakland squad hadn't been within sniffing distance of first place since the end of April—and losing six straight at the end of July and the beginning of August didn't help matters. "It's a disaster," fumed Charlie Finley on August 3, as his team slipped to third behind the Twins with an unimpressive 53–52 record. "I don't even know if I want to go out and see them play. When you're a fan, you can laugh at this. But when you're an owner, all you can do is cry."

A's players had long been numb to Finley's tirades, so it was probably just coincidental that the team started playing what Tanner termed "our best ball of the season" immediately thereafter, rattling off a nine-game win streak and going 17–9 for the rest of the month. The team kept on running, breaking the Athletics' single-season franchise record of 258 steals with two swipes during a 8–7 ninth-inning win over the Red Sox on August 15, but they were also winning with strong pitching (Vida Blue completed six of his seven starts in August, winning four of them, including a 3–0 shutout of the Orioles on August 23) and the long ball (Sal Bando, Phil Garner, Joe Rudi, and Gene Tenace all clubbed home runs in a 13–8 slugfest against the Angels on August 8). The A's August surge only pulled them within eight games of the Royals by the end of the month, but it was enough to get the team (and their owner) excited about their September prospects.

"Kansas City is looking over their shoulders," crowed Finley. "They can put it up on a big sign in their clubhouse: 'Finley Says

Kansas City Is Going to Choke.'" Starting pitcher Mike Torrez, who improved his record to 10–10 with two wins in August while lowering his ERA to 2.92, was likewise skeptical of the Royals' ability to hold on to first place. "They always could get an American Legion plague or something," he joked.

Bill Veeck failed to bring winning baseball to the South Side in the summer of '76, but he did deliver innovation and amusement. In addition to his endless procession of "Ethnic Night" celebrations, on-field beer-case-stacking contests, and giveaway promotions—like "Ragtime Night," where he gave away 10,000 copies of E. L. Doctorow's best-selling novel—Veeck also installed a shower in Comiskey Park's center field bleachers, and convinced boozed-up Sox broadcaster Harry Caray to lead the crowd in a sing-along of "Take Me Out to the Ball Game" during the seventh-inning stretch of every home game. The latter would become a time-honored Chicago tradition, while the former instantly entered Comiskey lore. "It had a utilitarian function," Veeck would later say of the shower. "It gets hot out there and people like to cool off. But it also attracts a number of young girls in bathing suits, and a certain number of young men who like to look at girls in bathing suits. People in the suburbs aren't going to say, 'Let's go to a game today because there's a shower in the bleachers,' but we create the impression that we are going to have some fun."

Indeed, fun was of utmost priority when it came to fielding a team whose innate lousiness was on display daily. By the end of the first week in August, with the Sox already 20 games out of first and struggling to stay out of the AL West cellar like an infant labors to lift its head off the surface of its crib, Veeck knew it was finally time to pull out the Bermuda shorts.

On July 4, *Chicago Tribune* sports columnist Bob Verdi reported that the shorts, so infamously introduced in March, had finally arrived at the ballpark, and that Veeck was just waiting for the right moment to have his team suit up in them. For the most part, the players seemed amused by the idea of the navy blue shorts, if not unanimously excited about actually playing in them. "Hope they give us a little notice, so I can buy some Nair," Goose Gossage told Verdi. "I'm not going to wear short pants unless they let me wear a halter top, too," cracked second baseman Jack Brohamer. Others, however, were decidedly into it. "I got the nicest thighs you ever saw," bragged first baseman and designated hitter Lamar Johnson. "I can't wait!"

The Sox shorts (and the accompanying knee socks with sliding pads) made their major league debut in the first game of the team's August 8 home doubleheader against the Royals, who found the spectacle of their Bermudas-clad opponents to be the very epitome of hilarity. "You guys are the sweetest team yet," hooted John Mayberry to Sox center fielder Ralph Garr as the "Road Runner" strode to the plate. "You get over to first base and I'm going to give you a big kiss."

The Kansas City players soon lived to regret their heckling—they lost the game 5–2, becoming the first team in major league history to be beaten by a team wearing short pants. Royals starting pitcher Marty Pattin and catcher Buck Martinez, clearly not expecting the bare-legged Sox to run, were victimized for five stolen bases, including the first-ever career steal by catcher Jim Essian and the first steals of the season by right fielder Jerry Hairston and Brohamer; the latter also delivered a key two-out single in the bottom of the sixth. Garr, for the record, made it to first twice on a pair of singles, though Mayberry unaccountably reneged on his offer to go to first base with the Road Runner.

The White Sox changed back into long pants for the second game, and lost 7–1. Only 15,997 fans bore witness to the shorts' debut, but Veeck got enough press out of the stunt that he decided to bring them back for a weekend series against the Orioles in late August. He'd promised NBC that his team would don the shorts for their August 21 game, which had been scheduled as the network's backup for their *Game of the Week* broadcast, and he put the word out in the local media that the shorts would also, weather permitting, make an appearance in the first game of the team's August 22 doubleheader. With an impressive Saturday crowd of 32,607 looking on, the White Sox beat the O's 11–10 in a raucous 12-inning affair; Brohamer hit a home run off Rudy May in the second inning, becoming the first shorts-wearing player to homer in a major league game. The luck of the shorts wore off on Sunday, though, as Jim Palmer beat the Sox 6–2 for his 17th victory.

That would be it for the White Sox shorts; disappointed by the smaller Sunday crowd of 16,991, and even more so by the lack of mentions the shorts received in the local papers' postgame write-ups, Veeck surmised that their novelty had worn off, and it was time to put his fashion innovation away. The Bermudas would reappear in 1977, however—the Topps '77 White Sox team card would feature a photo snapped at Comiskey of the entire '76 squad in shorts. A humorous memento of the Veeck years, the card triggered a false memory syndrome for more than a few traumatized White Sox fans, who would forever remain convinced that their team had once worn shorts for the entire season.

10.

Don't Go Breaking My Heart

(September 1976)

It all happened in little more than the blink of an eye: one moment, Steve Yeager was loosening up in the on-deck circle at San Diego Stadium; the next, the Dodger catcher was lying on his back, bleeding profusely with part of a baseball bat sticking out of his throat.

The September 6 contest between the Dodgers and the Padres had originally been notable for its pitching matchup between Don Sutton and Randy Jones, both of whom were in top contention for the NL Cy Young trophy. But for anyone who witnessed Yeager squirming in agony in the San Diego dirt, the other details of the game (including the final 4–1 score, and the four-hit complete game performance that gave Sutton his 18th win of the season) quickly receded in significance.

The freak accident that felled Yeager occurred in the top of the seventh. Dodger shortstop Bill Russell stepped to the plate to lead off the frame, and Yeager—an excellent defensive backstop whose .215 batting average consigned him to the eighth spot in the Los Angeles lineup—casually strolled out of the dugout behind him. After taking a few warm-up swings, Yeager knelt down in the on-deck circle, and turned his attention to the stands, where his new bride, Gloria, was sitting. Jones threw Russell a pitch that was slightly inside; the shortstop hit it off the handle, shattering his bat and sending the business end of it sailing toward Yeager, who never saw it coming. The jagged end of the broken bat stabbed the catcher in the left side of his neck, just above the collarbone, knocking him to the ground like a bull felled by a matador's sword. Yeager's teammates gathered around him, gaping in horror. "The first thing I heard Steve say was, 'I think I've broken my shoulder,'" said Dodger skipper Walter Alston, who rushed to Yeager's side along with team trainer Bill Buhler. "And he was bleeding so much. . . . Lord, it was an ugly sight. His neck looked like someone took a thumb and just pushed a hole in it."

Twenty tense minutes passed before an ambulance arrived at the ballpark. Yeager was rushed to the hospital, where it was determined that no bones had been broken; but his esophagus had been punctured, and multiple splinters from the bat were still lodged in his neck. It took over 90 minutes on the operating table to remove the splinters and close his wounds, but it could have been much worse—miraculously, Russell's bat missed a major artery in Yeager's neck by just a fraction of an inch. "Doctors said afterwards I was lucky to be alive," Yeager recalled. "The doctor who operated on me to remove the splinters, all from a half-inch to three-quarters of an inch long, said a difference in location of any of them by a quarter of an inch or so could have killed me."

With his wavy, sun-bleached hair, ruggedly handsome visage, and tinted aviator shades, Yeager looked like the quintessential L.A. playboy, and had a reputation for playing the part off the field. But between his recent marriage and his sudden brush with death, the 27-year-old catcher realized that it was time to start taking life at a more measured and contemplative pace, though his on-field approach would remain as intense as ever. The cousin of highly decorated Air Force test pilot Chuck Yeager—who in 1947 became the first man to break the sound barrier—Yeager demonstrated that toughness and resilience ran in the family when he returned to duty less than three weeks later, despite still feeling some pain in the puncture area and experiencing numbness in his fingers due to nerve damage. Yeager saw his first post-accident action on September 25, coming in as a defensive substitute in the eighth inning of a home game against the Reds. Joe Morgan immediately tested Yeager by trying to steal second base, but the newly recuperated catcher gunned him down—only the ninth time in 67 attempts that "Little Joe" had been caught stealing all year.

Concerned that a foul ball to the neck might aggravate Yeager's wound, Buhler worked with the catcher to create a protective plastic shield that would hang loosely from the bottom of his mask. Officially introduced in 1977, the Steve Yeager Throat Protector—or the "King Tut flap," as it was humorously dubbed, in reference to the ceremonial mummy beards seen in the traveling "Treasures of Tutankhamun" exhibition that reached American museums in November '76—would become standard equipment for major league backstops and umpires.

While Yeager was fighting for his life on September 6, a significant number of Philadelphia fans and sportswriters were calling for the Phillies to be given their last rites. Up by 15 games over the Pirates as of August 26, the team had mystifyingly plunged into a full-on nosedive. Beginning with a 4–1 loss to the Reds on August 27, they dropped eight straight, including three straight one-run decisions. The Phillies' lineup, which had been hitting like the Reds for most of the year, was suddenly rivaling the Expos for futility at the plate. "We're not getting that key hit, the double with men on first and second," Mike Schmidt explained to Sports Illustrated's Larry Keith.

"A lot of guys, including myself, are going for that whole ball of wax to break us out of it, but we're only becoming easy outs."

Larry Christenson broke the skid on September 5, scattering eight Mets hits in eight and a third innings, while also compensating for the team's recent power outage by blasting two massive home runs off Mickey Lolich in the 3–1 victory. But the Phils lost both ends of a doubleheader the next day in Pittsburgh, and lost again to the resurgent Pirates (who'd won 13 out of their last 14) on September 8, shrinking their lead in the NL East to a mere four and a half games. Formerly flush with the excitement of what had seemed like an easy ride to their first flag since 1950, Phillies fans were now seized by nightmarish flashbacks of 1964, when their team spent most of the season in first place before blowing a six-and-a-half-game lead to the Cardinals in the last two weeks of September. As the fans (and some of the players) began to panic, the once festive atmosphere at the Vet turned tense and ugly.

"A nightmare," was how Mike Schmidt would later describe it. "The hate mail, the letters saying we were choking, the abuse. I'd be out there trying to catch a tough grounder, thinking that what I did would decide whether we'd be 2½ in front the next day or 4½. 'Blow this one,' I'd think, 'and I'll need cops to guard my house.'"

"All the talk about '64 makes a lot of our players uneasy," lamented Tug McGraw to *New York Times* columnist Dave Anderson. "That was another team, not this team. But it's still part of our history." Backup infielder Tony Taylor, who had been the starting second baseman on that infamous '64 squad, agreed. "This team is not like the '64 team," he insisted. "That year we had only two pitchers, Jim Bunning and Chris Short, and only two guys who could hit the ball out of the ballpark, Johnny Callison and Dick Allen."

Allen was the only player other than Taylor on the '76 Phillies roster who had witnessed the '64 "phlop" firsthand. Along with Jim

Kaat, Dave Cash, and Garry Maddox, Allen and Taylor took the floor at a closed-door clubhouse meeting before a September 12 home game against the Cubs, and attempted to talk their fellow players off the ledge. "I was a guy who had been there, and I *knew* this wasn't '64," Allen later recalled. "We were just tired. I knew our talent would surface in time. With Schmidt, Bull, and me in the lineup, things weren't going to stay quiet for long."

The team then went out and beat the Cubs 8–0, with Christenson and McGraw holding Chicago scoreless on six hits. The Phillies then won two against the Expos, only to lose two more to the Pirates at the Vet, followed by a frustrating 4–3 extra inning loss to the Cubs at Wrigley Field on the afternoon of September 17. The Phillies were now only three games ahead of the Bucs, with 16 left to play.

Danny Ozark was completely beside himself. "I could throw things around the clubhouse, but what good would that do?" the Phillies skipper moaned to reporters after the Cubs loss. "I'm the most helpless person in the world under the circumstances. I just can't do anything about it. Anything you can think about has happened in the last few weeks." Ozark's rival, Pirates manager Danny Murtaugh, was feeling cautiously optimistic. "I've always thought that there were three main facets of baseball—pitching, hitting, and fielding," he mused while gnawing on a postgame spare rib following a September 17 win over the Mets, which gave the Pirates 18 victories in their last 22 contests. "About a month ago, we started putting them together. But we still have pressure on us every game. We have to do a lot of winning and the Phillies can lose a few more games."

Over in Kansas City, the Royals' grip on the AL West was becoming as precarious as the Phillies' on the NL East. "We're playing like we're scared to win," griped an exasperated Whitey Herzog, shortly before his team was shut out 2–0 by Angels hurlers Gary Ross and Dick Drago on September 8, the Royals' 10th loss in their past 12 games. The Royals bounced back the next night with a 6–5 win over the Angels—during which Freddie Patek scored the tying run in the bottom of the ninth on an errant pickoff play at third, and George Brett drove in the winning run in the bottom of the 10th with his fifth single of the game—then got blown out 18–3 by the Twins in Minnesota on September 10, dropping their division lead to five games. By September 15, the A's had cut it to three and a half.

During the past five seasons, the A's had literally fought their way to five AL West titles (not to mention three World Championships), battling each other, their managers, and their penny-pinching, endlessly meddlesome owner in the process. While the 1976 season had seen Charlie Finley make several attempts to dismantle his green-and-gold dynasty—and alienate his players to the point that several Oakland stars were actively looking forward to playing elsewhere in 1977—the surviving members of the Mustache Gang weren't about to let another team take the division for the first time since 1970 without a climactic gunfight.

"We're three-time world champions," Gene Tenace told the *Oakland Tribune*'s Ron Bergman. "We play for pride. We want to win this thing to show Mr. Finley that he's made a big mistake. He's torn this ball club up. I know I won't be around [after this season]. I've pretty much made a firm commitment not to play here anymore because of the way I've been treated. Well, if you go, you might as well go out a winner."

"I'm really surprised that we're this close considering all that's happened," added Joe Rudi, noting that the team's cut-rate travel itineraries—which typically involved no-frills commercial flights with multiple connections—were hardly conducive to winning. "All Charlie's interested in doing is saving money and making money," Rudi continued. "You can see he's not interested in winning."

Finley denied such charges, angrily telling the Oakland press that his players were "not going to win in spite of me, they're going to win *because* of me." And yet, his baffling personnel moves seemed designed to make the task of winning the West as challenging as possible. On August 30, Finley purchased the contract of Willie McCovey from San Diego. One of the most feared power hitters of the '60s and early '70s, the 38-year-old "Stretch" was currently in the midst of the worst season of his career, hitting only .203 with seven home runs and 36 RBIs and losing his first base job to 25-year-old Padres utility man Mike Ivie. The A's were already well stocked at first (Don Baylor and Gene Tenace had been handling the bag for most of the season, with help from veteran utility man Ken McMullen) and they already had another aging future Hall of Famer in their left-handed DH slot—38-year-old Billy Williams—although the once-sweet-swinging gentleman from Whistler, Alabama, was hitting only .211 with 11 homers and 40 RBIs at the beginning of September.

"The reason for getting McCovey was for getting us to the play-offs," insisted Finley, who then contradicted himself by trying to sell Sal Bando—the captain and emotional center of the team, who was currently leading the AL with 24 homers—to the Rangers via waivers. The transaction fell through when the Rangers balked at Bando's request for a four-year, $600,000 contract, but Finley's attempt to palm Bando off to a team that had already been all but eliminated from the pennant race was clearly intended as one final insult to a player he'd publicly denigrated for years.

McCovey seemed understandably confused by his new situation in Oakland, but—as befit a man who favored silver Cadillacs and white patent-leather loafers off the field—he played it cool. "To be honest with you, I don't know if they want me beyond this last month," he told Ron Bergman, adding that, "I was hoping to come back to the Bay Area, but to the other side. That was my secret dream." Still, the former Giants icon was profoundly moved by the standing ovations he received from the Coliseum faithful during his first game in Oakland. "It just felt good to be around some people who appreciate my ability," he enthused. "It did a lot for my morale." But two weeks later, with McCovey hitting .182 for the A's with no extra base hits or RBIs, Finley purchased the contract of yet another veteran left-handed first baseman: 38-year-old Ron Fairly, obtained from the Cardinals. The effect of the Fairly transaction upon McCovey's morale went unrecorded.

As veteran ballplayers went, Williams, McCovey, and Fairly were all veritable spring chickens compared to Saturnino Orestes Armas "Minnie" Minoso, the 53-year-old first base coach of the Chicago White Sox. The first dark-skinned Latin American player to make the majors, Minoso got his first cup of coffee in 1949 with the Indians and became a White Sox star (and the team's first minority player) as a rookie in 1951. Minoso hadn't played in the majors since 1964, but was active well into his 40s in the Mexican League, and Veeck had been scheming about a way to put Minoso back into the lineup ever since he'd hired him to join the coaching staff in January. On September 10, after a week of rumors that he would soon be returning to action, Minoso was officially activated as a player.

The return of fan-favorite Minoso was just Veeck's latest stunt to drum up ticket sales and local media attention for a team that had effectively staked its claim to last place in the AL West, but the "Cuban Comet" happily played along. "It's a new generation, but it's still baseball," he told reporters. "I don't think they'd ask me to play if they didn't think I could still hit." "I would speak out against [Minoso's reactivation] if we were in a pennant race," White Sox skipper Paul Richards admitted. "But I'm not so sure he can't still hit, either. He's looked great in batting practice, although that may not mean anything."

The White Sox were scheduled to face Nolan Ryan and the Angels at Comiskey on September 10, but Richards and Veeck knew better than to send Minoso to the plate against "The Ryan Express." Ryan wound up fanning 18 White Sox hitters and walking nine that night while improving his record to 13–17, and might have set a new MLB single-game strikeout record if Minoso had been in the lineup. Instead, the South Siders' newest and oldest DH made his debut the next day, batting ninth and going 0-for-3 with one strikeout against Frank Tanana, who cruised easily to his 16th win. On September 12, however, Minoso managed to knock a single off of Sid Monge in the second inning of Chicago's 2–1 victory in the first half of a Sunday doubleheader, making him the oldest player to hit safely in the majors at the time—though he would be downgraded to fourth-oldest many years later, after admitting that he'd padded his age by three years as a young man in order to join the Cuban army.

Like Bill Veeck's White Sox, Ted Turner's Braves finished out the season at the bottom of their division. Their average sales increase of nearly 3,500 tickets per home game bore ample testament to the effectiveness of Turner's and Bob Hope's promotional flair, though attendance at Atlanta–Fulton County Stadium dwindled abysmally during the final month of the season; only 970 people, the lowest number to watch a major league game all year, showed up for a Tuesday twi-night doubleheader against the Astros on September 14.

Five days later, Turner held an impromptu press conference to announce that he'd named Bill Lucas as the Braves' director of player personnel, making the 40-year-old Lucas—who first joined the team's front office in 1965 as an assistant farm director—the first African American to assume general manager–type duties for a major league club. Turner, however, declined to give Lucas the official GM title, "because I'm a lot more active [in personnel matters] than most owners and I intend to stay that way."

Hank Aaron's first wife was Barbara Lucas, Bill's sister; and though Hank and Bill's friendship had been strained by Hank and Barbara's 1971 divorce, plenty of mutual professional respect remained between the two men. This boded well for the future, as Turner was telling any reporter who would listen that he had his sights set on hiring Hank for a front office position with the Braves upon the Home Run King's retirement. "I've got a contract with the Brewers," Hank demurred. "Anything I have to say will come from my attorney. Other than that, no comment." But Hank was interested, knowing that Turner—unlike the Braves' previous owners—intended to give him a position with "real teeth," as opposed to the sort of honorary, do-nothing gig that most teams preferred to bestow upon their retired legends.

But job interviews with the Braves would have to wait until the season was over. On September 17, the AL East basement-dwelling Brewers bid Hank a formal farewell with "A Salute to Hank Aaron Night" at County Stadium. The team's largest turnout since Opening Day—40,383 fans—converged upon the Milwaukee ballpark to join such distinguished guests as President Ford, Commissioner Kuhn (who'd been conspicuously absent on the evening of April 8, 1974, when Aaron broke Babe Ruth's all-time home run record in Atlanta), Mickey Mantle, Willie Mays, Ernie Banks, and Aaron's former Braves teammates Warren Spahn and Eddie Mathews for a pregame pageant of testimonial speeches and standing ovations. Brewers owner and president Bud Selig announced that Aaron's number 44 would be retired after the season, and Hammerin' Hank's teammates presented him with the gag gift of a demolition derby car with the price of "44 Cents" scrawled on the windshield. "755 Home Runs," someone had painted on the side. "Who Cares—How Many Strikeouts?"

Despite the Brewers' welcome injection of humor, there was no ignoring the sense of melancholy that pervaded the event. "This is the end for me," Aaron told the crowd. "This is one of the saddest

times of my life, to reach the age when I have to bow out of baseball." Like Willie Mays before him, Aaron had stretched his brilliant
career out just a tad too far, as his depressing final-season numbers
(.229 batting average with 10 homers and 35 RBIs) would forever attest. "I have a lot of regrets about my home run production, my batting
average, this season and last," he told reporters, "but there's nothing
I can do about them."

The Brewers fans cheered mightily every time Aaron strode to the
plate that night, then groaned each time he made an out; instead of
giving them one more fence-clearer to remember, he went 0-for-5
as the Brewers lost 5–3 to the Yankees in 11 innings. Aaron didn't
hit safely in front of Milwaukee fans again until October 3, the last
day of the season, when he singled up the middle off the Tigers' Dave
Roberts in his final major league at-bat. It was the 3,771st hit of his
storied career, and his 2,297th RBI—no one in MLB history had hit
more home runs (755), knocked more extra-base hits (1,477) or collected more total bases (6,856) than Henry Aaron, and no one had
driven in more runs, either. Though it was only the sixth inning,
Brewers manager Alex Grammas sent rookie Jim Gantner in to pinch-
run for Aaron at first base, ensuring that he received the send-off he
deserved from the fans at County Stadium, who saluted the departing
icon with one more standing ovation as he walked off the field.

On September 18, the day after Aaron's official going-away party
in Milwaukee, Frank Robinson sent himself up to the plate in Cleveland to pinch-hit for shortstop Frank Duffy, and proceeded to stroke
a two-out, two-on, run-scoring single off the Orioles' Rudy May. It
was the 2,943rd hit of Robinson's career, his 1,812th RBI, and his
11,742nd and final plate appearance. After batting only .224 with
three home runs and 10 RBIs in 36 games, Robinson would be invited
back to Cleveland for 1977—but only as manager and at a substan-
tially reduced salary from the $200,000 he earned as player-manager

in 1976. Robby retired as a player with 586 home runs, at that point the fourth-highest total in major league history. He wouldn't reach 3,000 hits, but his Hall of Fame credentials were already more than assured.

"Mark Fidrych asks me to thank you for your good wishes and return your [amount]," read the form letter on Detroit Tigers stationery. "The Tigers also thank you for your interest." Tigers public relations director Hal Middlesworth was sending out as many as twenty of these letters a day to fans in Michigan and elsewhere who'd taken it upon themselves to supplement the Bird's meager rookie salary via a grassroots "Bucks for the Bird" campaign. Singles and five-spots arrived on a daily basis, along with cards and letters thanking the young pitcher for bringing joy and fun back to the game; Fidrych also received a blank check made out to him from a bank in Mount Carmel, Pennsylvania, and a donation from a hippie identifying himself as "The Mad Green," who extended an open invitation for the Bird to come and roost sometime at his Bay Area commune. All of the gifts were dutifully returned; Fidrych—whose initial reaction to this sudden influx of outside funding was "Whoa! I can go out and get drunk tonight and have a good time!"—was talked out of keeping the money by Ralph Houk. "You don't need it," the Tiger skipper told him, warning that there could also be unforeseen conflicts of interest involved in pocketing monetary gifts from fans.

As the Bird's star had risen, his pitching had begun to come back to earth. From the All-Star break to the end of the 1976 season, Fidrych went 10–7 with a 2.72 ERA in 18 starts—still very good, but nowhere near as magical as his first 11 starts. He continued to show flashes of brilliance, like his nine-hit 6–0 shutout of the Yankees at Yankee Stadium on September 12. Asked afterward by a New York reporter why he tossed the ball back to the home plate umpire after giving up each of those nine hits, Fidrych replied, "Well, that ball had a hit in it, so I want it to get back in the ball bag and goof around with the other balls there. Maybe it'll learn some sense and come out as a pop-up next time."

But there were also times when the ball flatly refused to do his bidding. On September 17, the Bird once again faced off against Luis Tiant—whose 21-win campaign was one of the few consistent bright spots for the beleaguered Red Sox in '76—only to be sent to the showers in the third inning after allowing Boston seven runs (six earned) on seven hits and two walks. It was his worst outing of the season.

Perhaps opposing batters were starting to figure him out, or maybe the accumulated pressure from his high-profile rookie campaign—the endless promotional appearances (he did signings at Detroit-area grocery stores and Little Caesars pizza franchises), the visits to hospitals and schools, and the constant attention from fans, groupies, and the media—was simply starting to take its toll. "It's a weird scene," he admitted to *Detroit Free Press* sportswriter Jim Hawkins. "You win a few baseball games and all of a sudden you're surrounded by reporters and TV men with cameras asking you about Vietnam and race relations and stuff like that. I don't even know who I am yet."

In September, *Go Bird Go!*, an unauthorized Fidrych bio penned by Hawkins and fellow *Freep* correspondent Jim Benagh, was rush-released by Dell Publishing to capitalize upon the pitcher's sudden celebrity. Lawyers from the William Morris Agency countered with a cease-and-desist letter, charging that the book invaded Fidrych's "personal and property rights," but the book stayed on the shelves, selling over 75,000 copies in its first month. Aside from not receiving a cut of the royalties, Fidrych was particularly miffed that *Go Bird Go!*—which was reportedly bashed out in about two weeks—

contained incorrect information about his upbringing. "If they had asked me," he ruefully reflected later, "I would have told them everything."

But even while *Go Bird Go!* was topping the best-seller lists at Michigan bookstores, and the Tigers' wives were preparing to auction off some of the Bird's freshly clipped locks at a charity fundraiser, the novelty of watching Mark Fidrych in action seemed to be wearing off for Tigers fans: only 7,147 of them were in the stands when the Bird beat the Indians 5–3 on September 21, his last home start of the season. Fidrych shut out the Indians in Cleveland on September 28, then beat the Brewers 4–1 in Milwaukee on October 2, finishing the season with a 19–9 record and a league-leading 2.34 ERA—pretty good for a rookie who hadn't started his first game until the middle of May.

September was also a challenging month for Randy Jones. The prolific Junkman went 2–4 with a 3.57 ERA in seven starts—including two one-run losses, bringing his total of narrow defeats to seven for the year—while dealing with the aftermath of a *San Diego Union* interview in which the usually self-effacing Padres lefty had admitted to being more inwardly confident about his pitching abilities than he'd previously revealed. Though quotes like "I thought all along that I had a chance to win 30 games this year" were hardly inflammatory in their honesty, they still triggered a flood of hate mail from San Diego fans who angrily accused Jones of being fake and deceitful; some even said that they were now rooting for him to lose. "I'm sorry to see him getting this kind of reaction," said Padres pitching coach Roger Craig. "If people knew what he was really like, well, they would be embarrassed about saying some of those things."

The angry Padres fans should have also been embarrassed about overlooking the incredible mound show that Jones had put on for them all season. In addition to tying Christy Mathewson's walk-less streak in 1976, Jones also set an NL record for pitchers by handling 112 total chances without making an error, and tied another NL record by participating in 12 double plays. Jones set the NL fielding record on September 28, when he successfully handled a grounder off the bat of Bill Plummer in the second inning of a game against the Reds at San Diego Stadium; unfortunately, it would also be his last play of the season. While throwing a slider to the next batter, Cesar Geronimo, Jones felt something snap in his left biceps; he came out of the game two pitches later with his arm looking, in his words, "like a flat tire." A torn biceps tendon was the initial diagnosis; exploratory surgery would later reveal that a nerve attached to the tendon had been severed.

Jones was done for the year, but he finished 1976 with a league-leading 22 wins (against 14 losses) and a 2.74 ERA, as well as league-topping totals in the starts (40), complete games (25), innings pitched (315.1), and batters faced (1,251) departments; he also led the NL in hits with 274, but made up for it by walking a mere 50 batters. And by fanning only 93 batters, he'd become the first NL pitcher since Johnny Sain in 1950 to win 20 games in a season while recording fewer than 100 strikeouts. The Junkman had pitched himself a gem of a season.

For John "The Count" Montefusco, the third in the season's trinity of charismatic, curly-haired hurlers, the final start of 1976 was the sweetest. Unlike Fidrych and Jones, Montefusco had garnered more press attention throughout the summer with his mouth than his arm, thanks in part to a particularly controversial outburst in August, wherein he alienated his manager and his teammates by telling the press, "Bill Rigney's a loser, and he's taking the club down with him. I want out." Giants owner Bob Lurie fined Montefusco $500 for his public tirade.

Going into his final scheduled start of the year on September 29 against the Braves in Atlanta, Montefusco was 15–14 with a 2.95 ERA for the season; he was also sick as a dog from a lingering virus. Given the option of making his final start of the season later in the week against the Astros, Montefusco ultimately decided to gut it out, but for once was less than confident about his chances. Giants announcer Al Michaels strolled by the Count during his pregame warm-ups, and playfully suggested that he end his season by pitching a no-hitter. "Oh no, not tonight," Montefusco groaned. "It's not in me."

Once he took the mound, however, the Count found himself in a groove that not even the flu could fluster; with the exception of a leadoff walk to Jerry Royster in the bottom of the fourth, not a single Brave made it safely to first base. Atlanta's only hard-hit ball of the night came off the bat of Dale Murphy, a September rookie call-up, who smoked a line drive directly at second baseman Marty Perez for the third out in the bottom of the eighth. "That one scared me," Montefusco admitted. "I thought it was all over right there. My heart stopped beating for a second." For the most part, though, Montefusco set the Braves down so easily it bordered on the clinical. "There are usually diving catches or great plays in a no-hitter," Rigney reflected, "but tonight it was all routine—ground balls right at people and little soft, lazy fly balls."

By the time Montefusco took the hill for the bottom of the ninth, his team was up 9–0 and he was all but assured of his 16th win of the season—yet he was determined not to leave the ballpark with anything less than a no-hitter under his belt. "I'll tell you, they weren't gonna get a hit off me in the ninth," he said afterward. "I wanted it bad then, and I was gonna get it." The Count got it, all right, fanning pinch-hitter Jimmy Wynn with a called strike three, then inducing Cito Gaston to fly to Bobby Murcer in right for the second out. Royster was up next, and catcher Gary Alexander warned his infielders to be on the lookout for a bunt off the bat of the speedy second baseman. "No way," Royster retorted. "If he pitches a no-no, he'll have to get me out swinging." Montefusco did just that, getting Royster to loft an easy fly to Murcer for the final out of the game.

As this was the last home game of the season for the Braves, Ted Turner had already invited everyone in the stands to join the team on the field afterward for a champagne toast to the Bicentennial Braves. But the postgame festivities quickly shifted to a celebration of Montefusco's pitching feat; most of the 1,369 fans in attendance had been cheering for him from the eighth inning on, anyway. "This ain't going to shut me up for a long time," exulted Montefusco, between swigs off a bottle of bubbly that Turner had pressed into his hand. "I'm going to be talking all winter now."

All season long, Sparky Anderson had downplayed expectations that the Reds would run away with the NL West like they had in 1975, when they'd clinched their division on September 7, the earliest pennant-grab in NL history. Sparky was right: the Big Red Machine's conquest of the division title in '76 was more of a leisurely jog, with the team taking an additional two weeks to put the Dodgers out of their misery.

On September 21, the Reds snagged their second straight NL West flag—and their fifth in seven years—with a 9–1 pasting of the Padres in front of 20,084 cheering Reds fans at Riverfront Stadium. The victory was carried off with typical Machine-like efficiency; highlights included George Foster knocking three hits (including his eighth triple of the year) and driving in his 118th and 119th runs, Joe Morgan going 2-for-4 and scoring twice while also stealing his 58th base, and Johnny Bench nailing Tito Fuentes at second after Doug Rader swung at a third strike. Rookie Pat Zachry recorded one of his strongest performances of the season, scattering eight hits, striking out nine batters, and allowing only one unearned run in a complete game victory, his 14th win of the year.

The mood in the Reds' clubhouse afterward was jovial, if subdued. Champagne corks popped and beer toasts were raised, but most of the celebrants were focused on the next tests they had to face. "It's been something we'd been expecting for a month, this Western Division championship," explained Pete Rose, relaxing in front of his locker. "But the real pressure is ahead of us, the playoffs and then the World Series." "It's been 54 years since a National League team has won consecutive world championships," added Sparky Anderson, referring to the New York Giants of 1921–22. "That's our goal."

Most of the Reds had been down this road before, but not Zachry, so it was understandable that the 24-year-old beanpole was more keyed up during the postgame celebration than the majority of his teammates. "This is beyond my wildest dreams," he whooped, donning a pair of Groucho Marx glasses and spraying Reds GM Bob Howsam with a blast of champagne. Zachry had another reason to celebrate: just the day before, assault charges pending against him had been dropped in Cincinnati Municipal Court. The charges stemmed from an ugly incident that occurred in the Riverfront Stadium parking lot following a game in August, when a Reds fan named Daniel Davis made an angry remark to Zachry after the pitcher refused an autograph request by Davis's 11-year-old brother. Davis claimed that Zachry responded to his complaint by punching him several times, then cursing out Davis's wife for good measure. The charges were dropped on September 20, after both sides agreed to an undisclosed out-of-court settlement. Zachry, who'd already had some run-ins with Sparky Anderson over his inability to control his temper, was apologetic. "I made a mistake," he said. "I'm sorry about it."

Despite Zachry's volatility, Anderson and his coaches were glad to have the 6'5" rookie on their staff, given how rickety the Reds' rotation had seemed at various points throughout the season—especially with Don Gullett missing over a month with neck and shoulder injuries, and former ace Jack Billingham posting an unimpressive 4.36 ERA in 29 starts. Though he hadn't even been a sure shot to make the team out of spring training, Zachry had turned out to be one of the Reds' most dependable pitchers in 1976, finishing the season with a 14–7 record, a team-high 143 strikeouts, and the lowest ERA (2.74) among the team's starters. Zachry's victories and innings pitched (204) were second on the staff to Gary Nolan (who went 15–9 with 3.46 ERA in 239.1 innings), and he only gave up eight home runs all season—as opposed to Nolan, who served up an NL-high 28.

With Gullett looking healthy again—the Kentucky southpaw went 4–0 over the last month of the season, lowering his ERA to 3.00 and raising his final record to 11–3—Anderson planned to hit the postseason with a four-man rotation of Nolan, Zachry, Gullett, and Fred Norman, who went 12–7 for the season with a 3.09 ERA in 180.1 innings, though he remained cagey about who would pitch the first game of the NL playoffs. "I'd like to wait until the day of the game before announcing the pitcher," he laughed. "Though I'll probably have to name him at least the day before."

There was no question about who Sparky's go-to reliever would be in tight late-game situations, however. Rawly Eastwick, who'd led the National League with 22 saves as a rookie in 1975, had been even better in '76, saving an NL-leading 26 games, winning 11 more, and striking out 70 with what Sparky dubbed a "here it is and now try and hit it" fastball, while posting a minuscule 2.09 ERA in 71 relief appearances and 107.2 innings. Eastwick's performance was impressive enough to nab the *Sporting News*'s NL Fireman of the Year award; the AL version went to Twins reliever Bill Campbell, who set a league record by throwing 167.2 relief innings while winning 17 games and saving 20.

Eastwick's brash competitiveness on the mound stood in stark contrast to the creativity and contemplativeness that the 25-year-old righty displayed off it. An avid antique collector, Eastwick spent much of his free time furnishing and renovating a 75-year-old Tudor-style house in the Queen City's Hyde Park neighborhood; the 11-room home contained a large sunroom, which Eastwick planned to turn into an art studio. "When I get the time," he told the *Cincinnati Post*'s Earl Lawson, "I plan to do some landscape paintings and some experimenting in modern art." Eastwick dreamed of spending a future off-season taking art lessons in London or the south of France—though as a firm believer in out-of-body experiences, he also hoped to be able to visit those locales without boarding a 747.

"I would like to travel spiritually to another country or maybe another universe and check them out," Eastwick was quoted in an Associated Press profile that ran in early September, and detailed some of the pitcher's experiences with astral projection and other psychic phenomena. "We have no idea what we can do with our brain power," Eastwick told the AP. "We can create positive energy, turn a thought into a reality. I believe in the phrase 'an object is a thought materialized.'"

Billy Martin and George Steinbrenner had spent the spring and summer visualizing the Yankees' return to the postseason for the first time since 1964, and their AL East flag finally materialized on September 25. The Yankees beat the Tigers 10–6 that afternoon at Tiger Stadium, and Steinbrenner threw a private dinner party for his players and coaches that night at Detroit's upscale Caucus Club; when word arrived midway through the meal that Luis Tiant and the Red Sox had beaten the Orioles 1–0 to knock the second-place O's out of the race, the relaxed repast turned raucous. Champagne flowed, and the players hollered and embraced each other. "Eight years," rejoiced a smiling Thurman Munson. "We've been waiting for this for eight years." Roy White, the stoic left fielder who'd been a Yankee since 1965, had tears in his eyes. "It was just one terrific thing," Steinbrenner told reporters afterward. "For the kids who had never been through this before, you could see what a great moment it was to them. And even guys like Catfish Hunter and Ken Holtzman who had won so many at Oakland still celebrated like it was the first time."

Steinbrenner felt that the divisional clinch thoroughly vindicated his controlling ways. "I know they always criticized me for wanting the players to cut their hair and wear coats and ties," gloated the Yankee owner, "but look where we are." He also took the opportunity to lash out at those around the game (most recently Tigers manager Ralph Houk), who'd accused the Yankees of having bought their pennant. "All you have to do is look at the facts," Steinbrenner retorted. "Catfish was the only player we bought. All the rest of the guys who contributed so much this year came in trades."

Steinbrenner conspicuously neglected to mention the contributions of Yanks GM Gabe Paul, the man who'd actually built the team through the aforementioned trades, or Billy Martin, whose aggressive managing style had kept the Yankees in first place since their third game of the season. After keeping Martin squirming in contract renegotiations for over a month, Steinbrenner finally gave his manager a three-year extension on September 9, telling the press, "Billy and I have a rapport that few people in sports have. . . . I've seen him go to Minnesota and Detroit and Texas and do a hell of a job and get fired. I don't think that will happen here because I know Billy. I know how to get along with him."

At the time, the Yankees were in the midst of an 11–3 surge; but when they lost six straight later in the month, their lead over the Orioles shrinking from 11 and a half to seven games, a panicked Steinbrenner began threatening to fire Martin. The AL East clinch quieted the Yankees' owner for the time being, but he showed no inclination to share the glory of the team's success with his manager—much to the disappointment of Martin, who'd honestly hoped that winning the division would bring him and Steinbrenner closer together as friends.

"At that point," Martin would later recount in his autobiography, "I began to feel that George was acting jealous of me. He seemed to resent that he didn't have a big enough hand in it, seemed to feel that he wasn't going to get enough credit, and it bothered him that I was getting so much publicity. The Yankees were supreme again. That was the real glory, and he should have been happy and let it go at that."

The Yankees indeed reigned supreme again, at least in the AL East; and if their lineup didn't exactly exude the awe-inspiring greatness of the legendary Bronx Bomber squads of yore, it was still a damn good team. Graig Nettles hit two round-trippers off Luis Tiant on September 29, giving him 32 for the year and his first AL home run crown. (Reggie Jackson and Sal Bando, who'd vied with each other for the home run lead, finished tied for second with 27 each.) Thurman Munson, who hit .302 with 17 homers, was one of only three AL players to drive in over 100 runs for the season, placing second in the category with 105—Lee May led the junior circuit with 109, and Carl Yastrzemski finished third with 102—while Chris Chambliss drove in 96 and Nettles another 93. Mickey Rivers didn't come close to his league-leading 1975 stolen base total of 70 (he led the team with 43), but he'd developed into an even deadlier leadoff hitter, setting career high marks in batting average (.312), doubles (31), home runs (8), RBIs (67), and runs scored (95); the Yankees were 84–48 on the season in games he started, and 13–14 in games he didn't. The ever-reliable White hit .286 in the two-spot behind Rivers, knocking 14 homers and 65 RBIs, and stole 31 bases while scoring a league-leading 104 times. Oscar Gamble, despite hitting a career low .232 for the season, still managed to blast 17 home runs while starting mostly against right-handed pitchers, tying Munson and Chambliss for second-most on the team.

"It wasn't our most talented club," Sparky Lyle would later reflect, "but it was the best all around. Everybody knew exactly what his job was, and everyone had a specific job. Oscar Gamble knew that when a left-hander started for the other team, he wasn't playing, and he knew that if it was a righty, he'd be playing. And he'd be ready to play that day. There was no guessing."

Lyle, ironically, had been forced to do the most guessing regarding his role on the team. Though nominally the Yankees' top fireman—he'd finish the season with a league-leading 23 saves while going 7–8 with a 2.26 ERA—Lyle suddenly found himself benched following three straight poor outings in August. Martin repeatedly assured Lyle that he'd call upon him again soon, but only used the lefty once between August 22 and September 11. "Whatever [Martin] says to you, you can count on it being the exact opposite," Lyle complained to the press, after watching Dick Tidrow rack up four straight saves during the first week in September. Lyle and Martin eventually cleared the air in a closed-door meeting, and on September 18, the pitcher got into a game in a save situation for the first time in a month.

But when it came to bad vibes at Yankee Stadium, nothing topped the night of September 28, when Ken Norton and Muhammad Ali squared off in a fight for the heavyweight boxing title while the Yankees were out of town. The fight itself would be forever shrouded in controversy—the judges and referees awarded the match to the fading Ali, despite what most observers believed was a clear-cut victory for Norton, who had beaten Ali in 1973. But the real battle royale occurred outside the stadium, where countless ticket-holders were beaten and robbed by roving bands of local hoodlums while NYPD cops—acting in mute solidarity with their off-duty counterparts, who were protesting the department's budget cuts and poor working conditions outside the ballpark that night—pointedly looked the other way. The boxing ring and on-field seating damaged the stadium's grass so badly that boxing matches would be banned from the ballpark for decades, while the violent and anarchic scene outside boded extremely ill for the return of October baseball to the Bronx.

Billy Martin kept his job, but September marked the end of the line for a handful of other managers. The Expos were preparing to leave the rickety confines of Jarry Park for the spacious, Space Age expanses of Montreal's new Olympic Stadium—which they'd finally get to call home in 1977 after years of delays—but they'd be making the move without the embattled Karl Kuehl, who was officially axed on the 4th of the month. "You can't be surprised with the record we've had," said Kuehl, who'd led the team to a major-league-worst 43-85 record during his tenure, which had been marked by public power struggles with both his players and the front office. Expos president John McHale, opining that "We feel we need an older person to handle the youngsters," replaced the 38-year-old Kuehl with 54-year-old Charlie Fox, an Expos scout who'd previously managed the Giants from 1970 to 1974. The Expos went 12–22 under Fox to finish at 55–107 for the year, their worst season since losing 110 games as an expansion team in 1969.

Bill Rigney could have managed the Giants for another season if he'd wanted to, but on September 21, just a few days after a fistfight broke out on a team flight between reserve infielder Bruce Miller and Giants traveling secretary Frank Berganzi, a the 58-year-old skipper announced that he'd had enough. "I never felt I lost control of the club," Rigney told reporters. "But it didn't perform as a team. It let a lot of minor things get it down, like the weather and lack of charter flights." Gary Matthews, who'd previously criticized Rigney for failing to enforce the rules he'd set for his players, admitted that the Giants' dismal performance—the team wound up in fourth place with a 74–88 record—wasn't Rigney's fault. "I want to see the players busting their butts," he said. "The manager calls the shots, but that is secondary. Sparky Anderson could not have made this club win."

Less than a week after Rigney stepped down, Walter Alston tendered a resignation of his own. Whether the 64-year-old Alston jumped or was pushed wasn't clear, but a "dump Alston" movement had certainly been gathering steam all season among Dodger fans and L.A. sportswriters who thought his managing style was stodgier than *The Lawrence Welk Show*, even though 1976 marked the 10th time that the Dodgers had won 90 games or more under Alston. The old skipper said that he was retiring before the end of the season in order to give the organization time to find his replacement, but it didn't take long for the Dodgers to make their decision—just two days later, to no one's surprise, they announced that third base coach Tommy Lasorda had been named as Alston's successor.

The 49-year-old Lasorda, who had been in the Dodger organization for 27 years as a player, scout, minor league manager, and major league coach—and who'd been angling for years to be Alston's successor—was about as different from Alston in personality and temperament as Oscar Madison was from Felix Unger. Nicknamed "The Quiet Man," Alston was a reticent, if occasionally intimidating, presence in the Dodger dugout and clubhouse; he typically spoke in even tones to his players and offered clipped, colorless sound bites to reporters. Lasorda, by contrast, was a boisterous and verbose "holler guy" on the diamond who socialized with players (and Hollywood stars like Frank Sinatra and Don Rickles) off the field, and who was often prone to dramatic hyperbole—especially when it came to the team he claimed to "bleed Dodger blue" for. Lasorda officially took the reins for the last four games of the season, winning two and losing two to bring the Dodgers' final record to 92–70, a 10-game, second-place finish behind the Reds. Once again, the Dodgers would have to wait until next year.

Darrell Johnson, who'd been let go by the Red Sox in July after the defending AL champions fell far short of expectations, was hired as the inaugural manager for the Seattle Mariners on September 3. Lou Gorman, Seattle's director of baseball operations, called Johnson "tactically as good as any man in the game," and told reporters that Johnson would help scout players before the November 5 expansion draft. Johnson told the press that he'd be looking for players with "pride, aggressiveness, and the right mental attitude," an obvious dig at the Red Sox. "People have to play together as a unit with one common object—winning—and with pride in the ballclub," he said. "But we lost that somewhat with all the things that happened in [Boston]."

Fred Lynn, Carlton Fisk, and Rick Burleson had all ended their contract holdouts in August—Lynn coming out the richest with a five-year, $1.6 million deal—but the '76 Red Sox never really got back on track until the season was almost over. Under the guidance of new manager Don Zimmer, the defending AL champions went 22–11 over their last 33 games, but only narrowly avoided finishing fourth behind the Yankees, Orioles, and Indians by winning their last three games of the season. They ended the year in third place with an 83–79 record, 15 and a half games behind the Yankees.

While their city's baseball team would be sitting out October, Bostonians could at least take some pride in the fact that their band was all over the radio. Boston, a rock group formed by guitarist, songwriter, and MIT graduate Tom Scholz, released its self-titled debut album during the last week of August; by the first week of September, the record—on the strength of such melodic and immaculately produced hard rock anthems as "More Than a Feeling" and "Peace of Mind"—was already being played on nearly 400 commercial radio stations nationwide. Though its total recording costs weren't much higher than that of the Ramones' low-budget debut (most of the album's tracks had been recorded at Scholz's basement studio in Watertown, Massachusetts), *Boston*'s crystalline vocal harmonies and interlocking layers of crushed-velvet guitar distortion sounded like they'd been dispatched directly from FM heaven, and American rock fans responded accordingly. The album went gold within two months of its release, selling 500,000 copies by late October, earned its million-selling platinum certification by the end of November, and would reach the two million sales mark early in the new year. If *Ramones* would go down in history as one of the most influential debut albums of all time, *Boston* would set the standard for the most successful debut, ultimately shifting over 17 million copies in the U.S. alone. Along with its music, *Boston*'s cover art—depicting guitar-shaped spaceships leaving Earth behind—undoubtedly struck a chord with more than a few Red Sox fans, who would have preferred to "Hitch a Ride" to another galaxy rather than watch the dreaded Yankees in the playoffs.

The day after the Yankees clinched their division, the Phillies did the same in the NL East, assuring the team of its first postseason appearance in 26 years. Just nine days earlier, the Phillies had looked like deer in the headlights of an oncoming Pittsburgh express, and their fans had been preparing for a collective leap from the top of Independence Hall. But the Phils had suddenly snapped out of their funk, taking six of their next eight games while the Pirates lost seven out of ten—including a 7–6 loss to the Mets on September 19, in which Dave Kingman blasted two homers and drove in five of the Mets' runs. The round-trippers were Kong's 36th and 37th of the year, temporarily giving him the lead in the NL home run race over Mike Schmidt, who had 35. But Kingman went homerless for the rest of the season, while Schmidt knocked three more over the fence before the end of September to earn his third straight NL home run title.

A 4–1 Philadelphia victory over the Expos in the first game of a September 26 doubleheader at Jarry Park sealed the deal, triggering a riotous between-game celebration in the visiting team's clubhouse. "Whatever I said last November still stands today," declared a visibly relieved Ozark as he wiped the champagne from his eyes. "I never felt we would let up. I've been confident all season long that we were going to win it. We've got the best club in baseball." "We've got pitching on this club," added Jim Lonborg, who nailed down the title with a four-hit, five-strikeout complete game victory, raising his record to 17–10. "We can hit. We've got some speed, experience and maturity. You've got to have all those things in order to become champions. Today, we're champions."

The Phillies had all of those things, it was true—but the Philadelphia ball club was also running increasingly low on brotherly love at precisely the point where they needed it most. They'd emerged from their September slide with serious cracks in their outward appearance of an emotionally centered team that had (in the words of *Sports Illustrated*'s Ron Fimrite) "toasted themselves at their team wine tastings, practiced their transcendental meditation, whiled away a perfectly splendid summer in the manner of gentlemen scholars on sabbatical." And the man at the center of the latest storm was, of course, Dick Allen.

The mercurial first baseman, who'd gone a dire 3-for-40 in his first 11 games after returning from the disabled list in early September, caught fire again for three days beginning September 21, going 8-for-12 with two doubles, a home run, four RBIs, and four runs scored in a key three-game sweep of the Cardinals at the Vet. For those three contests, Allen suddenly transformed himself into the franchise player he was paid to be, the intimidating slugger who could carry an entire team on his broad shoulders when the chips were down. And then, just as suddenly, his anger and internal demons once again got the best of him.

The catalyst for Allen's latest super-sulk was the Phillies' announcement that Tony Taylor would not be included on the team's 25-man playoff roster. The 40-year-old Cuban had only appeared in 26 games all year, mostly as a pinch-hitter, but Allen felt the roster move was disrespectful and unfair to Taylor, who'd not only been best man at Allen's wedding, but had also spent the bulk of his 19-year MLB career in Philadelphia, where he'd been an unfailingly positive presence on the team. In addition, Allen believed that the move had racial undertones—that the Phillies would have never cut a fan favorite and veteran player like Taylor from the playoff roster if he were white. "With God as my witness," Allen told reporters, "if the Phillies take Tony Taylor's uniform off his back, they'll have to take Dick Allen's too."

Angered by the Taylor situation, and disdainful of how his teammates were already "acting like we'd won the World Series," Allen refused to take part in the team's initial post-clinch celebration in Montreal. He opted instead for a quiet prayer of thanks in the visitors' dugout, followed by another prayer and a mellow champagne toast in the clubhouse with Dave Cash, Garry Maddox, and Mike

Schmidt while they sat out the second game of the doubleheader. "Dick gave thanks that we had a good season, that we were able to perform well and that no one got hurt," Maddox later recalled. "He prayed that God would help us play to the best of our ability in this playoff—not that He would let us win, but only that we play to the best of our ability and the Reds would play to the best of theirs."

Some of the Phillies were put off by Allen's separate celebration, and were doubly annoyed when Allen—saying he wanted to celebrate with his family—headed home to his horse farm in Perkasie, Pennsylvania, instead of flying with the rest of the team to St. Louis for a three-game series against the Cardinals. "I was happy to be on a winner," Allen explained later, "but I was torn up about how I felt about the Phillies organization. My shoulder was hurting. I needed to mentally recharge for the playoffs. I was wearing down. . . . I was worried about my horses. I was short-circuiting."

Allen's abrupt exit set off some additional short-circuits amongst his teammates. "He makes $250,000 a year," complained Tug McGraw. "If he was so hot to celebrate the championship with his family, he should have flown them here to St. Louis." During a contentious team meeting at Busch Stadium, McGraw accused several of the black players (the absent Allen included) of forming a clique and intentionally dividing the team along racial lines, a charge that incensed Garry Maddox. "Somebody's sure been fooling me this season," the smooth center fielder responded. "I never saw a sign all year of any race problems."

Allen, on the other hand, felt that the team was indeed racially divided, but that it was the fault of the Phillies' management, not the players. "Ollie Brown was being platooned with Jerry Martin," he later wrote, "and a lot of us felt he should have been given the job. Bobby Tolan was another guy who wasn't getting the shot he deserved. There was a sense that the Phillies were working a quota on us, and the clubhouse started getting divided because of it. We were starting to feel like two teams, black and white, though Schmitty was an honorary black. He seemed to understand what was going on. He was also sporting an Afro at the time, even if it was a bright red one."

Team president Ruly Carpenter visited Allen on his farm and assured him that Taylor would be in uniform for the playoffs, albeit as a coach instead of a player. While this compromise wasn't initially sufficient for Allen, Taylor intervened and begged Allen to suit up for the forthcoming National League Championship Series against the Reds. "If he hadn't done that," Allen would later reveal, "I would have watched that series from my farm."

With the Phillies' postseason berth sealed, it became the Royals' turn to flirt with a full collapse. After winning four straight in mid-September to widen their lead to six games, the Royals faced off against the A's in a three-game series at Kansas City. There was already no love lost between the two teams, as George Brett made clear. "I want to win it against them so bad," said the third baseman. "Let them break the stolen-base record by stealing when they're ahead by 12–1. We're a more civilized team. You don't see us popping off all the time. They're a bunch of individualists. When we talk over here, it's always about the Royals as a team, whether we're winning or losing."

Things grew even more acrimonious on September 21, the first night of the series, when A's righty Stan Bahnsen beaned Amos Otis in the first inning. The Royals center fielder—who was batting .286 at the time with 17 homers and 84 RBIs—was taken off the field on a stretcher, whereupon Bahnsen proceeded to dust Hal McRae and John Mayberry, both of whom had to be restrained from charging the mound. In the sixth inning, with the Royals up 2–1, a teenage member of the stadium grounds crew reported to Herzog that he'd spotted Rollie Fingers and Paul Lindblad using a pair of binoculars and a walkie-talkie in the A's bullpen, ostensibly to steal the Royals' signs. Herzog called time and led the umpiring crew out to the bullpen, where they searched in vain for the items until several fans in the bleachers yelled for them to check under a towel; the offending field glasses were thus discovered, though no one found any walkie-talkies. "Are you kidding?" scoffed one A's player. "How could we afford that sort of electronic equipment when we can't even charter a plane?"

Herzog announced that he was playing the game under protest, though the Royals' eventual 2–1 win rendered an official complaint unnecessary. Despite the victory, the Royals were fuming. "Chuck Tanner ordered [Bahnsen] to hit me," claimed Otis after returning from his visit to a local hospital, where X rays thankfully revealed no damage beyond a massive knot on the back of his head. "This puts us seven up with 11 to play," said Herzog. "I'd love to beat them the next two and put them nine back. Then they'd really be desperate."

But after Vida Blue held them to a lone run the next night in an 11–1 defeat, and the A's stole six bases on their way to an 8–1 victory in the rubber game of the series, it was the Royals who began to appear desperate. Their anxiety (and that of the Kansas City fans) intensified further when they lost two of three at Texas, and then flew into Oakland on September 27 to begin another three-game series against the A's. They lost the first one 8–3, in a contest that was mostly memorable for the massive brawl that occurred in the sixth inning, which was sparked when Dennis Leonard—retaliating for both Otis's earlier beaning and the solo home run that he'd just served up to Sal Bando—nailed Don Baylor in the back with a pitch. As the beefy Baylor stomped toward the mound with a murderous glint in his eye, Leonard made a beeline for the outfield, and both benches emptied onto the diamond for a wild rumble that lasted several minutes. "That fight went on for what seemed like forever," Otis recalled. "I kept walking around, looking for Bahnsen, but I could never find him. That night was a mess."

It got even messier when A's fans seated behind the Royals' bullpen began pelting the visitors with beer; the shouting between the Oakland fans and Kansas City players quickly escalated to shoving, and backup catchers Bob Stinson and John Wathan climbed into the stands to duke it out with their tormentors, while Tommy Davis—who'd just been purchased from the Angels a week earlier—provided some late-season offense by pummeling several unruly fans with a black umbrella he'd seized from one of them.

The Royals showed no fight at all the following night, going down quietly for their sixth loss in their last seven games. The A's won it 1–0 on Sal Bando's 27th homer, while Mike Torrez limited the Royals to two singles in the course of racking up his 16th victory. It was the sixth win and fourth complete game shutout of the month for the 6'5" right-hander; he seemed hell-bent upon personally delivering the A's to the postseason, having put them just two and a half games out with four left to play.

"This is just as exciting as the playoffs and the World Series," beamed Chuck Tanner, whose team had won six of its last eight games. "Our men are acting as if they want to get to the World Series. They know they have to win all of them and they are playing that way." "I'm seeing it, but I don't believe it," responded Herzog. "We caught Torrez on a night when he didn't have his good stuff, and still we get just two hits. We've shaken up the lineup, and that hasn't helped. What else can I do? Quit, maybe?"

On September 29, the Royals and A's convened for their final matchup of the season. If the Royals won the evening's contest, they would clinch at least a tie for the division title; if the A's emerged victorious, they would be only one and a half games back with three left to play. Instead of quitting, Herzog handed the ball to Larry Gura, who'd been hampered for much of the season by a groin pull, and had thus pitched almost exclusively in relief since coming over from the Yankees in May. Though many of his players questioned the move, Herzog felt that the A's lineup would have trouble against the lefty, whom they'd faced only briefly during the year. Herzog also put Otis, who'd been benched for a couple of games after hitting only 2-for-21 following the Bahnsen beaning, back in the lineup. Both moves paid off beautifully: Gura shut out the A's on four singles, while Otis doubled in a run in the third and added another in the fifth with his 18th homer of the year.

In the bottom of the ninth, with the Royals up 4–0, the A's sent Bert Campaneris, Joe Rudi, and Gene Tenace—three heroes of the Oakland dynasty—to the plate. Campy grounded back to the mound, and Rudi laced a drive to right that Al Cowens put away. Tenace followed by hitting a towering pop foul along the first base line; Big John Mayberry camped under it, reflecting upon the end of an era as he followed the ball's descent into his mitt. "Five straight pennants," he thought to himself. "World Champions three times. The mighty A's. We chased 'em and chased 'em, and now it's our turn." "We all wondered why they'd pitched Gura," Bando said afterward, "but we found out. He stuck our bats where the sun don't shine."

The Royals mobbed Gura on the field, and later they greeted Otis with a giddy chant of "A.O.! A.O.!" as he boarded the team bus. There were still three games left to play at home against the Twins, but they only had to win one of them—or watch the A's drop one of their next three games with the Angels—and they'd be the first Kansas City team in major league history to win a postseason berth.

The A's obliged by losing 2–0 to the Angels on October 1, as Frank Tanana pitched 11 scoreless innings with 14 strikeouts to earn his 19th victory; but the Angels-A's game finished so late that the Royals, who'd already gone home after a 4–3 loss to the Twins, weren't around to celebrate the good news. They rectified the situation the following night: after losing 3–2 to the Twins in a game populated mostly by Royals reserves, the team adjourned to the clubhouse and soaked each other with champagne, beer, and whatever other liquids they could get their hands on. Amos Otis sprayed beer all over owner Ewing Kauffman; George Brett poured a half-gallon of milk on the head of Jamie Quirk, then plunged Hal McRae's face into a ripe watermelon. Back when Royals Stadium first opened, Cookie Rojas had pledged to one day celebrate a Royals championship with a swim in the Kansas City ballpark's lavish right field fountains. Freddie Patek joined him, and the two infielders stripped to the waist and took their triumphant plunge. Luckily, someone on the Royals staff had the foresight to turn off the fountain's electricity before the two men jumped in.

The 1976 Oakland A's would go down in history as the most theft-happy team of the modern era, with 341 stolen bases to their credit; ultimately, however, they were unable to steal the AL West from the Royals. "It's over," said Chuck Tanner. "We did all we could. This is the finest bunch of players I have ever been associated with. We didn't quite make it, and I tip my hat to Kansas City."

The A's players were less gracious in defeat—"Kansas City, they backed into it," grumbled Sal Bando—though they largely focused their anger and disappointment on their owner. After losing 1–0 to the Angels in their final game of the year (in which Nolan Ryan struck out 14, bringing his major-league-leading total to 327), champagne and bile flowed in equal measure in the Oakland clubhouse. Players uncorked 36 bottles of bubbly—a farewell gift from their unsigned teammates Sal Bando, Joe Rudi, Rollie Fingers, Campy Campaneris, Gene Tenace, and Don Baylor, who officially became free agents at midnight. Willie McCovey, who'd only been on the team for a month, was also now a free agent.

"This is to celebrate the liberation of the Oakland Seven," whooped Bill North, who'd led the majors with 75 stolen bases. "This wasn't so much to celebrate leaving," Bando corrected him, "but to thank our teammates." "I feel sorry for anyone who has to play for this club next year," said Fingers, combing his handlebar mustache for the last time as a member of the A's. Vida Blue, who was still contractually bound to the team, seemed determined to put as much scorched earth as possible between himself and the A's owner. "I hope the next breath Charles O. Finley takes is his last," he spat. "I hope he falls flat on his face, or dies of polio."

With the division races all sewn up, all that was left to be decided on the final day of the 1976 season were the NL and AL batting races. In the senior circuit, defending batting champ Bill Madlock—who'd missed the last week of September with a slight concussion after being mugged for $50 in the hallway of New York's Waldorf-Astoria hotel, where he was staying during a Cubs-Mets series—came into the final game of the year hitting .333, five points behind league leader Ken Griffey. Unsure whether to play his right fielder in the Reds' final, meaningless contest against the Braves, Sparky Anderson asked Pete Rose, Joe Morgan, Johnny Bench, and Tony Perez their thoughts on the matter; they all advised that Griffey should sit the game out, thereby preserving his legs for the playoffs and his .338 batting average for posterity. "Pride is a lot of nothing," Morgan told Griffey before the game. "You shouldn't have played yesterday, and you shouldn't play today."

But when word reached Cincinnati that Madlock had taken the batting lead while feasting on Expos pitching during the Cubs' season finale at Wrigley Field, Anderson put Griffey into the game. Griffey struck out in his two plate appearances, dropping his average to .336; Madlock, who went 4-for-4, boosted his mark to a title-winning .339. "Going into the game, I really didn't think I had a chance," said Madlock. "I assumed Griffey had it wrapped up even if I got a hit every time up. If I had the lead going into the last day, I would have wanted to play regardless of the situation." "I did not lose the batting title," said a dejected-looking Griffey after the Reds wrapped up their 11–1 win over the Braves. "Bill Madlock won it." "Besides," Anderson reassured Griffey, "no one is gonna care tomorrow."

Anderson was right. Not only did the Reds have bigger fish to fry, but the bizarre end to the AL batting race would linger much longer in the collective memory than Griffey's sit-down. Hal McRae and George Brett had spent the last few months deflecting questions about competing against each other for the AL batting title; but here they were, running neck and neck in the race—McRae hitting .33078 to Brett's .33073, though the newspapers showed them both at .331—with Rod Carew of the Twins right behind them at .329. As fate would have it, all three men would be playing in the same final game of the season at Royals Stadium. (Carew's teammate Lyman Bostock was fourth in the batting race at .325, but a thumb injury prevented him from playing in the final game of the season. Ron LeFlore, whose breakout season had been ended in mid-September by a leg injury, sat a distant fifth at .316.)

Carew, who'd won the four previous AL batting crowns, went 2-for-4 in the contest, singling in his final at-bat in the top of the ninth to raise his average to .331. But it wasn't enough to catch Brett or McRae, both of whom had already gone 2-for-3 on the afternoon. With one out in the bottom of the inning, and the Twins up 5–2, Brett stepped to the plate against Jim Hughes; if he failed to hit safely, the batting title would belong to McRae, regardless of the outcome of McRae's next at-bat. Brett lofted what looked like an easy fly to left, but Twins left fielder Steve Brye pulled up short and let the ball drop 10 to 15 feet in front of him, then watched it take an AstroTurf-assisted bounce over his head and scoot to the wall while Brett circled the bases for an inside-the-park home run. McRae, batting behind Brett, then grounded out to short for the second out of the inning. Brett had won the batting championship.

As soon as he was thrown out at first, McRae began angrily gesticulating toward the Twins dugout, accusing Twins manager Gene Mauch of instructing Brye to let Brett's ball drop safely. As the exchange became increasingly heated, Whitey Herzog and several of McRae's teammates ran out onto the field in order restrain him from going after Mauch, who denied any wrongdoing.

"This is the worst thing that's happened to me in 35 years in baseball," a visibly upset Mauch told reporters afterward. "I would never, never do anything to harm the integrity of baseball. I trust Brye implicitly. If I thought for a second that he let that ball fall on purpose, I'd have him run right out of baseball." Brye, a usually surehanded fielder, claimed to have simply misplayed Brett's opposite field fly. "I didn't get a good jump on the ball," he said. "All during the series, balls I thought would fall in front of me were going over my head. It's tough to pick up the ball in Kansas City because there's a gray background, plus you don't hear the ball off the bat that well."

McRae wasn't buying it, believing instead that Mauch and Brye had intentionally conspired to let a white man win the batting title over a black man. "I knew it was going to happen this way," he seethed. "After all, this is America, and things haven't changed. I know what happened. It's been too good a season for me to say too much, but I know they let that ball fall on purpose. I don't mind losing to George. We were joking about it during the game. If he'd gotten a clean hit that last time, then that was fine. But that's not the way it was."

Brett, who finished with a .33333 average to McRae's .33269, suspected that something was up, as well. "Nothing occurred to me while I was running the bases," he said, "but after I got to the dugout I thought they may have given it to me. I kind of wondered about the double I got my second time up," he added, referring to a hit that right fielder Dan Ford appeared to misplay in the fourth inning. "It looked like he gave up and let it drop, too."

Carew, a black man born in Panama, flatly denied that there could have been any prejudicial plot behind the play. "There was no conspiracy and no racial prejudice," he snapped. "That racial stuff is a copout. McRae had a big lead going into the last month and lost the championship. He simply choked."

Enough controversy surrounded the incident that Commissioner Kuhn ordered an investigation, but after questioning everyone involved, AL president Lee MacPhail said he could find no evidence of conspiracy. Regardless, it left a bad taste in Brett's mouth. "I wish they could go back and find a mistake and saw the bat in half and give both of us half a bat," he mused. "If there is anybody on the team I would not like to beat out, it is Hal. He has helped me so much and we've gone through a lot together.

"This whole thing takes the edge off winning," he sighed. "I mean, I wanted to win, but I didn't want it to be this way."

11.

Still the One

(October 1976)

The publication of Jim 'Bouton's Ball Four in the spring of 1970 was a seismic event in the baseball world, one that would have far-reaching aftershocks regarding the way journalists covered sports, as well as how athletes penned their memoirs. Baseball fans were completely unprepared for the revelations the book contained; Bouton's amusingly profane tales of greenie-popping, skirt-chasing, Budweiser-pounding major leaguers like himself didn't jibe at all with the popular conception of ballplayers as All-American heroes, just as his rather sobering depictions of contract negotiations and being sent down to the minors flew in the face of the carefully constructed fiction that players were well paid, well taken care of, and fairly treated by their employers. *Ball Four* was so eye-opening—and the backlash against it from players and sportswriters alike so vicious—that David Halberstam compared it to investigative journalist Seymour Hersh's exposé of the My Lai massacre.

The fall 1976 debut of *Ball Four*, the CBS television series based on Bouton's eye-opening best-seller, was a far less earthshaking affair.

Scripted by Bouton (who also starred in the show as "Jim Barton," an aging pitcher who alienates his teammates on the fictional Washington Americans by writing tell-all articles for *Sports Illustrated*) with *Newsday* TV critic Marv Kitman and *New York Post* sportswriter Vic Ziegel, the boob tube version of *Ball Four* was intended as a *M*A*S*H*-style character comedy, but much of the ribald hilarity of the source material was lost in its transition to the small screen—not least because network censors insisted upon putting such tin-eared epithets as "horse-crock" and "bullhorse" in their characters' mouths. Despite tackling such hot-button topics as drug use, homosexuality, and female sportswriters in the locker room, the show—which featured a catchy theme song by folksinger Harry Chapin of "Cat's in the Cradle" fame—failed to connect with viewers, and was canceled at the end of October after only five episodes.

There was, of course, far more compelling baseball programming to be found on TV in October; you just had to switch over to ABC, which was broadcasting the playoffs. The first games of the AL and NL best-of-five championship series took place on Saturday, October 9, in Kansas City and Philadelphia. There was some concern going into Saturday that thundershowers would force the postponement of the NL opener, but the storm clouds hovering over Kansas City were of a more personal nature, thanks to a heated war of words in the press between Royals players George Brett and Larry Gura and Yankee manager Billy Martin. Brett claimed that Martin had lied to his older brother, Ken, assuring him that he wouldn't be traded two days before the Yankees shipped him to the White Sox in May; Gura, who was scheduled to start Game One of the ALCS, aired similar grievances about Martin's lack of honesty stemming from his time with the Yankees.

"When the season started, [Martin] said I'd be used as a spot starter or in long relief," complained Gura, who was traded to Kansas City in mid-May after not getting into a single game for New York. "But every time a situation would come up, he'd use someone else." "I got rid of [Gura] in Texas because he didn't get the ball over the plate," Martin shot back, "and I got rid of him this year because he wasn't as good as any of my four starters. And if I had him now, I'd get rid of him again."

Brett and Gura didn't realize it, but they'd just given Martin an edge. The Yankee skipper, who'd brought his team to Kansas City on October 5 in order to acclimate them to playing on the artificial turf at Royals Stadium—the first two games of the series marking the first time that the American League Championship Series was played on plastic grass—was always on the lookout for any possible advantage over his opponents. Realizing that he'd already gotten under their skin, Martin resolved to mercilessly heckle Brett and Gura in Game One, and his gambit drew blood almost immediately.

In the first inning, leadoff man Mickey Rivers tapped an 0–2 pitch down the third base line; Brett cleanly backhanded the ball, but then seemed to hesitate for a second before throwing the ball past John Mayberry at first, allowing Rivers to take second. Gura, a control pitcher by trade, suddenly had problems finding Roy White's strike zone, and walked the left fielder on four pitches. Thurman Munson then lined a single to center, loading the bases for Chris Chambliss with no outs. Chambliss bounced what looked like a rally-killing double play ball to Brett, who effortlessly fielded the ball and stepped on third to force White; but Brett's throw to Mayberry came in low and bounced past the first baseman's glove, allowing Munson to chug home behind Rivers. Only one out had been recorded, and the heavily favored Yankees were already up 2–0, thanks to two errors by one of the best young third basemen in the game.

Those two runs were all New York needed, though they added

two more off Gura in the ninth on a double by White that scored shortstop Fred "Chicken" Stanley (a .238 hitter during the season, who belied his easy-out reputation by going 3-for-4 off Gura) and Rivers. Catfish Hunter, whose 17–15, 3.53 ERA season had been considered a disappointment compared to his lofty past performances—despite still leading the Yankees in starts (36), complete games (21), innings (298.2), and strikeouts (173), while becoming the first pitcher since Cy Young and Christy Mathewson to win his 200th game before his 31st birthday—pitched like the Catfish of old, giving up just one hit in the first six innings (and five overall), while walking none and allowing the Royals' lone run on an Al Cowens triple and a fielder's choice grounder off the bat of Tom Poquette. Meanwhile, Munson demonstrated the accuracy of his throwing arm by nailing both Brett and Fred Patek on steal attempts, the latter of which diffused a potential Royals rally in the eighth.

"I don't think I choked, but I was nervous," Brett admitted to reporters after the Yanks' 4–1 victory. "I didn't appreciate the things Martin was saying to me about my brother, but it is not gonna affect the way I play." When asked to repeat what Martin had said to him during the game, Brett responded, "You can't print most of the stuff he was yelling at me. Things like 'Your brother stinks,' but not exactly those words if you know what I mean. If they put a microphone on him for comments during a game, it would be one bleeped tape." "I didn't really get upset about it," Gura insisted. "I have come to expect things like that from Billy Martin. When a guy is willing to win at any costs, even demeaning himself in front of his players like that, you just have to ignore it." "My players were the ones calling names," Martin claimed. "I didn't swear at [Brett]. I was a little hot at Gura," he admitted. "He's been taking some cheap shots at me."

More worrisome for the Royals than Martin's obnoxiousness was the state of Amos Otis's left ankle. The star center fielder sprained it while trying to beat out a first-inning bunt, and was forced to immediately leave the game; X rays of the ankle were negative, but it was so badly swollen that Royals club physician Paul Meyer pronounced Otis unlikely to appear in the second game of the series.

Adding to the Royals' general unease was a bomb threat phoned in following Game One by an anonymous caller, who told police that he'd placed an explosive device somewhere in the stadium, and would detonate it unless a payment of $250,000 was made; no bombs were turned up in the ensuing search, however. In a less deadly but still troubling development, the Royals also learned that Jerry Walker and Bobby Cox, two Yankee scouts, had been communicating with Yankee coach Gene Michael via walkie-talkie from their perch in the WPIX TV booth. Royals GM Joe Burke expressed concern that the scouts were stealing signs from the center field camera monitor and relaying them to Michael, but George Steinbrenner claimed that the Walker and Cox were merely using an "audio communications system" to help Michael position the Yankee defense. AL president Lee MacPhail allowed the Yankees to continue the practice, citing a lack of any rules on the books against the use of walkie-talkies.

While the Reds were favored to win their National League Championship Series against the Phillies, the consensus in the baseball press was that it would be a hard-fought playoff. The teams finished the year with similar records—102–60 for the Reds, 101–61 for the Phillies. Both were endowed with a surplus of speed, power, and stellar defense, and both were incredibly exciting to watch on their native AstroTurf. The Reds had the edge at the plate, having led the league in every major offensive statistic, but the Phils had the second-best offense in the league, and were stronger from a pitching standpoint: not only did their rotation boast two bona-fide aces in Steve Carlton (20–7, 3.13 ERA, 195 strikeouts) and Jim Lonborg (18–10,

3.08 ERA), but their bullpen had collectively racked up 44 saves and a league-best 2.55 ERA. "This is one of the finest matchups ever in the playoffs or a World Series," said Sparky Anderson. "I think the Phillies are an outstanding baseball team. I wouldn't be surprised if they beat us in the playoffs."

Still, for all his respectful comments about the Phillies, Anderson liked the Reds' chances in Game One. Not only was he starting Don Gullett in the opener, who'd looked strong while winning four games for Cincinnati over the last three weeks of the season, but Steve Carlton was starting the game for Philadelphia. Carlton was 0–0 with a 4.32 ERA in three starts against the Reds during the regular season, and his presence on the mound also meant that Tim McCarver, Carlton's personal catcher, would be behind the plate. While Bob Boone was below average in terms of throwing out would-be base stealers, McCarver was even worse, having nailed only eight of the 39 men who'd attempted to run on him in 1976. Even with Carlton's better-than-average pickoff move, the Reds—who'd stolen 210 bases during the season—would be able to run at will.

Indeed, the Reds wound up stealing four bases off Carlton and McCarver in Game One, but Gullett turned out to be the primary factor in Cincinnati's 6–3 victory. After a near-meltdown in the first inning—when he gave up a leadoff double to Dave Cash (who later scored on a Mike Schmidt sacrifice fly) and walked the bases loaded— the left-hander clicked into ace mode and shut the Phillies down through the eighth inning, allowing only a lone single to Garry Maddox along the way. Gullett, who'd hit a two-run homer in the 1975 NLCS, once again helped himself at the plate, going 2-for-4 with 3 RBIs, including a two-run double in the eighth off Tug McGraw that put the Reds up 5–1.

The Phillies were also surprisingly undone by their own defense: Mike Schmidt bobbled a Cesar Geronimo grounder in the sixth that kept the inning alive for the Reds and led to Dave Concepcion scoring on a single by Gullett, while Garry Maddox and Ollie Brown seemed lost in their own outfield, misplaying several balls into extra-base hits and throwing to the wrong bases. The Phillies' uncharacteristic ineptitude elicited loud boos from the Veterans Stadium crowd of 62,640, the largest in playoff history.

Gullett left the game after the eighth inning with a slight muscle strain in his left thigh, and the Phillies finally reconnected with their Bicentennial spirit in the ninth, rising up for four hits and two runs off Rawly Eastwick before he managed to quell the rebellion. "I don't think the Phillies played that badly," said Pete Rose, after Eastwick wrapped up the 6–3 victory. "I just think they are the second best team in baseball."

"I think they'll come back and show you a better team than you saw tonight," responded Danny Ozark, and for the first five innings of Game Two—highlighted by a fifth-inning Greg Luzinski rocket off Pat Zachry that landed in the distant 500 level of the Vet's left field upper deck—the Phillies once again looked like the team that had beaten the Reds seven out of 12 times during the regular season. But in the top of the sixth inning, with the Phillies up 2–0, the wheels came off. Jim Lonborg, who'd thrown five hitless innings for the Phils, walked Dave Concepcion to start the inning, then gave up the first Reds run of the afternoon on back-to-back one-out singles by Rose and Ken Griffey. Ozark brought in Gene Garber, the robustly bearded reliever who'd gone 9–3 on the year with a 2.82 ERA in 59 appearances, to put out the fire. But after Garber intentionally walked Joe Morgan to load the bases, Tony Perez smoked a searing liner down the first base line, which clipped Dick Allen's mitt and went bouncing into short right field; two runs scored, and George Foster plated another when Morgan headed home on his ground-out to second. The Reds scored twice more in the seventh to make it 6–2, and Pedro Borbon—who'd earned his "Dominican Dracula" nickname by biting Pirates hurler Daryl Patterson on the back of the neck during a 1974 brawl—came on to suck the remaining blood out of the Phillies' offense, holding them scoreless on four hits to earn the save. The Reds were going home to Cincinnati with a two-game lead; one more victory, and they'd have a return ticket to the World Series.

After the game, all anyone wanted to talk about was Perez's liner off Allen's mitt; the official scorers had ruled it an error, but Allen, the Reds, and even first base umpire Ed Sudol all disagreed vehemently with the call. Allen insisted that the only reason he was even able to get a glove on Perez's smash was that he'd been in the midst of breaking back to first on a pickoff play, hoping to draw a throw from catcher Bob Boone, when Perez made contact. "I'm running towards the bag and never saw the ball," he said. "If it wasn't a pickup play, I'm nowhere near it [and it goes for] a triple." Anderson agreed. "It wasn't his fault," said the Reds skipper. "Richie Allen shouldn't be blamed. There was a pickoff play on and he was out of position. If that ball had hit him in the head it would have killed him." Only Allen's manager, oddly enough, sided with the scorers. "The ball was catchable," Ozark said. "He got his glove on it. I thought it should have been called an error."

That evening, in Game Two of the ALCS, the Yankees kept the official scorers busy at Royals Stadium, committing a playoff-record five errors as the Royals evened up the series with a 7–3 victory. After looking like the efficient and indestructible "Damn Yankees" of yore in Game One, they now harked back to the hapless Bronx teams of the late '60s and early '70s, with Thurman Munson making two wild throws on Kansas City base stealers, Fred Stanley, Chris Chambliss, and right fielder Oscar Gamble all bobbling balls that were hit right at them, and the offense struggling to score despite outhitting the Royals 12–9. After Royals 17-game-winner

Dennis Leonard spotted the Yankees to a 3–2 lead in the third, lefty Paul Splittorff—who'd missed much of the second half of the season with a ruptured index finger tendon—came in and held the New Yorkers in check for five and two-thirds scoreless innings, while the Kansas City hitters slowly chipped away at 19-game-winner Ed Figueroa.

The Royals finally took the lead in the sixth on a George Brett triple (a drive to center that Mickey Rivers badly mistimed), a John Mayberry single, and a Tom Poquette double, then added two more in the eighth on a walk and three straight bloop singles off reliever Dick Tidrow. "Everything went wrong," grumbled Martin, who blew kisses and waved his cap to jeering Kansas City fans while walking to the mound to take Figueroa out in the sixth. "I'm not going to say anything about the sloppy play. I don't pay attention to errors. . . . I just worry about losing."

Overshadowed by the excitement of the playoffs was the sad demise of Pirates pitcher Bob Moose, who died on October 9, his 29th birthday, in a two-car collision on a wet road near St. Clarksville, Ohio. Moose, who'd played his entire 10-year major league career with the Bucs (and had pitched a no-hitter for them against the Mets in 1969), had gone 3–9 with a 3.68 ERA for Pittsburgh in 1976, a heartening comeback for a man who'd missed most of the two previous seasons after having part of a rib surgically removed to combat a blood clot. The right-hander had just finished playing in an annual golf tournament hosted by former Pirates second baseman Bill Mazeroski, and was on his way to meet teammates Jim Rooker, Dave Giusti, Manny Sanguillen, and Bruce Kison at Mazeroski's restaurant when the fatal accident occurred. (Dick Allen, a fellow son of Western Pennsylvania, would wear a black armband during the second and third games of the NLCS in Moose's honor.)

"Here's a young man in the prime of his life, alive and healthy one minute and not with us anymore the next," lamented Danny Murtaugh, Moose's last manager. "I can't tell you how depressing that is." Murtaugh—who'd enjoyed four different managerial tenures with the team dating back to 1957, including World Championships in 1960 and 1971—had retired less than two weeks earlier, citing health concerns. "I think it's time for a younger man to take over," he'd said at the time. Two months later, Murtaugh would join Moose on the great diamond in the sky, dying of a stroke at the age of 59.

The Pirates had yet to name Murtaugh's successor, but the Giants had already announced their new skipper for the 1977 season—twice. On October 6, the same day that Gerald Ford had put his foot in his mouth during a televised debate with Jimmy Carter by declaring that "there is no Soviet domination of Eastern Europe," the Giants made a massive public gaffe of their own by leaking word that they'd be introducing Vern Rapp as their new manager the next day. But before the press conference could take place, the Cardinals—who'd just fired Red Schoendienst after 12 years at the helm—offered their vacant managerial spot to Rapp, who'd previously managed in the Cards' farm system. A Redbird at heart, Rapp jumped at the offer, leaving the Giants in the lurch.

Scrambling to find another manager in time for the press conference, Giants owner Bob Lurie reached out to Joe Altobelli. Altobelli, who'd been managing in the minors for 11 long years, most recently in the Orioles' system, hadn't been included among Lurie's previous list of managerial candidates, but now Lurie offered him the job over the phone. "He was the best man available for the job," Lurie insisted at the October 7 press conference, which went off as originally planned, even though one San Francisco sportswriter greeted Altobelli with a hearty "Hello, Vern!"

Dick Williams had been one of the top names on Lurie's slate of

potential candidates, but the Expos (having decided to bump Charlie Fox upstairs at season's end, naming him vice president of baseball operations) dangled a two-year contract in front of the fired
Angels skipper before the Giants could get to him. Williams, who'd
played in Montreal as a minor leaguer in the '50s and served as a
third base coach for the Expos in 1970 before Charlie Finley hired
him to manage the A's, was delighted to return. "We will go after the
best two free agents we can get [in the November draft]," he told
the Montreal press, "and then we'll sell them on the advantage of
playing baseball here."

High on the Expos' free agent want list was one Reginald Martinez Jackson, who'd made it fairly clear to all concerned during the
last two months of the season that he would not be returning to the
Orioles for 1977. But because of baseball's tampering rules, which prohibited teams from negotiating with any of the 24 remaining free
agents before the end of the World Series—Ted Turner had already
drawn a $10,000 fine from the commissioner's office for his premature
interactions with the Giants' unsigned left fielder Gary Matthews—
the Expos would have to wait for a few more weeks to make their
pitch.

Reggie was busy at the moment anyway, serving as a guest color
man for ABC's ALCS broadcasts, joining veteran college football
commentator Keith Jackson and the legendarily loquacious Howard
Cosell in the booth. Cosell, best known for his *Monday Night Football* commentary (as well as his work with heavyweight boxing and
the Olympics), made no secret of his contempt for baseball's executive
class, and the feeling seemed mutual: when ABC signed its four-year
deal with Major League Baseball the previous winter, Bowie Kuhn
had specifically requested that Cosell not be included on any of the
broadcasts. "As we worked to better market the game, we did not
need Cosell dissecting baseball for the benefit of our ABC audience,"

the commissioner explained in his autobiography. But when ABC decided it was unhappy with the contributions of such regular season commentators as Bob Prince, Warner Wolf, and players-turned-sportscasters Bob Gibson and Norm Cash, Cosell got the call for the playoffs over Kuhn's strenuous objections.

Kuhn wasn't the only one who didn't dig Cosell: the Cosell-Jackson-Jackson trio's ALCS performance received mostly uncomplimentary notices from TV critics, who alternately took issue with Cosell's verbose delivery—which somehow simultaneously managed to sound both relentlessly staccato and lugubriously unctuous—or Reggie's less-than-polished "Wow, man!" interjections. But Reggie wasn't without his share of insightful points; Roger Angell, writing for *The New Yorker*, observed that Cosell seemed to take every one of Jackson's attempts to enlighten the audience as a personal affront, especially when Jackson's commentary was on the money. "Reggie Jackson is a perceptive young man," wrote Angell, "and by the middle of the second game from Kansas City it had become plain that he was no longer just describing a ball game; he was engaged in an open duel with his more-celebrated colleague for dominance in the proceedings."

But Reggie wasn't just there to set up a sideline for himself as a broadcast personality. The superstar slugger—whose 27 homers, 91 RBIs, and 28 stolen bases would have been impressive totals by 1976 standards, even if he hadn't missed all of April—was counting down the days until he could hit the free agency jackpot. "I'll soon be an overpaid athlete," he told *Sports Illustrated*'s Ron Fimrite. "I'll probably get a million more than I should, but I didn't make the rules. I'm just taking advantage of them."

Reggie insisted that he wasn't *just* in it for the money, however; he also had very specific ideas about the sort of city he'd like to play in, and the sort of team he'd like to play for. "I want to go to a place with a liberal attitude," he told Fimrite. "I know I'm not crazy about playing in the South, and the Midwest would be impractical for me because all of my business interests are either on the West Coast or in the East.

"But there are other considerations," he continued. "I'm not sure I'd fit in with teams like the Mets or the Dodgers that emphasize organization over individual personality. They may not even want someone like me. But I could see myself with a team like the Phillies, because with all their stars—the Schmidts, the Luzinskis—there wouldn't be so much pressure on me. And I'd like to be on a contender and a team that draws well. I've never been on a team that drew well. I like living near the ocean . . ."

Unfortunately for Jackson, the rules for the upcoming free agent draft stated that no more than 12 teams could attempt to negotiate with him—and the New York Yankees, who most closely fit Jackson's idealized description of his next team, would be among the last to draft due to their finish at the top of the AL East. With this in mind, Reggie had begun to not-so-subtly campaign (both in print and during the playoff broadcasts) to be drafted by the Yankees, as well as drop equally transparent hints to teams like the Twins, Indians, and Brewers that they shouldn't waste a draft pick on him, because there was no way in hell he'd consider playing for them. During the second game of the ALCS, Jackson watched Martin sarcastically blowing kisses to the Kansas City crowd. "I can play for a man like that," he announced to the viewers at home.

Jackson was also spotted chatting with George Steinbrenner on the field before Game One, though both men denied that there was anything untoward about their conversation. "We are discussing philosophies," deadpanned the Yankee owner. "He's permitted to tell me that New York City has great restaurants and lots of fine clothing stores," added Jackson. "And I am permitted to say that I work for

ABC, which is in New York; and I work for Puma, which is in New York."

After two losses at home, the Philadelphia Phillies came into Cincinnati with a notable absence of the "Phillies Fever" they'd proudly (if terribly) sung about earlier in the year. "We had beaten the Reds handily all season," Dick Allen would later recall, "but all the turmoil in the clubhouse over the final few weeks of the regular season had us feeling and playing like a broken team."

But in Game Three, on a sunny afternoon at Riverfront Stadium, the Phillies seemed to pull together and play like the team that had just won a franchise-record 101 games. They also seemed to finally be getting some breaks: in the bottom of the second inning, Garry Maddox unsuccessfully tried to make shoestring catch of a low liner off the bat of Tony Perez, missing the drive by several inches—but instead of bounding all the way to the dead-center wall and resulting in a triple or worse, the ball hit a dead spot on the stained and faded Riverfront carpet and bounced back toward the infield like a billiards trick shot. Maddox was able to grab it and hold Perez at first; the Big Doggie was erased two batters later, when Johnny Bench hit into an inning-ending 6-4-3 double play.

Back-to-back doubles by Mike Schmidt and Greg Luzinski off Gary Nolan gave the Phils a 1–0 lead in the top of the fourth, and Jim Kaat deftly kept the Reds scoreless through six. Nolan, who'd reaggravated a groin injury while covering first base in the third, got the hook after walking Allen and Johnstone to load the bases in the top of the sixth. Manny Sarmiento, a 20-year-old Venezuelan rookie who'd impressed Sparky Anderson as a late-July call-up, got the Reds out of that particular jam, but gave up two runs in the seventh on back-to-back doubles by Maddox (plating Larry Bowa, who'd walked) and Schmidt. The Phillies were up 3–0 and looking like they could very well stretch the series to at least four games.

Then, in the bottom of the seventh, the Big Red Machine roared back. Ken Griffey singled and Joe Morgan walked; Ozark pulled a double switch, yanking Kaat for Ron Reed, who'd done well against the Reds all season, while replacing Luzinski in left with Bobby Tolan. Reed went to a quick 0–2 on Perez, who fouled off another pitch before singling up the middle, scoring Griffey and bringing the Riverfront crowd of 55,047 to noisy life for the first time all day. George Foster flied to right, scoring Morgan from third, and Johnny Bench walked on a close pitch that Reed was sure should have been called a strike. After Dave Concepcion to popped out to Dave Cash at second, Cesar Geronimo blooped a Texas Leaguer to left; Tolan pulled up and let the ball drop in front of him, then watched in stunned disbelief as it shot past him on the AstroTurf. Schmidt, who'd hustled out into left in an attempt to flag the ball down, chased the ball almost all the way to the warning track before returning it to the infield. When the dust cleared, Geronimo stood on third with a triple, and the Reds were up 4–3.

Still, the Phillies refused to die. After Rawly Eastwick whiffed Dick Allen in the top of the eighth, Jay Johnstone hit a hot grounder that ricocheted off Perez's glove at first and landed in the stands for a double. Bob Boone walked, Larry Bowa hit a flare down the left field line that rolled into the Phillies' bullpen for a double that scored Johnstone, and a Dave Cash fly to right scored Terry Harmon (who was pinch-running for Boone) with the go-ahead run. After Reed regained his composure and held the Reds scoreless in the eighth, Jerry Martin—whom Ozark had brought in as a left fielder during the previous inning, moving Tolan to first and taking Allen out of the game—smacked a nasty grounder to Pete Rose at third, who handled it flawlessly but bounced the throw to Perez for an error. Johnstone then smoked one on the ground to the right of Joe Morgan, which skidded on the artificial turf all the way to the right-center wall for an RBI triple, and the Phillies were up 6–4 going into the bottom of the ninth.

Ozark stuck with Reed for the ninth, which immediately turned out to be a mistake. George Foster led off the inning, and he promptly deposited Reed's hanging first-pitch slider into the left field seats. Next up was Bench, who drove a 1–2 high fastball deep into the left-center stands to tie the game, a blast that eerily echoed his game-tying ninth-inning homer in the final contest of the 1972 NLCS against the Pirates. Ozark brought in Gene Garber to replace Reed, then yanked him after Garber gave up a first-pitch single to Concepcion. Ozark wanted to bring in Tug McGraw to face lefty batter Cesar Geronimo, but McGraw experienced a muscle spasm in his back while warming up in the bullpen, so Ozark went instead with 22-year-old lefty Tom Underwood, who'd gone 10-5 with a 3.53 ERA for the Phillies in 1976, albeit mostly as a starting pitcher.

Nervously chomping on his bubblegum, Underwood walked Geronimo on four pitches, then intentionally walked Rose to load the bases after pinch-hitter Ed Armbrister sacrificed Geronimo and Concepcion to second and third. With the bases loaded, one out and the score tied, Ken Griffey whacked a high, slow chopper toward first base; Tolan rushed in and vainly tried to come up with it, but it wouldn't have mattered even if he'd fielded the ball cleanly: Concepcion had already crossed the plate and was madly leaping about in celebration of the Reds' second straight NL championship. "As soon as I saw it hit off his glove, I knew it was over," said Griffey, as the champagne corks popped around him. "This is better than any batting championship!"

The mood in the Phillies' clubhouse was morose. As poetic and perfect as it would have been for Philadelphia to represent the NL in the 1976 World Series, the Phillies Fever and the Bicentennial spirit was ultimately no match for the pitiless onslaught of the Big Red Machine. "There was no luck involved," reflected Larry Bowa. "They had more experience. They took advantage of every mistake we made. There was no excuse. We just got beat.

"They simply don't quit," the shortstop continued. "I feel sorry for whoever plays them in the Series. I don't think there is a team over there [in the AL] who can compete with them."

Sparky Anderson agreed. "There isn't another club in baseball that can match the eight players we can put on the field every day," he said. "This isn't any three- or four-man team like most clubs, so how you gonna contain 'em? Sooner or later, these guys are gonna get you.

"I'll tell you one thing," he concluded. "Either Kansas City or the Yankees could beat us, but if they do, they will ache so much when they do that they won't ever feel relaxed."

An impromptu celebration broke out in downtown Cincinnati following the Reds' win, with a swarm of Reds fans (variously estimated at between 10,000 and 14,000) overrunning the city's Fountain Square Plaza, where official Reds victory rallies had been held in previous years. The unscheduled gathering, which began joyfully around 6:30 p.m., turned increasingly ugly as the evening wore on; rowdy fans smashed windows of local businesses, and tore banners reading "Reds Are Hot" from the front of a theater. Two shootings and one stabbing were reported, and over 70 people were arrested in the fracas. "I guess we should have had an organized program," shrugged Cincinnati City councilman James Cissell the next day. "At least the crowd would be occupied instead of just milling around and drinking beer."

That evening in the Bronx, the Yankee Stadium crowd of 56,808 (which included Secretary of State Henry Kissinger) barely had time to sip the foam off their first brews of the game before the Royals began hammering away at Dock Ellis, sending seven men to the plate in the first inning as they jumped out to a 3–0 lead. But Ellis, who'd finished the season 17-8 with a 3.19 ERA—despite walking more batters (76) than he'd whiffed (65) for the first time in his major league career—soon managed to settle down and defuse the Royals' attack, holding them scoreless on three hits from the second through the eighth. "On a scale of one to 10, I'd rate my performance about a four," admitted Ellis, who'd last pitched 10 days earlier, and was clearly shaking some rust out of his right arm. "The guys on Kansas City hit the ball hard but they hit it at people. That's why we won."

The Yanks also won Game Three because of their bats, which—after nine scoreless innings going back to the fourth frame of Game Two—finally woke up in the bottom of the fourth when Lou Piniella smacked a ball past George Brett at third for a two-out double, and Chris Chambliss tagged Royals starter Andy Hassler for a two-run homer that traveled 400 feet on a line into the right field bleachers. Chambliss drove in the tying run in the seventh by grounding into a force play with the bases loaded, then moved to second on an RBI single off the bat of Graig Nettles, and came home when Elliott Maddox doubled off Steve Mingori to make it 5–3. Maddox, who'd been used sparingly since returning from the DL in September, gave the Yankees their 10th two-bagger of the series, setting a playoff record. Though Sparky Lyle walked Brett to start the ninth, he set Mayberry, McRae, and pinch-hitter Dave Nelson down in order to clinch the victory and earn the save.

Down two games to one in the series, and scheduled to face the great Catfish Hunter in Game Four, the Royals expressed frustration at having let the Yankees off the hook in Game Three after a promising first inning. "We just let up," lamented Freddie Patek. "I hate to say that. We got three runs and could have buried them but we didn't. We turned from offense to defense and laid back a bit." Though Brett had gone 6-for-10 in the first three games, his difficulties at third—many thought he should have gotten to the Piniella grounder that opened the gate for the Yankees' first runs—caused even his own manager to compare him unfavorably to Graig Nettles. "I never realized until this year what a great third baseman [Nettles] was," Herzog told reporters. "He made some great plays tonight. He made some plays that our third baseman didn't."

Nettles homered twice in Game Four, while Brett went hitless, but neither third baseman was ultimately a deciding factor in the Royals' series-tying 7-4 win. With Amos Otis still out, Jim Wohlford hitting only .111 in the leadoff spot, Frank White hitting nearly as poorly (.125), and McRae hitless for the series so far, Herzog felt compelled to shake up his team's lineup. Al Cowens, who'd been playing center in Otis's absence, hit leadoff; rookie Jamie Quirk took over DH duties, while McRae was stationed in right, and right fielder Tom Poquette was moved to left. Most importantly, veteran second baseman Cookie Rojas got the starting nod over the slumping White. "Hey, I'm no genius," said Herzog. "This is my first time around at this thing. We just haven't gotten the job done in run production. Cookie's a better hitter and more of a clutch ballplayer."

Rojas made Herzog look like a genius in Game Four, going 2-for-3, scoring a run in the second, driving in another with a sacrifice fly in the fourth, and starting an inning-ending 4-6-3 double play in the sixth by snagging a hot grounder from Chris Chambliss. But Rojas wasn't the only unexpected hero of the Royals' 7–4 victory; Patek, hitting in the eighth hole, rapped a two-out second-inning double to right-center off Hunter—Mickey Rivers tried unsuccessfully to snag the ball with a backhanded shoestring catch—that scored Rojas and John Mayberry, then knocked another RBI double in the eighth to score Frank White (pinch-running for Rojas) for the team's final run of the game. Hal McRae got unstuck at the plate, cracking a double off Hunter, a triple off reliever Dick Tidrow, and scoring twice, while Quirk knocked the struggling Hunter out of the game in the fourth with an RBI triple, and drove in another run two innings later with a sacrifice fly.

That the top four hitters in the Kansas City lineup went a combined 0-for-16 ultimately proved irrelevant, as did Larry Gura's poor outing, which saw Herzog pulling him for Doug Bird after giving up six hits and two runs (both on Nettles's first homer of the afternoon) in two innings. Bird pitched a solid four and two-thirds innings in relief for the win, giving up only one run on an RBI single to Willie Randolph, and Steve Mingori gave up only one hit (Nettles's solo shot in the ninth) over the last two and a third innings while notching the save. The series was tied now at two games apiece.

"I feel we have the best momentum now," McRae rejoiced afterward. "I think we're in the best position. We beat their best pitcher—their big gun. They won't have the same faith in the guy they throw tomorrow as they had today." Billy Martin took umbrage at McRae's assertion, telling reporters that the Yankees had plenty of faith in Ed Figueroa. "Nineteen wins," he snapped, when asked why Figgy was still slated to start Game Five despite having pitched poorly in Game Two. "That's a pretty good reason." Martin said he had no interest in using the healthy and available Ken Holtzman, claiming that "he hasn't been pitching well lately," even though the veteran lefty had gone a solid 4–3 with a 3.17 ERA in his last eight starts.

Herzog, for his part, was still undecided as to who would take the mound for Kansas City in Game Five. "I have no idea right now," he admitted. "I have a choice of four—Dennis Leonard, Marty Pattin, Al Fitzmorris and Paul Splittorff. If I had Holtzman," he added, unable to resist needling Martin, "I'd pitch him." With Game Four ending shortly after 6 p.m., Herzog still had time to figure it out, and hoped that a night on Broadway would assist his decision-making process. "I'm going to see *A Chorus Line*, have a few scotches and come up with a winning pitcher," the White Rat announced.

The final game of the ALCS began at 8:30 on Thursday, October 14, following a performance of "The Star-Spangled Banner" by Melba Moore, a Tony Award–winning musical-theater-actress-turned-R&B-singer who'd recently enjoyed some chart success with the disco track "This Is It." Moore's strident rendition of the National Anthem reflected the energy and anxiety tautly vibrating throughout the packed Yankee Stadium, where 56,821 paying customers were gathered to witness the first do-or-die postseason game in the Bronx since Game Five of the 1958 World Series. "I think both teams are just as high as they could possibly be for the ballgame," announced Keith Jackson during the pregame show. The same thing could be said for the Yankee fans, who waved banners with such aspirational messages as "Think Series," "The Yankees Are Back," and "The Yankees Are Comin'—This Is Their Year," and cheered every strike and out call against the Royals so forcefully that their shouts repeatedly overloaded ABC's microphones.

The Royals tried to dampen the crowd's enthusiasm in the first inning, when Brett doubled on a 3–2 count with two outs, then came home on John Mayberry's two-run blast into the "short porch" in right. But the Yanks came out swinging in the bottom of the frame, bringing the fans back into the game when Mickey Rivers smacked an opposite field drive over the head of left fielder Tom Poquette, then turned on the jets to transform an easy double into a triple. Roy White singled Rivers home for the first New York run of the game, then stole second; Thurman Munson singled to left, and advanced to second when Poquette tried to nail White at third. Herzog, who'd seriously considered starting the left-handed Paul Splittorff instead of the right-handed Leonard, yanked Leonard and called for "Splitt." Chambliss, the next batter up, flied to left to bring White home, but Splitt made quick work of Carlos May and Graig Nettles, and emerged from the inning with the score tied 2–2.

The Royals fought back in the top of the second. Cookie Rojas, again playing in place of Frank White, singled to center. When Figueroa tried to pick him off at first, Rojas hustled to second and beat the throw from Chambliss, then scored when Buck Martinez singled him home to give the Royals a 3–2 lead. In the bottom of the third, Rivers once again sparked the Yankee offense with a leadoff hit, this time a single. George Steinbrenner had chewed Rivers out the previous evening for his inability to track down Patek's double in Game Four; now, up in the ABC booth, Reggie Jackson riffed on the Steinbrenner-Rivers "meeting" for the benefit of the television audience. "It's always amazing to me how someone who's never played the game can tell somebody how to play," he laughed. "Don't come down to the Oakland clubhouse or the Baltimore clubhouse and tell *me* what to do!"

Rivers moved to second on a Splittorff walk to Roy White, then scored on a Thurman Munson single. White followed him home shortly afterward, thanks to a Chris Chambliss grounder that forced Munson at second. Up 4–3, the Yankees threatened to widen their lead in the fourth, when Splittorff loaded the bases with two outs by sandwiching another single by Rivers with walks to Fred Stanley and White; but Herzog brought in Marty Pattin, who induced Munson to fly out to end the inning. The Yankees loaded the bases against lefty Andy Hassler with two out in the fifth, but again left the runners stranded as Stanley lined to Rojas for the final out.

The score remained frozen at 4–3 until the bottom of the sixth, when Rivers—now facing lefty Andy Hassler—got aboard on a bunt single, took second on a sacrifice bunt by White, and scored on a single by Munson, who was thrown out by McRae while trying to stretch his hit into a double. It was Munson's 10th hit of the series, a playoff record that Chris Chambliss immediately tied with a single off Hassler. Chambliss stole second, his second swipe of the series (he'd stolen only one bag all year), then trotted home when Carlos May hit a tapper to George Brett that the third baseman threw away for his third error of the series. The Yankees were now up 6–3, thanks to a textbook example of Billy Martin's hard-nosed brand of baseball, and the newly renovated ballpark sounded like it was readying for takeoff.

Though Figueroa was clearly tiring, Martin stuck with him until the top of the eighth, when he gave up a leadoff single to Al Cowens. "Ed-die! Ed-die! Ed-die!" chanted the fans as Figgy exited the field. Grant Jackson got the bullpen call from Martin, but the veteran lefty—who'd gone 5–0 with a 1.56 ERA over the last two months of the season—couldn't get the job done. Jim Wohlford (who'd come up as a pinch-hitter for Tom Poquette) looped a single to left, and then George Brett drilled the second pitch he saw from Jackson down the line into the lower right field stands for a game-tying three-run homer. Brett's blast abruptly hushed the Yankee Stadium crowd; it was as if an unseen hand had suddenly turned the ballpark's ambient noise setting from giddy pennant hysteria to dyspeptic murmur.

The dyspepsia turned to bitter impatience in the bottom of the eighth, when the top of the Yankees' order proved utterly ineffective against Royals reliever Mark Littell, Herzog's fifth pitcher of the night. Though Rivers, White, and Munson had already gone a combined 8-for-9 in the ballgame, Littell set them down in order, fanning Munson—who'd struck out only 38 times all season—for the final out. Yankee fans had been intermittently tossing empty bottles and other refuse onto the field throughout the game (the screen behind home plate had been festooned with toilet paper garlands since almost the first pitch), but now the garbage started to fall with a steady rhythm, like a foul Bronx rain.

Dick "Dirt" Tidrow replaced Jackson on the mound in the top of the ninth, and got Rojas and Patek to ground out to Stanley in rapid succession. But then Buck Martinez stroked a single to left, his third hit of the night, and Tidrow walked Al Cowens to put a Royal at first and second with two outs. With Brett (who was hitting a team-leading .444 for the series) on deck, Jim Wohlford, the next batter up, tapped a high chopper to Nettles; first base appeared to be the easier play, but Nettles threw to Willie Randolph at second instead. Cowens appeared to beat the throw—ABC's slow-motion replays subsequently reinforced that he was safe—but second base umpire Joe Brinkman signaled that he was out. Instead of Brett coming to the plate with bases loaded and two outs, the Royals' half of the ninth was over.

Though angered by Brinkman's call, Herzog chose not to argue it. "I didn't come out for two reasons," he revealed afterward. "First, I knew they weren't going to change the call. Second, the crowd had been throwing bottles and other things all night. I was hit by a tomato during the pre-game introductions. I didn't want to go out there and get killed." Herzog remained instead in the relative safety of the visitors' dugout, watching the umpires and grounds crew attempt another cleanup of the field before the Yankees came up to bat. He hoped that Littell would set Chambliss, Sandy Alomar—who'd come into the game in the bottom of the sixth as a pinch-runner for DH Carlos May—and Nettles down in order, thereby allowing Brett, Mayberry, and McRae to come to the plate in the top of the 10th.

But Brett and his teammates wouldn't get to take another cut until 1977. Chambliss, looking fastball all the way, swung from the heels and connected with the fireman's first pitch; the big first baseman stood frozen in the batter's box as he watched the flight of the ball to right-center-field, then took off for first as it cleared the wall. Chambliss had homered to win the game and the playoffs, and the Yankees were World Series–bound for the first time in twelve years.

The field was already overrun with ecstatic Yankee fans as Chambliss rounded first base; by the time he reached second, the bag was in the process of being looted for a souvenir, so he reached out and touched it with his right hand before it disappeared into the night. After taking a few steps toward third, Chambliss collided with a fan and fell to his knees; he quickly righted himself, but was set upon by several revelers who attempted to divest him of his batting helmet.

"What a way for the American League season to end!" exulted Howard Cosell on ABC, as Chambliss tucked his helmet under his arm like a football, feinted in the direction of third, then took off across the diamond for the safety of the Yankees' dugout, grimly plowing through the exponentially thickening mob like a reluctant fullback. "The look on his face now is not one of joy or fear or relief," wrote *The New Yorker*'s Roger Angell, "but just the closed, expressionless, neutral subway look that we all see and all wear when abroad in the enormous and inexplicable city." Roy White pleaded with the throng to give Chambliss room enough to touch home plate; instead, several fans picked up the outfielder and whisked him away on their shoulders, chanting "We're Number One!"

Afterward in the Yankee clubhouse, eyes stinging from a succession of champagne showers, Chambliss repeatedly insisted that he'd "touched all four bases." Just to be on the safe side, Elston Howard, Graig Nettles, and two NYPD officers had escorted him back out onto the field to touch the dirt where third base and home plate had formerly resided. Not that Herzog and the Royals were protesting the game's outcome; the condition of the field—which would require hundreds of man-hours and an estimated expenditure of $100,000 in order to make it presentable for Game Three of the World Series—and the impending start of the Fall Classic in roughly 36 hours would have rendered a replay all but impossible.

Perhaps things would have turned out differently for Kansas City if they hadn't lost their star center fielder in the first inning of the first game, if the Cowens call had gone their way, or if the time-out for trash removal between the top and bottom of the ninth hadn't thrown Littell off his rhythm. But the Royals were proud, not bitter, in defeat. "It was my best pitch," said Littell, who'd only given up one homer in 104 innings during the regular season. "You've got to give him credit, he hit it out." "We did our best and there's nothing to be ashamed of," said McRae. "It was a hell of a ball game. They just beat us." "The Yankees won, but we didn't lose," added Rojas. "I don't think anyone on this club will walk out of here with his head down."

From the Yankees' perspective, Chambliss's heroic homer was the dramatic final act of a season-long coronation, one that restored the Bronx Bombers to their rightful prominence after a dozen years of wandering in the wasteland. "New York has to win for baseball to be healthy," philosophized Billy Martin. For Martin, the only disappointment was that Casey Stengel wasn't around to see his apt pupil pilot the team to their 30th AL pennant. "Wouldn't Casey be happy?" asked the Yankee skipper, who'd worn a black armband on his uniform all season in honor of "The Old Perfessor," who'd passed away the previous September. "I'd love for him to be here. I guess he's smiling somewhere in the sky."

Even flushed with the joy of victory, Martin couldn't resist making a dig at his real and imagined foes in the press and elsewhere. "Those guys who didn't think this team could do it, who picked against us, who said I'd never win one, where are they now?" he shouted above the din of the clubhouse celebration. "Now they can kiss my dago ass. I won it. The Yankees are back where they belong, on top." "And it's not a one-year thing," promised George Steinbrenner, after Rivers doused him with bubbly. "We're back on top and we're going to stay there."

The Yankees' first pennant since 1964 represented more than just the storied franchise's return to greatness. Along with the Tall Ships extravaganza and the Democratic convention at Madison Square Garden, the resurrection of the Yankees was another high-profile 1976 event that seemed to herald the comeback of the beleaguered metropolis.

Despite having been portrayed for years by the media as a burntout husk of its former self, the Big Apple of the Bicentennial was vibrantly alive. From the squalor of the Lower East Side arose the downtown punk scene, personified by artists like the Ramones, Blondie (who released their debut single, "X Offender," in June), Mink DeVille, Television, Talking Heads, Richard Hell and the Voidoids, and Patti Smith, all of whom regularly played CBGB in the Bowery and Max's Kansas City near Union Square.

The city's disco scene was even livelier, with DJs like David Mancuso, Nicky Siano, and Larry Levan spinning records at predominantly gay SoHo and West Village nightspots like the Loft, the Gallery, and Paradise Garage, while a wealthier, straighter crowd gravitated toward uptown boogie palaces like the Hippopotamus and Regine's. In October, "Everybody Dance," a demo track by New York session musicians Bernard Edwards and Nile Rodgers, was driving dancers into a frenzy at the Night Owl, an upscale club in the Village; in a year's time, the song would form the cornerstone of the self-titled debut album by Chic, Edwards and Rodgers' elegant, groundbreaking, and platinum-selling disco band.

Up in the Bronx, a series of house and street parties thrown by local DJ Kool Herc had developed into what would come to be known as the hip-hop scene. Grand Wizzard Theodore, the young DJ who introduced "scratching" to the hip-hop vernacular, unveiled his new technique at a Bronx house party in late '76, using a drum break from Thin Lizzy's new *Johnny the Fox* LP to drive the revelers wild.

The influence of these movements would be profound and widespread, leaving their lasting mark on fashion and art as well as music for decades to come. Disco had already begun its move into the mainstream by 1976, but the punk and hip-hop scenes were still primarily underground, accessible only to those in the know. The Yankees, on the other hand, were in the public eye every day, and their season-long push to the American League pennant was both a point of pride for New Yorkers (at least those who weren't Mets fans), and a legitimate point of interest for the rest of the country. The mere presence of showbiz luminaries like Frank Sinatra, Telly Savalas, Cary Grant, and James Cagney—not to mention Henry Kissinger—at Yankee Stadium during the last three games of the ALCS said it all to the many millions watching the playoffs at home: despite rampant crime and corruption, urban blight and economic woes, New York City was once again the place to *be*, baby.

Those confusing the Yankees of 1976 with the dynastic Bronx Bombers of yore, however, were setting themselves up for disappointment. It was a very good team, to be sure; but with the possible exceptions of Munson, Hunter, and Lyle, none of the names on the roster exactly resonated with the greatness of Ruth, Gehrig, DiMaggio, or Mantle. There were some sportswriters who believed that Billy Martin's men had a shot to go all the way against the Reds ("The Yankees could have that intangible called momentum on their side," wrote the AP's Hal Bock), or thought that the Yankees' lineup would have an advantage against the Reds' much maligned pitching staff, but they obviously hadn't paid close attention to the self-assured ease with which the Reds had swept an excellent Phillies team earlier in the week.

They also neglected to factor in the hangover effect: after winning their physically and emotionally draining playoff series against the Royals, the Yankees had partied all night in celebration. "Then we had to catch an early bus to go to the airport and fly to Cincinnati," Nettles later recalled. "We weren't in any shape to play the World Series."

Not that Billy Martin would ever admit as much. "We're gonna take the windshield wipers off the [Big Red] Machine," rambled the bleary-eyed Yankee skipper to reporters, while overseeing his team's low-energy workout at Riverfront Stadium on the gray and drizzly afternoon of October 15. "You gotta see to drive. They might lead the league in popoffs, but I'm gonna be the Yankee loudmouth. All I gotta do is sober up before the game tomorrow."

Before the season began, shipping magnate Steinbrenner had magnanimously promised Martin the gift of one of his many tugboats if Martin reeled in the AL pennant for him in '76. Martin figured that a tugboat was worth about $300,000, a windfall he desperately needed; his 22-year-old daughter, Kelly Ann, had been arrested in November 1975 for attempting to smuggle a pound of cocaine from Colombia to Miami, and Martin had already shelled out tens of thousands of dollars in bribes and attorney fees in an effort to spring her from a Colombian prison. But when Martin asked for his tugboat following the Yankees' Game Five victory, Steinbrenner reneged. "You have to win the World Series to get the boat," he said.

Having thus annoyed his manager, Steinbrenner proceeded to anger his players by distributing the bulk of the team's ticket allotment for the World Series opener to his business cronies from Cleveland;

the Yankee players, most of whom had never appeared in a Fall Classic, were too busy trying to drum up tickets for their own families to fully focus on the impending contest. "Here we were," recalled Nettles, "five minutes before the national anthem of the first game in Cincinnati, and we're running around, still trying to find someone to give us our tickets. There was a lot of screaming and yelling. Everyone was upset. Thurman was furious. It was like George was telling us that he got us to the Series all by himself and screw the players."

Exhausted and pissed off was no way to go into any World Series, much less one against a well-rested Big Red Machine. With his three best starters worn out from their ALCS efforts, Martin named Doyle Alexander as his Game One starter, despite the fact that Alexander hadn't pitched since September 25. The 25-year-old right-hander had gone 10-5 with a 3.29 ERA in 19 starts for the Yankees after coming over from the Orioles in June, and Martin believed that his variety of off-speed breaking pitches would stymie the fastball-feasting Cincinnati lineup, which now also included Dan Driessen (who'd hit .247 with seven HRs and 44 RBIs as a backup first baseman and left fielder) as the first DH in Reds history.

"I still think the DH rule makes a mockery of the game," said Sparky Anderson, who'd initially threatened to let his pitchers bat in protest of the DH's incursion onto the World Series diamond. "But it's not fair to my ball club for me not to use it. If I didn't use it and we lost a game because of it, I couldn't face my own team."

The 1976 World Series opened on Saturday, October 16, on a sunny-but-crisp autumn afternoon in Cincinnati. Taking the mound for the Reds was Don Gullett, now fully recovered from the thigh muscle strain that knocked him out of the first game of the NLCS. Anderson had earlier expressed the opinion that stopping Rivers and Munson was the key to stopping the Yankees' offense, and

Gullett duly whiffed them both as he sailed through an easy first inning. Alexander, on the other hand, had difficulty getting his off-speed stuff over the plate, and was forced to rely on his fastball. He managed to get Pete Rose and Ken Griffey to fly out in the first inning, but Joe Morgan pounced on the first fastball he saw from Alexander and drove it deep into Riverfront's right field stands to give the Reds their first run of the series. It was the first career World Series homer for the compact second baseman, who'd hit 27 during the regular season.

The Yankees tied it up in the top of the second, with DH Lou Piniella doubling to left-center, moving to third on a Chris Chambliss grounder to second, and coming home on a long Graig Nettles fly ball to Cesar Geronimo in center. But thereafter, the game belonged to Gullett and the Reds. Dave Concepcion tripled in the third, scoring on a Pete Rose fly ball to center to make it 2–1. In the sixth, Ken Griffey reached first on a fielder's choice, stole second on a strike three pitch to Morgan, then came home on Perez's single to left. In the seventh, Martin finally pulled Alexander after George Foster singled and Johnny Bench blasted a ball off the right field wall for an opposite field RBI triple. Sparky Lyle came into the game, and promptly threw a wild pitch past Munson that scored Bench to give the Reds a 5–1 lead.

New York mounted a couple of rallies, but Gullett kept managing to work his way out of trouble, or at least let the Yankees do it for him. In the top of the sixth, with New York still down by only a run, Fred Stanley led off the inning with a walk; Rivers followed and tried to drag a bunt for a base hit, but Gullett made a nice grab of the ball and tossed it to second to force Stanley. Rivers—who'd bragged going into the series that he could "steal on anybody"—then tried to swipe second, but Bench gunned him down with a perfect peg to Morgan. With two outs and the bases empty, Roy

White cracked a drive to left-center that was dropped by the usually sure-handed Geronimo for a two-base error; Munson then singled to right, but Griffey pounced on the ball too quickly for White to head home. Piniella lined out to Morgan, and the inning was over. Four Yankees had reached base in the inning, and none of them had scored.

In the eighth, while facing Rivers, the ever-fragile Gullett stepped in a slight depression on the mound, causing some discomfort in his ankle; though he left the game shortly thereafter under his own power, X rays revealed a dislocation of the peroneus longus tendon, and his ankle was placed in a cast. The only member of the Big Red Machine planning to test the free agency waters in November, Gullett had most likely just pitched his last game in a Cincinnati uniform. Pedro Borbon came in to shut the Yankees down the rest of the way, and the Reds wrapped up the first game of the Series.

Afterward, neither manager claimed to be particularly impressed with the Big Red Machine's Game One performance; Anderson chided his team for not being aggressive enough at the plate or on the base paths, while Martin thought the Reds were more lucky than good. "We hit our line drives for outs more than they did for base hits," he said. "We just didn't come up with the big hits." Martin was also annoyed that Commissioner Kuhn had shut down the Yankees' "audio communication system" in the middle of the game, after the Reds—who'd previously agreed to let one walkie-talkie-wielding Yankee staffer sit among the fans in the upper deck—complained when three Yankee scouts planted themselves within sight of the TV monitors in the CBS radio booth. "It was nothing tricky, strictly for defense," Martin complained. "Apparently someone got to the Commissioner from the Reds and got it stopped. Why? Because baseball hasn't been doing it for 100 years. . . . I'm not going to ask for permission tomorrow. They're going to have to find it." Johnny Bench, a CB radio enthusiast whose handle was "Sidewinder," joked that he'd be bringing his own citizens band radio to rest of the games, so as to annoy Martin (CB handle: "Yankee One") with questions regarding the flow of traffic around second base.

The Yankees had been flat in Game One, which surprised their captain. "This was my first Series game, but it was not what I felt it would be," said Thurman Munson. "The last game of the playoffs is what I thought this Series game would be like." Chris Chambliss was equally baffled by his team's perfunctory performance, asking, "If you can't get up for the Cincinnati Reds, who can you get up for?" But with Catfish Hunter—a big-money pitcher in several senses of the term, who'd gone 4–0 with a 2.19 ERA in seven World Series appearances—slated to take the mound for Game Two, there was hope that the team would find a way to rekindle its competitive flame. In the end, the second game of the 1976 World Series would be its hardest-fought, though both teams would be colder than a Dairy Queen freezer by the time it was all over.

Of all of Commissioner Kuhn's controversial decisions and rulings in 1976, few elicited more howls of outrage from the sports press than his decision to have Game Two played on a Sunday night instead of its usual Sunday afternoon slot. The consensus among columnists was that Kuhn had sold out to TV interests (NBC had offered MLB an extra $750,000 to broadcast the game in the evening, so that it wouldn't interfere with their afternoon NFL coverage) without any regard for the well-being of the players or the enjoyment of the fans attending the game.

Kuhn countered that Major League Baseball had set an overall attendance record of 31,318,331 in 1976, despite what he characterized as "poor races," and the commissioner believed that the five night game broadcasts of the 1975 World Series had played a role in the sport's increased popularity. "I imagine a lot of fans would enjoy the opportunity to watch football Sunday afternoon and baseball Sunday night," he said. "But that is simply an incidental."

Kuhn also offered a nonverbal riposte to his critics by watching Game Two from his Riverfront box while wearing nothing heavier than a sports jacket, despite a chill factor that dipped into the low 20s. Meanwhile, the players huddled together in the dugouts, warming their hands over hibachi grills—Graig Nettles kept his bat warm with a hot water bottle, while Dan Driessen retreated several times into the Reds' clubhouse sauna without ever removing his uniform—and the 54,816 fans in attendance looked on in icy misery.

They—along the 20.3 million at home, a 45 percent increase over 1975's Game Two—witnessed a fine game, however. The Reds had Hunter on the ropes early, sending eight men to the plate and scoring three times in the second inning, including on Ken Griffey's fly ball to short center that scored Cesar Geronimo after Mickey Rivers's feeble throw to the plate all but rolled home to Thurman Munson. But as Reggie Jackson had explained to Howard Cosell during the ALCS, Catfish was the sort of pitcher who just got tougher as the game went on—and from the fourth inning through the eighth, he only allowed two hits, none of which did any damage. The Yankees, meanwhile, dinged Fred Norman for a run in the fourth on a Graig Nettles RBI single, then sent the diminutive lefty packing in the seventh when Fred Stanley doubled Willie Randolph home and went to third on a Roy White single. Jack Billingham, coming on in relief with one out, got Munson to ground to second, but Morgan was only able to get the force at second, and Stanley crossed the plate with the tying run.

The score stayed frozen at 3–3 going into the bottom of the ninth. Hunter, still pitching well, got Dave Concepcion and Pete Rose out on routine fly balls, then threw a slider that Ken Griffey bounced to short. It could have been the last out of the inning; but Stanley, mindful of Griffey's blazing speed (he'd legged out 38 infield hits during the regular season), fielded the ball off-balance and hurried his throw to first. The ball sailed into the Reds' dugout, and Griffey took second on the error. "The only thing I can do is try to get rid of it," Stanley explained afterward. "I could have taken it easy, taken an extra step and been surer of my throw, but then he would have been safe. I tried to get him out."

Martin then called for an intentional walk to Joe Morgan, setting up a force on Tony Perez. "I respect Perez as a hitter," Martin reasoned, "but I'd still rather pitch to him than the other guy." The Big Doggie, who'd been dogged for much of the season by rumors that the Reds were ready to replace him at first with the younger Driessen, stepped up to the plate and smashed the first pitch he saw from Hunter into left field for a single, scoring Griffey easily from second base. The Reds had won it 4–3, sending their fans home cold and tired, but happy.

The Series moved to Yankee Stadium on Tuesday night for Game Three, the Fall Classic returning to a stage that had hosted it 27 times before. The field miraculously bore little trace of the previous week's carnage, but the raucous "We're Number One!" chants from the stands made it clear that the Bronx crowd couldn't wait to victoriously rip it up all over again. Despite being down two games to none, Billy Martin invoked the ghosts of Yankee champions past. "We're gonna win," he insisted before the game. "Remember the 1956 Series with the Dodgers? They beat us in the first two games and we came back to win the next four out of five. We can do it again this time."

Dock Ellis wasn't so sure. After hearing a number of his teammates privately express sentiments along the lines of "No way we're going to beat Cincinnati," the fiery pitcher feared that the Yankees had already psyched themselves out of the Series. He went into his

Game Three start determined to single-handedly counteract the defeatism he sensed in the ranks; unfortunately, his pitching only made things worse.

"I got shelled," he'd later recall. "I think I was overreacting, trying to do more." Dock's sinker stopped sinking after the first inning, and the Reds knocked him around for three runs on four hits in the top of the second, taking advantage of some shoddy Yankee glove work (and Ellis's ineffectiveness at holding runners on first) in the process. In the top of the fourth, Driessen, who'd started the Reds' second-inning rally by singling off Ellis's glove and stealing second, clobbered a 1–0 pitch from Ellis some 400 feet into the right-center bleachers for a solo home run, the first homer by a designated hitter in World Series history. Martin sent Ellis to the showers two batters later.

Pat Zachry, who started the game for Cincinnati, wasn't particularly sharp, giving up six hits and five walks in six and two-thirds innings, but it almost didn't matter; once again, when the chips were down, it was the Yankees who took themselves out of the game. In an effort to take the bunt away from Mickey Rivers on the natural grass of Yankee Stadium (as well as generally mess with his mind), third baseman Pete Rose positioned himself several steps closer to the plate whenever Rivers came up. In the bottom of the first, Rivers tried to foil Rose by dropping a leadoff bunt to the right of the mound, and reached safely when Zachry overthrew Perez; one pitch to Roy White later, Zachry caught Rivers leaning and picked him off first. Martin angrily protested that the Reds pitcher had balked, but the call stood, and the Yankees proved unable to score in the frame. Rivers made an even more costly gaffe in the fifth inning: with Rivers on second and White on first with no outs, and the Reds up 4–1, Thurman Munson smashed a hot liner over the head of Tony Perez; the veteran first basemen leaped up and grabbed it, then instinctively threw to second to double up Rivers, who'd wandered too far off the bag. Zachry then struck out Chris Chambliss to end the Yankee uprising.

The Yankees tightened the score by a run in the bottom of the seventh, when Jim Mason, who'd been brought into the game in the top of the fifth as a replacement for the defensively shaky Fred Stanley—presumably at the behest of George Steinbrenner, who was still furious about Stanley's error in Game Two—clubbed a surprise solo shot off Zachry; that Mason, who'd hit .180 with exactly one home run all season, had just knocked the Yankees' only round-tripper of the Series, pretty much said it all about the sorry state of the New York offense.

"If we've been trying to make them overconfident, we've reached our limit," cracked Munson after the game, which—thanks to two eighth-inning RBIs by Joe Morgan and George Foster—ended 6–2 in favor of the Reds. "We've played lousy," said Ken Holtzman. "That's the only way you can describe it." Even Martin, who flashed his usual bravado by announcing plans to start Holtzman in Game 5, struggled to put a positive spin on the Yankees' three-game deficit.

"Listen, we're no quitters. I'm not a quitter and my guys aren't quitters," he said. "We've come back before and we plan to come back again. We'll be out there fighting all the way. They'll still have to beat us. . . . But I must admit we're not in a very good position." With a storm front moving into the New York area, it looked increasingly likely that Game Four would have to be pushed back to Thursday. Asked if the day off could potentially work in the Yankees' favor, Martin just shook his head. "A postponement would have helped us at the start of the Series," he said. "It won't help us now."

For a few moments on the cold and damp Bronx evening of October 21, it looked as if the New York rain—which had indeed caused

Game Four to be postponed a night—had somehow rendered the Reds mortal. In the top of the first, Pete Rose hit a ground-rule double down the left field line off Ed Figueroa, but hustled himself off the base paths when Ken Griffey hit a bouncer to short: Rose initially tried to advance to third, then tried to return to second when Fred Stanley tossed the ball to Graig Nettles; the third base-man tagged him out, then zipped a throw to Chris Chambliss to try and nail Griffey, who'd paused between first and second; Griffey broke for second, but was called out for running out of the baseline to avoid a tag from Willie Randolph. It was the sort of boneheaded base-running play one had come to expect from the Yankees in the Series, not the Big Red Machine. Maybe this would be the New Yorkers' night, after all?

The glimmer of Yankee hope grew brighter in the bottom of the first, when Thurman Munson bloop-singled off Gary Nolan with two outs, then thundered all the way home from first when Cham-bliss doubled to left-center. "This is the way the Yankees played all year!" raved Tony Kubek in the NBC booth, after Munson slid across the plate ahead of Johnny Bench's tag. The Yankees threat-ened again in the third, loading the bases on a walk to Fred Stan-ley, a two-out single from Munson, and a rare bobble by Joe Morgan of a Chris Chambliss grounder. But Nolan, unfazed by the jam or the baying crowd, defused the situation by getting Carlos May to line out to George Foster in left, and the Reds went into at-tack mode when they came up in the top of the fourth. Morgan walked, stole second without drawing a throw, and scored on a two-out Foster single. Johnny Bench, enjoying a stellar October on the heels of a miserable season in which he hit only .234 with an unim-pressive 16 homers and 74 RBIs, ripped a 1–1 pitch from Figueroa off the left field foul screen to give the Reds a 3–1 lead.

In the bottom of the fourth, the Yankees resumed their self-defeating ways. Graig Nettles knocked a leadoff single, then moved up a base when Oscar Gamble grounded to Tony Perez at first and Dave Concepcion dropped Perez's throw to second. But Nettles wound up getting picked off second, Willie Randolph struck out looking, and Nolan got Fred Stanley to fly to right for the third out. The Yankees did manage to score the following inning, when Rivers singled, stole his first base of the Series, and came home on a Munson single to make it 3–2 Reds. Munson singled again in the seventh, giving him six straight World Series hits (a record) and convincing Sparky Anderson that it was time to give Gary Nolan the hook. While waiting for lefty reliever Will McEnaney to enter the game, Sparky Anderson stood at the mound with Pete Rose and Johnny Bench and marveled at Munson's performance against his pitchers. "That fella can flat-out hit, now," he said. "Ooh, is he a good hitter! He just stays with the ball."

The 3–2 score held into the top of the ninth, when a tiring Figueroa walked Perez on a full count, then bounced a curve to Driessen that skipped past Munson and allowed Perez to take second. Billy Martin, frustrated all night by home plate umpire Bill Deegan's strike zone, was further angered when a scuffed ball that Deegan tossed out of play hit him on the chest; the Yankee skipper petulantly tossed the ball back onto the field. First base ump Bruce Froemming, who witnessed Martin's juvenile act, tossed him out of the game. It was the first ejection of a manager from the World Series since Earl Weaver in 1969.

Perhaps Martin sensed what was coming and couldn't bear to watch it in person. After Figueroa walked Driessen, Dick Tidrow came out of the bullpen and got Foster to fly to center, but then served up a fat first pitch to Bench that the catcher lined into the left field seats, just over Roy White's glove. The Reds added another run on back-to-back doubles by Cesar Geronimo and Concepcion, whereupon disgruntled Yankee fans let loose with another barrage of trash—though the gesture seemed almost halfhearted, compared to their almost feral boisterousness in the fifth game of the ALCS.

With the score now 7–2, the Yankees came up in the bottom of the ninth to take their last licks against McEnaney. Otto Velez, pinch-hitting for Jim Mason, struck out swinging. Mickey Rivers finally managed to smack a searing liner at Pete Rose, but the third baseman nonchalantly snagged it with a smile. As *Sports Illustrated*'s Ron Fimrite recounted, Rose "then held his glove up, as if to say, 'Better luck next time, sucker.'" Roy White stepped to the plate, hoping to get on and give Munson (who'd already gone 4-for-4) a chance to become the first player in World Series history to rack up five hits in a game and six straight over two. But White hit a lazy fly ball to Foster, and it was all over. McEnaney raised him arms victoriously, then hustled with his teammates into the dugout before the field could become a battleground between fans and security.

The Cincinnati Reds had just become the first team to sweep a World Series since the Baltimore Orioles in 1966, the first team in history to sweep seven games through the playoffs and the World Series, and the first NL team to win back-to-back Fall Classics since the New York Giants of 1921–22. The question was no longer whether the Big Red Machine was the best team in baseball, but how well they stacked up against such legendary squads as the 1927 Yankees or the 1929 Athletics. "It'll be up to you gentlemen to judge this team now," Anderson told reporters during the relatively low-key postgame celebration, during which most of the Reds players behaved as if they'd just enjoyed a particularly satisfying round of golf. "I'm glad to know that we can now be considered in the same class with the other great teams of baseball. That's what I wanted in this series." Joe Morgan put it more succinctly. "How can you have a much better team than this one?" he asked.

While a couple of the games had been close, there was no question that the Reds had dominated, if not steamrolled, the Yankees. Of the nine regulars who swung bats for the Reds in the World Series, only Rose (.188) and Griffey (.059) had subpar performances at the plate; everyone else in the lineup hit .308 or better, combining to outhit the AL champs .313 to .222 while outscoring them 22 to 8. Driessen, the Reds' DH, hit .357, while the Yankees' three designated hitters—Lou Piniella, Carlos May, Elliott Maddox—hit a combined .070 in the Series. The Cincinnati staff posted a sleek 2.00 ERA, while the supposedly superior Yankee arms produced an ugly 5.45 mark. Even the Bad News Bears had come closer to winning it all than Martin's Yankees had. "Our World Series was the playoffs," reflected Dick Tidrow. "Their World Series was the World Series."

The '76 Series received largely bad reviews from sportswriters across the country, most of whom cited the one-sidedness of the competition and the overall lack of drama as its chief disappointments, especially compared to the white-knuckle ride of the 1975 Fall Classic, or even the nail-biting excitement of the Yankees-Royals ALCS. But as far as the Reds, their fans, and their legacy were concerned, it couldn't have been scripted any better.

Johnny Bench, who'd led all players in the Series with a .533 average, two homers, and six RBIs, was named the Series MVP. "I always said he would have more bearing on this game than Babe Ruth and I still say it," Anderson raved. "The man is so talented. I've never seen one man play his position the way he plays it." When reporters asked Anderson his opinion of Munson, who'd hit .529 over the four games (a World Series record for batting average in service of a losing team), the Reds skipper responded, "I think Thurman Munson would hit .300 in the National League, but like I've said many times before, gentlemen, don't ever embarrass a man by comparing him to Johnny Bench."

Munson, who was standing three feet away on the press conference platform at the time, was deeply wounded by Anderson's remarks. "For me to be belittled after my season, after my Series," he told reporters, "It hurts. . . . We have a good team. I'm embarrassed to lose in four straight, but I'm not embarrassed to lose with this team. I just don't appreciate it rubbed in my face by a man I'm standing right next to." Anderson claimed he meant no insult; indeed, NBC's microphones had picked up his "flat-out hit" comment, which would be included in the official World Series highlights film. Three weeks later, he sent a handwritten letter of apology to Munson, care of the Yankees. The irascible Munson would forever claim he never received it.

In the Yankees' clubhouse, the players sat in stunned silence, unwilling or unable to process the fact that they were done for the year. "These kids have nothing to be embarrassed about," George Steinbrenner calmly told reporters. "There were 550 other players watching this game on television. Our guys were playing in it. It was their first taste. They were a little nervous, but we'll get them next year."

Off camera, though, the Yankee owner was harsher in his assessment. In Steinbrenner's mind, the glory of winning the American League pennant had been negated by his team's failure to win even one game on baseball's biggest stage. "You oughta hang your heads," he growled at his players, before stomping off in search of his manager. He found Martin seated on the floor of the trainer's room, red-eyed from weeping bitter tears of frustration at having come so far for naught. Steinbrenner said nothing, but shot him a murderous look before making his exit. "If daggers could have come out of that man's eyes," Martin later recalled, "they would have."

12.

Take the Money and Run

(November 1976 and Beyond)

Twelve nights after he and his partner Tony Kubek called the last out of the 1976 World Series at Yankee Stadium, NBC broadcaster and former major leaguer Joe Garagiola spent the evening inside another legendary American edifice—the White House—watching the presidential election returns with Gerald Ford. While Ford's bid for another term ultimately died harder than the Yankees' bid for their 21st World Series championship, Jimmy Carter's early leads in key states Pennsylvania, Texas, and Wisconsin boded ill for Ford that night. "The President took all the news very calmly," wrote Garagiola, who'd befriended Ford at a celebrity golf tournament. "I'd seen Enos Slaughter get more upset about an umpire saying 'Strike Two' than Gerald Ford did when he realized he wasn't going to win a presidential election."

Carter's win came via a much narrower margin—50.1 percent of the popular vote to Ford's 48—than anyone would have predicted back in July, when opinion polls showed the Georgia governor maintaining a commanding 33-point lead over the president. But aside from his "no Soviet domination of Easter Europe" misstep, Ford had done well in the televised debates against Carter, whose vagueness on many of the issues bolstered the Ford campaign's repeated assertion that the Georgia governor lacked the necessary experience to be the "Leader of the Free World." Carter also shot himself in the foot (and perhaps elsewhere) with his admission in the November issue of *Playboy* magazine that he'd "committed adultery in my heart"— having lusted after women other than his wife, Rosalynn—a statement that didn't play particularly well with the women or evangelical Christians who comprised a substantial part of his support base.

Carter's Southern roots also continued to be seen as something of a liability in a country that hadn't elected a Deep Southerner to the White House in over 125 years; the near-constant presence of his wacky family members in the news (most notably his outspoken mother, "Miss Lillian," and his beer-swilling good ol' boy brother, Billy) offered little reassurance to those who feared that Carter and his clan were just hicks from the sticks. But thanks to his Southern base—he swept every state in the South, save Virginia—as well as strong support from unions and black voters, Carter and his running mate, Walter Mondale, were ultimately able to defeat Ford and Bob Dole in November.

"Well, we came from way back," Ford said to Garagiola. "Nobody can say we didn't give it a helluva try." Indeed, given the virulently anti-Nixon sentiments that still permeated the electorate in the years following the Watergate scandal, Ford—who'd pardoned America's most despised political figure in decades—had no business making such an impressive showing in the election. "The only reason it was close was that I as a candidate was not good enough as a campaigner," Carter told a gathering of supporters upon returning to his hometown of Plains, Georgia, following his victory. "But I'll make up for that as President."

With the election of Carter, who'd promised to pardon the hundreds of thousands of young men who'd fled the country or otherwise dodged the draft during the Vietnam War, America was officially closing the books on the Vietnam/Nixon/Watergate era, and preparing to step into a challenging new chapter. During his victory speech in the wee hours of November 3, the president-elect pledged, "It's time for us to get together, to correct our mistakes, to answer difficult questions, and to make our nation great." After a year of reveling in their collective past, it was time for Americans to embrace their shared future.

"As our first resolution of the New Year, let us pledge to keep the spirit of '76 alive," a weary-looking President Ford encouraged the nation on December 31, during the final *Bicentennial Minutes* broadcast. But the red-white-and-blue souvenirs of the star-spangled summer of '76 would soon be packed away, discarded and forgotten, largely supplanted in 1977 by an endless array of Carter memorabilia, much of it featuring the cartoonish "smiling peanut" that had become his unofficial mascot during the campaign. The American tchotchke industry would have a field day cranking out smiling peanut piggy banks, AM radios, ashtrays, pendants, belt buckles, and everything else imaginable; Michigan model company AMT even offered a kit for a "Peanut 1" funny car that bore Carter's distinctive choppers on its nose. Carter's smile, manufactured or otherwise, would become even more ubiquitous in the new year than the pearly whites of Farrah Fawcett-Majors, the lithe blond actress whose red-swimsuit pinup poster—released in the fall of 1976, shortly before the debut of *Charlie's Angels*, the hit ABC crime drama starring Farrah, Jaclyn Smith, and Kate Jackson as bra-less private investigators—would go on to sell a reported 12 million copies.

The city of Philadelphia took its final Bicentennial curtain call as the gritty backdrop for *Rocky*, a low-budget film about the titular small-time boxer and loan shark thug who gets a chance to fight the undefeated heavyweight champion, which hit U.S. theaters in late November. While the urban realism of *Rocky* was of a piece with much of the American cinema of the '70s, the film's uplifting, Horatio Alger–tinged "roaches to riches" story contrasted starkly with the downbeat, pessimistic, antihero-oriented flicks that had been so popular in the Nixon-Ford era—films like 1974's *Chinatown*, 1975's *Dog Day Afternoon*, and such 1976 hits as *Taxi Driver*, the dystopian sci-fi thriller *Logan's Run*, and *Carrie*, a supernatural horror film based on the 1974 Stephen King novel of the same name, which opened just a few weeks before *Rocky*.

"I've really had it with anti-this and anti-that," Sylvester Stallone, the previously unknown actor who wrote the film's script and starred as the "Italian Stallion" boxer of the title, told *The New York Times*. "I want to be remembered as a man of raging optimism, who believes in the American dream. Right now, it's as if a big cavernous black hole has been burned into the entertainment section of the brain. It's filled with demons and paranoia and fear. Where are all the heroes? Let other people suffer and do all those pain things and put their demons up on the screen. I'm not going to."

Though the film (directed by John Avildsen) was predictable and often schmaltzy, American audiences responded to Stallone's ragingly optimistic reaffirmation of the American dream by making *Rocky* a surprise hit; the film (which was made for a little over a million dollars) earned $5.6 million in its first week of general release, eventually raking in $225 million worldwide and winning three Academy Awards. There would be no shortage of feel-good underdog tales coming out of Hollywood during the rest of the decade.

American popular music was changing, too, though not necessarily in such immediately definable ways. Disco music was becoming slicker and more mechanical, and soul music—led by Stevie Wonder's

Songs in the Key of Life, which in October became the first American album to debut at Number One on the *Billboard* charts—was becoming lusher and glossier; over the next few years, it would become increasingly difficult to differentiate between disco and soul. Blue Oyster Cult and Boston set the tone for FM rock of the late '70s with their meticulously layered, heavy-yet-sleek tracks like "Don't Fear the Reaper" and "More Than a Feeling," both of which were major hits in the autumn of 1976. The Band, one of the most critically lauded American groups of the late '60s and early '70s, finally called it quits after years of diminishing commercial and artistic returns; the rootsy rockers' farewell concert, performed November 25 at San Francisco's Winterland Ballroom with a long list of special guests that included Eric Clapton, Van Morrison, Neil Diamond, Neil Young, Joni Mitchell, and their former boss Bob Dylan, was filmed by Martin Scorsese for a documentary later released as *The Last Waltz*. Though it wasn't necessarily what Scorsese and Band leader Robbie Robertson were getting at with the title, the film wound up as something of a requiem for the Woodstock era, as many of the artists featured struggled to maintain artistic direction or relevance amid the changes of the coming years.

The Eagles, one of the most popular American bands of the '70s, skirted irrelevance by hardening their sound and darkening their lyrics on *Hotel California*, a new concept album released in early December. "It's our Bicentennial year," the band's drummer and vocalist Don Henley explained to *ZigZag* magazine shortly before the record's release. "The country is 200 years old, so we figured since we are the Eagles and the Eagle is our national symbol, that we were obliged to make some kind of a little Bicentennial statement using California as a microcosm of the whole United States, or the whole world, if you will, and to try to wake people up and say

'We've been okay so far, for 200 years, but we're gonna have to change if we're gonna continue to be around.'"

Baseball would have to change, too. The day after Jimmy Carter was elected president, a new chapter in major league history began with the landmark session of the free agent reentry draft, held on the afternoon of November 4 at New York's Plaza Hotel. Of the 24 players offering their services on the open market to the 24 established major league teams (the Blue Jays and the Mariners, who held their own expansion draft on November 5, were not allowed to participate), only two—aging sluggers Willie McCovey and Nate Colbert—failed to draw any interest, while 12 would eventually sign deals worth a million dollars or more. The economics of the game were thus drastically transformed.

The first player to cash in was Bill Campbell, the *Sporting News* AL Fireman of the Year, who inked a four-year, $1 million deal with the Red Sox just two days after the draft was held. Campbell and his wife liked the idea of moving to Boston; and when the Red Sox made him their top draft pick, he and his agent decided to go straight into negotiations with the team. The Red Sox, who'd spent most of the season locked in bitter negotiations with Fred Lynn, Carlton Fisk, and Rick Burleson, now seemed completely cool with the idea of dumping a truckload of cash into a free agent's lap. "Look, this business seems insane to me," admitted Campbell, who'd made all of $22,000 with the Twins in 1976. "No player is really worth what they're paying me, but if they want to, then fine."

The Reds were the only team to stay completely out of the reentry draft. Aside from not having any glaring holes in their World Series–winning lineup that needed to be filled, Reds GM Bob Howsam felt that there were more sensible options available for the replacement of

Don Gullett, the Reds' lone free agent defector. As a 19-year-old rookie in 1970, the Kentucky-born left-hander had pronounced his profound dislike for New York City during a Reds-Mets series. "All you can see is buildings and long-haired people," he'd told reporters at the time. "There's no fresh air. I can't take that, not even out on the mound when you're pitching. You're surrounded by so many people that the air smells."

On November 18, Gullett signed a six-year, $2 million contract with the New York Yankees, who were apparently willing to overlook his chronic fragility in their search for top-level left-handed starting pitching, just as Gullett was willing to overlook the fact that the Big Apple's odor hadn't appreciably improved in the last half-decade. "It wasn't a hard decision for me," he said, while posing for photos with George Steinbrenner and Catfish Hunter. "There's something special about pitching in Yankee Stadium."

The rich contracts being offered to baseball's first free agent class were mind-boggling, not least for the players themselves. Wayne Garland, who'd gone 20–7 with a 2.67 ERA for Baltimore in his first full year as a starting pitcher, was stunned when the Indians offered him a 10-year contract for a total of $2.3 million. "You gotta be kidding," he told his agent, Jerry Kapstein. "Quick, gimme a pen before they change their mind." Garland's Orioles teammate, Gold Glove second baseman Bobby Grich, signed a five-year, $1.75 million deal with the California Angels, despite Angels owner Gene Autry's professed reluctance to dabble in the free agent market. Autry also signed Joe Rudi and Don Baylor to five- and six-year contracts worth over $2 million apiece, or about what Autry had paid for the entire expansion franchise in 1961.

"Four or five teams are spending themselves right out of baseball in a hurry," huffed Twins owner Calvin Griffith, shooting angry glances in the direction Autry and Ted Turner, the latter of whom was in the process of signing Gary Matthews (who'd finished the season with a .279 average and career highs of 20 homers and 84 RBIs) to a five-year, $1.2 million deal. "I'm not going to help make any of [the players] millionaires," added Griffith, who'd gone ahead and drafted several of the unsigned players anyway, though his tight-fisted fiscal philosophy failed to attract any of them to Minnesota.

While Griffith and many others wondered how baseball would be able to afford these blockbuster deals (and the inflated player salaries that would inevitably result), others questioned why owners who for years had aggressively nickel-and-dimed their players during contract negotiations were now spending money like sailors on shore leave. "If this kind of money has been there all the time," asked Furman Bisher in a *Sporting News* editorial, "why hasn't it been put to use to pay the players a satisfying wage beforehand?" Players Association director Marvin Miller had once opined that the reserve system primarily existed "to protect the owners from themselves," and the current free agent feeding frenzy seemed to be proving him right.

"I thought the owners were smarter than this," grumbled Jim Palmer, Garland and Grich's former teammate. "I thought they'd show more restraint." Palmer, who'd just won his third American League Cy Young Award in four seasons (thus tying Sandy Koufax for most Cys) after finishing the season 22–13 with a 2.51 ERA, was making slightly over $180,000 annually on an Orioles contract that had two more years to run. While a pitcher of Palmer's caliber could certainly earn much more than that by offering his services on the open market, Palmer said he had no plans to hawk his services to the highest bidder when his current contract ran out. "I don't want to be known as a ballplayer who was just interested in getting as much money as possible," he said. "I don't want people to think of me as someone who's not really interested in winning and losing."

Palmer's runner-up in the AL Cy Young voting had a similar, if somewhat more naive, perspective on the matter. Mark Fidrych, who won the AL Rookie of the Year award in a landslide, had been deluged throughout the second half of the season by offers of representation from agents promising that they could procure him a multiyear, million-dollar deal from the Tigers. But Fidrych, still just happy to be pitching in the majors, turned them all down; instead, he had his schoolteacher father represent him in negotiations with Tigers GM Jim Campbell, who happily took advantage of the situation. After less than 30 minutes of contract talks, Fidrych and his father emerged from Campbell's office with a $34,500 bonus for 1976, and a three-year deal worth $165,000. Since Fidrych had already made $26,500 in 1976 ($19,000 base salary, plus a $7,500 contractual bonus for staying in the majors for 90 days) on top of Campbell's bonus, his new deal meant that the most popular young baseball player in the country would actually be taking a six-grand pay cut in 1977—and once all the new free agent contracts inflated the median 1977 MLB player salary from $51,501 to $76,066, Fidrych would essentially be earning $21,000 less than his average colleague.

"An agent probably could have gotten me more money," the Bird admitted at the time. "I could have signed a one-year contract for a lot of money, but what if I died out next year? This should make it easier for me. Now I know I'll be able to pitch next year and the next year and the next year without anybody asking me all the time if I'm going to get an agent." Sadly, Fidrych would badly injure his knee in March 1977 while horsing around in the outfield during spring training; an arm injury would follow, and answering questions about agents would be the least of his problems. The Bird would never pitch another complete season in his career, much less enjoy a glorious flight like the one he'd taken the entire country on in 1976.

Randy Jones would never experience a season quite like 1976, either. Deprived of the NL Cy Young award by Tom Seaver in 1975, Jones—who finished with a 2.74 ERA, leading the league in victories, starts (40), complete games (25), and innings pitched (315.1)—handily beat out Seaver's rotation mate Jerry Koosman (21–10, 2.69 ERA) and Don Sutton (21–10, 3.06 ERA) for the award in '76. (Seaver, doomed by lousy run support to a 14-11 record despite posting a 2.59 ERA and leading the league in strikeouts for the fifth time with 235, finished a distant eighth in the voting.) But with his left arm still recovering from surgery for the ruptured tendon, Jones was unable to lift the coveted trophy, and there was considerable concern that the Junkman's career might be over. The Junkman would resume his place in the Padres' rotation in '77, however, albeit without anywhere near the same degree of effectiveness.

Still, Jones could at least take heart at Tommy John's unexpected comeback success in 1976. A soft-tossing sinkerballer like Jones, the Dodger lefty had been in the midst of a brilliant season in 1974 when he'd permanently damaged the ulnar collateral ligament in his throwing arm. Such injuries were typically considered career-enders, but orthopedic surgeon Dr. Frank Jobe tried experimental surgery on John, replacing the ligament in his left elbow with a tendon from his right arm. Mike Marshall assisted in John's recovery, putting him on a special exercise regimen and teaching him a new pitching motion that would put less pressure on his knee and his arm. John, who missed the entire 1975 season, returned to the Dodgers in 1976 and pitched a miraculous 207 innings in 31 starts without injury, going 10–10 with a 3.09 ERA. The *Sporting News* named John their NL Comeback Player of the Year, and the pitcher's name would be forever associated with Jobe's procedure—one that would become increasingly common for injured hurlers in the ensuing decades.

———

After ending the season with Sparky Anderson's words ringing acridly in his ears, Thurman Munson—who'd long felt that his skills were underappreciated, especially by the press—thoroughly enjoyed the vindication of being named the American League's Most Valuable Player for 1976 by the Baseball Writers Association of America. Munson received 18 of the 24 first-place votes; AL batting champ George Brett received two, while Mickey Rivers, Rod Carew, Amos Otis, and Mark Fidrych all received one apiece. "I know one thing," said Munson, speaking at the press conference the Yankees called to commemorate the occasion. "I didn't win the damn thing on politics."

Indeed, winning the award did nothing to mellow Munson's longstanding refusal to kiss the media's collective ass; invited to appear on a major network TV morning show shortly after winning the award, Munson declined, citing the earliness of the hour. "They wanted me to get up at six in the morning to be interviewed from 7:10 to 7:14, four minutes, for no pay," he laughed. "That would really go over big with my wife. I get up at six for television, but I'd never do it for her? I'd never hear the end of it."

To no one's surprise, Joe Morgan was named the National League MVP, receiving 19 of 24 first place votes—the other five went to teammate George Foster—and becoming the only NL player not named Ernie Banks to win the award in back-to-back seasons. "As happy as I am for Joe Morgan," said the Reds' second baseman when he received the news, "I am sad for George. He had a tremendous year." Foster, who'd finished the season hitting .306 with 29 home runs, a league-leading 121 RBIs, and 86 runs scored, had indeed put up some impressive numbers; but they couldn't quite compare with those of Little Joe, who'd hit .320, led the league in both on-base percentage (.444) and slugging (.576), and hit 27 homers with 111 RBIs, 113 runs, with 60 stolen bases.

A Red also took home the NL Rookie of the Year award—or, rather, half of it. For the first time in the 25-year history of MLB rookie honors, the writers' ballots produced a tie: Pat Zachry was named co–NL Rookie of the Year along with Padres reliever Butch Metzger, who'd put up an 11–4 record with 16 saves, and posted a 2.93 ERA in 77 appearances. Zachry, reached at home in Waco, Texas, by Cincinnati sportswriter Earl Lawson, was pleased by the news, but also revealed that he was in mourning for Bronco, the two-year-old German shepherd he'd raised from a pup, who'd been stolen from his parents' backyard at the end of the season. "My dad didn't tell me about Bronco being stolen until after the World Series," he said. "He knew how much that dog meant to me."

Morgan, Zachry, and their teammates would receive more sad news in December, when it was announced that the Reds—needing a left-hander to replace the departed Gullett, and with Dan Driessen waiting in the wings for a full-time shot at first—had dealt Tony Perez and reliever Will McEnaney to the Expos in exchange for veteran lefty starter Woodie Fryman and righty reliever Dale Murray. Perez, a 10-and-5-year man, approved the deal once the Expos offered him a multiyear, no-cut/no-trade contract worth $150,000 per season, or about $50,000 more per year than he was making on the Reds. "I am both happy and sad," said Perez at the news conference where the transaction was announced, noting that the "multi-year contract will give my family security. That is important."

Perez then turned to hug Johnny Bench good-bye—"Thanks for all the years," he said—and left to phone his sons in Puerto Rico with the news. With that, the Reds' all-time RBI leader (and the man Sparky Anderson had often referred to as the "heart and soul" of his team) was gone. Reds GM Bob Howsam would later admit that dealing the Big Doggie was the biggest mistake of his career; while Driessen was a solid first baseman with a good bat, neither

Fryman nor Murray pitched well in Reds uniforms, and the team would never again function as lethally without Perez in the lineup. The Dodgers, reenergized by Tommy Lasorda, would win the NL championship in 1977 and '78; when the Reds regained control of the NL West in 1979, it would be with a weaker team that no longer included two of the Big Red Machine's other main cogs: Pete Rose and Sparky Anderson.

The Phillies were now missing the entire right side of their infield, thanks to Dave Cash's departure for the greener pastures of free agency, and what could politely be described as a mutual parting of ways with Dick Allen. Cash, who'd been denied during the summer when he asked the Phillies for a five-year, million-dollar contract, got what he was looking for from the Expos. Allen, who'd once again overstayed his welcome in Philadelphia, asked the Phillies to make him a free agent, and they happily complied. The Phillies quickly filled the vacancy at first, plucking former Pirate Richie Hebner from the free agent pool. Hebner, who played third base for the Bucs, had originally been a first baseman, and Danny Ozark was confident that he could take over for Allen. "I'm tickled," said Phillies GM Paul Owens. "This gives us the left-handed power hitter we've been after for four years." Hebner was pretty tickled, as well; a man who'd once dug graves in the off-season to make ends meet, Hebner would now be earning $150,000 a year in Philadelphia.

After finally breaking into the postseason in 1976, the Phillies and Royals would return in 1977 and 1978, though neither would reach the World Series until 1980, when they faced off against each other in the first all-AstroTurf Fall Classic. The A's, on the other hand, were essentially done for the '70s, devastated by free agent defections and Charlie Finley's overzealous dealing. "We have a good chance of losing 100 games next summer," said Bill North, one of only three players (Vida Blue and Claudell Washington were the others) left from Oakland's dynastic period. North wasn't far off; the A's would lose 98 games in 1977—followed by a 93-loss season in 1978, and a brutal 108-loss campaign in 1979.

Meanwhile, the diaspora of former Mustache Gang members continued to make headlines in November and December, with Rollie Fingers and Gene Tenace moving south to San Diego (Fingers received a six-year deal worth $1.6 million, while Tenace signed for five years and $1.8 million), Bert Campaneris inking a five-year, $750,000 deal with the Rangers, and team captain Sal Bando signing a five-year, $1.4 million deal with the Brewers. Thirty-eight-year-old DH Billy Williams, left unprotected in the expansion draft, announced his retirement after the Mariners and Blue Jays both declined to claim him. (Seattle and Toronto's respective first picks were Royals outfield prospect Ruppert Jones and Orioles infield prospect Bob Bailor.) "I wouldn't want to go through another season like the last one," he said. "Too much sitting around. Too much designated hitting." Williams, who joined the A's in 1975 after spending his entire career with the Cubs, never had a chance to swing his Hall of Fame–worthy bat in the World Series. He retired with 2,711 career hits, 426 home runs, and a lifetime .290 batting average.

A's manager Chuck Tanner was on the move, too, traded by Finley to Pittsburgh in exchange for Pirates catcher Manny Sanguillen and $100,000 in cash. The seeds of this rare manager-for-player swap were sown in early October, when AL president Lee MacPhail finally got around to ruling on the long-running question of whether Bill Veeck or Charlie Finley was supposed to be paying Tanner's salary. MacPhail decreed that Veeck owed Tanner $35,000 for 1976, but that Finley was on the hook for the next two years of Tanner's contract. Loath to renegotiate Tanner's deal, Finley was all ears when new Pirates vice president Pete Peterson contacted him about the possibility of bringing Tanner to Pittsburgh.

"I run a finishing school for managers," explained Finley with typical modesty, once news of the Tanner-Sanguillen deal got out. "I get them when they're coarse and rough, and it takes me at least a year to develop them into exceptional managers. It costs me a lot of time and money to conduct this school, so I should be reimbursed. Or, I should say, indemnified when someone wants to take away the jewel I have created." Finley's next "jewel," former Royals manager Jack McKeon, would last all of 53 games in 1977 before Finley fired him. Tanner, on the other hand, would go on to lead the Pirates to victory over Earl Weaver's Orioles in the 1979 World Series.

Having to pay a substantial chunk of Chuck Tanner's salary for the season in which he'd managed the A's was only one of the issues troubling Bill Veeck in November. There was also a long-standing spinal issue that required surgery to remove pressure on his neck nerves, and the fact that Paul Richards, who seemed to have lost interest in piloting the White Sox as the season wore on, had decided to vacate the manager's position. Seated in a wheelchair and clad in a brown robe with gold polka dots, Veeck convened a press conference at Illinois Masonic Medical Center, where he was awaiting surgery, to announce that the new White Sox skipper would be Bob Lemon, the recently inducted Hall of Famer who'd pitched for Veeck in Cleveland back in 1948, and who'd most recently been employed by the Yankees as Billy Martin's pitching coach.

Perpetually short of cash, Veeck could not afford to make a big splash in the free agent market; instead of picking up any marquee names from the draft, the White Sox signed Cubs pitcher Steve Stone (who was coming off an injury-plagued 3–6, 4.08 season) and Twins third baseman Eric Soderholm (who'd missed all of 1976 with a bad knee) to one-year deals at $55,000 each, and picked up Orioles reserve outfielder Royle Stillman for $25,000. Knowing that these weren't the sort of players that would pack Comiskey

Park by themselves, Veeck hit upon the "rent-a-player" concept, which involved trading for stars from other teams who were currently unsigned and preparing to play out their option year; Veeck would only be able to "rent" these players for a single season before losing them to free agency, but they would at least improve the team (and attendance) during their stay on the South Side. The strategy would pay ample dividends for Veeck and the White Sox in 1977, when Richie Zisk and Oscar Gamble led the team through a memorably explosive season that saw the "South Side Hitmen" throw a legitimate scare into the defending AL West champion Royals. But health problems and the inability to compete in baseball's increasingly challenging financial landscape—the average player salary would rise to $143,756 by 1980, nearly $100,000 higher than it had been when Veeck resumed ownership—would force him to sell the White Sox in January 1981. Ironically, the man who had been one of the most ardent and articulate opponents of the reserve clause was ultimately done in by its removal.

Finley would also be gone by the 1981 season. After losing his lawsuit against Kuhn over the latter's negation of his deals to sell Vida Blue to the Yankees and Rollie Fingers and Joe Rudi to the Red Sox, Finley realized that he would never recoup the $3.5 million from his failed "fire sale" that he hoped would finance the rebuilding of his team. For the next four seasons, Finley would repeatedly try to sell the A's to out-of-town buyers—only to be repeatedly thwarted by Oakland officials, who refused to let the A's break their Coliseum lease. Finley finally found a local buyer in Levi Strauss chairman Walter A. Haas Jr., and announced in August 1980 that he was leaving baseball. "I can no longer compete," he announced at his final press conference. "During the time we were winning championships, survival was a battle of wits. . . . It is no longer a battle of wits, but how much you have on the hip."

The departure of Veeck and Finley would leave Ted Turner as baseball's last maverick owner. Turner's pockets were much deeper than Veeck's or Finley's, thanks in part to his rapidly growing media empire based around satellite-broadcasting "superstation" WTBS (the cable butterfly that evolved from WTCG's UHF caterpillar), which would soon include 24-hour cable news channel CNN. Turner, who hired Hank Aaron to work directly under him as vice president in charge of Braves player development, stayed focused on his mission of trying to rebuild the Braves while providing enough of a spectacle to keep the team's fans happy—à la the "Wet T-Shirt Night" promotion that drew 27,000 fans to a game at Atlanta-Fulton County Stadium in the summer of '77. "The Mouth of the South" also remained gleefully committed to running things his way, even donning a Braves uniform and appointing himself temporary manager in an attempt to turn around a lengthy 1977 losing streak. Turner's antics further endeared him to Braves fans, a contingent that would increase exponentially in size during the '80s, thanks to WTBS's nationwide broadcast of Braves games.

When asked about life on the 1976 Yankees, Oscar Gamble just shook his neatly coiffed afro at the daily chaos engendered in the Yankee clubhouse by Billy Martin and George Steinbrenner, and uttered his famous phrase, "They think it don't be like it is, but it do." After the season's end, Gamble was too busy opening Oscar Gamble's Players Club—an upscale disco in his hometown of Montgomery, Alabama—to pay close attention to what was happening with his team. But if he had, he might have realized that 1976 was just a warm-up for the tension and insanity that would grip the team in 1977.

Going into the postseason, George Steinbrenner promised Billy Martin that he would obtain a starting pitcher and a big bat via the free agent reentry draft. Steinbrenner made good on the former pledge by signing Don Gullett, but bringing home a solid hitter proved more challenging. Martin was pushing for Joe Rudi to offset the preponderance of left-handed batters in the Yankee lineup, though Steinbrenner and GM Gabe Paul were more interested in Bobby Grich or Don Baylor. But when Baylor signed with the Angels, Grich—who saw the opportunity to be reunited with one of his favorite former teammates and play ball in Southern California, where he'd grown up—quickly followed suit. And once Rudi signed an Angels contract, only one impact offensive player was still left on the market: Reggie Jackson.

Jackson, who'd told reporters back in 1973 that "If I played in New York, they'd name a candy bar after me," had of course been angling to play for the Yankees. But the Yankees, feeling that Baylor, Grich, Gullett, Gary Matthews, and Wayne Garland were all bigger priorities, had only drafted him sixth. Jackson had more ardent suitors, however: McDonald's magnate Ray Kroc offered Reggie and his agent, Gary Walker, $3.6 million for five years to play for the Padres; but when Walker and Jackson came back asking for an additional tax-free loan of $1 million, Kroc angrily rescinded his offer.

Expos owner (and multimillionaire Seagram's boss) Charles Bronfman rolled out the red carpet in his effort to sign the magnetic slugger, spending a reported $20,000 to fly Jackson and four of his associates up to Montreal for a whirlwind weekend that included a tour of Olympic Stadium from Jackson's former manager Dick Williams, and a lavish dinner party at Bronfman's palatial estate. Jackson's visit was marred by an embarrassing incident with Canadian customs, who discovered marijuana in his luggage and notified the Royal Canadian Mounted Police. After further investigation, federal officials declined to press charges against Jackson, since the amount of weed involved was under an ounce, and his bags had been out of his control for at least 12 hours. Bronfman dismissed the incident as a "nothing thing," adding that the Expos organization was "satisfied that he has absolutely no problem with any type of narcotic." "I didn't know it was illegal in this country," added the slugger.

Jackson was tremendously impressed with Bronfman's hospitality; Bronfman's offer of nearly $5 million over five years spun his head, as well. But when it came to sales pitches, Bronfman had nothing on Steinbrenner. Belatedly convinced that Jackson was both the big bat he needed to beef up the Yankee lineup, as well as the sort of superstar who would generate additional publicity and ticket revenue, Steinbrenner set his sights on signing him. Paul and Martin were adamantly opposed to the idea, Paul fearing the negative effects that Jackson's ego (and the high salary that it would take to land him) would have on the chemistry and morale of their pennant-winning team, while Martin just actively disliked Jackson, whom he viewed as a gutless player. But neither man had any say in the matter, and Steinbrenner pulled out all the stops to make sure that Jackson would be his.

The Yankee boss met Jackson (who was fresh off the plane from Montreal) at LaGuardia airport, and whisked him off in a limo to lunch at New York's prestigious "21" Club. "George was at his best that day," Jackson would later write in his autobiography. "He sold tradition. He sold the pinstripes. He sold himself. He sold the city." Specifically, he sold Jackson on the tremendous business and endorsement opportunities he'd have as a New York Yankee.

"Let's just you and me take a walk," Steinbrenner suggested to Jackson after they finished dining, and the two men set off on foot up Fifth Avenue. It was a gorgeous Indian Summer afternoon, in glorious contrast to the windy and frigid weather Jackson had just experienced in Montreal; even warmer and more welcoming were the spontaneous outbursts of affection he received from New Yorkers as they strolled uptown to Steinbrenner's brownstone in the East 60s. Cab drivers honked their horns and shouted to him; passersby stopped Jackson on the street, imploring him to come and play for the Yankees; a group of schoolkids mobbed him on the street, asking for his autograph. "This is what it's like," Steinbrenner told him with a warm smile. "This is the greatest city in the world, isn't it? Can't you feel how much it wants you?"

Jackson could feel it, all right, and he wanted it right back. A few days of negotiating later, Jackson was officially a Yankee, signing a contract for five years at $2.96 million. The Expos, who'd offered considerably more money, were angry and disappointed. "I'm sure that Jackson and his people were able to use our offer as a lever," observed Expos president John McHale. But it wasn't just about the money; as Jackson explained at the Yankees' introductory press conference for him at the Americana Hotel, he felt a sense of comfort and kinship with Steinbrenner. "His expression of humanism is the reason I'm a Yankee," he said. "I feel I'm a friend of his. I feel I can go and ask him to let me borrow his sports coat, and he'll give it to me. He's like me, he's a little crazy and he's a hustler."

Thurman Munson was spotted at the press conference looking uncharacteristically happy. Three weeks earlier, the Yankee captain had encouraged Steinbrenner and Paul to go after Jackson instead of Bobby Grich. "I told them I didn't feel Grich was what we really needed," he recalled to the press. "He's a great player, but we needed a power hitter and an outfielder who could throw." But Munson was smiling for another reason: before the season began, he'd obtained what he believed was a verbal agreement from Steinbrenner that, with the exception of Catfish Hunter (who'd signed a five-year, $3.75 million contract with the Yankees before the 1975 season), he would always be the highest-paid player on the team. Now that Jackson had just signed the second-largest contract in Yankee history, Munson was cheerfully waiting for his own contract to be adjusted accordingly. But the Yankee captain wouldn't be smiling for long, once he realized that Steinbrenner had no intention of making good on their agreement.

Billy Martin was already seething. Not only had Steinbrenner refused him a say in the matter of signing Jackson, but now Jackson was speaking as if he and Steinbrenner were the closest of friends. Martin, who desperately craved Steinbrenner's approval and friendship, would spend the winter holed up in his New Jersey hotel room, brooding as he thought about the Yankee owner and his new multimillion-dollar prize enjoying lunch after lunch together at "21." "George hadn't taken me out to lunch even once," Martin would recall in his 1980 autobiography, still fuming like a spurned girlfriend.

"I didn't come to New York to prove I'm a star," Jackson told reporters. "I brought my star with me." Over the next two seasons, Jackson would help power the Yankees to two World Championships, earn the nickname "Mr. October," and, yes, even get a candy bar named after him. But the explosions that resulted when his star alighted in the already combustive Yankee clubhouse would make the July 4th fireworks of Operation Sail look like a game of Lite-Brite.

Acknowledgments;
Baby, I Love Your Way

As anyone who's done it can tell you, writing a book can be an arduous and lonely process—and as much as I loved immersing myself daily in the games, politics, and cultural milieu of 1976, there were certainly times where I wondered what the hell I'd gotten myself into, and how the hell I was ever going to get myself (and this book) out of it. Thankfully, I was blessed with an incredible support system of colleagues, friends, and loved ones who helped keep my spirits high and my aim true throughout this project.

The heartiest thanks, of course, goes out to my editor, Rob Kirkpatrick, a fellow baseball and music nut (and a very talented author in his own right) who all but grabbed me by the collar and insisted that I write this book, then repeatedly went to bat for the project at St. Martin's. I am also endlessly grateful for the steadfast support of Lyn DelliQuadri and Jane Lahr, my loyal agents at Lahr & Associates, and for my friendship with Peter Schilling Jr., a fellow Tigers fan (and another fine writer) who very generously took the time to read (and give me invaluable advice regarding) my original manuscript.

Profound thanks are also due Donnell Alexander, Phil Allen, Shawn Anderson, Michael Ansaldo, Marty Appel, Mike Aronstein, Michael Azerrad, Tom Beaujour, Michael Bouton, Michael Bramlage, Craig Calcaterra, Matthew Callan, Chris Case, Kevin Cashman, Abbot Chambers, Robert Chancey, Ted Coe, Ron Coomer, Peter J. Cooper, Chris Cortez, Bill Crandall, Scott Crawford, Tim Cronin, Irwin and Fran Epstein, Rebecca Epstein, Bob "Skates" Farinelli, John and Becky Ford, Jeff Garlin, Jay Goldberg, Peter Golenbock, Sam Graham, Lieutenant Colonel (Retired) Dave Grob, Ed "Hoggy" Herrmann, Ken Holtzman, Caroline Howerton, Thomas Andrew Jackson, Josh Kantor, Maxwell Kates, Sean Kelly, Ben Kufrin, Adam Langer, Dr. LaWanda, Handsome Dick Manitoba, Michaelangelo Matos, Jim Merlis, Josh Mills, Morgan Neville, Rob Neyer, Ben Platt, Greg Prince, Domenic Priore, Eric Colin Reidelberger, Stuart Shea, Matthew Silverman, Christophe Silvey, Jay Smith, Mike Stax, Mick Stingley, Erik Sugg, Paul Francis Sullivan, Paul Turner, Tom Underwood, Josh Wilker, and Andrew Woolley; Michael Baker, Joe Bonomo, Ted Cogswell, Kevin Crane, Dave Davis, Gilbert Giles, David Jordan, Scott Milslagle, Stace Sisco, Darren "Repoz" Viola, Bailey G. Walsh, and the rest of the Baseball Freaks; Nicole Sohl, Jennifer Letwack, and Fred Chase at St. Martin's; everyone who has supported the *Big Hair and Plastic Grass* page on Facebook; my boys Oscar and Otis; and everyone else I'm surely forgetting who lent their ideas, enthusiasm, expertise, personal memories, and/or moral support to my star-spangled labor of love.

I also have to thank the Internet for making a project like this far easier to research than it would have been, say, 15 years ago. I am particularly indebted to the archival sites PaperOfRecord.com, NewspaperArchive.com, and Google News (news.google.com/archivesearch) for enabling me to page through every issue of the *Sporting News* and countless daily newspapers from 1976; the *Time* magazine (http://content.time.com/time/archive) and *Sports Illustrated* (www.sportsillustrated/cnn.com/vault) archive sites were similarly helpful. And of course, Baseball-reference.com was absolutely indispensable.

Saving the best for last, I must humbly thank Katie Howerton, the gorgeous love of my life, for her endless affection and encouragement—and for devotedly enduring my distractedness, occasional depression, free-floating stress, impossibly messy desk, moments of sheer panic, periods of financial uncertainty, and all the other "glamorous" things that go along with sharing life and lodgings with a published author. By the time you read this, Miss Howerton will be Mrs. Epstein . . . and that's about the happiest ending to a book that anyone could ask for.

Selected Bibliography

Allen, Dick, and Tim Whitaker. *Crash: The Life and Times of Dick Allen*. Ticknor & Fields, 1989.

Anderson, Sparky, and Si Burick. *The Main Spark: Sparky Anderson and the Cincinnati Reds*. Doubleday, 1978.

Angell, Roger. *Five Seasons: A Baseball Companion*. Simon & Schuster, 1977.

——. *Once More Around the Park: A Baseball Reader*. Ivan R. Dee, 2001.

Ballew, Bill. *The Pastime in the Seventies: Oral Histories of 16 Major Leaguers*. McFarland, 2002.

Bashe, Philip. *Dog Days: The New York Yankees' Fall from Grace and Return to Glory, 1964–1976*. Random House, 1994.

Bench, Johnny, and William Brashler. *Catch You Later: The Autobiography of Johnny Bench*. Harper & Row, 1979.

Bryant, Howard. *The Last Hero: A Life of Henry Aaron.* Anchor, 2011.

———. *Shut Out: A Story of Race and Baseball in Boston.* Beacon, 2002.

Cameron, Steve. *Moments Memories Miracles: A Quarter Century with the Kansas City Royals.* Taylor, 1992.

Carew, Rod, with Ira Berkow. *Carew.* Simon & Schuster, 1979.

Conner, Floyd. *Baseball's Most Wanted.* Potomac, 2000.

Delson, Steve. *True Blue.* William Morrow, 2001.

Dickson, Paul. *Bill Veeck: Baseball's Greatest Maverick.* Walker, 2012.

———. *The Dickson Baseball Dictionary,* 3rd ed. W. W. Norton, 2009.

Down, Fred. *Major League Baseball 1975.* Pocket Books, 1975.

———. *Major League Baseball 1976.* Ballantine, 1976.

———. *Major League Baseball 1977.* Ballantine, 1977.

Edelman, Rob. *Great Baseball Films.* Citadel, 1994.

Fidrych, Mark, and Tom Clark. *No Big Deal.* J. B. Lippincott, 1977.

Fletcher, Tony. *All Hopped Up and Ready to Go: Music from the Streets of New York, 1927–1977.* W. W. Norton, 2009.

Garruth, Gorton. *The Encyclopedia of American Facts and Dates,* 10th ed. HarperCollins, 1997.

Golenbock, Peter. *George: The Poor Little Rich Boy Who Built the Yankee Empire.* John Wiley & Sons, 2009.

———. *Wild, High and Tight: The Life and Death of Billy Martin*. St. Martin's, 1994.

———. *Wrigleyville: A Magical History Tour of the Chicago Cubs*. St. Martin's, 1996.

Gossage, Richard "Goose," with Russ Pate. *The Goose Is Loose: An Autobiography*. Ballantine, 2000.

Green, G. Michael, and Roger D. Launius. *Charlie Finley: The Outrageous Story of Baseball's Super Showman*. Walker, 2010.

Gutman, Dan. *Baseball Babylon*. Penguin, 1992.

Hall, Donald, with Dock Ellis. *Dock Ellis in the Country of Baseball*. Fireside, 1989.

Hermes, Will. *Love Goes to Buildings on Fire: Five Years in New York That Changed Music Forever*. Faber & Faber, 2011.

Herzog, Whitey, and Kevin Horrigan. *White Rat: A Life in Baseball*. Harper & Row, 1987.

Honig, Donald. *The American League: An Illustrated History*. Crown, 1983.

———. *The National League: An Illustrated History*. Crown, 1987.

Hope, Bob. *We Could've Finished Last Without You: An Irreverent Look at the Atlanta Braves, the Losingest Team in Baseball for the Past 25 Years*. Longstreet, 1991.

Jackson, Reggie, with Mike Lupica. *Reggie: The Autobiography of Reggie Jackson*. Villard, 1984.

Johnstone, Jay, with Rick Talley. *Temporary Insanity*. Contemporary, 1985.

Jordan, David M. *Occasional Glory: The History of the Philadelphia Phillies*. McFarland, 2002.

———. *Pete Rose: A Biography*. Greenwood, 2004.

Kuhn, Bowie. *Hardball: The Education of a Baseball Commissioner*. Times Books, 1987.

LaBlanc, Michael L. *Hotdogs, Heroes and Hooligans: The Story of Baseball's Major League Teams*. Visible Ink, 1994.

Lee, Bill "Spaceman," with Dick Lally. *The Wrong Stuff*. Penguin, 1988.

LeFlore, Ron, with Jim Hawkins. *Breakout: From Prison to the Big Leagues*. Harper & Row, 1978.

Lyle, Sparky, with Peter Golenbock. *The Bronx Zoo*. Triumph, 2005.

Maadi, Rob. *Mike Schmidt: The Phillies' Legendary Slugger*. Triumph, 2010.

Maddon, Bill. *Steinbrenner: The Last Lion of Baseball*. HarperCollins, 2010.

Markusen, Bruce. *A Baseball Dynasty: Charlie Finley's Swingin' A's*. St. Johann Press, 2002.

Martin, Billy, and Peter Golenbock. *Number 1*. Delacorte, 1980.

Matthews, Denny, with Matt Fulks. *Tales from the Royals Dugout*. Sports Publishing, 2004.

McCollister, John. *The Tigers and Their Den: The Official Story of the Detroit Tigers*. Addax, 1999.

Nash, Bruce, and Allan Zullo. *The Baseball Hall of Shame*. Wallaby, 1985.

Nettles, Graig, and Peter Golenbock. *Balls*. G. P. Putnam's Sons, 1984.

Neyer, Rob. *Rob Neyer's Big Book of Baseball Blunders: A Complete Guide to the Worst Decisions and Stupidest Moments in Baseball History*. Simon & Schuster, 2006.

Okkonen, Marc. *Baseball Uniforms of the 20th Century*. Sterling, 1993.

Pepe, Phil. *Talkin' Baseball: An Oral History of Baseball in the 1970s*. Ballantine, 1998.

Preston, Joseph G. *Major League Baseball in the 1970s*. McFarland, 2004.

Reichler, Joseph. *Baseball's Great Moments*. Bonanza, 1987.

Reidenbaugh, Lowell. *Take Me Out to the Ball Park*. Sporting News Publishing, 1983.

Rieland, Randy. *The New Professionals: Baseball in the 1970s*. Redefinition, 1989.

Ritter, Lawrence S. *Lost Ballparks: A Celebration of Baseball's Legendary Fields*. Penguin Studio, 1992.

Rivers, Mickey, and Michael DeMarco. *Ain't No Sense Worryin'*. Sports Publishing, 2003.

Rodgers, Nile. *Le Freak: An Upside Down Story of Family, Disco and Destiny*. Spiegel & Grau, 2011.

Roeper, Richard. *Sox and the City: A Fan's Love Affair with the White Sox from the Heartbreak of '67 to the Wizards of Oz*. Chicago Review Press, 2007.

Rosen, Ira. *Blue Skies Green Fields: A Celebration of 50 Major League Baseball Stadiums*. Clarkson Potter, 2001.

Ryan, Nolan, with Bill Libby. *The Other Game*. Word, 1977.

Shea, Stuart, with George Castle. *Wrigley Field: The Unauthorized Biography*. Brassey's, 2004.

Thorn, John. *The Relief Pitcher: Baseball's New Hero*. E. P. Dutton, 1979.

Thorn, John, et al. *Total Baseball*, 6th ed. Total Sports, Inc., 1999.

Thorn, John, ed. *The Complete Armchair Book of Baseball*. Galahad, 1997.

The Editors of Total Baseball. *Baseball: The Biographical Encyclopedia*. Total/Sports Illustrated, 2000.

Veeck, Bill, with Ed Linn. *Veeck—As in Wreck*. University of Chicago Press, 2001.

Weaver, Earl, with Berry Stainback. *It's What You Learn After You Know It All That Counts: The Autobiography of Earl Weaver*. Doubleday, 1982

Williams, Dick, and Bill Plaschke. *No More Mr. Nice Guy: A Life of Hardball*. Harcourt Brace Jovanovich, 1990.

Wilker, Josh. *Cardboard Gods: An All-American Tale Told Through Baseball Cards*. Seven Footer Press, 2010.

Wilson, Doug. *The Bird: The Life and Legacy of Mark Fidrych*. Thomas Dunne, 2013.

Zimmer, Don, with Bill Madden. *Zim: A Baseball Life*. Contemporary, 2001.

Index